THE SELFLESS MIND

THE SELFLESS MIND

Personality, Consciousness and Nirvāṇa in Early Buddhism

Peter Harvey

CP
CURZON
PRESS

First published in 1995
by Curzon Press
St John's Studios, Church Road, Richmond
Surrey, TW9 2QA

Typeset in Times by
Florencetype Ltd, Stoodleigh, Devon

Printed in Great Britain by
Biddles Limited, Guildford and King's Lynn

British Library Cataloguing in Publication Data
A catalogue record for this book is available from the British Library

Library of Congress in Publication Data
A catalog record for this book has been requested

ISBN 0 7007 0337 3 (hbk)
ISBN 0 7007 0338 1 (pbk)

Ye dhammā hetuppabhavā tesaṃ hetuṃ tathāgato āha
Tesañ ca yo norodho evaṃvādī mahāsamaṇo ti (Vin.I.40)

Those basic processes which proceed from a cause,
Of these the *tathāgata* has told the cause,
And that which is their stopping –
The great wandering ascetic has such a teaching

ACKNOWLEDGEMENTS

I would like to thank Dr Karel Werner, of Durham University (retired), for his encouragement and help in bringing this work to publication. I would also like to thank my wife Anne for her patience while I was undertaking the research on which this work is based.

CONTENTS

INTRODUCTION

(I.1) This work is concerned with exploring certain key features of the world-view of early Buddhism: its attitude to notions of self and its understanding of the nature and role of *viññāṇa*: 'consciousness' or 'discernment'. Both of these topics are of intrinsic interest in themselves, and exploration of them in early Buddhist literature both facilitates a better understanding of early Buddhism and adds a different perspective to the current debate on these topics. In order to carry out this analysis, though, it is necessary to have an understanding of certain basic concepts of early Indian thought.

KEY NON-BUDDHIST CONCEPTS

(I.2) Prior to Buddhism, the Brahmanical (proto-Hindu) tradition had started to produce compositions known as *Upaniṣad*s. In these, the spiritual quest was seen as, at heart, the quest for knowing the Self (Skt. *ātman*), which came to be seen as an essence underlying the whole of reality: both the external world and personality. It was not a personal 'self', though, but lay beyond both body and mind, as a transcendent, yet immanent reality that was a person's true nature. Lying beyond empirical individuality, it was a universal Self, the same in all beings. Such ideas were among those debated by the non-Brahmanical *samaṇa*s, or religious wanderers, that the Buddha (circa 484–404 BC) moved among. One group of *samaṇa*s was the Jains. They saw a person's true Self as the 'Life-principle' (*jīva*), a luminescent inner Self which lay within a person, trapped in matter until it was liberated. Such a 'Life-principle' was, unlike the Upaniṣadic Self, seen as an individual entity: each being had a separate Life-principle. In Buddhist texts, though, the word *atta* (Pāli) or *ātman*, meaning self or Self (Pāli and Sanskrit have no capital letters) is used for all such concepts. Another *samaṇa* group was the Ājīvakas. These were fatalists who felt that there was a Life-principle or individual Self that was impelled from rebirth to rebirth by an iron law of destiny. Another group, dubbed by the Buddhists as 'Annihilationists', were materialists who held that a person was completely destroyed at death. In this, they were unlike the Brahmins, Jains, Ājīvakas and Buddhists, all of whom believed that beings went through a series of rebirths, as humans, animals, or other kinds of beings. All but the Ājīvakas also thought that *how* a person was reborn depended on the quality of their karma, or action. Simply put, good, unselfish actions were seen as leading to pleasant rebirths, and bad, selfish ones were seen as leading to unpleasant rebirths. All, though, sought to attain liberation from this age-old round of rebirths, so as to gain final peace in some form. In his summary of the religious scene of his day, the Buddha often grouped others under three heads: the 'Eternalists', who believed in some form of eternal Self or Life-principle; the 'Annihilationists', who felt that a person is destroyed at death, and the 'Eel-wrigglers', referring to a group of Skeptics who felt that human beings were incapable of having knowledge of such matters as Self and rebirth.

KEY BUDDHIST CONCEPTS

(I.3) Turning to the Buddhists, they have believed in a number of kinds of rebirth (Harvey, 1990: 32–46). The most unpleasant are various forms of hellish existence which, though long-lasting, are not eternal. Other unpleasant ones are the realms of the frustrated 'departed' or ghosts, and animals/birds/fishes/insects. The human realm is among the relatively pleasant rebirths, as are a number of heaven worlds, populated by (non-eternal) gods (*deva*s) of a progressively refined nature. The lower ones belong, like all the worlds mentioned so far, to the 'realm of sense-desire', where beings experience things largely in terms of what seems desirable or undesirable. More refined are those heavens belonging to the realm of '(pure) form', where things are experienced in a somewhat less partial way. Such rebirths correspond to, and are seen as attained by achieving, certain refined meditative states known as *jhāna*s, of which there are four. Perhaps the most important type of god is Great Brahmā, who dwells in one of the lower (pure) form heavens. Such a being is seen as full of lovingkindness and compassion, but as thinking, mistakenly, that he created the world. Most refined of the heavens are the four 'formless' rebirths, which exactly correspond to certain meditative states. Such 'formless' worlds are seen as entirely mental in nature. The *jhāna*s are developed by careful concentration on such things as the breath or the attitude of lovingkindness to all. The formless states focus on such objects as 'infinite space'. Together, they form a sequence in which the whole body-mind complex is progressively calmed and stilled.

(I.4) The goal of Buddhism, *nibbāna* (Skt. *nirvāṇa*), is said to entail an end to all rebirths. Such a goal is attained by an *Arahat*, who experiences *nibbāna* during life, and then finally 'enters' it at death. The *Arahat* is one of several 'Holy' or 'Noble' (*ariya*) persons: saints who have fully experienced *nibbāna* or glimpsed it from afar. The first of these saints is the Stream-enterer, who has definitively entered the 'stream' (path) which will lead to *nibbāna* within seven lives at most, and will never be reborn at less than a human level. The second is the Once-returner, who will return only once to the realm of sense-desire in future rebirths. The third is the Non-returner, who will not return to this realm, but be reborn in one or more 'pure abodes', part of the realm of (pure) form, before becoming an *Arahat*. Lastly, there is the *Arahat*. These saints, along with the four types of person well established on the way leading to these states, comprise the 'Holy *Saṅgha*', the community of saints. There is also the monastic *Saṅgha* of monks and nuns who, in the Buddha's day, are mostly said to have been Holy persons. The monastic way of life was established by the Buddha as a disciplined spiritual way which was particularly conducive to spiritual progress. Its material needs were supplied by the Buddhist laity. While conditions for a lay practitioner were less ideal, there are plenty of early references to lay Stream-enterers and even Non-returners, plus a few lay Arahats. All followers of the Buddha expressed their commitment by going to the Buddha, *Dhamma* and (Holy) *Saṅgha* as 'refuges', i.e. looking to them as the embodiment of good qualities which inspire and generate inner strength when reflected on. In this trio, Dhamma refers to the Buddha's path and its goal, *nibbāna*. It can also mean the Buddha's teachings, the eternal Truth at which these point, and various spiritual realisations along the path. The Buddhist way, then, was, and still is, one of understanding, practising and realizing Dhamma.

(I.5) At the heart of the Buddha's teachings are the four 'Holy' Truths. These are essentially that:

i) life is frustrating, subject to *dukkha*, or 'suffering', and all components of personality are *dukkha*, in the sense of being 'unsatisfactory';
ii) the main cause for this situation, and for repeated rebirths, is craving of various kinds;
iii) if craving is destroyed, *dukkha* is destroyed, this end of suffering being *nibbāna*
iv) the Path to the end of *dukkha* is the Holy Eightfold Path, which consists of cultivating various aspects of virtue, meditation and wisdom (Harvey, 1990: 47–72).

Among the spiritual qualities to be developed on the Buddhist path are lovingkindness (*mettā*): the heartfelt aspiration for the happiness of oneself and others – ultimately all beings –, and the four 'foundations of mindfulness (*sati*)': careful moment-to-moment observation of the arising and passing of states, be they bodily sensations, feelings, states of mind, or patterns of existence such as the four Holy Truths or analyses of personality.

(I.6) The main Buddhist analysis of personality is that it consists of the five *khandha*s, 'groups', or *upādāna-kkhandha*s, 'groups of grasping'. These are five groups of processes that we normally grasp at as 'I' or 'me'. They can, thus, loosely be described as the 'personality-factors' (and they will be referred to in this way in this work). The five are:

i) *rūpa*: '(material) form', meaning the body;
ii) *vedanā*: 'feeling', the hedonic tone of any experience, its aspect as being pleasant, unpleasant or neutral;
iii) *saññā* : 'cognition', that which recognizes, classifies and interprets objects of the senses and mind;
iv) the *saṅkhāra*s: a number of 'constructing activities', of which the typical one is *cetanā*, or volition; others include such things as emotional states and attention;
iv) *viññāṇa*: generally translated by the rather vague term 'consciousness', but, as argued in chapter 9, better seen as 'discernment': sensory or mental awareness which discerns the basic parts/aspects of its object.

Another analysis is that of the 'twelve sense-spheres' (*āyatana*s): the five sense organs, with mind-organ (*mano*) as a sixth, and the six kind of objects these are aware of. A third analysis is in terms of the 'eighteen elements' (*dhatus*): these twelve with the addition of the kinds of discernment related to each sense-organ. Personality is also analysed in a more dynamic way, according to the principle of *paṭicca-samuppāda*: 'Conditioned Arising' or 'Dependent Origination'. The principle is that nothing (other than *nibbāna*) arises or ceases except in dependence on certain conditions. The application of this principle to personality is most often done in terms of a series of twelve *nidāna*s, or causal links, each one conditioning the one which follows it in the sequence:

i) '(spiritual) ignorance' (*avijjā*) (of the four Holy truths), in the form of persistent mis-perception of the nature of reality.
ii) 'constructing activities' (the *saṅkhāra*s): the fourth factor of personality, emphasized here as that which generates karmic effects.
iii) 'discernment' (*viññāṇa*), the fifth factor of personality.
iv) 'mind-and-body'(*nāma-rūpa*): a person in their mental and physical aspects, i.e. the sentient body, particularly at the start of a new rebirth.
v) 'the six sense-spheres' (the *āyatana*s): the six sense-organs.
vi) 'stimulation' (*phassa*): the mind's bare awareness of sensory contact.
vii) 'feeling' (*vedanā*): the second factor of personality.
viii) 'craving' (*taṇhā*): the key cause of suffering.
ix) 'grasping' (*upādāna*): clinging to things and views.
x) 'becoming' (*bhava*): perhaps meaning the continuing process of life.
xi) 'birth' (*jāti*): the start of a new life.
xii) 'ageing, death, sorrow, lamentation, pain, grief and despair ... this whole mass of *dukkha*'.

The weak points in this sequence are ignorance and craving. Meditative calming (*samatha*), by the *jhāna*s, is seen to weaken craving, and direct meditative insight (*vipassanā*), based on strong mindfulness, is seen to destroy both craving and ignorance.

(I.7) It is emphasized, again and again, that each personality-factor, sense-sphere, element and link has three qualities: qualities which mean that one should not cling to or be attached to them. These are that they are:

i) impermanent (*anicca*): subject to change and decay
ii) *dukkha*, causing suffering, and being unsatisfactory

ii) not-Self (*anatta*, Skt. *anātman*): not a substantial, real Self or I.

It is the interpretation of this latter point that this work is largely concerned with. Essentially, if many things are not-Self, is this because there *is* no Self or, in a way similar to the *Upaniṣads*, was early Buddhism counselling people to find their genuine, true Self? It is said that 'all *dhammas* (basic processes or patterns) are not-Self': but what is implied by this, and why is it so emphasized in the early Buddhist texts?

(I.8) Among the early Buddhist teachings relevant to its position on 'Self', is that concerning the 'views on the existing group' (*sakkāya-diṭṭhis*). The 'existing group' (*sakkāya*) (or, possibly, 'own group') is the five personality-factors, as described above (M.I.299). The views on these are a set of beliefs held on them by a *puthujjana*, an 'ordinary person' who has not yet become a Stream-enterer, nor is poised for becoming one. As these beliefs are only held by a spiritually undeveloped person, they are clearly seen as unacceptable. The views in question concern a putative 'Self' and its relation to the personality-factors. Of feeling, for example, the views hold: i) Self is feeling, or ii) Self has the property of feeling, or iii) feeling is in Self, or iv) Self is in feeling. Parallel views are held with respect to each of the other four personality-factors, so that there are twenty such views in all, covering all the ways that an ordinary person might look on the personality-factors and 'Self'. This means, for example, that it is wrong to say that the body is Self, or that the body is a property of Self, or that the body is contained within (i.e. part of) Self, or that the body contains a Self! A related set of theories are those enshrined in what are known as the 'undetermined (*avyākatā*) questions': a set of questions which were frequently put to the Buddha, but which he set aside with the response 'say not so' to each and every one. This set of ten questions is:

i) 'Is the world (*loka*) eternal?'
ii) 'Is the world not eternal?'
iii) 'Is the world finite?'
iv) 'Is the world infinite?'
v) 'Is the life-principle (*jīva*) the same as the mortal body (*sarīra*)?'
vi 'Is the life-principle different from the mortal body?'
vii) 'A *tathāgata* (enlightened person) is after (his) death?'

viii) 'A *tathāgata* is not after death?'
ix) 'A *tathāgata* both is and is not after death?'
x) 'A *tathāgata* neither is nor is not after death?'

The possible implications of the Buddha's reaction to these questions, particularly on the intriguing and mysterious '*tathāgata*', are most thought-provoking!

'NOT-SELF' AND SCHOLARS

(I.9) In the history of modern scholarship on Buddhism, many words have been spilled on the implications of, and potential philosophical problems in, Buddhism's teaching that all components of personality are 'not-Self'. The Buddhist tradition, in general, is seen as taking this as implying that, as no permanent, metaphysical Self can be found in personality, then such a thing does not exist. Indeed the tradition is often taken as explicitly *denying* the existence of such a Self. Thus Paul Williams, for example, in an otherwise excellent recent book, persists in translating *anātman* as 'no-Self' (1989: 77). Certainly some modern followers of the Theravāda school see the Buddha as having 'denied' the existence of Self. This is also the line taken in the most recent book-length study of the not-Self teaching according to the Theravāda school, Steven Collins's *Selfless Persons* (eg. pp. 7, 10, 71). As will be shown below, though, the early sources used by the Theravāda are bereft of any such explicit denial. The idea that Buddhism, 'denies the self', though, has become a commonplace of Religious Studies. While sophisticated treatments like Collins's are clear that the Buddhist perspective does not rule out psychological continuity within a person, it is quite common to find that newcomers to Buddhist Studies see in 'there is no Self' a denial of *any* kind of self, metaphysical (Self) or empirical. This is plain wrong. Moreover, in teaching that the factors of personality are not-Self, the Buddha has been portrayed as engaged in an attack at the concept of Self, rather than as getting his disciples to recognize an important truth about the empirical factors of personality. Again, this portrayal does not seem true to the sources of early Buddhism. Collins fails to recognize this, though, when he says that, for the scholar and meditator, the not-Self teaching functions merely as 'a linguistic taboo in technical discourse' (p. 77): that is, a declaration that Self-talk is a philosophical no-go area.

(I.10) The not-Self teaching is not without its potential problems, such as: what is it that is reborn after death? Who is the agent of action and the locus of moral responsibility? As Collins and others have argued, there are classical Buddhist answers to these questions which do not require the assertion of a Self. Nevertheless, worry over such problems has been recurrent. Indeed, one quite influential early Buddhist school, the Puggalavādins, or 'Personalists', was prompted by such questions to posit some kind of genuine Self. This was the 'person' (*puggala*), which was seen as neither the same as nor different from the empirical personality-factors: just as a whole is not identical with or different from its parts. Over time, it was neither changing nor unchanging.

(I.11) Such questions have also caused a number of modern western and Indian writers to assert that, in saying that many things are not-Self, early Buddhist sources implicitly, or even explicitly, asserted the existence of such a Self, beyond the realm of empirical personality. The list of such interpreters includes Mrs C.A.F. Rhys Davids, Ananda Coomaraswamy, George Grimm, K. Bhattacharya, J. Pérez-Remón, and even two of the most illustrious translators of Buddhist texts, Miss I.B. Horner, late president of the Pāli Text Society, and Edward Conze, renowned for his work on Mahāyāna Perfection of Wisdom texts, and author of many fine books on Buddhism. Given such different views on the subject, it seems appropriate to add to the literature on not-Self by attempting an impartial assessment of what the teaching actually says, both explicitly and implicitly, and what the *intention* behind the teaching is. For if the teaching is as central as it certainly seems, it is crucial to understand what it is about, and what it is *not* about. Unlike Collins (1982: 77), I hold that a sensitive approach *does* allow the scholar, *qua* scholar, to explain what the use of the not-Self teaching 'means'. In doing so, of course, one must seek carefully to allow the texts to speak for themselves, being alive to the fault of imposing one's own prejudices on the material. Once the question of Self has been fully dealt with, this work will then analyse the nature of 'discernment', which seems to be assigned a central role in the empirical personality and also allows an increased understanding of the nature of *nibbāna* and the mysterious *tathāgata*, he who is literally 'Thus-gone'.

SOURCES

(I.12) The primary sources for this work are drawn from the 'Pāli Canon', the early collection of scriptures, in the Pāli language, of the Theravāda school. Of the early schools of Buddhism, which developed prior to the arising of the Mahāyāna movement (*circa* first century BC/first century AD), this is the only one for which we have a full Canon of scriptures. It is all seen, traditionally, as having been taught by the Buddha (or his immediate disciples) and, though some parts of it clearly post-date the Buddha, many parts of it are ancient and may date from his day or soon after. Its teachings generally have an overall harmony, which strongly suggest 'authorship' of a system of thought by one mind. The Pāli Canon was originally transmitted orally, by communal chanting, and was first committed to writing, in part or whole, in the first century BC on the island of Ceylon. Steven Collins (1990) has argued that the Theravādins were the only Buddhist school to have developed a closed 'Canon' of scriptures, and that this took place in the early centuries AD in the context of sectarian rivalries in Ceylon. He therefore sees the Canon as the product, rather than the pre-existing basis of this school. I would agree that certain portions of the Canon, whenever they were composed, do show evidence of a specifically *Theravādin* orientation. But, on the other hand, much of the material is not specifically 'Theravādin', but is simply the collection of teachings that this school happened to preserve from among the early, non-sectarian body of teachings. That this is so can be seen from the fact that it contains material which is at odds with later Theravādin orthodoxy. A good example of this is the material analysed in ch.6, which shows that the early Buddhists believed in an intermediary period between rebirths, unlike the Theravādin view which sees no gap between the end of one life and the start of the next. The Theravādins, then, may have *added* texts to their Canon for some time, but they do not seem to have tampered with what they already had from an earlier period. It is the texts of this earlier period that I shall take as the main focus of my investigation. I do so both because of the rich and fascinating nature of the material itself, and because an examination of it helps us to see what later ideas and formulations were building on. Some see a focus on the early Pāli material as a sign of a purist 'Protestant' approach. I contend, however, that the early material is far richer and diverse than modern Theravādin 'Protestant' reformers hold it to be.

(I.13) The basic structure of the Pāli Canon is:

i) *Vinaya-piṭaka*, the section on monastic discipline.
ii) *Sutta-piṭaka*, the section on the 'discourses' of the Buddha.
iii) *Abhidhamma-piṭaka*, the section on 'further teachings', in the form of a psycho-philosophically exact and systematic formulation of the Sutta-teachings.

Of this material, the most relevant to the subject of this work is the Sutta section. This consists of five '*Nikāya*s'. Other than parts of the *Vinaya*, the oldest sections of the Canon lie in the first four *Nikāya*s and parts of the fifth. The first four are known as the *Dīgha Nikāya*, *Majjhima Nikāya*, *Saṃyutta Nikāya* and *Aṅguttara Nikāya*. Of the fifth, or *Khuddaka*, *Nikāya*, the sections I shall refer to most are: the *Suttanipāta*, *Udāna*, *Itivuttaka, Dhammapada*, *Theragāthā* and *Therigāthā*, all of which are in verse. I shall also make some use of the *Vimānavatthu*, *Petavatthu*, *Jātaka*s (all from the *Khuddaka Nikāya*), and Sutta-like sections of the *Vinaya*. I do not see any of these as specifically Theravādin in content. They constitute a unit of texts, of broadly the same period of composition, which for want of a better phrase I shall refer to as the 'early Suttas', though parts of the *Vinaya* are included, and parts of the *Khuddaka Nikāya* are excluded. These shall be my main focus of interest. It would have been good to consult parallel versions of many of such texts, in the Tibetan and Chinese Canons, but this goes beyond my linguistic abilities.

(I.14) My second group of primary sources are those texts which can be seen as the early interpretative literature of the Theravāda school. These are their Canonical Abhidhamma texts, sections of the *Khuddaka Nikāya* such as the *Niddesa* and *Paṭisambhidāmagga*, and the post-Canonical *Milindapañha* (approximately first century AD, though portions may be as late as the fourth century, and it is probably not exclusively Theravādin). In the main, these works are concerned with an analysis and systematisation of the teachings of the first group of texts, with the Abhidhamma focussing on a moment-by-moment analysis of reality. The second group of texts is consulted to expand on topics not dealt with in sufficient depth in the 'early Suttas'. It is also consulted to find and assess interpretations of the earlier material, which interpretations are only accepted – as plausible readings of what was originally meant – if they cohere with that material. In a similar way, a third group of primary sources are consulted: the Theravādin commentaries and the *Visuddhimagga* of Buddhaghosa (sixth century AD). These texts are clearly later than the second group of texts (except, perhaps, for portions of the *Milindapañha*), and generally expand on rather than diverge from the latter. Nevertheless, when going beyond the 'early Suttas', the second group of texts is referred to in preference to the third, so as to keep as near as possible to the early period. I am thus primarily concerned with analysing the ideas expressed in the 'early Suttas', but have consulted later Theravādin literature for the reasons stated, and to note where certain changes in ideas have occurred.

(I.15) All the texts cited so far are in Pāli, and belong to the Theravāda school. A few other texts have also been consulted. They include certain *Upaniṣad*s and Mahāyāna works (originally in a form of Sanskrit), along with certain Jain works (in Prakrit). These have been consulted so as to shed further light on aspects of 'early Sutta' concepts and to trace how certain of these concepts were developed in the Mahāyāna. Similarly, in order to follow up certain topics raised in the 'early Suttas', particularly relating to the status of the 'person' and the 'between-lives' state, there has also been some reference to the *Abhidharmakośa* of Vasubandhu (fifth century AD), a work in Sanskrit expressing the ideas of the (Vaibhāṣika) Sarvāstivāda school. This was one of the three major pre-Mahāyāna schools which generated an Abhidhamma and other systematic interpretative treatises, the others being the Theravāda and Personalist schools. To better understand the ideas of the Personalists, the translation of their *Sāmmitīya-nikāya Śāstra*, from Chinese, has also been consulted. This was translated into Chinese some time between 381 and 431 AD, and is one of the few surviving texts of this school. In understanding their views, then, we must rely on it as well as sections of the *Abhidharmakośa* (ch.9; fifth century AD) and the Theravādin Abhidhamma work known as the *Kathāvatthu* (pp.1–69; 250 BC or later). These texts allow us to investigate another important non-Theravādin perspective on the 'early Sutta' material.

METHODOLOGY

(I.16) When dealing with the Pāli literature, one finds that one is confronting a single world-view, though admittedly one which is very rich and with many aspects to it. Not only between texts in the same group, as defined above, does one find a remarkable homogeneity of ideas, but there is also a large degree of coherence even between texts of different groups. One can thus treat the literature as one 'world' in which there is a generally coherent body of ideas, but also certain tensions and divergences. My method has thus been to try to gain an understanding of this world in its own terms, drawing out the nuances of its thought.

(I.17) Now it should be noted that Edward Conze was critical of the idea Buddhism as a coherent body of truths:

> statements of Buddhist writers are not meant to be propositions about the nature of reality, but advice on how to act. . . . If one, however, isolates the Buddha's statements from the task they intend to perform, then they become quite meaningless (1951: 16–17).

This formulation of the situation suggests that, because the Buddha only made statements *useful* for helping persons towards *nibbāna*, such statements are not also to be seen as intended to be objectively *true*. However, to point out that statements attributed to the Buddha were practically orientated does not show that, in being so, they were not also seen as true. It only implies that the Buddha would not have been seen to teach things which were true but not useful. Indeed the 'early Suttas' portray the Buddha as having gained knowledge of many things, but having only taught those which were conducive to *nibbāna* (S.V.437–38). He is said (M.I.395) to have uttered speech only if it was true and spiritually useful, not if it was true and not spiritually useful, or false and not spiritually useful. There is no reference to speech which is false but spiritually useful: the Buddha held that only what is true is of potential spiritual use.

(I.18) Certainly, Conze was right to insist that passages be understood in their practical context of use: this helps to clarify meaning and avoid misunderstandings. *If*, however, the context of a passage is properly consulted, then the passage *can* be extracted, like a plant *and* some of its immediate environment, to compare and fit together with similarly extracted passages. If 'There is only one truth; there is no second . . .' (Sn.884), it would seem reasonable to see 'early Sutta' statements as intended to form a coherent and mutually compatible set of teachings, even though they are portrayed as having been originally given in a variety of contexts, to people of different backgrounds and levels of understanding. Taking this approach of contextual understanding is certainly fruitful. In order to assess the meaning of an 'early Sutta' passage, consultation of parallel 'early

Sutta' passages, and ones using similar language, often shed much light on the material. The Buddha may not have been a philosopher, as such, but it is quite possible to extract a coherent philosophy from the far-ranging, practically-oriented and inter-related teachings attributed to him in the 'early Suttas'. Of course, this must be done sensitively, so as to avoid partial interpretations, or reading ideas *into* the material rather than seeking to extract them *from* it. The method followed, in this work, then, is as follows:

a) treat passages from the 'early Suttas' as presenting a coherent body of ideas-cum-practical-guidelines, unless there are clear contradictions. This still allows that different passages may stress or concentrate on different aspects of a particular topic.
b) where the meaning of a passage, in context, is not clear, parallel passages should be sought to help illuminate it, providing that their context is taken into account.
c) build up a coherent pattern of ideas by such a method.
d) where information is lacking in the 'early Suttas', consult later material, provided it is in harmony with the former, in order to provide a fuller picture.

Except when noted, I take responsibility for all translations as my own.[1]

Part I

EXPLORING THE NOTION OF SELFLESSNESS

1

THE QUESTION OF SELF

If Self and what belongs to Self are truly, reliably not being apprehended . . . (M.I.138).

SCHOLARS WHO SEE A METAPHYSICAL SELF IN THE 'EARLY SUTTAS'

(1.1) In order to explore the implication of the teaching that 'all *dhamma*s are not-Self (*an-atta*)', it is useful to refer to the interpretations of some of those who see the 'early Suttas' as positing or allowing the existence of a metaphysical *atta* : a permanent, substantial, autonomous self or I. To refer to such a supposed entity, I will refer to it as 'Self', reserving the lower case 'self' for an empirical, changing self of any kind. As the general trend in the literature on Buddhism is simply to see it as *denying* a Self, it seems appropriate to calmly listen to those who have gone against this consensus. One can then use their interpretations as, at least, hypotheses to be tested against what the texts actually say. Even if they are wrong, they may be wrong in interesting ways!

(1.2) Miss I.B. Horner, while allowing that the early Pāli texts often use '*atta*' simply in the conventional sense of 'oneself', held that it is also used as the logical opposite of not-Self, i.e. as Self (1971: 32). Her view seems to have been that there is a 'Higher' or 'Greater' Self and a 'Lower', individual one that can *become* the 'Higher' Self by perfecting itself: 'Man was not to be regarded as That Self which is the Highest, but as potentially capable of becoming even as That Self' (1936: 103). She also talked of the individual self as coming to attain 'union with' the Higher Self (1936: 238). Nevertheless, she wished to avoid saying too much as to the nature of Self. She saw the Pāli Canon as not regarding *atta* as a permanent core to personality, nor as a permanent entity which survived death, nor as an underlying principle of the universe, as in the *Upaniṣad*s. Moreover, *nibbāna* was included among those things which were 'not-Self' (1977: 288–89).[1]

(1.3) Another great translator of Buddhist texts (mostly Mahāyāna) who seems to have posited some kind of Self was Edward Conze. In *Buddhism, its Essence and Development* (1951), he says that 'our true self gets estranged from itself' when we identify ourselves 'with what we are not' (p.109). He then seems to identify the 'true self' with the 'Unconditioned' or 'Absolute', i.e. *nibbāna* (p.111). In a 1959 article, though, he says that it has been the 'curse of Buddhist studies' that people have tried to 'attribute to primitive Buddhism the Upanishadic teaching on Self or *ātman*' (1967: 12–13). In his *Buddhist Thought in India* (1962), while still affirming that 'I am nothing else than the Absolute' (p.43), he makes clear why he sees no Upaniṣadic 'universal *ātman*' in early Buddhism: because it is identified with 'consciousness' (*viññāṇa*), which is counted as not-Self by Buddhism (p.127). All in all, his considered view is that the Buddha did not deny the Self but only said that it 'cannot be apprehended' (p.39). The passage on which this view is based will be considered carefully below. Conze also warns that 'The non-apprehension of a self – essential to a religious life along Buddhist lines, is greatly cheapened when it is turned into a philosophical statement proclaiming that the self does not exist' (p.130). This warning is, I hold, well given. Conze's own reasons for giving it are that the Buddha taught 'self' to coarse materialists, 'non-existence of self' to egoists, and to those near *nibbāna* and free from all love of self, he taught 'that there is neither self nor not self' (p.208). In a 1963 article, he talks of *nibbāna* as a 'state in which the self has become extinct' (1967: 211), by which he must mean that the empirical self becomes extinct. Finally, in a 1967 article, he says that (Mahāyāna) Buddhism aims at 'some kind of union with the transcendental One, which is identical with our true Self', also seeing the latter as a 'divine spark' (1975: 17 and 19).

(1.4) Among scholars who have devoted full books to outlining a Self-interpretation of Buddhism is George Grimm, in his *Doctrine of the Buddha* (1958, English version). In this he runs into a number of problems. One is that, in order to explain why the Self is not liberated, he has to attribute craving to it, but as the latter is clearly said to be not-Self, he has to see it as an 'inessential quality' (p.233). One part of his interpretation which is of real interest, though, is his view that 'you are not Something, but you are indeed Nothing' (p.133), ie. one's Self is no-*thing*, nothing knowable: it is beyond the categories of 'being' and 'non-being', which only apply to the finite world (p.6). This seems similar to Conze's view that the Self 'cannot be apprehended'. J. Pérez-Remón has produced a somewhat more sophisticated version of a Grimm-type position in his *Self and Non-self in Early Buddhism* (1980), but it still fails to avoid the problem of coherently relating craving to the 'Self'.

(1.5) Having outlined the views of selected Self-interpreters, it is clear that they raise certain possibilities which must thus be borne in mind when investigating the 'early Suttas' on the question of self/Self:

i) there is a real Self, which is not *nibbāna*, and a changing self which *becomes* the real Self (Horner).
ii) there is a 'true Self' which is the 'Unconditioned', *nibbāna*, but which is 'not apprehended' (Conze).
iii) such a real or true Self is beyond the categories of 'existence' and 'non-existence' (Grimm).

USES OF THE WORD 'SELF' (*ATTA*) IN THE 'EARLY SUTTAS'

(1.6) Before examining passages which might support or disprove the above hypotheses, it is first useful to clear the ground of possible confusions. It is clear that the 'early Suttas' often use the word '*atta*' (literally 'self') in such a way that no metaphysical Self is implied, only a changing empirical self. One common usage of this type has '*atta*' simply meaning 'oneself', 'himself', or 'myself', according to context. For example, when it is recommended that one should not act in a way that would be displeasing if someone else acted in this way towards one, it is said, 'self (of another) ought to measured against self (i.e. oneself)' (M.I.97).[2]

(1.7) A second, related meaning of '*atta*' is when it refers to 'character'. For example, at A.IV.114, a monk is said to be a 'self-knower' (*attaññū*) when he knows of himself that his spiritual qualities such as faith are developed to a certain degree. Pérez-Remón sees such a usage as evidence for a real Self, which is the 'substrate' of such qualities as faith (1980: 65, cf. 82 and 92). As such qualities must be seen as part of the personality-factor of 'constructing activities', however, this view seems to be a form of 'view on the existing group' (*sakkāya-diṭṭhi*), all of which are rejected by the Buddha. This is because it would see Self as 'endowed with' the constructing activities, or these as 'in' Self. Other passages use '*atta*' to refer to one's 'self' (character) as 'uprooted and injured' if one prevents someone from giving alms (A.I.161), and as 'become pure' when one lives virtuously (M.I.179). Such 'character', as it is clearly changeable, may be what I.B. Horner refers to as the changing 'Lower' self, but it cannot be the supposed Self that is different from the '*not*-Self'. As it changes, it is impermanent, and so must be not-Self (S.III.67).

(1.8) Thirdly, *atta* also occurs in the compound '*atta-bhāva*', literally 'selfhood'. At A.V.202, this is used to refer to the (living) body of an elephant, and at D.II.210, to refer to the visible, bodily aspect of the god Brahmā. At M.III.53, it is said that a harmful 'assumption of selfhood', when followed, leads to the growth of unwholesome states of mind: here the compound means something like 'personality'. Likewise, there is reference to a 'formless assumption of self *(atta)*', i.e. a personality in a formless rebirth realm (D.I.195).

(1.9) Fourthly, '*atta*' can be used as equivalent to '*citta*', which is variously translated as 'mind', 'heart' or 'thought'. This is evident from an investigation of Dhp. 160, a verse which is often picked on by Self-interpreters:

> Self is protector of oneself (*attā hi attano nātho*),
> for what other protector would there be?
> For with a well-controlled self (*attanā'va sudantena*)
> one gains a protector hard to gain.

Here, the 'protector' self is one which is 'well-controlled', paralleling a line at Dhp.35: 'a controlled (*dantam*) *citta* is conducive to happiness'. A self/*citta* identity is also seen at A.II.32 and Dhp.43: the first refers to 'perfect application of self' as leading to prosperity, the second to a 'perfectly applied' *citta* as of more benefit than the action of relatives. Now something which must be controlled or well applied is evidently changing, and not an unchanging metaphysical Self. The 'protector' self is simply the empirical *citta* , which is said to be very changeable, so that it should not be seen as 'my Self' (S.II.94). Again, as the arising of *citta* is said to depend on the arising of mind-and-body (*nāma-rūpa*, S.V.184), which is not-Self, it must itself be not-Self, following the principle enshrined in the following: 'How will the eye, which is arisen from what is not-Self, be Self?' (S.IV.130). *Citta* as 'self' seems to refer to one's psychological/emotional 'centre', which can be uncontrolled, badly applied and agitated, or well controlled, well applied and calm. It is 'self' in this sense which can upbraid one, as can other people, for lapses from virtue (A.V.88). It is also a 'self' which can be 'unguarded' even if a person is protected externally by an army (S.I.72–3).

(1.10) Among the non-Buddhist religious groups of the Buddha's day, the Annihilationists held that a person was completely destroyed at death. It appears, though, that they believed in up to seven 'Selves', the physical body, and various kinds of mental Selves, perhaps seen as psychic 'centres' (D.I.34–6). While all such Selves were seen as destroyed at death, they seem to have been regarded as unchanging during life, for the Buddha describes the Annihilationists as teaching the cutting off of a 'real being (*sato sattassa*)': i.e. they saw death as destroying a substantially real being/Self. The implication is clearly that an unchanging 'real being' is synonymous with a Self, and that it is contradictory to posit such an entity but then say that it can be destroyed.

PASSAGES WHICH MIGHT INDICATE THE ACCEPTANCE OF A SELF

(1.11) I.B. Horner has pointed to a passage at Vin.I.23 as indicating an early Buddhist belief in a Self (1971: 33): 'What do you think of this, young men? Which is better for you, that you should seek for a woman or that you should seek for self?'. This passage has been seen as an allusion to the Upaniṣadic *ātman*, for at BU.I.4.8, it is said 'One should meditate on the Self alone as dear'. However, the Vin.I.23 passage need mean no more than 'look within', particularly if the young men that the Buddha spoke to would have taken 'seek for one's self/Self' as simply a call to spiritual practice. Indeed, at the time, it seems that the religious life was popularly equated with 'seeking for Self'. Thus at M.III.155, a non-Buddhist gatekeeper simply assumes that some Buddhist monks meditating in a grove 'appear to be desiring Self (*atta-kāma-rūpā*)'.

(1.12) I.B. Horner (1971: 34) also refers to a passage at Ud. 47, where king Pasenadi and his wife agree that there is no one 'dearer than self'. Later, the Buddha says, 'Since self is so dear to others, let the self-lover not harm another'. Whatever Pasenadi meant by 'self', it is clear that the Buddha does not here refer to a metaphysical Self: for such a thing, being permanent, would be beyond suffering and harm. Reference to it would thus not be a reason for not harming others. The Buddha is here saying: everyone cares for their own happiness, just like oneself, so don't inflict suffering on them.

(1.13) A passage which both I.B. Horner (1971: 34) and K. Bhattacharya (1973: 62) refer to as showing a 'Great Self' or Upaniṣadic Self is A.I.149–50:

> There is nowhere in the world, indeed, for hiding evil action,
> O man, your self knows whether it is true or false,
> Indeed, dear witness, you scorn the good self,
> (You) who hides the existing evil self in yourself.
> The *tathāgatas* and gods see the fool who walks crookedly
> in the world.
> Thus let he who has self as master wander mindfully . . .

Horner translates: '. . . Indeed, my friend, thou scorn'st the noble self, thinking to hide the evil self in thee from the self who witnessed it. . . .' This gives the impression that there is a good/noble self which co-exists with and is witness to the acts of an 'evil' self. However, the Pāli word translated as 'witness' or 'who witnessed it', '*sakkhi*', is in the nominative or vocative case, the latter being most likely after '*bho*', 'dear', or 'my friend'. It is not in the ablative, as implied by Horner's translation. The passage thus seems to mean: your self witnesses good and bad actions, but you neglect to cultivate good aspects of yourself and only hide the real evil parts: but not only yourself, *tathāgatas* and gods see through you! The passage does refer to good and bad selves, but one is not a witness to what the other does. The two refer to good and bad aspects of personality, and the 'self' which witnesses both is identical with neither, but probably refers to deeper aspects of *citta* acting as 'conscience'. As for having 'self as master' (*attāhipako*), the context (A.I.147) indicates that 'dominance of the self (*attādhipateyyaṃ*)' refers to striving energetically, so as not to be ashamed of one's laxity, just as 'dominance of the world' refers to doing so lest gods intuit the bad states in one's mind. Having 'self as master', then, means being in charge of oneself, preserving one's integrity by not doing anything that one would be ashamed of. No underlying 'Great Self' is implied.

(1.14) Such passages as the above, while they do not indicate that the early Buddhists believed in a metaphysical Self, do indicate that they regarded the empirical self as a definite quantity to be reckoned with. It can and should be blamed (Sn.778, 913), censured (Dhp.379), upbraided (A.I.157) and controlled, if this is necessary, and should be 'conquered' (Dhp.104), for 'self, indeed, is hard to tame' (Dhp.159). As has been seen above, the 'self' which needs such treatment is *citta*.

NIBBĀNA AS NOT-SELF AND NOT RELATED TO A SELF

(1.15) In investigating whether a Self is posited in the 'early Suttas', it is useful to eliminate one possibility: that *nibbāna* might be a Self, or what a liberated Self merges into and becomes, or that it might be not-Self, but be what is enjoyed by a liberated Self (cf. Para.1.5)? A good place to start, here, is with the refrain (eg. A.I.286) that 'all constructed things (*saṅkhārā*) are impermanent, all constructed things are *dukkha*, all basic patterns (*dhammā*) are not-Self'. Now it is clear that the five personality-factors are what are normally to be regarded as impermanent, *dukkha* and not-Self (S.III.167): for they are what are normally grasped at (wrongly) as what 'I' am. If *nibbāna* is a *dhamma*, though, it also falls within the range of those things which are not-Self. That *nibbāna is* a *dhamma* is clear from A.II.34: 'As far as *dhamma*s constructed or unconstructed (*saṅkhatā vā asaṅkhatā*), dispassion is reckoned best of those *dhamma*s, that is to say . . . *nibbāna*'. This shows that, among *dhamma*s, some are constructed, i.e., 'constructed things', and some are unconstructed, i.e. *nibbāna*. The above refrain thus clearly indicates that while only constructed *dhamma*s are impermanent and *dukkha*, they and also the unconstructed *dhamma*, *nibbāna*, is not-Self.

(1.16) If *nibbāna* is not-Self, might it, though, be enjoyed by a liberated Self? When Ud.28 talks of a monk as knowing '*nibbāna* of self' or perhaps 'his own *nibbāna*', is this using 'self' in anything more than a conventional sense? A good indication that a purely conventional sense is meant is at M.I.4. Here, a spiritually undeveloped person is said to 'conceive (ideas)' (*maññati*) on a number of items, including *nibbāna*. The verb '*maññati*' is frequently used to refer to I-centred thought, such as seeing oneself as 'better', 'equal' or 'inferior' (Sn.918, S.I.12): thoughts which are the stuff of 'conceit' (*māna*)' (Vibh.346). This is surely the sense that *maññati* has here: relating things back to 'I', or Self. While the enlightened Arahat is free from such conceiving, the spiritually undeveloped person conceives that: i) ('I' am) *nibbāna*; ii) ('I' am) in *nibbāna*; iii) ('I' am) (different) from *nibbāna*; iv) '*nibbāna* is mine'. As all these positions are seen as inappropriate, *nibbāna* cannot be seen as standing in any relation to a real 'I', or Self.[3]

SELF AS 'NOT BEING APPREHENDED'

(1.17) A passage of crucial importance in ascertaining the early Buddhist position on Self is found at M.I.138:

> 'If, monks, there were Self, could it be said "it belongs to my Self"'. 'Yes, Lord'. 'Or, monks, if there were what belongs to Self, could it be (said) "it is my Self"?'. 'Yes, Lord'. 'But if Self and what belongs to Self are truly, reliably not being apprehended (*saccato thetato anupalabbhamāne*), is not the view and causal relation that "this the world, this the Self, this after dying I will become, permanent . . . ", is this not, monks, absolute, complete folly?'

At MLS.I.177, I.B.Horner translates '*saccato thetato anupalabbhamāne*' as 'although actually existing, are incomprehensible'. The passage is also clearly that alluded to by Edward Conze when he says that the Buddha did not deny the Self but only said that 'it cannot be apprehended' (Para.1.3). Again, K. Bhattacharya holds the passage as indicating that any self that can be objectively seized is not the true, durable Self (1973: 67, note 3). The key question is, which of the following is being said by the passage:

i) a metaphysical Self exists (or, perhaps, lies beyond 'existence' and 'non-existence'), but is inapprehensible, ineffable;
ii) there is absolutely no evidence for a metaphysical Self, as it is not apprehended in experience; Self can thus be seen as an empty concept alluding to something that does not exist.

(1.18) Firstly, what is the most reliable translation of '*saccato thetato*'? In some contexts, '*sacca*' (adjective or neuter), *not* accompanied by '*theta*', can mean 'real': as used of the *present* personality as opposed to past or future ones (D.I.201), or of *nibbāna* (Sn.756–58). However, where '*sacca*' is found with '*theta*', the former has the sense of 'truth' and the latter 'reliable'. For example, 'Having abandoned false speech, the *samaṇa* Gotama . . . is a speaker of truth (*sacca-vādī*), joined to truth (*sacca-sandho*), reliable (*theto*), trustworthy, not a breaker of his word' (D.I.4). As the two words occur together at M.I.138, this indicates that '*sacca*' here means 'true', not 'real' or 'existing'. Indeed, the two words occur together in a similar context at M.I.8:' ' "There is for me a Self" the view arises to him as true, as reliable (*saccato thetato*)'. Changing this from the adjectival to the adverbial mode (truly, reliably) thus gives the best rendering at M.I.138.

(1.19) What, then, of the implications of Self 'not being apprehended'? Two parallel passages help to shed some light, here. At A.I.174, the Buddha is criticizing three types of doctrine of 'inaction', and says that of those holding such views, 'there is no desire, nor effort, nor this is to-be-done, nor this is not-to-be-done. So that, as to-be-done-not-to-be-done are truly, reliably not being apprehended (*saccato thetato anupalabbhiyamāne*), the term *samaṇa* is not justly used specifically of you'. Now it might be said that those things which are 'to-be-done' or 'not-to-be-done' are realities which exist even if not apprehended, and thus that we have an example of something's 'not being apprehended' not precluding its existence. However, the context does not allow this. The possessive construction 'is not . . . of them' is used, meaning that the people involved do not have desire or (we must say) the *sense* of 'to-be-done' etc. As the phrase about 'not being apprehended' follows on from this, it must summarize it, and mean that 'to-be-done-not-to-be-done' is truly *not found to exist* in such people. This is in line with usage in later portions of the Pāli Canon, where '*anupalabbhiyamāna*' is synonymous with 'non-existent' (*asanta*) (Nd.I.253, 273, 277, 436). Indeed, in the Abhidhamma, the Personalist is at pains to argue, against the Theravādin, that the 'person' (*puggala*) *is* 'apprehended (*upalabbhati*)' (Kvu.1 ff.). This clearly implies that, when the text was composed, 'not apprehended' was equivalent to 'does not exist', whether in a limited context, or at all.

(1.20) Another related passage is found at S.III.118 and S.IV.384. Here, after various ways of regarding the relationship between a *tathāgata* and the five personality-factors have been dismissed, it is said: 'as here in this visible world, truly, reliably a *tathāgata* is not being apprehended[4] by you, is it proper for you' (to explain as you have on the state of a *tathāgata* after death)? Now it would be rather rash to read this as saying that a tathagata *does not exist*, as '*Tathāgata*' refers to an enlightened being, one who is 'deep, immeasurable, hard to fathom as is the great ocean' (M.I.487). At S.III.120, in the Sutta after that at S.III.118, though, there is an indication as to the meaning of what is said. There, the Buddha says, 'Enough, Vakkali, what is there for you in this vile visible body? Vakkali, who sees Dhamma sees me; who sees me sees Dhamma'. Now the Buddha often used the word '*tathāgata*' in place of 'I' or 'me', to refer to himself inasmuch as he was enlightened[5]. S.III.120 thus says: whoever sees Dhamma sees the *tathāgata*. As the mysterious *tathāgata* can thus be (metaphorically) 'seen', his 'not being apprehended' cannot imply his non-existence.

(1.21) Note, though, that the *tathāgata* is said to be 'not being apprehended' *by you* (someone who is spiritually undeveloped, who has not yet 'seen' Dhamma), that is, there is a qualification. With (the sense of) to-be-done, the only qualification is that the text is talking of a particular kind of person: but something's 'not being apprehended' in them still amounts to its non-existence in them. In the case of Self, there is no qualification given to its 'not-being apprehended'. The Pāli word order in the three passages may also be of relevance. In literal English, these run:

i) 'by you . . . truly, reliably, a *tathāgata* is not being apprehended'.
ii) 'to-be-done-not-to-be-done truly, reliably are not being apprehended'.
iii) 'Self and what belongs to Self, truly, reliably are not being apprehended'.

This suggests that the implication in iii) is of the same type – something does not exist – as in ii), unlike the implication in i): something exists but is not found. Moreover, related passages and the context of M.I.138, on Self, also indicate that Self's 'not being apprehended' implies that it does not exist.

(1.22) A well known passage at S.I.135 is on a 'being' (*satta*) as not 'apprehended'. Now as it has been seen above that the Buddha saw 'a real being' and 'Self' as synonymous (Para.1.10), this passage seems directly relevant to Self as 'not being apprehended'. It is addressed to Māra, a perverse god who encourages people in attachment and delusion, so as to keep them within the round of rebirths:

Why do you harp on 'being'
Māra, you are afflicted with speculative views,
A pure heap of constructed things, this
Not, here, is a being apprehended (*na-y-idha satt-ūpalabbhati*).
For just as when the parts are rightly set,
The word 'chariot' is (used),
So, when the personality-factors are, there is the agreed usage 'being'.
It is just *dukkha* which arises, which persists and passes.

None apart from *dukkha* arises, none other than *dukkha* ceases.

Here, the nun Vajirā makes the point that 'being' is merely a conventional designation for the personality-factors in functional relationship, just as 'chariot' does not refer to any special entity over and above the properly configured parts of a chariot. 'Being', or 'self', then, is not a name for a real essence or Self within what we call a 'being' or 'self'; such an essence is not apprehended because it does not exist. The relevance of S.I.135 to M.I.138 is strengthened by a passage in the same Sutta (the *Alagaddūpama-sutta*), at M.I.140. Here, the Buddha denies that he teaches the 'cutting off of a real being' (at the death of a *tathāgata*): he simply teaches the cessation of *dukkha*. As 'being' is just a label for the collection of empirical components of a person, which are also equivalent to '*dukkha*' (S.IV.39), when these end, what we conventionally call a particular 'being' ends, but this is no destruction of a 'real being'. If a 'real being' is not accepted, at M.I.140, then this implies that the Self referred to earlier in the Sutta is also not accepted.

(1.23) It is now fruitful to examine M.I.138 in its context, to get a full appreciation of its meaning. The *Alagaddūpama-sutta* begins by saying that one should not learn Dhamma simply so as to be able to reproach others. It then goes on to discuss six views: five varieties of 'This is mine, this I am, this is my Self', as well as the view which M.I.138 says is absolute folly: 'This the world, this the Self, this after dying I will become, permanent. . . . ' All these views are seen as leading to anxiety (p.136), and one who holds the view seen as absolute folly is seen as particularly anxious as, when he hears the *tathāgata*'s teaching on *nibbāna*, he feels that death will bring his annihilation, rather than the permanence that he had previously thought (p.137): that is, it is seen as bringing the cutting off of a 'real being'. Next, the Buddha gets his monks to admit that one could never permanently, eternally possess anything. The monks then admit that there is no 'Self-doctrine-grasping' nor 'dependence on a view' which does *not* lead to grief and suffering. At this point, the passage on Self as 'not being apprehended' is given, followed by one which says, on each of the five personality-factors, that it is 'not fitting to regard that which is impermanent, *dukkha*, liable to change as "This is mine, this am I, this is my Self".'

(1.24) This context shows the Buddha condemning the idea of gaining a permanent state for oneself, after death, and sees *all* doctrines of Self as leading to suffering. This makes sense of the fact that at M.I.138, 'it belongs to my Self' and 'it is my Self' are in quotes, representing something which is verbalized or thought, ie. some form of view. Indeed, at S.III.114, a spiritually immature person, afflicted by views on Self, is said to be assured, with respect to each factor of personality, 'it is my Self'. One can thus see M.I.138 as saying: *if* there were a Self, or what belongs to Self, then the *views* 'it belongs to Self' or 'it is my Self' would be appropriate. The context of the passage completes the meaning:

i) any Self-doctrine leads to suffering,
ii) if there were a Self, a Self-doctrine would be appropriate:
iii) but no Self is found to exist;
iv) so a doctrine on Self is *truly* foolish, as it leads to suffering, and is not even grounded on reality.

That is, M.I.138 does not allude to a real Self which is inapprehensible, but implies that such a thing is impossible: *if* there is a Self, one can have views on it; as no view on it is acceptable, no Self can exist. In logical notation: if A, then B; if not-B, then not-A.

(1.25) The most that a Self-interpreter could get from M.I.138 is to say that Self is so inapprehendable as to be beyond even 'existence': if it is admitted to exist, then *views* can be held on it, and these are inadmissible. However, not even the *Upaniṣad*s take this line: 'Not by speech, not by mind, not by sight can he be apprehended (*prāptuṃ*). How can he be comprehended (*upalabhyate*) except by him who says "He is" ' (KU.II.3.12). Again, even *nibbāna* is said, in Buddhism, to exist (*atthi*, Ud.80). However, it still might be possible that the 'early Suttas' do posit a Self beyond existence: unless it is proved otherwise.

A SELF BEYOND 'EXISTENCE' AND 'NON-EXISTENCE'?

(1.26) A passage of direct relevance to this is S.IV.400–01. Here, the monk Vacchagotta directly asks the Buddha whether 'a self' exists (*atthi*) or not (as Pāli has no capital letters, this can be seen as a question on self or Self). In response to both questions, the Buddha remains silent. The passage is thus appropriately placed in the *avyākata-saṃyutta*, which deals with 'undetermined questions': ones which the Buddha set aside without giving any answer. The Buddha later explains his responses to Ānanda:

i) to have replied 'a s/Self exists' would have been to side with the Eternalists (those who believe in an eternal Self which survives death) and would not have been 'in accordance with' the knowledge that all *dhammas* are not-Self.
ii) to have replied 'a s/Self does not exist' would have been to side with the Annihilationists, and 'it would have been more bewilderment (*sammohāya*) for the bewildered Vacchagotta, for he would have said "It is, then, that formerly my self existed, (but) now it does not exist?".'

(1.27) This clearly says that it is inappropriate to assert that 'a Self exists'. Might this allow that, nevertheless, there is a Self beyond 'existence'? To escape the rebuttal in i), Self would have to be not a *dhamma*, and also be beyond time, so as not to be even 'eternal', in the sense of existing forever in time. However, the wording of the passage does not allow such an interpretation. In Indian logic, it is meaningful to say that something 'is neither x nor not-x', or 'neither is nor is not'. Indeed, the Buddha was often asked if a *tathāgata* after death 'neither is nor is not': another 'undetermined question'. The point is, that if 'a Self neither exists nor does not exist' were *true*, then both 'a Self exists' and 'a Self does not exist' (and 'a Self both exists and does not exist') would be *false*. The Buddha could have said that they were false, but he did not: he simply responded with silence. In other cases of 'undetermined questions', he is said to have 'set aside' the questions (M.I.426), or said that such things were 'not a proper question' (S.II.13–14). This response implies that the questions are wrongly put, misconceived, with a mistake built into them. They are unanswerable, like the question 'have you stopped beating your wife?', when put to an innocent man. The problem in this case probably arose from the ambiguity of the word 'self'; for to say, for example, that an empirical 'self' exists might well be mistakenly seen as meaning that a metaphysical 'Self' exists.

(1.28) Now, as it happens, an empirical self, strictly speaking, 'neither exists nor does not exist': so if it were also true that Self 'neither exists not does not exist', the Buddha could have unambiguously said: 's/Self neither exists nor does not exist'; for whichever way the reply was taken, it would be true! The demonstration that an empirical self is seen to neither exist nor not exist is:

> Now for him, Kaccāyana, who with right insight sees, as it really is, the arising of the world (*loka-samudayaṃ*), there is not non-existence in respect of the world. For him, Kaccāyana, who with right insight sees, as it really is, the stopping of the world (*loka-nirodhaṃ*), there is not existence in respect of the world (S.II.17).

This passage makes the point that one who sees the world as a flow of changing, conditioned phenomena, sees that it neither totally lacks existence, nor exists in a substantial, unchanging way. While the passage is on the 'world', at S.IV.39 'world', 'a being' and '*dukkha*' are said to be alternative ways of describing the same eighteen 'elements' (Para.I.6). That is, 'world' and 'a being' are equivalent. As empirical 'self' must be equivalent to an empirical 'being' (cf. Para 1.10), it can thus be said that self = being = world, and that all of these 'neither exist nor do not exist'. Of course, as they are equivalent to *dukkha*, they are all not-Self. It can therefore be said:

i) if there was a Self beyond existence and non-existence, the Buddha could have safely said so;
ii) the only 'self' which is beyond existence and non-existence is the empirical self, which is not-Self.

(1.29) Returning to Vacchagotta's questions to the Buddha, two queries remain:

i) is it possible to deduce an answer to the question 'does Self exist?', rather than to the ambiguous 'does s/Self exist?';
ii) if the Buddha felt that Self did not exist, why did he not directly say so to Vacchagotta, having first made a distinction between self and Self?

The first question will be addressed next and then, after a discussion of Upaniṣadic concepts of Self and the Personalist's 'person', the second.

PROOF OF THE IMPOSSIBILITY OF A SELF

(1.30) The basis for developing such an argument is found in the *Mahā-nidāna-sutta*, at D.II.66–68. Here, three concepts of Self are discussed:

i) 'My Self is feeling (*vedanā*)'
ii) 'No, my Self is not feeling, my Self is without experience (*appaṭisaṃvedano*)'
iii) 'No, my Self *is* not feeling, nor is it without experience, my Self *feels*, it has the property of feeling'.

The first view is refuted on the grounds that feeling fluctuates from being pleasant to being unpleasant or neutral, such that each of these modes is impermanent. If any of them were taken as Self, one would have to say 'My Self has departed' when that kind of feeling passed (but a permanent Self cannot pass away). If, on the other hand, one took feeling in general as Self, then one would take Self as something which was 'impermanent, a blend of pleasure and pain, and liable to rise and fall': this is clearly seen as unacceptable. So, feeling is not Self. The refutations of views ii) and iii), are:

ii) 'My friend, where there is entirely no feeling, would "I am" be there?' 'No, venerable sir'.
iii) 'My friend, were feeling of every sort or kind to cease without remainder, all feeling not existing, from the cessation of feeling, would "this I am" (*aham asmīti*) be there?'. 'No, venerable sir'.

(1.31) These two refutations show that, for the authors of the 'early Suttas', a real Self must have self-awareness, having a sense of 'I am' or 'this I am'. The argument is, though, that the sense of 'I am' or 'this I am' only arise when feeling exists. As they thus depend on feeling, which is itself not-Self (refutation i), they are themselves not-Self, from the principle mentioned in Para 1.9. The 'I' that is Self would thus turn out to be not-Self, which is a contradictory situation. That is, if there can only be a Self under conditions which would make it *not*-Self, then it is clearly impossible for there to be such a thing as a Self. While the above passage may not be intended to 'refute' Self, but only deny certain views on Self, it clearly has the effect of showing that *the concept itself is self-contradictory.*

In fact, S.III.105 says that there is only 'I am' by clinging (*upādāya*) to the personality-factors, which are, of course, not-Self. That is, a sense of Self only arises with respect to the factors of personality, but it is not *legitimately* applied even here. As is said at S.III.46, all who 'consider Self in various ways consider it as all these five personality-factors, or as a certain one of these'. The self-contradictory Self-concept, then, concerns something which is supposed to be *both* permanent *and* aware of itself as 'I'. But to get even an illusory sense of I-ness, it must be feeling, or one of the other personality-factors, which work in unison with feeling (or all the factors), but these are all *im*permanent.

(1.32) At S.III.127ff., the Arahat is said to lack the sense of both 'I am' and 'this I am': both must thus be based on illusions transcended at enlightenment. The passage also makes clear what both of these feelings/views are. The monk Khemaka explains that he does not consider any of the personality-factors as Self or what belongs to Self, such that he is without 'views on the existing group' (*sakkāya-diṭṭhi*). This shows that he is at least a Stream-enterer, one of the types of Holy persons. However, he still has the 'conceit' and 'latent tendency' of 'I am', and so he is not yet an Arahat, the highest type of Holy person. He then explains by saying that though he has the attitude 'I am' with respect to the personality-factors, he does not consider 'this I am'. That is, he does not say 'I am' with respect to any specific personality-factor, nor 'apart from' any of them, but he has the attitude 'I am' with respect to *all* of them, just as the scent belongs to the whole flower, not just to a particular part of it. Only later does he become an Arahat, without the 'I am conceit (*asmī-māno*)'. Thus:

i) thinking 'this I am' is to have a 'view on the existing group': identifying Self with, or relating it to, a specific personality-factor;
ii) thinking 'I am' is a more deep-rooted conceit, more a vague attitude than a conceptualized view, which can exist even after i) is destroyed, but not once Arahatship is attained.

Both Self-view and Self-attitude, then, evaporate under the light of knowledge developed on the path to Arahatship. An Arahat has feeling, but does not misinterpret this so as to hold the conceit that he is a permanent, substantial Self feeling that which is other than Self. Feeling is simply observed to arise as a conditioned process.

He or she no longer clings to the personality-factors, and it is only by so clinging that he can consider 'this is mine, this I am, this is my Self' (S.III.181–82). When he considers 'this is not mine, this is not I am, this is not my Self', therefore, he has merely transcended craving ('this is mine'), conceit ('this I am') and views on the existing group ('this is my Self'). He is not alluding to any real Self or I which is *not* the personality-factors.

(1.33) In interpreting D.II.66-8, though, George Grimm applies his idea of a Self beyond existence, thus seeing it as saying that one cannot say of the true I, 'I am': 'Thus the Buddha here expressly declares the cupola "to be" possesses meaning only within the realm of sensations . . . if we rid ourselves of sensations, it can no longer be said that our self *is*' (1958: 149). Though it has been shown above that there is no evidence that the Buddha postulated a Self beyond existence, Grimm's suggestion is still worthy of careful assessment. His notion is that, though there "is" 'mine' 'I' and 'Self', it is wrong to *identify* them with anything, making them *be* something (rather than no-*thing*; see Para. 1.4). The context of D.II.66 does not fit this suggestion, though. The Buddha is simply asked whether Self can be identified in certain ways, and shows that this cannot be so: as it would be to take something which is impermanent, or something beyond 'I am', as Self, which is contradictory. That is, the Buddha *uses* the link between Self and 'I *am*' in the disproof of the offered views.

(1.34) Summarising the findings so far, it can thus be said that, while an empirical self exists – or rather consists of a changing flow of mental and pysical states which neither unchangingly exists nor does not exist – no metaphysical Self can be apprehended. This does not imply that it is real but inapprehensible, as the Buddha of the 'early Suttas' saw views on it as appropriate, *if* it was real. Moreover, even *nibbāna* is not-Self and not related to a Self, and the Buddha did not accept that Self exists, or that it even lay beyond existence and non-existence. Indeed, the concept itself is seen as self-contradictory, for 'Self' is dependent on a sense of 'I am', and this can *only* arise by clinging to the conditioned factors of personality, which are *not*-Self.

BUDDHISM AND THE *UPANIṢADS* ON SELF

(1.35) Several authors, such as K. Bhattacharya, have tried to see the Buddha as having agreed with the *Upaniṣads* that there is an inapprehensible permanent Self (Skt. *ātman*), a universal essence which underlies all individual beings and the whole world. The above clearly shows how the Buddha of the 'early Suttas' differs from such a view. For him, only *nibbāna* was beyond impermanence, and it was also, precisely, not-Self. As *nibbāna* was attained by one without clinging (S.II.279), no 'I am' attitude could arise with regard to it. Self, though, is the ultimate reality of the *Upaniṣads*. Even 'in the beginning', when only it existed, it said 'I am' (BU.I.4.1). The *Upaniṣads* agree that Self requires the sense of 'this I am' (Skt. *ayan aham asmīti*; CU.VIII.11.1), so that Self cannot be the state of dreamless sleep; but unlike Buddhism, they hold that Self can get this sense from something beyond the conditioned factors of personality. Whereas the *Upaniṣads* see Self as underlying the whole world, being 'below', 'above', and in the four directions (CU.VII.25.1-2), the Buddhist Arahat says 'Above, below, everywhere set free, not considering "this I am" ' (Ud.74). Some *Upaniṣads* seem closer to Buddhism, though. The post-Buddhist *Maitrī Upaniṣad* (III.2) holds that only the defiled individual self (Skt. *bhūt-ātman*), rather than the universal one, thinks 'this is I' or 'this is mine'. This is very reminiscent of Buddhism, and may well have been influenced by it to divorce the universal Self from such egocentric associations. Nevertheless, the earlier, pre-Buddhist *Upaniṣads* (BU and CU) clearly linked Self to 'I am'. Though Self shares certain qualities with *nibbāna* (both being permanent, beyond suffering, and unconditioned), it is clear why the Buddha would have shunned any attempt to see the spiritual goal in terms of 'Self'. Both in the *Upaniṣads* and common usage, self/Self is linked to the sense of 'I am': but this ego-sense is seen as the very thing which keeps a person in the round of rebirth, preventing him or her from attaining *nibbāna* (S.III.46). If the later *Upaniṣads* came to see ultimate reality as beyond the sense of 'I am', Buddhism would then say: why call it 'Self', then?

THE STATUS OF THE 'PERSON'

(1.36) Of course, within the Buddhist fold, a school developed which upheld the reality of the Self-like 'person' (*puggala*): the Personalists (Puggalavādins). It is appropriate at this juncture to describe and assess its views. Its characteristic doctrine was that the 'person' is neither the same as nor different from the five factors of personality (Kvu.11-13 and 20, SNS.179). If it were different from them, it would be an eternal Self, as in the views of the Eternalist. Moreover, as the 'person' is the same as the 'life principle' (*jīva*) (Kvu.25–26), this would mean that the life-principle was different from the 'mortal body' (*sarīra*), which the Buddha did not accept. Moreover, a person separate from the personality-factors could not produce an effort in them to end rebirth, nor would it make sense to talk of its bondage or liberation (SNS.180–01)[6]. As regards the view which identifies the person with the factors of personality, the Personalists saw this as implying Annihilationism, and that the life principle was the same as the mortal body: again, views not accepted by the Buddha. Their 'person', in other words, was carefully described so as not to come obviously under any of the views which the Buddha had not accepted.

(1.37) The 'person' is said to be related to the personality factors by the relation of *upādāya*: 'derivation from', 'relation to' or 'correlation with' (Kvu.34, L'AK.V.323). It is like the relationship between fire and burning fuel, the fire getting its name from what it burns (SNS.182). Perhaps the most useful image, though, is one suggested by Venkataramanan (SNS.225). This is that of a whole (the person) and its parts (the personality-factors). That is, the Personalists held the 'person' to be a kind of whole which was more than the sum of its parts. In this, it is different from a mere complex of elements, such as 'milk', which they admitted to be no more than its component parts (L'AK.V.232–33). It must thus be seen as an *organic* whole; thus Venkataramanan refers to it as an 'organismic whole' (SNS.159), and Conze sees it as kind of 'structural unity' (1962: 128). Such a 'person' is said to be neither constructed nor unconstructed, neither eternal nor non-eternal (Kvu.24). It is 'ineffable' (*avaktavya*) (L'AK.V.237).

(1.38) The main point of contention between the Personalists and their opponents – principally the Theravādins and Sarvāstivādins –, was as follows. The Personalists held that the 'the person is apprehended (*upalabbhati*) in accordance with real and ultimate meaning' (Kvu.1), while their opponents held that it was not (Kvu.2), holding that 'person' is merely a conventional label for the personality-factors, which *are* genuinely 'apprehended'. As a well known passage in the *Milindapañha* puts it, a person's name, such as 'Nāgasena' is 'but a denotation, an appelation, a designation, a current usage . . . indeed no person is apprehended here' (Miln.25). In this passage, Nāgasena explains that 'Nāgasena' is not any specific personality-factor, nor all of them merely listed together, nor apart from them, just as a 'chariot' is not so related to its parts (Miln.26–7). It is simply that the designation 'Nāgasena' is 'dependent on' (*paṭicca*) each personality-factor. Nāgasena then (p.28) quotes S.I.135 (Para.1.22):

> For just as when the parts are rightly set,
> The word 'chariot' is (used),
> Thus, when the personality-factors are, there is the agreed
> usage 'being'.

Now Nāgasena did not accept that the 'person' 'Nāgasena' was simply all the personality-factors listed together, just as a 'chariot' is not all its parts layed out on the ground. Just as the chariot parts have to be 'rightly set' for there to be a 'chariot', so the personality-factors have to be in functioning relationship for there to be a 'being' or 'person'. On this, the Personalist and non-Personalist agree. The Personalist, though, sees this relationship as constituting a new entity, while the non-Personalist sees 'person' as just a label, a nominal reality. For the Personalist, 'When the personality-factors are, the person is apprehended' (L'AK.V.238), for the non-Personalist, no such extra entity can be found. In this, the non-Personalist are clearly supported by the early texts, for at S.I.135, just before the lines quoted by Nāgasena, it is said, 'not, here, is a being [equivalent to 'person'] apprehended'.

(1.39) It is apparent that the Personalist's 'person' is rather like 'I am', discussed above. This is because 'I am' is said to be '*upādāya*' each of the personality-factors (S.III.105). At Para 1.31, this was translated 'by clinging to', but it can also mean 'derived from', as when the Personalists say the person is 'derived from' the factors. Moreover, at S.III.127ff. (Para 1.29), Khemaka has the attitude 'I am', but does not see 'I am' as being any of the factors or as 'apart from' them. It is thus like the 'person': not the same as or different from the factors. Now while the *attitude* 'I am' is a reality, the 'I' it postulates is simply a delusion, for the Arahat transcends it. If 'I am' were the 'person' of the Personalists, the Arahat would no longer be such a person. Yet he still has the personality-factors and the early text still refer to him as a 'person' (eg. S.III.159–60). Such reference to 'person', then, can only be seen as conventional language, not a reference to some mysterious inner 'person', as the Personalists thought.

(1.40) A favourite proof-text of the Personalists (e.g. at L'AK.V.256) was the 'Burden Sutta', S.III.25–6. The essential points made in this passage are:

i) there is a 'burden' (*bhāra*), which is the five personality-factors;
ii) there is the 'taking hold of the burden' (*bhārahāra*): 'the person . . . that venerable one of such and such a name';
iii) there is the 'taking up of the burden' (*bhārādāna*): craving, which brings suffering;
iv) there is the 'laying down of the burden' (*bhāra-nikkhepa*): the complete cessation of craving, in one who attains *nibbāna*.

The Personalist argues that 'the burden cannot be the taking hold of the burden' (L'AK.V.256), that is, the personality-factors cannot be the same as the 'person'. That this is so is by no means clear, for craving, the 'taking up' of the burden, *is* seen as an aspect of the conditioned factors of personality: it is said to be conditioned by feeling in the Conditioned Arising sequence. Craving, in fact, is said to 'cause a person to be' (S.I.37): that is, craving causes a new rebirth, constituting a 'new' person. Such a person, 'of such and such a name' is a concatanation of personality-factors which are 'taken hold of': held together by the momentum set up by past craving. When a person attains Arhatship, then he has 'put down the burden (*ohita-bhāro*)' (It.38). That is, he has no present craving for the personality-factors, but he continues as a person, with his personality-factors cohering together and functioning, till he dies.

(1.41) The 'Burden Sutta' does not, then, indicate any Personalist 'person'. Indeed, as S.I.37 says that craving 'causes a person to be', the 'person' of the Suttas cannot be the Personalist one, for this is said *not* to be conditioned. However much the Personalist hedges on the relationship of 'person' and personality-factors, he must still say that it 'grasps' at this burden. As pointed out by Vasubandhu, though (L'AK.V.260), the Buddha sees the question, 'Who, now, venerable sir, is it who grasps (*upadiyati*)?', as not a proper question, for 'I do not say "he grasps" ' (S.II.14). A proper question would be to ask what condition grasping arises from: the answer being 'craving'. That is, the grasping at the personality-factors etc. is itself a conditioned factor just like other factors within a person.

(1.42) Among the functions ascribed by the Personalists to the 'person' was that of being the subject of discernment/consciousness. This is seen by their reference to a 'support' (Skt. *āsraya*) of discernment 'he who discerns (Skt. *vijñātam*)' (L'AK.V.279), and to 'he who sees', who is 'derived from the eye' but does not cease when it ceases (Kvu.37). The 'early Suttas', though, argue against the reality of any subject lying behind discernment. It is simply discernment (*viññāṇa)* itself which 'discerns (*vijānāti*)' (S.III.87). In fact, the Buddha saw the question 'Who, now, venerable sir, is it who feeds on (*āhāreti*) the discernmemnt-nutriment (*-āharāṃ*)?', as another improper question (one without an answer) (S.II. 13). A proper question would be simply to ask 'Of what is discernment the nutriment?', the answer being that discernment acts as a condition for future rebirth. There does not, then, appear to be any support in the 'early Suttas' for the 'person' of the Personalist, just as there is no support for a Self.

WHY IS SELF NOT DENIED?: THE BUDDHA AND THE ANNIHILATIONISTS

(1.43) If Buddhism, then, does not accept the existence of a Self, why did the Buddha not deny its existence when asked by Vacchagotta, regarding a denial of 's/Self' as equivalent to Annihilationism? The simplest answer to this is that the Buddha accepted a changing empirical self which was not destroyed at death, but flowed on into a future rebirth. The Annihilationist 'denial' of s/Self rejected any idea of rebirth, and thus denied 'self' in this sense.

(1.44) Moreover, we see elsewhere that Vacchagotta frequently pestered the Buddha for answers to the undetermined questions, such as on the state of a *tathāgata* after death (eg. S.IV.391–402), and was generally affected by 'bewilderment' at his responses (e.g. M.I.487). Thus, if he had been told that s/Self did not exist, he would (wrongly) have assumed this to have impled that a *tathāgata* did not exist after death, but was annihilated. He would have been bewildered as he would have been like the Eternalist who, on hearing the teaching on *nibbāna*, would think, 'I will surely be annihilated', so as to 'grieve' and be 'bewildered' (M.I.136–37). Such an Eternalist is thus said to be anxious about something 'internal that does not exist', this being like someone who grieves over something 'external that does not exist', which the commentary explains to mean the case of losing some external possession. This suggests that Vacchagotta would have been 'bewildered' at the denial of s/Self because, having formerly suspected that he had an eternal Self, he would feel that he had *lost* it if told that such a s/Self did not exist. He would grieve at what he would see as the non-existence of the Self he thought that he had, and at the non-attainment of eternal existence after death.

(1.45) It is a curious fact that the 'early Suttas' see even Annihilationism, which the Buddha equated with denial of s/Self, as tied up with belief in a Self. At S.IV.286, Annihilationism is among a range of views all of which arise due to 'views on the existing group': i.e. on there being a Self in some sort of relationship to the personality-factors. As has been seen, Annihilationists believed in various kinds of Self that existed unchangingly throughout life before being destroyed at death (Para.1.10). The Buddha saw it as nonsense, though, to say that a genuine Self or 'real being' could be destroyed. The Annihilationist, then, is one who denies that anything of a person exists after death, but who believes in a one-life Self, typically identifying this with the body. He is still preoccupied with 'I' and 'Self', then. As S.III.46 says, the attitude 'I am' leads, among other things, to the idea 'I will not be', i.e. Annihilationism. Similarly, M.I.8 sees the wrong views 'there is for me a s/Self' and 'there is not for me a s/Self' as *both* arising from unmethodical speculation on whether or what one was in the past, whether or what one will be in the future, or thinking, as to the present, 'Now am I? Now what am I?'. That is, preoccupation with 'I' even leads to the idea that 'I' do not exist. Thus, if the Buddha had said 's/Self does not exist', he would have been legitimizing such preoccupation. He thus did not see it as a true statement, or choose to say that 's/Self exists' is *false*.

(1.46) While Annihilationists believed in a one-life Self, seen by the Buddha as a type of 'real being', they could also sound like nihilists, denying not only that there is a world beyond death, but also saying that 'this world does not exist' (D.I.55). There may have been different groups of Annihilationists, but it is perhaps more likely that Annihilationists held that anything which does not last *forever* does not really 'exist'. If this is so, the Buddha's criticism, that they accepted a 'real being' that is destroyed at death, would amount to the accusation that their beliefs were inconsistent. The point would be that, in accepting the destruction of a Self at death, the Annihilationists denied it true existence as a 'real being', but in accepting an unchanging Self during life, they implicitly accepted it as a truly existent 'real being'. Moreover, if Self is wholly unchanging during an entire life-time, it can't suddenly succomb to the catastrophic change that is destruction; only the changeable can be destroyed. This seems the most plausible reading of the situation as regards to the Annihilationists. As seen above (Para. 1.28), the Buddha held that, while the world lacked unchanging 'existence', it was an experienced reality, and so could not be said to be totally 'non-existent'. In this, he differed from the nihilist/Annihilationists. The empirical self did not exist in an unchanging way, but nor was it non-existent. For him, what is occurring in the present could be said, in a relative sense at least, to 'exist', unlike what is past or what is still to come (S.III.72).

THE 'I AM' ATTITUDE: ITS CAUSE, EFFECT AND ITS ENDING

(1.47) If the 'early Suttas' did not accept a Self, and saw views on Self (even those denying s/Self) as rooted in the 'I am' attitude, the question arises as to how this attitude could itelf come to be. A passage at S.III.46 gives a clue to this:

> Monks, but when there is the attitude 'I am', then there is descent (*avakkanti*) of the five sense-faculties of eye . . . body.
>
> Monks, there is the mind-organ (*mano*), there are mental objects (*dhammas*) there is the element of knowledge (*vijjā-dhātu*); monks, the uninstructed ordinary person, touched by feeling born of stimulation by spiritual ignorance (*avijjā-samphassa-jena*), thinks 'I am'.

That is, due to having the 'I am' attitude in a previous life, one once more has sense-organs, i.e. is reborn. Once the mind-organ gets to work processing the input of the senses, and its own objects, then there is potential for the attitude to emerge again. In this, feeling plays a crucial role. This accords with Paras.1.30–1, which show that the 'I am' attitude is impossible where feeling is absent. In producing the attitude, one conditioning factor is spiritual ignorance: the misperception of the true nature of things. The immediate cause of the attitude, though, seems to be the mind-organ, *mano*. Now the word '*mano*' is from the same root as '*maññati*', the word used for conceited 'conceiving' at e.g. M.I.4 (Para.1.16). One commentary (Asl.140) explains *mano* in terms of 'knowing by measuring', as with a balance, while the 'I am' conceit (*māno*) is very often seen in terms of inter-personal *comparisons*, in terms of 'I am superior', 'I am equal' and 'I am inferior' (e.g. S.IV.88). It is surely this comparing/measuring aspect of *mano* that moves from inter-personal comparisons to build up the conceit of a substantial 'I' that is compared to other 'I-s'. This process seems to be described at Sn.917–18. The first verse refers to an internal or external object as having been 'fully known', just as S.III.46 refers to 'the element of knowledge'. Verse 918 then continues: 'Let him not conceive by that "better", "inferior" or "equal". Touched by diverse forms, let him not stay thinking around Self'. That is, *mano*, as it allows knowledge to arise, also introduces interpersonal comparisons and, based on misinterpretations of the data by which 'oneself' is stimulated, thus suggests a stable 'I' unchanged by what surrounds and impinges on it. One could say, here, that 'a little knowledge is a dangerous thing', especially when it is admixed with spiritual ignorance. One is, indeed, even reminded of the Christian story of evil arising after Adam and Eve eat of the fruit of the tree of knowledge! The above also shows that a translation which well captures the nature of *mano* is 'conception': the activity of 'conceiving', often in a 'conceited' way.

(1.48) It can thus be seen that, though rebirth requires no permanent Self, as some have argued that it did, one cannot be reborn if one lacks the *idea* of Self, or at least its root, the deluded attitude or conceit 'I am'. Having caused rebirth, the attitude arises again in a new life, as the mind-organ processes the 'diverse forms' presented by the senses, and particularly feelings stimulated by sense-input, comparing and measuring what is known in a way which is distorted by spiritual ignorance. Thus, when qualities in 'oneself' and 'others' are compared, this leads to the conceit that there is an underlying, unchanging 'I' which *has* these qualities, and is superior, inferior or equal to other 'I-s'.

(1.49) The Arahat, though, has transcended this 'I am' conceit (*asmi-māno*). As the verses after Sn.918 (above) say, he grows inwardly calm, being one for whom there is nothing possessed: thus there is nothing to be got rid of (Sn.919). He is like the unmoved depths of the ocean, unstirred by the waves (of 'diverse forms', v.918), so as to have no thought of personal prominence (Sn.920). Though he may say 'I say' or 'they say it's mine', he has gone beyond all conceit, for he would 'speak merely conforming to popular usage' (S.I.15). He does not take 'I' and 'mine' in ordinary conversation as implying a substantial, unchanging 'I'. He is fully aware of the changing nature of personality, which is thus no grounds for positing a substantial 'I': he knows that 'whatever he conceives (himself as), it becomes different from that' (Ud.32). Such a person lives without any idea of 'Self' or 'I', he 'does not conceive that he is anything, or anywhere, or in anything' (M.III.45): he is certainly not one who has discovered some true Self or I.

(1.50) What, then, is the overall conclusion of this chapter? It is that the 'early Suttas' neither posit not allow the existence of a metaphysical Self, i.e. a permanent, substantial, autonomous I-essence, however subtly such a concept is formulated. While such an entity is never directly denied, this is because such a denial would have had an inappropriate effect on the hearers of such a denial. The Self-concept is alluded to and made use of in the instruction to see things as not-Self but it is not endorsed. It is even implied, indirectly, that it is a self-contradictory concept, attempting to combine permanence and real I-ness. Only apparent I-ness can be found, however, and then only in relation to the impermanent personality-factors. While a metaphysical Self is not accepted, a changing empirical 'self' *is* accepted: as 'oneself', 'character', 'personality' (the term *attabhāva*)', or *citta* , 'mind/heart'. And yet the Personalists' interpretation of the 'early Sutta' position is invalid. They saw these texts as alluding to a 'person'/Self which neither eternal nor non-eternal and is the organic whole which contains all the personality-factors but is not the same as them. There is, however, no genuine support for such an idea in the texts, and all the supposed functions of the 'person' are carried out by the personality-factors themselves. Reference to an empirical 'self' is simply a way of talking about the functioning personality-factors, not a reference to some hidden extra entity or structure. Why, though, is there such an emphasis on seeing everything as 'not-Self'? This will be examined in the next chapter.

2

THE MEANING OF 'NOT-SELF'

. . . *the ultimate empty thing, nibbāna* (Ps.II.240).

(2.1) In his book *Selfless Persons*, Steven Collins discusses the role of the not-Self teaching for the 'specialist scholar and meditator' of classical and contemporary Theravāda societies. He holds that the 'intellectual position of specialist Buddhism' is that 'there is a radical refusal to speak of a self or permanent person in any theoretical contexts. It is, I think, fruitless for the scholar to try to explain, in his own more or less technical terms, what this "means". . . . Rather, he should see Buddhism's ideological stance as a social, intellectual and soteriological strategy' (p.78). While agreeing that the not-Self teaching clearly is a 'soteriological strategy', I would argue that this does not preclude the scholar from teasing out what the teaching 'means': how the strategy works and what its purpose is. It is the aim of this chapter to do just that with regard to the outlook found in the Pāli Suttas.

THE ROLE OF VIEWING PHENOMENA AS NOT-SELF

(2.2) The 'tone' of the not-Self teaching is seen in numerous passages, indicating that anything subject to the 'three marks' (being impermanent, *dukkha* and not-Self) should not be grasped at, but be dropped like hot bricks. The 'Discourse on the characteristic of not-Self' (*Anatta-lakkhaṇa Sutta*: S.III.66–8), seen as the Buddha's second sermon, first asserts that each of the personality-factors is not-Self. This is then reinforced by emphasizing that they are impermanent and *dukkha*: 'But is it fit to consider that which is impermanent, *dukkha*, of a nature to change, as "This is mine, this I am, this is my Self"?'. The Sutta concludes by saying that one who rightly understands in this way '*nibbindati*' – 'disregards', 'turns away from' or is 'disgusted by' – each of the personality-factors, such that he is free from attachment, is liberated, and knows that the chain of rebirths and all its suffering is ended. Elsewhere the negative aspects of the personality-factors are highlighted by saying that they are to be seen 'as impermanent, as *dukkha*, as a disease, as a boil, as a dart, as a misfortune, as a sickness, as other, as disintegrating, as empty (*suññato*), as not-Self' (S.III.167). They are to be seen as an enemy with a drawn sword (S.IV.174), a burden (S.III.25), a devourer (S.III.87–8.) and murderous (S.III.112–13)!

(2.3) While the 'early Suttas' have no place for a metaphysical Self, then, two things are also clear:

i) an actual denial of s/Self would have sounded like Annihilationism, and legitimated the conceit-founded preoccupation with 'I' and 'Self' (Para.1.45)
ii) seeing things as *not*-Self was clearly regarded as playing a vital soteriological role.

Given that a Self is not asserted, nor explicitly denied, and that seeing things as *not*-Self is so important, it becomes apparent that the concept of 'Self', and the associated deep-rooted feeling of 'I am', are being utilized for a spiritual end. The not-Self teaching can in fact be seen as a brilliant device – a skilful means – which uses a deep-seated human aspiration, ultimately *illusory*, to overcome the negative products of such an illusion. Identification, whether conscious or unconscious, with something as 'what I truly and permanently am' is a source of attachment; such attachment leads to frustration and a sense of loss when what one identifies with changes and becomes other than one desires. The deep-rooted idea of 'Self', though, is not to be attacked, but used as a measuring-rod against which all phenomena should be compared: so as to see them as falling short of the perfections implied in the idea of Self. This is to be done through a rigorous experiential examination: as each possible candidate is examined, but is seen to be not-Self, falling short of the ideal, the intended result is that one should let go of any attachment for such a thing. The aim of seeing things as not-Self, then, is to make one see that this, this, this . . . *everything* one grasps at, due to identifying it as 'Self' or 'I', is *not* Self, such that one should *let go* of it, which letting go brings *nibbāna*. Contemplation of phenomena as impermanent, *dukkha* and not-Self is a way of undermining craving for and clinging to such phenomena.

By seeing things 'as they really are', attachment and its attendant suffering will be undermined.

(2.4) One uses 'not-Self', then, as a reason to let go of things, not to 'prove' that there is no Self. There is no need to give some philosophical denial of 'Self'; the idea simply withers away, or evaporates in the light of knowledge, when it is seen that the concept does not apply to *anything* at all, or, as the Suttas put it, when it is seen that everything is 'empty' of Self. A philosophical denial is just a view, a theory, which may be agreed with or not. It does not get one actually to examine all the things that one really *does* identify with, consciously or unconsciously, as Self or I. This examination, in a calm, meditative context, is what the 'not-Self' teaching aims at. It is not so much a thing to be thought about as to be *done*, applied to actual experience, so that the meditator actually *sees* that '*all dhamma*s are not-Self', 'Self is not being apprehended'. A mere philosophical denial does not encourage this, and may actually mean that a person sees no need for it. One can, then, perhaps see the Self idea as fulfilling a role akin to a rocket which boosts a payload into space, against the force of gravity. It provides the force to drive the mind out of the 'gravity field' of attachment to the personality-factors. Having done so, it then 'falls away and is burnt up', as itself a baseless concept, which arises as part of the unsatisfactory personality-factors.

(2.5) As described in the Suttas, the Buddha was clearly very wary of mere theories or 'views' (*diṭṭhi*s), holding that they led to quarrels (A.I.66) and conceit (Sn.842–43). One should not even cling to the view that all views displease one, but get rid of whatever view one has, and not take up *any* other (M.I.497–501). To be sure, there are what might be called 'Buddhist views', such as belief in the goodness of giving and in karma and rebirth. Such beliefs are termed 'ordinary' (*lokiya*) 'right view', and, though they lead in the right direction, they are still associated with clinging (M.III.72), as they can be clung to if not tested by wisdom (M.I.133). Views, like all else in the conditioned world, are seen to be arisen according to conditions, to be impermanent, and bringing *dukkha* if clung to (A.V.187–88). Wisdom (*paññā*), analytically directed intuitive insight, though, is said to be 'transcendent' (*lokuttara*) 'right view' (M.III.72). When it knows 'all *dhamma*s are not-Self', this is 'well seen, as it really is' (A.V.188), in a way that goes beyond all speculative reasoning or acceptance of ideas from others. The aim, then, is not to have a view or belief, even if it happens to be true, but to have direct knowledge 'not dependent on another' (S.III.135). In other words, to replace a view-point with a direct *seeing*. In the case of the existence of rebirth, for example, this is regarded as a correct view-point (which, according to Buddhism, can be confirmed by direct meditative experience), but a denial of s/Self is not even a correct view-point, for the reasons already given (Paras.1.43–6). Seeing things as not-Self is a tool to cut off identifying with and clinging to things, including views. It should not itself generate a view 'there is no Self'. Seeing things as not-Self is a constructed process, and is itself not-Self: it should not be clung to.

THE CRITERIA FOR SELF-HOOD

(2.6) If seeing phenomena as *not*-Self is so important in early Buddhism, it is worth examining what criteria of Self-hood everything, including *nibbāna*, fail to satisfy. In other words, what would a true Self be like, *if* it existed? What is the ideal that all things fall short of? It is clear from many passages (e.g. S.III.66–8, Para.2.1) that anything which is impermanent and *dukkha* cannot be Self, so Self would have to be permanent and without *dukkha*. It has also been seen that a Self must have self-awareness, knowing 'I am' and 'this I am' (Para.1.31). D.II.66–8 adds, as reasons for something being not-Self, that it is 'constructed (*saṅkhatā*), conditionally arisen . . . a blend of pleasure and pain, liable to arise and fall'. Thus a real Self would have to be: permanent, not liable to arise and fall; entirely free of *dukkha*; unconstructed and not conditioned by anything. One of the reasons that Self must be unconditioned is that whatever arises from a condition that is impermanent, *dukkha* and not-Self will itself have these qualities (S.IV.130 and 131). Perhaps the most crucial aspect of a putative Self would be its freedom from all *dukkha*, such that it only had the opposite quality, *sukha*: happiness or bliss. This is because something's being *dukkha* is usually the most immediate reason for its being not-Self. For example, 'Whatever, sirs, is become, constructed, thought out, conditionally arisen, that is impermanent, that is *dukkha, what is dukkha, "That is not mine, that is not I am, that is not my Self"* ' (A.V.188). That is, a real Self would be a self-aware I which was *totally happy, because* it did not change, because it did not depend on anything else.

(2.7) What do the early Theravadin interpretative texts add to what we have seen from the 'early Suttas'? The Pāli Text Society version of the text of the *Culla-niddesa* (pp.278–82) usefully collects together its passages on 'not-Self', so as to provide a sweeping panorama of its meaning, and thus of the implied meaning of 'Self'. This is done by way of a commentary on 'regard the world as empty (*suññato*)' (Sn.1119), that is: see it as 'empty' of Self (eg. M.II.263). The passage is given below, complete with the headings provided in the PTS. text, and indications of the sources of the 'early Sutta' passages it cites:-

A. In two ways is the world seen as empty: (I) either because of the consideration of the non-exercise-of-power, or (II) because of seeing constructed things (*-saṅkhatā-*) as hollow (*tucchato*).

(I) How, because of the consideration of the non-exercise-of-power does he consider the world to be empty?:-

a) Power is not got over material form . . .

b) This was said by the Lord (*Anatta-lakkhaṇa Sutta*: S.III.66–7, Vin.I.13–14): 'Material form, monks, is not-Self. If, monks, material form were Self, it would not tend to sickness, and one might get the chance of saying in regard to it "Let my material form be thus; let it not be thus". But inasmuch, monks, as it is not-Self, then it tends to sickness, and one does not get the chance of saying this of it. [This is then repeated of the other four personality-factors].

(II) How, because of seeing constructed things as hollow, does he consider the world as empty?:- An essence (*sāro*) is not got in material form, nor in any of the other personality-factors. Material form is without essence, with no essence, with essence gone, in the sense of essence as permanence-essence, or essence as happiness-essence, or essence as Self-essence, or of permanence, or of stability, or of eternity, or of being of a nature not to change. [Nd.II.279:-] . . .

B. Moreover, in six ways does he consider the world as empty: eye (and the other of the eighteen 'elements': Para.I.6)) are empty of Self, or what pertains to Self, or of permanence, or of stability, or of eternity, or of being of a nature not to change . . .

C. Moreover, in ten ways does he regard the world as empty: He considers material form as devoid (*rittato*), as hollow (*tucchato*), as empty, as not-Self, as without an Overlord, as incapable of being made into what one wants, as incapable of being had (as one wishes), as insusceptible to the exercise of power, as other (*parato*), as variegated. [The same is repeated of:] the other personality-factors; decease; arising; relinking; becoming; essence (*sāra-*); the round (of rebirths). [Nd.II.280:-].

D. (I) Moreover, in twelve ways does he consider the world as empty: Material form is not a living being (*satto*), not a life-principle (*jīvo*), not a person, not a man, not a female, not a male, not a Self, not what pertains to a Self, not an I, not a mine, not anyone. [The same is repeated of the other personality-factors].

(II) This was said by the Lord (S.II.64–5): 'This body, monks, is not yours, nor another's: it is to be seen as old karma which is constructed, thought out, felt. Therefore, monks, a learned disciple of the Holy ones attends well, methodically, to Conditioned Arising . . . '

This, too, was said by the Lord (S.III.33–4, M.I.140–41): ' "What, monks, is not yours, put it away; putting it away will be, for a long time, for your welfare and happiness. And what, monks, is not yours? The personality-factors. Just as if, monks, a person were to gather or burn or do as he pleased with the grass, twigs, branches and foliage in this Jeta Grove, would it occur to you: 'This person is gathering *us*, he is burning *us*, he is doing as he pleases with *us*?' " "No, Lord". "What is the reason for this?". "It is, Lord, that this is not our Self nor what pertains to Self". "Even so, monks, what is not yours, put it away . . . " '. [Nd.II.281:-]

E. 'There is no fear, for one who sees, as they really are, the pure and simple arising of *dhamma*s (in 'oneself'), and the pure and simple continuity of constructed things, chieftain. He sees the world, with wisdom, as like grass and wood, [thus far, as at Thag.716–17] there is no other. He wishes for whatever is elsewhere, not for relinking (i.e. rebirth)'.

F. Venerable Ānanda said this to the Lord (S.IV.54):

> ' "The world is empty, the world is empty" is the saying, revered sir, how far does this saying go?'. 'Since, Ānanda, the world is empty of Self or what pertains to Self, therefore is it said that the world is empty [this is explained to refer to the eighteen 'elements', beginning with the eye]'.

This was said by the Lord (S.IV.197): 'Even so, monks, a monk investigates material form as far as the scope of material form; . . . he investigates discernment as far as the scope of discernment. Of him investigating, whatever there is of "I" or "mine" or "I am", there is none of that for him'.

(2.8) What does this long passage add to our picture of the meaning and criteria of use of 'not-Self', and thus of 'Self'? The *first* aspect to be mentioned (A.(I)) is that anything which cannot have complete power and control exercised over it must be not-Self. This is the aspect of not-Self emphasized in the *Anatta-lakkhaṇa Sutta*, as quoted in A. (I). While one can control one's body and mind to a certain extent, there are clear limits: one can move an arm, but not stop it ageing, or make it invulnerable to injury, or make it twice as long as it is. By implication, a Self would have total control over itself. This connects with it having to be totally happy, as this can be ensured only by Self having total control over its parts or aspects. It must have an Overlord (see C.) which is itself. This is the sense, surely, in which Self is not 'other' (C.). Buddhaghosa's *Visuddhimagga* (p.612) comments on this: 'as other because of the inability to have mastery exercised over them, and because of intractability'. Now in the phrase 'as other, as *dukkha*, and not as Self' (A.II.18), the commentary[1] sees 'other' as linked to impermanence, which can be seen in terms of inability make something *stay* the same and not *become* other. However, the phrase 'as other and not as Self' is found (Thag. 1160, 1161; Thig. 177), suggesting that 'other' can be equivalent to 'not-Self', rather than to impermanence. Indeed, it is classified as equivalent to 'not-Self', rather than to 'impermanent' at Ps. II.241–42. Something which is 'other', in this sense, is unruly and not within the ambit of one's full control.

(2.9) What is Self, then, would have to be fully *controlled*, and controlled by *itself*: it must be fully *self-controlled*. The aspect of Self as putative controll*er* is implied in a standard passage (e.g.at M.III.18–19) which explains that knowing and seeing the personality-factors as not-Self gets rid of the 'latent conceits that "I am the doer, mine is the doer" in regard to this discernment-endowed body and all sensory indications external to it'. Self, then, is the supposed agent of actions. This is also seen at Ud.70, where it is said that a wise man is without any ideas of '*I* act' or 'I am the agent'. This is not, of course, because there is a 'true I' which does not act: for the wise man, as has been seen, also lacks ideas of 'I' or 'I am'. As is said in the Abhidhamma, there is action, but no (separate 'Self as) agent of it (Kvu.54).

(2.10) The *second* important aspect of Nd.II.278–82 is that a Self would have an 'essence' of permanence, happiness and Self (A.(II)). Ps.I.53, in fact, sees things as being not-Self 'in the sense of having no essence'. Vism.610 comments on this that Self-essence is 'Self, an abider, a doer, an experiencer, one who is his own master'. Vism.612, on the other hand, says 'as without essence because of feebleness and because of decaying soon like sapwood'. Again, Nd.I.409 f. (commenting on Sn.937), says that the world is 'without essence' as it is like a reed, a lump of foam, a mirage, or the trunk of a plantain tree (which has no core, like an onion). Thus a Self would have to have a real, *substantial* essence, unlike the insubstantial personality-factors. As described at S.III.142, these are 'devoid, hollow', as:

> Material form is like a lump of foam,
> Feeling is like a bubble,
> Cognition is like a mirage,
> The constructing activities are like a plantain tree,
> And discernment is like a conjurer's illusion.

As described at D.II and E., they have no more worth than grass and twigs.

(2.11) A *third* aspect of Nd.II.278–82 is that Self is practically equivalent to 'what pertains to Self', I, mine, 'I am' (D. (I), F.), to a life-principle, being, person, or to 'someone' (D.(I)). This firmly roots Self, as understood in early Buddhist texts, as a personal, individual Self, an *I*. If it were real, it would be no merely abstract entity. D. (II) show that something is not-Self as it is not 'us', or 'our' Self. This compares to 'not-Self' as equivalent to 'other'. Thus, the Buddha did not say 'do not cling to this because it is not some "Self" of speculative thought', but 'do not cling to this because it is *other* that what *you* should take as "I", the "I" you certainly feel you have. *You* should let go of all the things that you can't *really* take as your essential Self or "I": don't be satisfied with *anything* that can't be that'. In this way, disciples were fully encouraged to let go of everything, which process is fuelled by the very ideal of 'Self' which eventually gets burnt away in the process itself.

(2.12) It can thus be seen that the Self-ideal which early Buddhism worked with was of an unconditioned, permanent, totally happy 'I', which is self-aware, in total control of itself, a truly autonomous agent, with an inherent substantial essence, the true nature of an individual person. Of course, not all Self-views may explicitly say this, but the 'early Suttas' and the early Theravāda interpretative texts imply that such ideas are implicit in these views and in the more deep-rooted 'I am' attitude.

NIBBĀNA AND THE SELF-IDEAL

(2.13) The reason for contemplating things as impermanent, *dukkha* and not-Self, is, ultimately, to experience *nibbāna*: the ending of *dukkha*. It can thus be said that *nibbāna* is that for the sake of which the impermanent, *dukkha*, not-Self personality-factors are dropped. This would only make sense if it lacked the imperfections of these factors. And indeed, it is seen as beyond all that is impermanent and *dukkha*, while still being not-Self (Paras.1.15–16). However, the *Paṭisambhāmagga*, an early Theravādin interpretative text, sees it as coming very close to the Self-ideal. Under contemplation of the personality-factors as i) impermanent, ii) *dukkha* and iii) not-Self, they are to be seen, respectively, as:

i) impermanent, wavering, perishable, unstable, of a nature to change, destruction, constructed (*saṅkhata-*), of a nature to die;
ii) *dukkha*, a disease, a boil, a dart, a misfortune, a sickness, a plague, a distress, a danger, a menace, not a protection, not a cave of shelter, not a refuge, devoid (*ritta-*), a disadvantage, the root of misfortune, murderous, with-cankers, a prey to Māra (the evil tempter-god), of the nature of birth, ageing, grief, lamentation, despair and defilement;
iii) other (*para*), disintegrating, hollow (*tuccha-*), empty (*suñña-*), not-Self, lacking an essence (Ps.II.241–42).

The opposite of all of the qualities under i) and ii) are applied to *nibbāna*, according to the pattern: 'Seeing the five personality-factors as *impermanent*, he gets patience accordingly, seeing "the stopping (*nirodho*) of the five personality-factors is the *permanent*, *nibbāna*", he enters into the perfect way' (Ps.II.238–41). Using this pattern, with respect to the 'not-Self' predicates under iii), *nibbāna* is said to be, respectively: 'not conditioned by another (*apara-paccayaṃ*)', 'not of a nature to disintegrate', 'not hollow', 'the ultimate empty thing (*parama-suññaṃ*)', 'the ultimate goal (*paramatthaṃ*)'[2], 'essence'.

(2.14) Here, half the predicates applied to *nibbāna* are straightforward opposites of those equivalent to 'not-Self'. *Nibbāna*, as 'not of a nature to disintegrate', is seen as a reality which does not crumble away, or break into parts. Like Self, it must not only be permanent, but must also have a unitary nature which cannot be split. As regards *nibbāna* being 'essence', Para.2.7 shows the relevant kinds of essence to be permanence, happiness and Self. *Nibbāna* is an essence as it has the first two of these, though not the third. It is the 'real (*santaṃ*)' (A.V.322), something which is not insubstantial like a lump of foam or a mirage (to which the personality-factors are compared), a true essence which is yet empty of Self.[3] *Nibbāna* as 'essence' is clearly also 'not hollow', for in Para.2.7, the 'hollowness' of things is explained in terms of their lacking an essence. It is also not a trivial thing: Vism.612 comments (with respect to the personality factors): 'as hollow because of their devoidness, or because of their triviality'.

(2.15) *Nibbāna* as 'not dependent on another' is not a straightforward opposite of the personality-factors as 'other'. Among the meanings of 'other', discussed in Paras. 2.8 and 2.11, are 'becoming other' i.e. changeable, and other-than-(supposed)-Self: unruly/intractable. Clearly, *nibbāna* is not Self, but it is the opposite of changeable. Like a supposed Self, it is not dependent on anything else, and so is quiescent, unruffled, and unchanging. While this means that it is not 'unruly', it cannot be seen as fully 'tractable', in the sense of being totally controllable at will: for much effort is needed to attain it! *Nibbāna* is also 'the ultimate empty thing' as it is empty of Self, and it is the 'ultimate goal'. Here the pattern of *nibbāna* being the clear opposite of the personality-factors is decisively broken: it is *not* said to be 'not-empty' or 'Self'. Like everything, it is empty of Self, though it is the highest of all empty things. While it is not Self, which is usually taken as the ultimate goal, it is the genuine ultimate goal. Self is thought of as located within the personality-factors in some way, but when attachment to these ends, all idea of Self evaporates, and *nibbāna* is experienced as the real 'ultimate goal'.

(2.16) Thus *nibbāna*, like Self, is permanent (and not wavering, unstable, constructed etc.: see Para. 2.13), happiness (and not a disease, a sickness, but a protection, cave of shelter, refuge, unborn, etc.: see Para. 2.13), and it is even undisintegrating, not hollow, an essence, and not dependent on another. Where Self and *nibbāna* differ is with respect to the very aspect of *Self*-hood, I-ness. Firstly, being the stopping of the personality-factors (Para.2.13, also Sn.727–37), *nibbāna* is the stopping of anything that could allow self-awareness as 'I am' or 'this I am', essential for Self-hood (see Para.1.31). Secondly, while it is not itself dependent on anything else, it cannot be controlled at will. Similarly, it does not make sense to see it as the agent-controller of action, as Self is seen to be.

(2.17) *Nibbāna* is realized, and the personality-factors stopped, by fully knowing the personality-factors as not-Self, thus ending all attachment. As *nibbāna* is the stopping of the factors, this further shows their impermanence, and thus that they are not-Self. *Nibbāna* itself is not-Self as it is the stopping of the breeding-ground for the 'I am' attitude, beyond all possibility of I-ness. Thus, where there was formerly impermanence and a supposed 'I', there is now permanence and no grounds at all for 'I'. All the personality-factors are dropped because they fall short of the Self-ideal. The moment this ideal might be attained, though, in *nibbāna*, the very possibility of Self drops away: yet most of what it stood for remains. *Nibbāna* might thus be seen as the virtual attainment of Self-hood. It is everything that Self might be except that it is empty of I-ness, controllability and agency. It is that which is 'not dependent on another' attained by not depending on *anything* as 'Self'. It is the 'ultimate empty thing', which is true permanence and happiness.

3

DEVELOPING A SELF WITHOUT BOUNDARIES

This is the Path by which those with great selves . . . have fared (It.28–9).

(3.1) Having seen that *nibbāna* shares most, if not all, of the characteristics of a supposed metaphysical Self, it will now be shown that the 'early Suttas' see an enlightened person as one whose *empirical* self is highly developed. Thus, while Self is seen as a baseless concept, this does not preclude the development of a strong empirical self. Indeed, the most developed self is one which is, precisely, known as Selfless and I-less. Thus, paradoxically, the way to attain the Self-like *nibbāna* and to develop a fully mature empirical self, is, at least in part, to know everything as Selfless.

LIVING WITH *CITTA* AS AN 'ISLAND'

(3.2) The path which leads to Arahatship is portrayed, in the 'early Suttas', as one which builds up self-reliance and an inner centre of calm:

> Herein, monks, a monk fares along contemplating the body in the body, ardent, clearly conscious, mindful, so as to control covetousness and dejection with respect to the world; he fares along contemplating feelings in feelings . . . *citta*s in *citta*s . . . basic patterns (*dhammā-*) in basic patterns . . . Thus, monks, a monk lives with himself as an island (*atta-dīpo*), with himself as a refuge, with no other (person) as a refuge, (he lives) with Dhamma as an island, Dhamma as a refuge, with no other (Dhamma) as refuge[1]. Keep to your own pastures, monks, range in your own native beat. Ranging there Māra will not get a chance, he will not get an opportunity (for attack). It is thus by reason of undertaking wholesome states, monks, that this goodness-power[2] grows' (D.III.58).

S.V.148–49 explains that what is 'not one's own pasture but another's native beat' are objects of the five senses which excite sense-desire (known as the (*kāma-guṇa*s). Through these, the evil god Māra 'gets a chance' over one. One's 'own pasture', on the other hand, consists of the four foundations of mindfulness: body, feelings, *citta*-states and key patterns of existence, inasmuch as they are objects of mindful contemplation. We thus see that the above quote counsels one to keep aloof, by means of mindful alertness, from the things that excite sensual desire, this being what it is to live with oneself and the (taught and practised) Dhamma as 'island' and 'refuge'. One should live quietly overseeing one's body and mind so that one's mind is unperturbed and not excited to desire. The 'self' which one thus has as an 'island' is *citta*, the heart/mind, which Para.1.9 has shown to be a common meaning for 'self' in the 'early Suttas'. That it is the meaning in the present context can be seen, again, from S.V.148–49. This speaks of a monkey which lives where only monkeys range, but is trapped by a hunter in the area where humans also range. The hunter represents Māra, who 'gets a chance' over a person by means of the five *kāma-guṇa*s. As the monkey is often used as a symbol for *citta* (e.g. S.II.94), one can see that *this* is what should keep to its 'own range' and should be an 'island', so as to be out of Māra's reach. Indeed, at Dhp.40 one reads:

> Realizing that this body is as fragile as a jar,
> Establishing this *citta* as a (fortified) city,
> He should attack Māra with the weapon of wisdom,
> He should guard his conquest and be without attachment.

DEVELOPING A 'GREAT SELF'

(3.3) The *citta* of one on the Buddhist path, then, should not be at the mercy of outside stimuli, nor of its own moods etc. (the object of the third foundation of mindfulness), but should be an island of calm, imbued with self-control, self-contained. It should no longer be scattered and diffused but should be more integrated and consistently directed towards one goal, *nibbāna*. Indeed, at S.V.5–6, it is said that a term for the Holy Eightfold Path is 'Dhamma-vehicle', with the meaning of this explained in verse:

> Who has faith and wisdom, (these) yoked states ever lead
> him on,

Moral integrity (*hiri*) is the pole, mind-organ (*mano*) the
yoke,
Mindfulness is the watchful charioteer.
The chariot is furnished with virtue,
Meditation (*jhāna*) its axle, strength its wheels,
Equanimity, concentration, its shaft; desirelessness its
drapery,
Goodwill, non-injury and seclusion are his weapons,
Endurance is his leather coat of mail:
(This chariot) rolls on to attain rest from exertion [*nibbāna*].
This is become Self-like (*attaniyam*),
It is the unsurpassed Brahma-vehicle,
(Seated in it) the self-relying leaves the world,
Certainly they win victory.

Thus the components of the Path, integrated into a consistent whole, in a consistent *citta*-state, can be called a 'Self-like' Dhamma-vehicle which leads to *nibbāna*. It cannot, of course be a metaphysical Self as it is a composite, constructed entity – the Holy Path is said to be the best of all constructed things (A.II.34) – but it is characterized by Self-like qualities.

(3.4) The Holy Path is also described as the way by which 'one with a great self (*mahattā*)' travels. Thus at It.28–9, the Buddha says of the religious life which goes to *nibbāna*, 'This is the Path by which those with great selves (*mahattehi*), great seers have fared'. This idea of a 'great self' is amplified at A.I.249. Here the Buddha explains that the same small (evil) deed may take one sort of person to hell to experience its karmic fruition, while another sort of person will experience its fruition in the present life, and not beyond. The first sort of person is 'of undeveloped body, undeveloped virtue, undeveloped *citta*, undeveloped wisdom, he is limited (*paritto*), he has an insignificant self (*appātume*), he dwells insignificant and miserable'. The second is 'of developed body, developed virtue, developed *citta*, developed wisdom, he is not limited, he has a great self (*mahattā*), he dwells immeasurable (*appamāṇa-*)'. This contrast of fates is illustrated by saying that a grain of salt will make a cup of water undrinkable, but not the great mass of the river Ganges. As the person who has a 'great self' can still do a small evil action, which brings some karmic fruition, he must be someone who is not yet an Arahat. As he is of developed virtue, and does not experience karmic fruition in hell, he is probably at least a Stream-enterer, who has transcended all bad rebirths. As for the 'self' which is 'great', this is no metaphysical Self, but the very 'self' which would have been 'insignificant' when the person in question had not yet developed 'body', virtue, *citta* and wisdom: it must thus describe such qualities.[3]

(3.5) What transforms a person's empirical self from being 'insignificant' into being 'great' can clearly be seen as such practices as the cultivation of lovingkindness (*mettā*) and mindfulness (*sati*). The relevance of lovingkindness can be seen from A.V.299, where a disciple whose *citta* is 'grown great' and 'immeasurable' through lovingkindness knows: 'Formerly this *citta* of mine was limited (*parittaṃ*), but now my *citta* is immeasurable (*appamāṇaṃ*), well developed'. The wording of this shows its relevance to the A.I.249 passage above. As for the relevance of mindfulness, this can be seen from M.I.270, which says that one who feels no attraction or repugnance for any of the six sense-objects, and who has mindfulness of the body, dwells 'with a mind that is immeasurable (*appamāṇa-cetaso*)', in contrast to someone with the opposite qualities, who dwells 'with mind that is limited (*paritta-cetaso*)' (p.266).

'ONE OF DEVELOPED SELF'

(3.6) As the path towards Arahatship is building up a 'great self' and a personality that has 'become Self-like', then it is no wonder that the Arahat is called 'one of developed self (*bhāvit-atto*)', a title which differentiates him or her from a 'learner (*sekho*)' (It.79–80, cf.57 and 69). A long explanation of this term is found in the *Culla-niddesa* (pp.218–19), commenting on its application to the Buddha at Sn.1049. Summing up the various strands of the explanation, one can say that for one who is '*bhāvit-atto*':

i) virtue, wisdom, the Path and the spiritual faculties are well 'developed';
ii) 'body' (*kāya*) is 'developed' and 'steadfast';
iii) *citta* is 'developed', 'steadfast', 'well-released' and without ill-will;
iv) he is 'unlimited, great, deep, immeasurable, hard to fathom, with much treasure, arisen (like the) ocean' (cf. M.I.486–87);
v) in the face of the six sense-objects, he has equanimity and is not confused; he sees only what is seen, hears only what is heard etc. [i.e. does not project and elaborate on what is actually

sensed], and he has no desire or attachment for such sense-objects;

vi) the six senses are 'controlled' and 'guarded';

vii) he is 'self-controlled (*atta-danto*)', and 'with a well-controlled self (*attanā sudantena*)'.

(3.7) The above explanation of why someone – a Buddha or Arahat – is 'one of developed self' certainly shows that such a person has developed all the good aspects of their personality. It also makes clear, though, that such a person has two groups of qualities that might be seen as in opposition to each other:

i) he is self-controlled and has a *citta* that is not shaken by the input of the senses: he is self-contained;

ii) he has a *citta* which has no limit or measure: he has no boundaries.

How can someone be self-contained and yet have no boundaries? To answer this, further aspects of i) and ii) need to be explored.

THE ARAHAT AS SELF-CONTAINED AND 'DWELLING ALONE'

(3.8) The Arahat's self-contained nature is shown in many ways. For example, at A.I.124, he is described as 'one with a *citta* like a diamond (*vajirūpama-citto*)': his *citta* can 'cut' anything and is itself uncuttable: it cannot be affected by anything. Thus, at S.II.274, the Buddha's chief disciple, Sāriputta, says that he does not know of *anything* from whose alteration he would be caused sorrow or *dukkha*, and at Thag.715–17, the Arahat Adhimutta shows complete equanimity when his life is threatened: nothing can dismay him (see E in Para.2.7). Again, the Arahat is 'unsoiled' by anything. At S.III.140, it is said that a *tathāgata* is like a lotus flower which 'stands unsoiled by the water' (water runs off it 'like water from a duck's back'), as he dwells 'unsoiled (*anupalitto*) by the world'. Similarly, at Thag.1180, Moggallāna says of himself, 'he is not soiled by constructed states, as a lotus is not soiled by water'. Elsewhere, the image of a lotus flower or leaf being unsoiled by water is used to illustrate various qualities: 'Thus the sage, speaking of peace, without greed, is unsoiled by sense-desire and the world' (Sn.845); 'lamenting and envy do not soil him' (Sn.811); 'Thus the sage is not soiled by what is seen, heard or sensed' (Sn.812). Similarly, there is reference to Arahats 'having put evils outside, unsoiled' (S.I.141). Such passage show that an Arahat is 'unsoiled' by the world or conditioned things in the sense that he does not react to them with greed, lamentation etc., he has no attachment for them and is unaffected by them.

(3.9) One can see, in fact, that the Arahat is, in a sense, cut off from the world of the six sense-objects. Thus, at M.III.274–75, the Buddha outlines a simile: a butcher who cuts off the hide from a dead cow and then drapes it back over the carcase would be wrong to say 'This hide is conjoined with the cow as before'. Here, the carcase stands for the six senses, the hide stands for the objects of these senses, and the tendons and ligaments which are cut stand for 'delight and attachment'. As attachment is only fully got rid of by an Arahat, the simile is surely meant to apply to him. He is thus portrayed as being such that his senses are in no way tied or bound to the objects of which they are aware. He passes through the world without sticking to it. He is thus one who 'dwells alone (*eka-vihārī*) even if he is in the midst of a crowd, for he has destroyed 'delight' and 'attachment' with respect to the six desirable sense-objects (S.IV.36–7). Similarly, at S.II.283–84, a monk living alone is told by the Buddha that to perfect 'dwelling alone (*eka-vihāro*)', he should abandon the past, renounce the future and give up 'desire and attachment' for what is 'presently (his) assumption of selfhood (*attabhāva-*)'. He then gives a verse:

Who overcomes all, knows all, very wise,
Unsoiled by any *dhamma*,
Who, letting go of all, is freed in the destruction of craving,
That is the man of whom I say 'he dwells alone'.

The Arahat thus dwells totally 'alone' as he has let go of *everything*, is not 'soiled' by anything. By ending attachment, he has 'abandoned' the personality-factors (S.III.27), and the 'home' which they constitute (S.III.9–10).

(3.10) This 'aloneness' seems to apply not only to the Arahat, but also to *nibbāna*. 'Seclusion (*viveko*)' is a synonym for 'detachment' (*virāga*) and 'stopping' (*nirodha*) (e.g. at S.IV.365–68) and, as these are themselves synonyms for *nibbāna* (e.g. at It.88), *nibbāna* can be seen as such a 'seclusion'. Thus *Mahā-niddesa* 26–7, commenting on this word at Sn.772, says that it can be of three kinds:

i) of body (*kāya*): physical seclusion in the form of forest-dwelling;
ii) of *citta*: as in the case of *citta* in any of the eight states of meditative *jhāna*, or of an Arahat or lesser saint such as a Stream-enterer, such *citta*s being 'secluded' from various unwholesome states;
iii) from 'substrate (*upadhi*): this refers to *nibbāna*, which is 'secluded' from 'substrate' in the form of defilements, personality-factors and constructing activities which generate karma (cf.Ps.II.220 and Nd.II.251).

THE ARAHAT'S BOUNDARYLESS *CITTA*

(3.11) The Arahat is in several places described in such a way as to suggest that he has broken down all barriers between 'himself' and 'others'. At M.I.139, he is said to have:

i) 'lifted the barrier', i.e. got rid of spiritual ignorance;
ii) 'filled in the moat', i.e. ended rebirth;
iii) 'pulled up the pillar', i.e. got rid of craving;
iv) 'withdrawn the bolt', i.e. got rid of the five spiritual fetters which lead to rebirth in the realm of sense-desire;
v) become 'a pure one with flag laid low, burden dropped, without fetters', i.e. he has got rid of the 'I am conceit'.

The Arahat can thus be seen as no longer waving the flag of 'I am', and so no longer has boundaries; for he no longer identifies with any particular group of phenomena such as his 'own' personality-factors. There is no longer spiritual ignorance to act as a barrier. Thus the Buddha refers to himself as having broken the 'egg-shell of spiritual ignorance' (A.IV.176). In a similar, but more striking way, the non-Theravādin Sanskrit text the *Avadāna-śataka* says of the Arahat, 'He lost all attachment to the three worlds; gold and a clod of earth were the same to him; the sky and the palm of his hand were the same to his mind; . . . he had torn the egg-shell (of ignorance) by his knowledge . . . ; he obtained the [meditative] knowledges, the *abhijñā*s'.[4] Again, A.II.166 compares the 'break up' of spiritual ignorance to the 'breach of a dyke' which will occur in 'a village pond that has stood for countless years' when all the inlets are opened, the outlets blocked, and it rains down steadily. Thus spiritual ignorance is like a 'barrier' to be lifted, an 'egg-shell' to be broken, and the 'dyke' of an ancient pond, to be burst. The Arahat is one who has destroyed such an enclosing boundary.

(3.12) The lack of boundaries to the Arahat's mind is perhaps well illustrated at M.I.206–07 (cf. M.III.156). Here, the Buddha approaches the monks Anuruddha, Nandiya and Kimbila, greeting them simply as 'Anuruddhas̱'. He then asks them, 'And how is it that you, Anuruddhas, are living together on friendly terms and harmonious, as milk and water blend, regarding one another with the eye of affection?' To this, Anuruddha replies that this is because he has developed lovingkindness, with respect to acts of body, speech and mind, for his companions, and thus gone on to become such that, 'I, Lord, having surrendered my own *citta*, am living only in accordance with the *citta* of these venerable ones. Lord, we have diverse bodies (*kāyā*) but assuredly have only one *citta* '. He then explains that they help each other with various chores and (p.210) that he has read the minds of his companions so as to know that they have mastery of all eight meditative *jhāna*s, and destroyed the spiritual 'cankers' (*āsava*s) (i.e. they are Arahats). In this passage, one thus finds three Arahats being regarded as having *one citta* and being all called 'Anuruddha', even though this is the actual name of only one of them. This merging of *citta*s is motivated by lovingkindness, a quality which when fully developed means that a person no longer has the barriers which make him prefer his own happiness to that of others, and make the *citta* 'immeasurable' (see Vism.307–08, Sn.368 and 705). One must also assume that such a merging is enabled by the three monks being Arahats, whose *citta*s are no longer enclosed in an 'egg-shell' of spiritual ignorance, and who no longer wave the 'flag' of 'I am'.

(3.13) The reason why the Arahat's *citta* has no boundaries, why he 'dwells with a *citta* made to be without boundaries' is explained in a number of places. It is because he is 'escaped from, unfettered by, released from' the personality-factors, being like a lotus standing above the water, unsoiled by it (A.I.152); because he feels no attraction or repugnance for the objects of the six senses and so is 'independent (*anissito*)', 'released, unfettered' (M.III.30); and because he has fully understood the satisfaction of, misery of, and 'leaving behind (*nissaranaṃ*)' (i.e. *nibbāna*, from Ud.80–81) of the personality-factors, so as to be 'escaped, unfettered, released' (S.III.31).

THE ARAHAT'S NOT-SELF, BOUNDARYLESS, SELF-CONTAINED SELF

(3.14) The above, then, enables a resolution of the apparent tension outlined in Para.3.7. It is *because* an Arahat is so self-contained, having abandoned everything, being 'unsoiled' by anything, without attachment or repugnance for sense-objects, independent, 'dwelling alone', and having experienced *nibbāna*, 'seclusion', that his *citta* has no boundaries. *Citta*, being completely 'alone' *has* no barriers or boundaries. When a person lets go of everything, such that 'his' identity shrinks to zero, then *citta* expands to infinity. Whatever one grasps at and identifies with as 'I am' limits one. As can be seen at Sn.1103 and S.I.12, it allows Māra to 'follow' a person, and gods and humans to 'search him out'. The Arahat, however, does not invest anything with I-ness and so cannot be 'found' anywhere. Though he is completely 'alone', he 'is' no-one, he 'does not conceive that he is anything, or anywhere, or in anything' (M.III.45). He is a 'man of nothing (*akiñkano*)' who has broken through the binding-energy of I-centred existence, being one of those 'who fare in the world with self as an island, entirely released, men of nothing' (Sn.501).

(3.15) The Arahat dwells with 'self' (i.e. *citta*) as an island, but he knows that 'himself', 'others' and the world are all, equally, not-Self, and that there is no real 'I' anywhere: he has nothing on the island, so to speak. Thus Adhimutta was not afraid when his life was threatened, as there was no 'I am' attitude there to cause a feeling of threat and fear, only a flow of conditioned *dhamma*s (Thag.715–17): the threat passed straight through him, so to speak, without meeting any target. Again, the Arahat's senses are 'cut off' from their objects, not because he invests identity in his sentient body and shuns all else[5], but because he sees *both*, the inner and the outer, as equally not-Self. He is undisturbed by the world, not because he is protected from it by a barrier, but because he knows that no such barrier exists, separating a 'Self', an 'I', from 'others'. All is equally not-Self, so there are no grounds for I-grasping to arise and give his *citta* limiting boundaries. Paradoxically, by realizing that all he had taken as Self and 'I' is really not-Self and insusceptible to control (S.III.66–8), the Arahat is no longer controlled by such things – they have no hold over him – and he is more able to control them – he has mastery over mental processes. As Edward Conze says, one aware of things as not-Self will see that 'possessions possess you, see their coercive power and that "I am theirs" is as true as "they are mine" ' (1962: 37). Nyanaponika expresses a similar thought when he says 'Detachment gives, with regard to its objects, mastery as well as freedom' (1969: 68)

(3.16) In sum, it can be seen that the Holy Eightfold Path, when properly integrated into someone's personality, is regarded as 'become Self-like', and those on the Path are such as to live with 'self' – *citta* – as an 'island', by means of the foundations of mindfulness. By such factors as mindfulness and lovingkindness, the Path can be seen as developing good qualities and inner strength, such that Stream-enterers etc. are referred to as 'those with great selves'. Each can be seen as a truly 'big person'. At the culmination of the Path is the Arahat, 'one of developed self', who has carried the process of personal development and self-reliance to its perfection. He or she is thus very self-contained and self-controlled, with a 'diamond-like *citta*', unperturbed and 'unsoiled' by anything. His or her senses are not tied to their objects and he has perfected 'dwelling alone' by letting go of everything, such as the personality-factors, with no attachment or repugnance. He is independent, and has experienced *nibbāna*, the ultimate 'seclusion', the 'leaving behind' of the conditioned world. It is because of these self-contained qualities that the Arahat is one who has made his *citta* be without boundaries and has broken the 'egg-shell', burst the ancient 'pond', of spiritual ignorance, and is such that his *citta* can merge with that of other Arahats. He is an independent 'man of nothing' who does not identify with anything as 'I', but who surveys everything, internal and external, as not-Self. He is thus i) completely 'alone', with 'self' as an island: he does not identify with anything, does not 'lean' on anything for support, is not influenced by anything, as nothing can excite attachment, repugnance or fear in him, and ii) he has a boundaryless *citta*, not limited by attachment or I-identification, and immeasurable with such qualities as lovingkindness.[6] He has, then, a developed, boundless 'self', this being, paradoxically, because he is completely devoid of any tendency to the conceit 'I am', having realized that no metaphysical Self can be found: that the thought of 'I am' can only arise with respect to the personality-factors, which cannot possibly give it genuine validity. As seen at Sn.19, he is one whose 'hut', i.e. *citta*, is open and whose 'fire', i.e. attachment, hatred and delusion, which are centred on the 'I am' conceit, has gone out.

4

PERSONAL CONTINUITY AND RESPONSIBILITY

. . . *the pure and simple continuity of constructed states* (Thag.716).

(4.1) If the enlightened person has a well-developed empirical self, what of the empirical self of non-enlightened people? Given that the 'early Suttas' and early Theravādin interpretative texts see a person as a cluster of interacting, changing states, what is their position on the following questions:

i) does it make sense to hold a person karmically responsible for past actions, if he or she is not unchangingly the *same* person?
ii) to what extent is there a continuity of character from life to life?
iii) how is such continuity accounted for?

Such questions were among those that the Personalists raised regarding the view that 'person' is simply a conventional label for the personality-factors (see Paras.1.36–42). They saw their 'person' as that which travels through the round of rebirths (L'AK.V.271), though it was neither eternal nor non-eternal (Kvu. 24); over time, it was neither 'the same', 'different', 'both the same and different', 'neither the same nor different', nor all of these together (Kvu. 28–9)! It was seen as the structural unity of the personality-factors, though the factors which it unified were admitted to be ever-changing. In support of their position, they pointed to such passages as It.17–18, which says that the bones of 'one person', in many lives, would make a huge pile. They also saw the 'person' as the substantive agent of action (SNS.177–78), as necessary for the ascription of moral responsibility (SNS.170), and as that which explained how karma could produce results in the future. The Personalists were right to be concerned about questions of responsibility and continuity, and to resist any view of personality which saw it as so changeable as to undermine these. Nevertheless, there is no need to posit a substantial 'person' to account for such things: this chapter will show how the 'early Suttas' and subsequent Theravāda (and to some extent Sarvāstivāda) literature did this in a convincing way.

THE PERSON AS A CONTINUITY

(4.2) The understanding of personality as a flux of causally-related states is well expressed in some verses by the Arahat Adhimutta, said to have been spoken when his life was threatened:

> I do not have the thought "I have been", nor do I have the thought "I shall be"; conditioned things will cease to exist. What lamentation will there be in respect of that?
>
> There is no fear, for one who sees, as they really are, the pure and simple arising of *dhammas*, the pure and simple continuity (*-santati-*) of constructed stated states . . .'
>
> (Thag.715–16).

Similarly, at M.I.265, it is said that one who understands Conditioned Arising will not wonder on whether or what 'I' was in the past, will be in the future, or am now. There is a flow of conditioned states, but no substantial, unchanging 'I' is found to exist. The states which make up this flow or 'continuity' are seen as ceaselessly changing. The Abhidhamma is based around the idea that at each micro-moment, a new cluster of states, conditioned by each other and those that went before, arise and help condition those that come after. In the Suttas, it is said that, in the present, only the present empirical self is real, not the past and future ones, but that these are causally related, just as milk turns to curds, which turns to butter (D.I.201). This simile is taken up in the post-Canonical *Milindapañha*, where it is said that the milk itself is not the curds or butter, but that they 'come into being in dependence on just this' (Miln.41). Just so, 'a continuity (*-santati*) of *dhammas* runs on; one uprises, another ceases. . . .' The same text illustrates the idea of a 'continuity' by the simile of a seed which is planted, so as to grow and yield fruit, from which a seed is taken and planted . . . etc. (Miln.50–1). That is, it is a series where what comes after grows out of what came before, in an ongoing process.

(4.3) It is as a conditioned and conditioning series of processes, then, that a person comes into existence. As said by a nun at S.I.134, a being has no 'maker', for the personality-factors are neither 'self-made' nor 'made by another', but arise in dependence on a cause, just as a seed grows when it has earth and moisture. Similarly, at S.II.19–20 (cf. S.II.33–4 and S.II.38), it is said that painful feeling is not made by self, other, both, or neither (i.e. without any reason). Were it to be self-made, this would be Eternalism, with both the agent of past karma and the present experiencer of its result being the same unchanging I. Were it to be other-made, this would be Annihilationism, with the agent of past karma being totally unrelated to the person experiencing its result in the present life. Both these extremes are avoided by understanding life as the flow of conditions outlined in the Conditioned Arising series. At M.III.19, the Buddha thus rebukes a monk for asking, 'Then what Self do karmas affect which are done by what is not-Self?'; his response is to remind his monks that he has trained them to understand things in terms of not-Self conditions. As expressed by the *Milindapañha*, over time a person 'is not the same and he is not another' (Miln.40). The link between rebirths is like lighting one lamp from another: the transmission of a process, not the passing over of some substantial entity (Miln.72). As Vasubandhu expresses it, 'of the flame which burns a jungle, one says that it travels, although it is only moments of flame, because those constitute a series; similarly the combination of personality-factors incessantly renewed receives the figurative name "a being"; supported by craving, the series of personality-factors travels in the round of rebirth' (L'AK.V.271).

RESPONSIBILITY FOR ACTIONS

(4.4) Without an unchanging 'I', and indeed without any agent other than the process of action (Para.2.9), how is responsibility to be accounted for? That it is important in the 'early Suttas' is shown from M.III.179–80, where Yama, king of the dead, reprimands an evil-doer who has arrived in hell, saying that a certain deed was done by *him*, and not by any friend or relative, so that *he* must experience its karmic result. This passage need not imply that such a past action was done by a substantial, still existent Self, but only that it was done by an earlier portion of the 'continuity' that the person now is: rather than by any other continuity. He, no-one else, is responsible. Moreover, he cannot evade responsibility by saying that he had no control over what actions he performed, like the fatalist Ājīvakas (D.I.53): for there is an 'element of initiating (*ārabbha-dhātu*)' in people, which allows them to initiate actions (A.III.337–38). Karma, literally 'action', is seen as the volition behind an overt action, 'It is will (*cetanā*), O monks, that I call karma; having willed, one performs an action through body, speech or mind' (A.III.415). Willing is a conditioned process, but most of its conditions lie within a person, and some are simultaneous with it, such as mindful awareness. There is a sense, then, in which a person has control over the actions he performs.

(4.5) Is it fair, just or appropriate, though, that a later portion of a 'continuity' should suffer for the actions performed by an earlier portion of it? This problem, along with the related one of why the changes which occurs through rebirth do not destroy karma and its results, is dealt with at Miln.46–8 and 72. Nāgasena says that, though the mind-and-body (*nāma-rūpa*) of one life is different from that of previous ones, one is not, thereby 'freed from evil karma'. He then explains this by similes. The first of these (pp. 46 and 72) is that of a someone who steals a man's mangoes, but then denies that they belonged to the owner, as the mangoes planted by the man were different from the ones he had taken (they had grown bigger!). King Milinda agrees that, 'these mangoes, revered sir, come into existence in dependence on (these others), therefore he would still deserve punishment' (Miln.72). The second simile is that of a man who lights a lamp which then sets fire to his house, and thence the whole village. He is still responsible for burning the village, even though the fire which burnt it was not precisely the same as the one he had lit (Miln.47). The point made by these similes seems to be that even the *objects* of an action are not static, but change and develop in a causally ordered series: so why cannot action (karma) and the person who does it change in this way without wiping out his responsibility for past actions?

(4.6) Karma done in a past life, and which has not yet produced its results, can still be seen as existing in the 'continuity' that a person is: karmic potency will be passed on as a pattern within the continuity, conditioned by the past performance of the appropriate past action (i.e. past volition). As regards the continuity itself (the person), it cannot occur in one rebirth cut off from the effects of karmas previously performed by it: as there would *be* no continuation into another rebirth except 'in dependence on' such past conditioning karmas. As Nāgasena puts it, mind-and-body 'reconnect' *because* of past karma (Miln.46–7). Karma is like a seed (A.I.134–35), and the term for a karmic result is a 'fruit' (*phala*) or 'fruition' (*vipāka*); the one develops into the other, contributing to the process whereby the earlier portion of a 'continuity' evolves into and brings about the later portion. There is no danger that a person might, unjustly, get the 'wrong' karmic results: it is not a question of a 'reward' or 'punishment' finding the 'right' person. It is said that 'beings are heirs to karma, karma is matrix, karma is kin' (M.III.203); so a person is actually the *product* of his past karma: without it, he would not exist. Karma can never bring results to the 'wrong' person, just as, when two mango seeds are planted, each produces a specific mango, and each mango only grows from one seed and not from the seed which produced the other mango (Vism.555). To ask how karma 'catches up' with the 'right person' is like asking how a seed produces the 'right mango'. A seed simply develops into the mango that develops from it. Similarly, a being is what past karmas have made it and is the 'evolute' of a being in the past, as T.W. Rhys Davids expresses it (1910: 46). To a large extent, he actually *consists* of the fruitions of past karmas. In the Abhidhamma, the states comprising the mental aspects of a person are either the result of past karma (of a past or the present life), part of the generation of new karma, or, in a few cases, non-karmic 'functional' states.

THE STABILITY OF CHARACTER TRAITS OVER LIVES

(4.7) To what extent, though, is there a consistency of character over lives? How close does the continuity of a being over time approximate to unchanging identity? As the round of rebirths has no discernible beginning (S.II.178), and the past is often discussed in terms of huge 'eons' (*kappa*s) of time, the 'continuity' that a being is must be seen as ancient without measure. While all the component processes of the continuity are marked by change and impermanence, various character-traits are, in fact, seen as very long-lasting, and take time to manifest their impermanency. That is, the psychic heritage of a being contains many conditioned patterns, and some of these repeat themselves over many lives.

(4.8) One such trait or pattern is sex. In the Suttas, when reference is made to the sex of a being in more than one life, in most cases it is the same. For example, in all of the *Vimānavatthu* – a text on heavenly rebirths –, there is no place where it is *said* that there is a sex-change between lives. In many cases, the sex is definitely the same, though in some cases this is only said in the commentary. *Vimanavatthu* sections 1–15 and 44 all concern women, most of whom are said to be goddesses (*devīs*) in their next life (the rest are, neutrally, described as *devatās*). In section 53, a male Brahmin is reborn as a male god, while in 51, a male *frog* is even said to be reborn thus. The *Petavatthu* is a similar text, on those reborn as ghosts. Here, there is even a case of a woman reborn as the *queen* of a king 'Brahmadatta' 86,000 times! (Book II, story 13).

(4.9) Nevertheless, sex is not seen as a completely unchangeable component of a being's ongoing personality, for this very woman is told, 'You were a woman, you have been a man and as an animal also you were born'. The commentary here explains that this was said in answer to her question as to whether one is *always* born with the same sex. The story then goes on to tell of a woman who, 'having faded out the *citta* (mind-set) of a woman', and developed the *citta* of lovingkindness, is reborn among the *brahmā* gods, who are sexless (Vibh.418). Elsewhere, a male god says that he had been a woman, but by faith in the Buddha, Dhamma and Sangha, and living ethically, 'having faded out the *citta* of a woman, and developed the *citta* of a man', (s)he was reborn in her present male status (and in a higher rebirth than some monks she had known; D.II.272). J.III.93–4 reports a sex-change in the opposite direction, concerning a *brahmā* god reborn as a virtuous woman who marries the Bodhisatta (Gotama in a past life) and then becomes an ascetic with him. Thig.400–47 reports a male-female sex-change in the case of a (once) *un*virtuous person. Here, an Arahat nun says that, in a past rebirth, she had been a male adulterer, who had then gone through a rebirth in a hell, then as three kinds of animals who were castrated, as a hermaphrodite human, as a troublesome co-*wife* and, in her current life, as a woman rejected by several husbands. Such passages demonstrate that the sex of a being *is* seen as changeable, but that it will stay the same, as if by force of momentum, unless, i) some specific re-direction of the mind is made to this end, or ii) the fruition of karma makes a sex change particularly appropriate.

(4.10) The Thig.400–47 reference also demonstrates that the effects of karma are seen as a long-lasting feature of a being's 'continuity'. This is even more clear from M.III.169–71. Here it is said that a being reborn in hell will take a very long time before regaining a human rebirth, for this is harder than a blind turtle putting its neck through ring floating on the ocean, when it only surfaces once a century. Even when a human rebirth *is* regained, the person will be poor, ugly, ill or deformed *and* will behave badly, so as to return to hell! In contrast to this, M.III.177–78 says that wise man who upholds the ethical precepts will be reborn in a heaven and only 'once in a very long while' will he be reborn as a human. When this does occur, he will be rich and handsome, etc., will behave virtuously, and so return to a heaven. In both case, the effects of karma are seen as lasting a very long time, and even the patterns of good and bad actions, and thus the character-traits which prompt these, are seen as similarly recurring. As with a being's sex, then, the form and directedness of character is seen as continuing over the ages. Thig.400–47 shows, though, that a pattern can be broken: the woman come from hell becomes an Arahat. A past evil-doer only *tends* to continue in evil, then. The pattern can be changed, perhaps by a bad person coming under the good influence of others (or vice versa), or consistently acting in the best way his or her character will allow.

(4.11) A further factor sometimes seen as carrying over between lives is the relationship between people, such that one can say that 'karmic links' are forged between them. Such stable relationships are prominent in the *Jātaka*s, stories purportedly about past lives of the Buddha, as a Bodhisatta . Here, the past forms of several of the Buddha's disciples crop up. In particular, the Buddha's attendant monk, Ānanda, accompanies the Bodhisatta in *many* of his previous lives, as pointed out by John Garrett Jones (1979: 105-16). His mother and father were also his mother and father in at least one past life (J.I.136). Such links might be seen as due to similarity of inclinations, attachments and karma: at A.II.61–2, it is said that a husband and wife wishing to be reborn together should be *equally* virtuous etc. However, the evil monk Devadatta also crops up, as an evil-doer, in *Jātaka* stories. Irrespective of inclinations and nature, then, people are seen to form long-lasting links with each other.

(4.12) Commenting on such long-lasting links in the *Jātaka*s, Jones says that 'this shows how determinedly the doctrine of *anatta* (selflessness) is ignored in the *Jātaka* s' (1979: 107, cf.39 and vii). It would be wrong, though, to assume that the not-Self teaching implies that certain phenomena cannot be very long-lasting, repeating themselves over long periods. A god of the heaven of the 'Four Great Kings' is said to remain as such a god for 9,000,000 human years (though in this time, only 500 divine years pass; Vibh.422). By comparison, this is as nothing compared to the life-span of a god in the realm of neither-cognition-nor-non-cognition, which Vibh.426 says is 86,000 *kappa*s, each such *kappa* being the time it takes for a physical universe to evolve and decay! Such a life-span might seem almost infinite, but the important point, from the Buddhist perspective, is that it *does* have an end: the sequence of lives then continues, and may at some time include a hellish rebirth. Thus, prior to his Buddhahood, Gotama is said to have been dissatisfied with the level of meditation which led to this rebirth (M.I.166). Even while in this rebirth, the Abhidhamma says that the *citta* of a being 'arises moment by moment, it ceases moment by moment' (Kvu.208): it is a stream of mind-moments. The components of such a being, and its life-span, are thus impermanent, and so not-Self.

(4.13) The Personalists saw the Buddha's statements, in the *Jātaka*s, that 'I was so-and-so' in a past rebirth, as evidence for a substantial 'person' who was (non-different-from) that past being and also the Buddha (L'AK.V.253). The Theravādin, though, argues that such reasoning means that, were a buffalo reborn as a human, the human would *be* the buffalo, as it would be the 'person' the buffalo had been (Kvu.30). Such 'I was' phraseology, then, need only mean, in more exact language: this mind-and-body is in the same 'continuity' as that. Remembrance of past lives, indeed, is not seen as necessarily intensifying the idea of oneself as a permanent 'I', provided it is done in the proper way, without jumping to wrong conclusions. The Buddha is said to have attained such a memory just prior to his enlightenment, with the memory being 'the first breaking through as a chick from the egg-shell' (M.I.357; cf. Paras.3.11 and 16). This simile suggests the breaking of the illusion of one's personality as having a real and permanent I-ness to it. Remembrance of past lives would undermine this illusion by showing:

i) the great changes (cf. impermanence) that one has actually undergone (as well as any relatively unchanging features): the differences of sex and type of being, and having crossed paths with nearly all beings, when they were once a close relative or friend (S.II.189–90);
ii) the great suffering (cf. *dukkha*) that one has experienced, particularly in unpleasant rebirths;
iii) the fact that one has experienced, at one time or another, what any other being now experiences (S.II.186), thus overshadowing the differences between 'oneself' and 'others' (cf. not-Self).

WHAT CONSERVES CHARACTER TRAITS AND THE UNITY OF THE 'CONTINUITY'?

(4.14) In spite of changes within the ancient 'continuity', it is still seen as containing some very long-lasting character-patterns. Indeed, the memories of long-past lives must be seen as laying deep in the mind as traces or patterns awaiting to be meditatively uncovered. There may not be unchanging personal *identity*, then, but personal continuity is seen as very strong. If a 'continuity' at any time is a product, or 'evolute' of what it was before, then, what is seen as 'binding together' its component processes, preserving its patterns and preventing it splitting into more than one 'continuity' at rebirth? As Karel Werner has expressed it, what makes the universal, non-personal elements of the universe 'combine into an individual structure?' (1988: 76).

(4.15) If a 'continuity' is a stream of conditioned and conditioning processes, it is natural that any pattern in these processes will be reproduced over time for as long as the conditions for it remain. These might include a particular past karma or karmas, which take time to bring all their 'fruits' before their impetus decays. This could perhaps be likened to a push given to a railway truck, which movement is then gradually communicated down a line of trucks to which it is connected. Moreover, as seen Para.4.10, an action may lead to a character-trait which then leads to similar actions: a trait is reinforced by being acted on, thus becoming a habit.

(4.16) Within one life, the body, which is crystallised past karma (D.II, Para.2.7), unifies the states of a person. As is said in the *Milindapañha*, a person's processes are 'all held together as a unity in dependence in this body itself' (Miln.40). More specifically, as pointed out by S. Collins (1982: 229), the Theravādin Abhidhamma and commentaries see the physical and the mental 'life-faculties' (the *jīvit-indriya*s) as 'maintaining the (conventional) unity called a person'. What prevents the unity of a continuity splitting at rebirth, though? M.I.185 suggests that craving is a key binding-force of the continuity. This discusses the physical elements within a person's body and refers to the body as 'appropriated' 'grasped at' or 'taken up' (*upādiṇṇa*) by craving. The passage discusses this in a universal way, not suggesting any exceptions, so that even a craving-free Arahat must have a body 'appropriated by craving'. The craving involved must thus be *past* craving [1], of the time prior to the development of a new being in the womb. As craving is inevitably associated with the 'I am' conceit, and 'I' is surely felt to be a singular entity, craving could be seen as an ego-centric energy which drives a 'being' to 'appropriate' only *one* new body. Working through the constructing activities, which are said to construct each of the personality-factors (S.III.87), the structure of a new person is woven, building on the desires, inclinations and karma of the previous personality.

(4.17) Karel Werner (1988) has sought to develop an alternative explanation of how character-continuity is conserved. He takes early Buddhist terms such as *viññāṇa* (discernment) and *citta* as referring, in certain instances, to a 'personality structure' with changing contents, but an ongoing identity (p.89). He sees this, in turn, as similar to the Vedic idea of *tanū,* the 'likeness' which when 'filled' with phenomenal elements is a person's 'character', but which momentarily exists without content after death (pp.78–9). Such an 'empty structure' is not an unchanging entity but a 'structural continuum which registers and preserves . . . the imprints of past experiences, volitions and capabilities' (p.79). The 'personality-structure' of such a model, though, seems indistinguishable from the 'person' of the Personalists, which has already been shown to lack any foundation in the 'early Sutta' world-view (Paras.1.36–42). The continuum of changing personality-factors itself contains structuring processes, and will naturally pass on character-patterns as part of its ongoing flow of conditions. There is no evidence that the 'early Suttas' posited any transmitter of these patterns other than processes within the flow-of-conditions itself. To postulate a 'container' of these processes is tantamount to one of the unacceptable 'views on the existing group': taking the personality-factors as 'in' a Self (Para.I.8). While opposing the Personalists, the Sarvāstivādins came up with the idea of a particular type of state, *prāpti*, or 'possession', whose only function was to act as a kind of 'glue' unifying the states in a 'continuity', from life to life (e.g. Conze, 1962: 139–41). Such an idea, though, goes against the 'early Sutta' idea that the conditions comprising a being are not owned by anyone or anything (S.II.13–14).

TO WHAT EXTENT ARE 'CONTINUITIES' ISOLATED FROM EACH OTHER AND THE WORLD?

(4.18) If beings are ancient 'continuities' driven and unified by the force of ego-centric craving, to what extent are they seen as interacting with each other and their environment? Winston King points out that the long psychic heritage of a being, including its stable traits, can be seen to provide a 'core of solid character, or hidden roots', which can be seen to explain the differences between similarly nurtured beings (even identical twins), and to provide a store of unpredictable tendencies or power for good or evil (1964: 64–5). Though this does not imply a metaphysical Self, it might nevertheless be seen to imply that the 'continuity' that a being is, is radically isolated within itself, an inviolate stream of events that can have no real interaction with the world or other beings. For King, such 'continuities' must be seen as 'each an indissolubly joined linkage that possesses an eternal individuality that is never crossed, confused or blended with any other chain or process'; though each has passed through countless existences, it 'has remained continuous and separate, something like a tube or channel hermetically sealed from pollution or interference from any other stream of being' (p.38–9). He goes on to refer to 'iron-bound continuities of separate units'.

(4.19) King aims to articulate the views of contemporary Burmese Buddhism, but these are largely based on the 'early Suttas' and later Theravāda literature. To what extent does his understanding fit the world-view of the 'early Suttas'? The very personal nature of karma might be seen as lending him support:

> No others have a share in it,
> And robbers cannot steal this store;
> So let the steadfast make goodness-power,
> The store that is their follower (Khp.7).

Nevertheless, the working out of karma can actually reduce the supposed isolation of a 'continuity'; for the fruition of karma can come through events in the world and the actions of other beings. The karmic results of harming the harmless include 'loss of relatives, or destruction of wealth, or ravaging by fire that will destroy his houses' (Dhp.139–40). At A.II.74–5, it is said that, due to the unrightiousness of a king and his people:

> moon and sun revolve unevenly. This being so, constellations and stars do likewise; days and nights, months and fortnights, seasons and years revolve unevenly; the winds blow unevenly, out of season. The gods are thus annoyed. This being so, the sky-god does not bestow sufficient rain.

Consequently, the crops are poor and the people are short-lived and sickly. Whatever one makes of the details of this passage, it views immoral actions as upsetting the natural order, and karmic fruitions as arising through environmental and climatic intermediaries: the world reacts to the moral and spiritual level of its inhabitants. A similar idea is expressed in the *Aggañña Sutta* (D.III.85–93), which describes the evolution of human society from the sexless beings that inhabited the earth at the start of a world-cycle. Here, as the beings degenerate morally from a god-like beginning, the physical world evolves and becomes more solid and diversified. For example, due to the greed of the beings, they horde rice, so that while it originally grew to maturity in a day, it comes to grow in the normal way. At the individual level, the reaction of the environment to karma can be seen at J.I.167, where a thunderbolt causes a rock to split and so kill a goat, due to its karma of a past life.[2]

(4.20) Karmic fruitions also come through the actions of other people. In the story of the nun's past lives in Para.6.9, karmic results include being an animal which is castrated and a wife rejected by several husbands. Moreover, a layman who gives alms will, if he becomes a monk, be 'often asked to accept alms' (A.II.32), and the murder of the monk Moggallāna is seen as the result of past karma (J.V.126). Even karma, or action, can itself be influenced by others, for in the above A.II.74–5 passage, the king's people are unrightious because they come under the sway of the king's bad influence.

(4.21) Some aspects of karma's working strengthen individuality: its direct effects on character, and the arising of its results through 'internal' means such as ineptitude in business (D.II.85, A.II.81–2) or illness (Sn.p.125). But the other aspects weaken the individuality and isolation of a being by tying it to the world and other beings. Even through something as personal and intimate as karma, then, a being is not 'hermetically sealed from pollution or interference'. A being is inter-related with the world and others, and its karmic dependence on what is outside its 'continuity' shows how it is conditioned and not-Self. By practising the Buddhist path, though, a person's 'continuity' can attain greater consistency, strength and integration, so that he or she comes to have a 'great self' (ch.3). On attaining Arahatship, such a person becomes independent from and untouched by the world: but in doing so the mind also becomes 'immeasurable', and can even blend with that of other like-minded people!

(4.22) In sum, the 'early Suttas', and such Theravādin texts as the *Milindapañha*, present what could be called a process-view of a person, and also of non-human beings. A being is seen as a collection of rapidly changing and interacting mental and physical processes, though it has character-patterns re-occurring even from life to life. The not-Self process-view, then, does not see a person as a chaotic flux lacking in such persistent traits. The Personalists saw the 'person' as the 'structural unity' of a being, perhaps in the form of such long-lasting, though slowly changing character-patterns (Venkataramanan, 1953: 217). They saw it as neither eternal nor non-eternal, neither constructed nor unconstructed (Kvu.24). However, as character-patterns eventually change, and are seen as set up by constructing activities such as karma, they must therefore be seen as constructed and non-eternal. The early Pāli texts did not ignore these patterns, but saw no need to regard them as the kind of mysterious substantial things that the Personalists thought. The view of a person as a stream of conditioned processes can be perfectly adequately used to account for persistence of such traits over long periods. It can likewise account for the appropriateness of ascribing responsibility to a particular person-process for actions performed by an earlier 'segment' of the specific process-stream that he or she is a contemporary 'segment' of. Moreover, while craving and the constructing activities ensures that each such 'stream' carries on into the future with its own particular individuality, such streams can only continue by constantly interacting with their environment in a variety of ways: they are not isolated from the world and each other, even in regard to the outworking of their karma. Of course, what I have called the process-view is not how we normally view ourselves, for we tend to think of mental and physical states as 'owned' by an I or Self. The not-Self teaching, though, seeks to challenge the attachment that such an attitude leads to, while at the same time not denying the relative character-continuity that clearly does exist. Why, though, should a person care about what happens to 'him' in the future, if there is no permanent 'I' that will be there then? The answer, here, is two-fold. For the unenlightened, the 'I am' attitude will still exist, so there is still a motive for benefiting the supposed 'I' in the future. For the enlightened, compassion for *any* suffering being should mean that efforts are made to avoid suffering for this-person-stream-in-the-future. Such a motive can, of course, also be drawn on by the unenlightened (cf. Harvey, 1987).

5

MY WORLD AND ITS END

It is in this fathom-long carcase . . . that, I declare, lies the world . . . (S.I.62).

(5.1) The last chapter ended by touching on the relationship between a person and the world in which they live. In this chapter, the focus will be on what is meant by the 'world' in the 'early Suttas', how it is related to notions of Self, and how beings contribute to the construction of their own world-of-experience, interpreting it from the perspective of the 'I am' conceit. Such a discussion then paves the way for an analysis of the Buddha's response to the 'undetermined questions' on the 'world'.

THE SELF-WORLD LINK AND THE MEANING OF 'WORLD' (*LOKA*)

(5.2) In the Buddha's day, there seems to have been a clear conceptual link between the ideas of 'Self' and 'world'. At D.I.14–16, there is a view 'Self and world is eternal . . . it definitely exists eternally', this being based on the idea that beings transmigrate from from life to life. This talks of Self and world, together, as singular, not plural, suggesting their identity, and it sees Self-and-world as equivalent to transmigrating beings. This identity is more clearly shown at M.I.135–36: 'This the world, this the Self, this after dying I will be, permanent, stable, eternal'. The 'this . . . this' ('*so* . . . *so*') construction utilised here shows, according to Pāli usage, that Self and world were seen as identical by the holders of this view. The meaning of such an idea is suggested by D.I.29, where someone who disbelieves in the idea of past rebirths holds 'Self and world are arisen by chance. Why? Formerly I was not, but now I am. Having not been, I have come into existence'. Here, as at M.I.135–36, 'Self and world' are equivalent to 'I'. This would make sense if 'Self and world' meant 'Self and *my* world', i.e. 'I and *my world of experience*'.

(5.3) If '*loka*' means a being's 'experienced world', then this would explain why there are no views in the Suttas which link an eternal Self with a non-eternal world, or vice-versa. Even those who are 'Semi-eternalists' (D.I.17–21) do not make the eternal/non-eternal split a Self/world split, but say that some Self-and-(experienced)-world is eternal, and some not: e.g. *citta* is eternal but the physical sense-organs are not, or the god Brahmā is eternal, but the beings he supposedly created are not. In both of these contrasts, Self and world are still linked to beings: no one seemed interested in whether a world apart from (transmigrating) beings was eternal or not; they were interested in beings and their experienced world. That this also applies to questions of the infinity/finitude of the world is shown at M.II.233, which refers to views on 'Self and the world' as finite or as infinite. The 'world', then, was often understood, in the Buddha's day, as having the same qualities as the supposed 'Self' of which it was the world, the realm. If Self was seen, as was most usual, as permanent, fixed and stable, then so was its world. If it was seen, as by Annihilationists, as coming to an end, so was its world. As seen above, some thought that a person's mind and mental world was eternal, but that their body and sensory world was not.

(5.4) The linguistic derivation of the word '*loka*' also indicates it as meaning 'experienced world'. Related words in Pāli are '*oloketi*', 'he looks at', and '*āloka*', 'light'. Related Sanskrit words are *locate*, 'he perceives', and *locana*, 'eye' (PED.586f.). Thus the *primary* meaning of *loka* is 'visible (or perceived) world'. In general usage, *loka* is always linked to beings in some way, thus the Buddha says 'I quarrel not with the world (*lokena*), the world quarrels with me' (S.III.138), and it is said 'Indeed the world has fallen on trouble; one is born and grows old and dies . . . ' (D.II.30).

THE BUDDHIST PERSPECTIVE ON THE WORLD

(5.5) While the Buddha did not accept any Self, and so was not concerned with Self-and-its-world, he is portrayed as seeing the empirical self as intimately related to *loka*, its experienced world. A remarkable fact is that *loka* is seen as comprised of the same group of phenomena as a 'being (*satto*)'. At S.IV.38–40, both 'the world' and 'a being' (and also '*dukkha*') are seen as terms for the eighteen elements (Para.I.6) and states discernible by discernment. That is, the totality of empirical phenomena, the 'all (*sabbaṃ*)' (S.IV.16–17), is a set of natural processes which comprise both 'beings' and their world(s). For example, the visible appearance of one being is part of the world of both that being and others. A sound is part of the 'world', but when it is perceived by ear-discernment, it contributes to the content of what the listening being 'is'. The mind-organ also contributes to the kind of world which a being experiences.

(5.6) In their discussion of the 'world', the 'early Suttas' focus very much on the world of lived experience. While a purely external, physical world is not denied, this is not the world that people actually *live* in. They live in the world-as-sensed-and-thought-about, which exists as a constructed experience within a sentient organism. As the Suttas put it: 'It is in this fathom-long carcase, (which is) cognitive (*saññimhi*) and endowed with conception (*-mana-*), that, I declare, (lies) the world, and the arising of the world, and the stopping of the world, and the course that goes to the stopping of the world' (S.I.62). This is a statement of the four Holy Truths – on *dukkha*, its arising, its stopping, and the course going to this – with 'the world' replacing *dukkha*, and this 'world' being seen as within the mentally-endowed physical body. The sense of this passage is elucidated by a similar one at S.IV.95: 'Sir, that by which, in the world, one is cognitive (*saññī*) of the world, holds conceits (*-manī*) on the world, is called the world in the discipline of the Holy ones'. This is then explained to mean the six sense-organs. Similarly, at Sn.169–71, it is said that 'the world has arisen in six . . . is from clinging to just six', the 'six' being the five 'strands of sensual pleasure' (the *kāma-guṇa*s), and conception (*mano*), the mind-organ (Para.1.47). As the *kāma-guṇa*s) are desirable sense-*objects* (A.IV.430), this sees the 'world' as not so much the six sense-organs, as that which arises from the operation of the sixth of these, mind-organ, on the five sense-objects. It is the product of the mind-organ and cognition (*saññā*) working on the input of the five physical sense-organs, interpreting and processing it. Here the mind-organ acts as conception, that which 'conceives (*maññati*)' so as to produce the 'I am' conceit. Indeed, while this conceit exists 'from clinging (*upādāya*)' to the personality-factors (S.III.105), the 'world' exists 'from clinging' to the mind-organ and alluring sensory objects (see above). That is, the 'experienced world' is one which is moulded by the distorting effects of clinging and the 'I am' delusion. It is seen as '*my* world', that which has 'I' at its centre.

(5.7) In S.IV.95, above, 'world' seems to be being used in more than one sense: 'that by which, *in the world*, one is cognitive of *the* *world* . . . is called *the world*. . . .' The third occurrence of the word, here, refers to the 'internal' world, as constructed by conception and cognition. The second must refer to the 'external' sense-input which is interpreted by these, for the 'strands of sensual pleasure' alone can also be seen as the 'world' (A.IV.430). The first must refer to the 'world' in the most general sense, internal and external, as in Para.5.5, where it refers to both 'internal' and 'external' phenomena. Rune Johansson, though, uses the passages given in Paras.5.6–7 to reach a different conclusion on the view of the Suttas: 'There is no independently existing world. The world is a dynamic process, constantly being produced and deliberately constructed by our senses, our thoughts and our desires' (1979: 28–9). I would agree with this as said of what I have called the 'internal' world, but not of the 'external' world.

(5.8) Johansson sees even solidity, cohesion, heat and motion (literally 'earth', 'water', 'fire' and 'air': the four 'great elements' (*mahā-bhūta*s)), the most basic ingredients of 'material form' (*rūpa*), as constructed by our thoughts etc. (p.34). These elements, though, are also included in the six 'elements' (*dhātu*s), along with space and discernment. They are not seen as any *less* basic than discernment/thought, and indeed at A.I.176, these six are seen as the basic ingredients for the production of a being in the womb, from the time of conception, before any active thoughts exist. 'Material form', indeed, can be seen to be more than a construct of the perceiving mind. At D.III.217, it is said to be of three kinds: i) 'visible and reacting', ii) 'invisible and reacting', and iii) 'invisible and non-reacting'. These are explained in the Abhidhamma thus:

i) the sphere of visible objects;
ii) the spheres of the other four physical sense-objects, and the five physical sense-organs;
iii) the remaining aspects of 'material form', such as the faculties of femininity and masculinity and life, all of which are included in the sphere of mind-objects (Dhs.751–56 and 980).

This shows that early Buddhism accepted that there were types of 'material form' that could not be known by the physical senses, but only by the mind. The only way that one can differentiate such a thing from a pure fantasy, as an object of mind, is to say that it *exists* as a type of 'material form' known either by direct meditative intuition or by reasoning, just as e.g. electrons are imperceptible but known to exist by reasoning (aided by certain instruments).

(5.9) Johansson thus seems to be incorrect when he says:

> The objects are there but our perceptions of them are constituent and essential parts of them . . . it is not mere subjectiveness. It is only that the cleavage into 'objective' and 'subjective' was never made: the subjective process of image-formation was thought to be part of the object itself' (p.29).

The Suttas clearly make a distinction between, say a 'visible form' (also *rūpa*) and the cognition (*saññā*) of a visible form. Johansson in fact admits that the Buddha knew that the senses can deceive (p.79, as e.g. at M.I.507): but this amounts to an admission that a subjective/objective distinction, between how things appear and how they are, *is* made in the Suttas. If this were not so, indeed, a real 'I' or Self would exist simply because people thought and felt that it did.

(5.10) Johansson has a similar perspective on the heavenly 'worlds' and gods of Buddhist cosmology. As specific meditative states are seen as parallelling specific heavenly worlds (D.III.263 and D.I.195), he feels that this proves that 'purely subjective states . . . are projected as objective worlds, populated by gods' (p.35). However, a modern psychologist's view that gods do not exist is as much a commitment as the belief that they *do* exist. Johansson's view of gods as 'projections' could, indeed, be seen as a projection of his own world-view. It is certainly not the view of the Suttas. The Buddha does not appear to have accepted the existence of gods simply because it was a 'popular idea prevalent at his time' (p.23). In the 'early Suttas', he clearly distinguished between his 'certain knowledge' that gods existed, and the commonly held belief that they did (M.II.212–13). He was aware that projection could enter into people's beliefs about gods, leading, for example, to the view that Brahmā was an eternal creator; but such projections were about beings which were as real as human beings, and could be known about by specific meditative techniques: they were not mere subjective impressions. Gods and humans were seen as influencing each other to a certain extent, and being able to communicate, but the heavenly worlds were seen as existing whether or not they were perceived by humans. As M.I.402 says, 'And because there is, indeed, an other world, the view of anyone that there is not an other world is a false view of his'.

(5.11) Still, the world (and worlds) should be seen as 'untrue' (Sn.9) and as like a bubble or mirage (Dhp.170). Para.1.28 shows that the world (in whatever sense: see Para 5.7) does not 'exist' in a solid, eternal way, nor does it 'not exist', as it *does* arise in the form of fluxing phenomena. 'This' and 'other' worlds do not consist of compact, unitary realities, but collections of such fluxing phenomena. The different worlds can be seen as being different ranges of these. To be born 'in' the human world, or a particular heavenly world, means that one is sensitive to certain types of sense-objects[1], and that there is a certain range of such phenomena available to be sensed (according to the Abhidhamma, which ones a particular person tends to notice depends on his karma: see Para.9.19). The perceived sense-objects are also operated on by the conceiving mind-organ, in a way characteristic of a particular being. The range of available experiencable sense-objects, and the way they are operated on, can be changed either by rebirth or attaining *jhāna*: meditative altered states of consciousness. Rebirth 'tunes one into' a particular range of such sense-objects, while meditation allows one to actively tune into such a range. In a specific world, a particular 'wave band' of experiencable sense-objects are available to a being, and those that are noticed are operated on in a particular kind of way by his mind-organ so as to produce a particular kind of internal experienced world. Meditative 'tuning' seems to be illustrated at A.IV.302–03, where the Buddha gradually comes to know about gods by first recognizing their 'radiance', then seeing their 'forms' (*rūpa*s), then talking to them and going on to learn about them. The 'world' of a human being is normally based on perception and interpretation of a limited range of experiencable sense-input, but by refining the mind's sensitivity, through meditation, a wider range of phenomena can be known: other worlds and their inhabitants. All are impermanent, *dukkha* and not-Self, though, and *nibbāna* lies beyond them all.

THE UNDETERMINED QUESTIONS

(5.12) The Buddha was frequently asked[2] a set of ten 'undetermined (*avyākatā*) questions' (Para.I.8), four of which are on the 'world' (*loka*): is it eternal, not eternal, finite or infinite? The Buddha 'set aside' all such questions, saw them as improper, or met them with silence. He clearly saw them as a timewasting distraction from the spiritual life (M.I.429), but also as linked to the Self-illusion. This can be seen from S.IV.395, where he says that others give answers to the undetermined questions because they have some kind of 'view on the existing group' (*sakkāya-diṭṭhi*): a view which sees a Self as somehow or other related to the personality-factors; he does not answer them as he has no such view.[3] Likewise, the monk Isidatta says that the views enshrined in the questions cannot exist without such Self-views (S.IV.287). Clearly, the questions are asked by those who projected the concept of Self onto the ideas of 'world', 'life-principle' and '*tathāgata*'. Their questions are about the nature of 'Self's world', 'Life-principle-Self' and '*tathāgata*-Self', even though 'Self' is a baseless concept. As such, no answer can be given to the questions, just as an innocent man cannot answer either 'yes' or 'no' to 'have you stopped beating your wife?'.

(5.13) The reasons for the Buddha's not answering the undetermined questions, though, seem to be not *only* those of avoiding timewasting and not legitimating the Self-delusion built into the questions. There is also the issue of people misunderstanding the nature of the the world etc. in other ways, as is indicated by S.V.447–48. Here, holding the views enshrined in the questions is first refered to as 'thought about the world (*loka-cintaṃ*)'. The Buddha then gives a story on a man who, indulging in such thought next to a lotus pond, thinks that he is mad when he sees an army entering a lotus-stalk. He is wrong to think that he sees what does not exist, though, for there *is* an army of *asura*s (demi-gods) entering the lotus, fleeing from the gods! If the nature of the 'world' etc. is misunderstood, then, views on its qualities are bound to be misguided. Relevant misunderstandings on the 'world' will be dealt with next; those on the life-principle and the *tathāgata* will be dealt with in chapters 6 and 13 respectively.

THE UNDETERMINED QUESTIONS ON THE WORLD

(5.14) Of the undetermined questions on the world, two concern whether it 'has an end (*anta-vā*)' or not. D.I.22–3 shows that a spatial end is meant: is the world finite or infinite? In the same Sutta as S.IV.95, on the inner, psychological 'world' (Para.5.6), it is said that one cannot reach the 'end (*antaṃ*) of the world' by travelling (S.IV.93). This is clearly because wherever one is, even in pitch black empty space, away from all stars etc., one would still, if alive, have a body and thoughts: one would *bring* one's world *with* one. That is, wherever one went, there would always be an inner world of thought and an external world, for example of the body in black empty space. The Sutta affirms, though, that if one rightly understands the world, it can be seen to have an end, indeed it *must* have an end if one is to 'make and end of *dukkha*' (S.IV.93). The nature of such a salvific 'end' is indicated in a parallel passage (S.I.61) as 'where one is not born, nor ages, nor dies, nor falls away, nor arises': i.e. *nibbāna*.

(5.15) At A.IV.428–32 is a passage which shows that *nibbāna* is the 'end' of all worlds, in the sense of being that which transcends them all. Here the emphasis is on the 'worlds' of 'external' experientiable phenomena that may be tuned into. The passage begins by the Buddha setting aside the questions on the world as finite or infinite. He then emphasizes that, however fast one travelled, one would die before reaching any 'end' of the world. The true way to reach the 'end' of the world is not like this. He then says, 'These five strands of sensual pleasure (the *kama-guṇa*s) are called the world in the discipline of the Holy ones', explaining these as the physical sense-objects as 'longed for, alluring, pleasurable, lovely, fraught with sense-desire'. A person can reach the 'end' of such a world by transcending sense-desire and attaining the first *jhāna*, or lucid meditative trance. There are then other worlds to pass beyond, which may be done by successively entering, and then passing beyond, each of the remaining three *jhāna*s and the four formless altered states of consciousness. Even then, he has not yet 'passed through the world's entanglements'. He is only one who is 'gone to the end of the world (*lokantagū*)' when he transcends even the highest formless state and, in (or immediately after?) the state known as the 'cessation of cognition and feeling', comes to destroy the spiritual cankers and thus attain *nibbāna*.[4] Here there is, 'in this fathom-long carcase . . . the stopping of the world', a 'world's end' where 'one is not born, nor ages, nor dies' (S.I.61–2). All 'external' worlds are transcended and no 'internal' world is generated.

(5.16) The questions on the 'world' as finite or infinite can thus be seen to have been set aside by the Buddha as:

i) Views of this kind take the 'world' to be closely associated with, or identical to a Self. To say that the *loka*, the experienced and experiencable world, is finite or infinite, would be to imply that there was a Self which experiences it, this also being finite or infinite.

ii) The questions also contain another misconception on the nature of the 'world': that it could meaningfully be said to be with or without an end in a spatial sense. No end can be found to it by travelling: not because it is, as a contingent fact, infinite, but because, *a priori*, it is impossible to ever *travel* to where one no longer experiences anything. The only 'end' of the world is when consciousness is tuned beyond any internal world and beyond the perception of any external world.

(5.17) What then of the questions of whether or not the world is 'eternal' (*sassata*), whether it has an 'end' in time? The Buddha is portrayed as being able to remember his past lives 'as far as' he wished (M.I.482). On the basis of such a meditative recollection, he said, 'Inconceivable is the beginning of this *saṃsāra* (round of rebirths), a past extreme of which is not known' (S.II.178). This asserts that no beginning *can be found*. The situation of remembering further and further into the past is analogous to that of travelling further and further in space. Just as travelling will not bring one to any 'end' of the world, so remembering will, it is held, always uncover *some* past experienced-world. That one with unlimited recall has not *found* an ultimate beginning does not mean, as such, that there was none. Such a beginning, though, is also described as 'inconceivable'; this is probably because everything in the world is seen as arising according to conditions, which are themselves conditioned (the doctrine of Conditioned Arising). As is said at Miln.50–1, just as there might be a series of seed leading to fruit, leading to seed, etc., 'is there ever an end to this series? . . . Even so, sire, an earliest extreme of (*saṃsāric*) time cannot be known either'. At any time in the past, then, the (physical and mental) world must have had something *before* it to condition it. This still leaves the question of the eternity of the world open, however, for it does not touch on whether the world will continue to exist in the future, forever.

(5.18) To ask this is, in effect, to ask whether all beings will some day attain *nibbāna*. Were this to occur, there would be no beings to have any 'internal' worlds, and there would be no need for an 'external' world to exist, given that it is seen as evolving mainly in response to the karma of the beings in it (D.III.84ff.), and would thus peter out without them. However, when the Buddha was actually asked whether the 'whole world' would end *dukkha* (attain *nibbāna*, the 'end' of the world), he was silent (A.V.194), thus leaving the question undetermined. His disciple Ānanda then explained that those who *do* end *dukkha* will do so by practising the Holy Eightfold Path. That is, the attainment of *nibbāna* is not pre-determined but depends on effort, so it cannot be predicted whether all will attain it: or that they won't. Thus the *Abhidharmakośa* (L'AK. V.267), giving the Sarvāstivādin view, says that the Buddha set aside the questions of the eternity of the world because of: i) the perceived link between the world and Self, and ii) if the world, as *saṃsāra* were eternal, no-one would ever attain *nibbāna*; and if it were non-eternal, this would mean that everyone would attain it, spontaneously and not by personal effort.

(5.19) Because of the supposed link between the world and Self, taking the world as eternal would imply Eternalism: the view that there is an eternal Self. Taking it as non-eternal would imply Annihilationism: the view that there is a substantial Self which is, yet, destroyed at death. The Buddhist perspective is that it consists of a cluster of ephemeral, conditioned phenomena. For all but the enlightened, it flows on after death, when there is a new rebirth-world. Within the general flow of worldly phenomena, the experienced world of a being arises by the mind tuning into and interpreting certain ranges of phenomena. In the experience of *nibbāna*, that which is beyond space and time, such a world is transcended.

(5.20) In sum, it can be seen that the 'early Suttas' see 'the world' as having different sense:

i) the external world of sense-objects, of which there are different ranges, corresponding to the different worlds that can be tuned into by meditation or rebirth;
ii) the internal world generated by cognition interpreting, and mind-organ egocentrically conceiving on, whichever sense-objects are noticed from the range currently available to a being;
iii) the 'world' in the largest sense, including both the internal and external.

Here, the conceit-prone mind is active in both tuning into and interpreting/misinterpreting sense-objects, to generate a lived world of experience. This idea seems to be an implicit 'early Sutta' explanation of why non-Buddhists saw Self and world as so closely linked. The lived world (ii) of an unenlightened person is always centred on 'I' in some way. When *nibbāna* is experienced, though, such a world comes to an end, be this because no external world is tuned into, or because such external worlds are perceived in a way which is not distorted by the perverse influence of the 'I am' delusion.

6

THE LIFE-PRINCIPLE AND THE BETWEEN-LIVES STATE

When a being lays aside this body and it is not (yet) arisen in another body . . . (S.IV.399–400).

(6.1) Having explored, in the last chapter, the undetermined questions on the 'world', this chapter will begin by an examination of such questions as they relate to the 'life-principle'. It will then move on to show that the 'early Suttas' accepted a type of empirical 'life-principle', just as they accepted an empirical self. The 'early Sutta' understanding of the period after death will then be examined, showing that discernment (*viññāṇa*) was regarded as a key link between rebirths, and that a between-lives existence was accepted. It will then be shown that this was seen as a time of restless searching, in which a person exists in the form of a kind of 'spirit'. Such an idea, however, is perfectly compatible with the not-Self teaching.

THE UNDETERMINED QUESTIONS ON THE LIFE-PRINCIPLE

(6.2) As with the other 'undetermined questions', the Buddha gave no answer to the questions 'Is the life-principle (*jīva*) the same as the mortal body (*sarīra*)?'[1] and 'Is the life-principle different from the mortal body?'. The primary reason for this was that the 'life-principle' asked about was taken as a metaphysical Self (Para.5.12). The questions amount to asking whether there is an eternal Self which survives the death of the body (Eternalism) or whether a supposedly substantial Self is nevertheless destroyed at death, this being the total end of a being (Annihilationism). Apart from the falsity of taking the empirical self as either eternal or destroyed at death, the questions were strictly speaking meaningless, for they asked about the nature of a substantial Self, which was not found to exist: they were analogous to asking about the real colour of a unicorn's horn!

(6.3) '*Jīva*' is the word used in Jainism for the Self. Their *Bhagavati Sūtra* (XII.7.495) sees it as both the same as and different from the body, a view which is strangely absent from those enumerated in the Buddhist Suttas. In the post-canonical *Milindapañha* (p.54–5), king Milinda asks the monk Nāgasena about an 'experiencer', by which he means 'The life-principle within that sees visible forms with the eyes . . . and discerns mental objects with the mind-organ'. This probably represents how the life-principle was seen by non-Buddhists: a substantial inner subject of experience. Nāgasena's reply, when asked if an 'experiencer', i.e. life-principle, is 'apprehended (*upalabbhati*)'[2], is that the different types of sense-discernment (awareness of visual forms etc.) arise only due to each organ contacting its respective object, this being a causally-ordered process giving rise, among other things, to the 'life-faculty' (*jīvit-indriya*). Thus 'these states are produced from a condition, and no experiencer is apprehended here'. That is, there is no unitary, unchanging life-principle that is the subject of all experiences, though there are conditionally arisen states, including discernment and the life-faculty.

(6.4) In the Suttas, the questions on the 'life-principle' are seen as equivalent to asking about an owner of the conditioned links of Conditioned Arising. Thus:

> 'Now what, Lord, is ageing-and-death, and whose is this ageing-and-death?'. 'Not a proper question', said the Lord. 'You might ask this double question, monk, or you might say, "ageing-and-death are one thing but he who has them is another"; if you did, both would be the same in meaning, different only in form. There being the view "the life-principle is the same as the mortal body", there is no living of the holy life. There being the view "the life-principle is different from the mortal body", there is no living of the holy life. The *tathāgata*, monks, goes to neither of these two extremes, he teaches Dhamma by the middle way: conditioned by birth is ageing-and-death [as in the sequence of Conditioned Arising] (S.II.60–1).

Similarly, the questions 'Who, now, feels?' and 'Who, now, grasps?' are seen as improper questions, to be replaced by questions on what feeling and grasping are conditioned by (S.II.13–14). Thus there is no life-principle as owner of the links of Conditioned Arising, whether it is seen as the mortal body subject to ageing-and-death, or as different from it. The links do not 'belong' to anyone, but just occur according to conditions such as past karma, as at D.(II) in Para.2.7. If there were an eternal life-principle, it would be unchangeable, and no spiritual progress would be possible. If there were a life-principle that was destroyed at death, any spiritual progress would be cut off at death. Either way, there is no motivation for living of the 'holy life'.

THE 'LIFE-PRINCIPLE' ACCEPTED BY EARLY BUDDHISM

(6.5) Just as the 'early Suttas' did not posit a metaphysical Self, but accepted an empirical, changing self, so they did not accept a substantial Life-principle, but did accept one which was changing. It would appear that this was seen as neither the same as nor totally different from the 'mortal body', but as partly *dependent* on it, in such a way that it was not destroyed at the death of the body. The evidence for this is as follows. At D.I.157–58, the Buddha is asked the undetermined questions on the life-principle. Part of his reply is that one attained to any of the four meditative *jhāna*s would not give either answer. The same is then said of someone in the fourth *jhāna* who applies his mind to 'knowledge-and-vision', elsewhere said to consist of a series of meditation-based knowledges (D.I.76–7). The first of these is where one comprehends:

> This body (*kāyo*) of mine has form (*rūpī*), it is made from the four great elements, produced by mother and father . . . is subject to erasion, abrasion, dissolution and disintegration; this is my discernment (*viññāṇaṃ*), here supported (*sitaṃ*), here bound'.

The next 'knowledge-and-vision' is where one applies oneself to calling up a 'mind-made body' (*mano-maya kāya*):

> He calls up from this body another body, having form, mind-made, having all limbs and parts, not deficient in any organ. Just as if, O king, a man were to pull a reed out of its sheath, he would know 'This is the reed, this the sheath. The reed is different from the sheath. It is from the sheath that the reed has been drawn forth' (D.I.77).

This suggests that one who is proficient in meditation is aware of a kind of life-principle in the form of discernment (perhaps with some accompaniments), this being *dependent* on the mortal physical body. Such a life-principle, though, can leave the physical body by means of a mind-made body. The latter could be seen as a kind of 'subtle body', for a being with a mind-made body is said to feed on joy (D.I.17), not on solid nutriment (D.I.195): it must thus lack the four great elements of the physical body. It occupies space, but does not impinge on physical matter, for the 'selfhood' of a certain god with a mind-made body is said to be as large as two or three fields, but to cause no harm to anyone (A.III.122).

(6.6) That the mind-made body could itself be seen as a kind of life-principle is shown by a passage in the Jain *Sūtra Kṛtāṅga.*[3] Here one who denies rebirth says:

> Those who maintain that the life-principle is something different from the body do not see the following (objections): . . . nobody can draw (the life-principle from the body) and show it (you saying), 'Friend, this is the life-principle and this is the body', as a man draws a fibre from a stalk of Munja grass and shows it (you saying), 'Friend, this is a stalk, and that is the fibre' . . .

Clearly, according to this criterion, the Buddhist mind-made body and accompanying discernment is a life-principle and, but for its dependence on the physical body, would be wholly *different* from it. It is like *citta*, which is said to be 'without a mortal body (*asarīraṃ*)' (Dhp.37) but to be 'born of the mortal body (*sarīra-ja*)' (Thag.355).[4]

(6.7) The early Buddhist understanding of the life-principle, in the context of rebirth, can be seen at D.II.332ff. Here, the materialist prince Payāsi feels that he has disproved rebirth as, when he put a criminal in a sealed jar and let him die, he saw no life-principle leaving the jar when it was opened. In order to show that this gruesome 'experiment' does not disprove rebirth, Mahā-Kassapa argues that, as the prince's attendants do not see his life-principle 'entering or leaving (*pavisantaṃ vā nikkhamantaṃ va*)' him when he dreams, he cannot expect to see the life-principle of a dead person 'entering or leaving' (D.II.334). That it, the life-principle is not denied, but accepted, as an invisible phenomenon.

(6.8) The language used in the above is reminiscent of that found in an Upaniṣadic passage (BU.IV.4.2) on the process of death:

> this (i.e. the individual) self (*ātman*) leaves (*niṣ-krāmati*) through the eye or the head or from any other point of the mortal body (*śarīra-*); in the wake of him ascending (*ut-krāmantam*), vital breath (*prānaṃ*) ascends; in the wake of vital breath ascending all the vital functions ascend; (he, i.e. the *ātman*) becomes with-discernment (*sa-vi-jñānaḥ*); as that very (*eva*) discernment with which he is identified (he) descends (*ava-krāmati*) (into the womb) over again . . .

This passage concerns the changing, individual *ātman*, rather than the supposed universal *ātman* (Werner, 1988: 82–3), and says that it 'leaves' (*niṣ-krāmati*) the body at death, just as Mahā-Kassapa says that the life-principle 'leaves' (*nikkhamati*, from Sanskrit *niṣ-krāmati*) it then. Prince Payāsi is clearly trying to detect such a life-principle or individual self leaving, via some part of the body.

(6.9) The above Upaniṣadic passage also shows other parallels to Buddhist ones. It sees the individual *ātman*, after death, as becoming with-discernment, or discernment itself, and as 'descending' in this form into a new womb (i.e. rebirth). To this may be compared D.II.62–3:

> 'Were discernment, Ānanda, not to fall (*okkamissatha*) into the mother's womb, would mind-and-body (*nāma-rūpaṃ*) be constituted there?' 'It would not, Lord'. 'Were discernment, having fallen into the mother's womb, to turn aside (*vokkamis-satha*) from it, would mind-and-body come to birth in this present state?' 'It would not, Lord'.

Just as the Upaniṣadic passage says that it is *ātman*-as-discernment which 'descends' (*ava-krāmati*) into the womb (at conception), so this says that discernment 'falls into' (*o-kkamati*) the womb at conception. '*O-kkamati*' is, in fact, equivalent to *ava-kkamati*, which is the Pāli form of '*ava-krāmati*'. Similarly, just as the *ātman* 'ascends' (*ut-krāmati*) from a person at death, so discernment must not 'turn aside' (*vo-kkamati*) from the womb, if a live birth is to follow. Here the Pāli prefix '*vo*' is equivalent to '*vi*' + '*ut*', and so the similarity of language persists. It can thus be seen that the life-principle referred to by Mahā-Kassapa seems to be, in the main, the process of discernment which enters the womb at conception and leaves the body at death. In this, it is talked of in much the same way as the individual, transmigrating *ātman* of the *Upaniṣad*s, though it clearly is not seen as having any metaphysical Self/*ātman* as an underlying support, as does the transmigrating *ātman*.

(6.10) In arguing against another 'experiment' of Payāsi concerning a life-principle, Mahā-Kassapa says that a body 'endowed with vitality, heat and discernment' is lighter and more pliable than a dead body, just as a heated iron ball 'endowed with heat and (hot) air' is lighter and more pliable than a cool one (D.II.334–35). Moreover, only a body so endowed can be aware of sense-objects, just as a conch-shell-trumpet will only make a sound when 'endowed with a man, an effort and air' (D.II.337–38). A third simile is that of a fire-drill which will only make fire when properly used, not when chopped up to look for the 'fire' in it (D.II.340–42). That is, the life-principle is not a separate part of a person, but is a process which occurs when certain conditions are present, namely 'vitality (*āyu*)', 'heat (*usmā*)' and discernment. This life-principle-complex relates to the body like heat and surrounding hot air to heated iron.[5] A more modern analogy might be to see it as like the magnetic-field of a piece of magnetised iron: both heat and magnetism may be a property of iron, but this does not prevent them being transferred to something else: an analogy for rebirth.

(6.11) If the language of the iron-ball and conch analogies is examined, a specific analogy between discernment and air becomes apparent:

i) 'vitality (*āyu*), heat (*usmā*) and discernment (*viññāṇaṃ*)';
ii) 'iron (*ayo*)', 'heat (*tejo*) and (hot) air (*vāyo*)';
iii) 'a man (*purisa-*), an effort (*vāyāma-*) and air (*vāyo*)'.

If '*ayo*' is taken as a pun on '*āyu*', and the two words for heat as equivalent and also analogous to an effort, the *viññāṇa*/*vāya* parallel is seen. This suggests that discernment, the main process contributing to the life-principle process, is analogous to air or, an abstract meaning of *vāya*, motion. Some seem to have taken this kind of analogy literally, though, for at Miln.30–1, someone takes 'Nāgasena' as 'the inner air (*vāyo*), the life-principle which enters and leaves', seemingly taking this as 'wind (*vāto*)', i.e. breath. The analogy to air or breath is suggestive, though, for the English words 'inspiration' and 'expiration' – literally breathing in and breathing out – are derived from the Latin word for breathing, '*spirare*', which is related to '*spiritus*', breath, from which comes 'spirit'. 'Spirit', of course, is that which moves us, in 'inspiration', and that which is seen as leaving us at death, when we 'expire'. It is thus appropriate to refer to the 'early Sutta' 'life-principle', of which air-like discernment is a crucial factor, as a person's 'spirit'. Of course, it is still to be seen as impermanent, *dukkha* and not-Self.

(6.12) It can thus be seen that the 'life-principle' or 'spirit' accepted by the 'early Suttas' is 'vitality, heat and discernment', or perhaps discernment and the subtle 'mind-made body'. It consists of conditionally arisen changing processes, which are not identical with the mortal body, nor totally different from it, but partly *dependent* on it. If the life-principle is taken as a substantial Self, it is meaningless to say that 'it' is the 'same as' or 'different from' the mortal body, but if it is recognized as not-Self, then these views can be seen as actually false. The life-principle is neither the same as nor different from the mortal body, as the relationship is that of the mingling of mutually-dependent processes. Thus at S.I.206, when a nature-spirit (*yakkha*) says ' "Material form is not alive (*na jīvan*)" say the Buddhas, then how does this [life-principle] find this mortal body?', the Buddha replies by outlining his view of the stages of embryonic growth. As seen above, the mortal body of a person develops because discernment, the crucial factor in the life-principle-process, enters the womb at conception; discernment then remains supported by and bound to the body.[6]

DISCERNMENT AND REBIRTH

(6.13) At M.I.256, the monk Sāti is said to have the view, 'In so far as I understand Dhamma taught by the Lord, it is that this discernment itself (*tad-ev'idaṃ viññāṇaṃ*) runs on, wanders on (in rebirth), not another'. On being asked about this discernment, he explains, 'It is this, Lord, that speaks, that feels, that, now here, now there, experiences the fruitions of karmas that are lovely and that are depraved' (M.I.258). This view is also found at M.I.8, where it is about a permanent Self. Thus Sāti is portrayed as taking discernment as a permanent Self which transmigrates, is the agent of karma, and the experiencer of karmic results. Accordingly, the Buddha rebukes him (M.I.259–60), arguing that different forms of discernment arise dependent on different sense-organs and sense-objects – visual-discernment on eye and visual objects, etc. – so that there is no one, unchanging, discernment which performs all the functions of discernment. That is, he criticizes the idea of a self-identical discernment which stays the same, being 'not another', i.e. an unchanging Self. The Buddha goes on, though, to refer to discernment as a 'nutriment' (*āhāra*) (p.260) which, with three others – 'food-', 'stimulation-' and 'mental-volition-' nutriments – are 'for the maintenance of beings come to be or for the assistance of those seeking to be' (p.261), with S.II.13 seeing these four nutriments as conditions for future rebirth. That is, while discernment is not unchanging, it is a crucial condition for rebirth. That there is a danger that discernment-nutriment might be easily clung to as a Self is then emphasized: the Buddha is careful to stress that his monks should not cling to the above 'purified view' about what is conditioned by that nutriment.[7]

(6.14) It has been seen in Para.6.9 that an embryo develops after discernment has 'fallen into' the womb. This indicates that discernment is the crucial process which is transmitted from a previous life, to trigger off another rebirth. The transmission of such a discernment from a past life is referred to at M.II.262. Here it is said of a monk seeking to make his *citta* 'immeasurable' that, 'if he is serene, either he comes to imperturbability now, or he is intent on wisdom. At the breaking up of his body, after dying, this situation exists, that the conducive (*saṃattanikaṃ*) discernment may accordingly reach imperturbability'. The following passage shows that 'imperturbability' refers to any of the formless rebirths (and to the mystical states they correspond to). This passage thus describes 'conducive' discernment as outlasting death and reaching rebirth in a formless rebirth, to which it had previously conduced by being meditatively 'tuned' to that level of existence. Similarly, M.III.259–61 indicates that rebirth occurs because, by grasping at various things, discernment is made to be 'dependent' (*nissita*) on them. S.II.66 complements this by saying 'When discernment is supported (*patiṭṭhite*) and growing, there is descent (*avakkanti*) of mind-and-body', i.e. a being develops in the womb to begin another rebirth.

(6.15) The nature of the discernment which links rebirths is suggested by S.II.67:

> That which one wills (*ceteti*) and that which one plans, and that for which one has a latent tendency: this is an object

> (*ārammaṇam*) for the maintenance (*ṭhitiyā*) of discernment; when the object is, there is a support (*patiṭṭhā*) for discernment. When discernment is supported and growing, there is inclination (*nati*); inclination being, there is coming and going (*āgati-gati*); coming and going being, there is falling away and arising (*cutūpapāto*); falling away and arising being, there is, in the future, birth, age and death, grief, lamentation, suffering, sorrow and despair originate. This is the arising of the entire mass of *dukkha*.

This is clearly a version of the Conditioned Arising sequence. This normally ends: . . . grasping → becoming (*bhava*) → birth (*jāti*) → ageing etc.: this mass of *dukkha*. As 'becoming' normally conditions 'birth', S.II.67 seems to describe such 'becoming' in terms of three phases: 'inclination' → 'coming and going' → 'falling away and arising', and to see these as occurring when discernment is supported by objects with which it is preoccupied. Indeed, S.III.54–5 speaks of the phases of becoming as, in fact, phases of a 'growing', 'supported' discernment: '. . . the coming or going, or the falling away and arising, or the growth, increase or abundance *of discernment*'. Thus at death, if discernment is still associated with grasping, it is supported by its objects, goes through the phases of 'becoming', and conditions the generation of a new mind-and-body in a new rebirth.

(6.16) The association between discernment and 'becoming' is also shown in the explanation of 'becoming' at A.I.223:

> 'Ānanda, if there were no element of sense-desire (*kāma-dhātu*), and no karma to ripen (there), would there be any sense-desire-becoming manifested?'. 'Surely not, Lord'. 'In this way, Ānanda, karma is the field, discernment is the seed, craving is the moisture: for beings hindered by ignorance, fettered by craving, discernment is supported (*patiṭṭhitaṃ*) in a lower element. Thus, in the future, there is re-becoming and production. Thus, Ānanda, there is becoming. [parallel statements are then given for the 'element of (pure) form', which is 'middling', and the 'formless element', which is 'excellent'].

The following Sutta says precisely the same except that 'will (*cetanā*)' and 'aspiration' are 'supported' in one of the three 'elements', i.e. rebirth realms, with discernment still being the 'seed' for this.

THE QUESTION OF AN INTERMEDIARY EXISTENCE (*ANTARĀ-BHAVA*)

(6.17) It has been argued above that early Buddhism accepted a kind of spirit-like life-principle whose primary process is discernment. This life-principle is not identical with the mortal body, nor wholly different from it; though it is 'supported' by and 'bound' to it, it leaves it at death. It has also been seen that discernment is the 'seed' of rebirth, with its nature conducing to specific kinds of rebirth. It links lives and goes through the phases of 'becoming'. It is thus appropriate to ask about the 'early Sutta' view of what happens when the mortal body ends: is death immediately followed by conception at the start of a new life, or is there a time interval between rebirths? Does 'becoming' occur in a time *after* death but *before* conception? On this question of an 'intermediary existence' (*antarā-bhava*), the early schools of Buddhism were more or less equally divided. It was accepted by the Sarvāstivādins, Sammitīyas (a Personalist subschool), Pūrvaśailas, the later Mahīśāsakas, and Dārṣṭantikas, but denied by the Mahāsāṅghikas, early Mahīśāsakas, Dharmaguptakas, Vibhajyavādins and (practically identical) Theravādins (Bareau, 1955: 291).

(6.18) The Theravāda position, argued for at Kvu.361–66, is not the only possible conclusion that can be drawn from the rest of the Theravādin Abhidhamma. *Paṭṭhāna* I. 312–13 (CR.338–39) asserts that arising-*citta* immediately follows falling-away-*citta*, but this may mean no more than that in the last phase of 'becoming', 'falling away and arising', there is an immediate transition from becoming to 'arising' in a new rebirth.[8] D.II.63–4 talks of the conditions under which one might 'grow old, or die, or fall away, or arise', so 'falling away' is not the same thing, as such, as death.

(6.19) There are, indeed, a number of positive indications that a between-lives state was included in the world-view of the 'early Suttas'. An important passage is found at S.IV.399–400, where the Buddha says:

> At a time when a flame, Vaccha, flung by the wind, goes a very long way, I declare that flame to be fuelled by the wind (*vāto*). At the time, Vaccha, wind is the fuel (*upādānaṃ*)[9] . . .

> At the time, Vaccha, when a being lays aside this body and is not arisen (*anuppanno*) in another body, for this I say craving is the fuel. Indeed, Vaccha, craving is the fuel at that time.

In *Kindred Sayings* IV., F.L.Woodward translates '*anuppanno*' as 'rises up'. Here he must be following Leon Feer, the editor of S.IV., who says that 'The true reading *ought* to be *anuppatto*' (my emphasis), thus making the word into the past participle of '*anupāpuṇāti*', 'attains', rather than the negative past participle of '*uppajjati*', 'arises'. The only actual variant reading at S.IV.399–400 is '*anupapanno*', but this means practically the same as '*anuppanno*', which reading is also found in the commentary (S.A.III.114).[10] Feer's 'ought', therefore, can only be based on a wish to defend Theravādin orthodoxy on the question of an intermediary existence. This is hardly a good reason for changing a reading, especially on such a contentious issue! The text as it stands *clearly* refers to a time between the 'laying aside' of the body, at death, and the 'arising' in a new one, and likens this to a time when a flame is carried by the wind across a gap.

(6.20) The time period before 'arising' cannot be construed as that of gestation in the womb. 'Arising' is an aspect of the third phase of 'becoming', 'falling away and arising', and 'becoming' is the condition for 'birth (*jāti*)' in the Conditioned Arising sequence. Such 'birth', though, refers to *conception* (or perhaps implantation), as shown by its definition at S.II.3: 'birth (*jāti*), generation, descent (*okkanti*), production, appearance (*pātubhāvo*) of personality-factors, gaining of sense-spheres'. Here '*okkanti*' is linguistically equivalent to '*avakkanti*', the word used for the 'descent' of discernment into the womb at the start of an organism's development in the womb (Para.6.9), and for the 'descent' of the 'embryo' which takes place when there is sexual intercourse at the right time in a woman's monthly cycle (M.I.265–66). The 'gaining of sense-spheres', i.e. the development of sense-organs is seen, by the different schools of Buddhism, as taking place from conception onwards. In the Theravādin Abhidhamma, the mind-organ and body-organ (of sensitivity to touch) are said to be present from the beginning of pregnancy, while the others develop later; an opposing Buddhist view which it refers to is that all the sense-organs are present from the beginning (Kvu.493–94). It can thus be seen that 'birth' refers to the process beginning at conception or at implantation, and that the 'falling away and arising' which conditions it must thus be prior to conception/implantation; though probably immediately leading up to it, with 'arising' actually equivalent to 'birth'. A period between the 'laying aside' of one's body in death, and conception in a new life is thus clearly referred to.

(6.21) A passage cited by the Sammitīyas,[11] Pūrvaśailas [12] and Sarvāstivādins (L'AK.II.37) in support of the intermediary existence is one concerning 'Non-returners': the type of saints who will not 'return' to rebirth in the sense-desire realm of humans etc., as they are almost Arahats (those who have experienced *nibbāna*). The passage is found at D.III.237:

> Five classes of persons who become Non-returners: those who attain *nibbāna* inbetween (*antarā-parinibbāyī*); those who attain *nibbāna* cutting short (*upahacca-*); those who attain it without (further) activity (*asaṅkhāra-*); those who attain it with (further) activity (*sasaṅkāra-*); those going up-stream to Akaniṭṭha [the highest of the 'five pure abodes', where only Non-returners are reborn (also at D.III.237)].

On its own, however, this passage does not prove that an intermediary existence was accepted in the early Suttas. It does do so, though, when supplemented by similar passages.

(6.22) S.V.69–70 discusses the five types of Non-returners, in the same order as at D.III.237, listing them after someone who has become an Arahat 'at the time of dying': clearly this implies that the order represents a decreasing speed of spiritual attainment. This would certainly make it likely that that the first of the five types of Non-returners attains *nibbāna* 'inbetween' death and rebirth. The interpretation given in the Theravādin Abhidhamma and commentaries, though, is that this Non-returner attains *nibbāna* immediately after 'arising' in a new rebirth, or at some time before the middle of the life-span there (Pug.16 and A.A.IV.7). Less contentiously, the next of the Non-returners is seen as one who comes to attain *nibbāna* between the mid-point of his life span and his death; the fifth type is one who is reborn in each of the five 'pure abodes' until he attains *nibbāna* in the last of these (Pug.17).

(6.23) The above Theravādin interpretation of one who 'attains *nibbāna* inbetween', however, can be seen from A.IV.70–4. to be a rather weak and strained one.[13] This passage discusses the five kinds of Non-returners, and compares them, respectively, to:

1a. a bit which comes off from a hot, beaten iron slab, and then cools down;
1b. a bit which comes off, flies up and then cools down;
1c. a bit which comes off, flies up, and then cools down before cutting into the ground (*anupahacca-talaṃ*).
2. a bit which cools after cutting into the ground.
3. a bit which flies up and falls on a little fuel, igniting it, then cools down after the fuel gets used up.
4. a bit which falls on a large heap of fuel, but cools down after it is used up.
5. a bit which flies up and falls on a heap of fuel such that a fire spreads, but then goes out when it reaches e.g. water or rock.

The Theravādin interpretation of the *antarā-parinibbāyī* Non-returner hardly fits this illustration. Not to 'cut into the ground' means, surely, not to begin a new rebirth. In the case of Non-returners, there is not even any question of whether this might mean conception or leaving the womb: they are of immediate 'spontaneous arising (*opapātiko*)' (M.I.465), rather than being born from a womb or egg (M.I.73). Thus to 'cut into the ground' alludes to the very start of a rebirth. For the 'fire' to spread and then go out (illustration 5, above) means to go through several rebirths before the Non-returner 'cools (*nibbāyati*)' by attaining *nibbāna*. As the Theravādin interpretation of the *antarā-parinibbāyī* (1a-c.) is that he attains *nibbāna* at some time between the start and middle of the next life, and the 'cutting-short (*upahacca-*)' Non-returner (2) attains it after this, then the 'cutting into the ground (*upahacca-talaṃ*)' of the simile would have to represent the middle of this life, which seems *most* artificial. Even the commentary (A.A.IV.39) sees similes 1a-c. as involving a 'bit' which is still in 'space', 'not having reached the earth'; reaching the earth would most naturally apply to the very *start* of a life. The *antarā-parinibbāyī* must thus be one who attains *nibbāna* after death and *before* any rebirth.

(6.24) A.II.134 shows that the between-lives period in which the *antarā-parinibbāyī* Non-returner attains *nibbāna* is in fact called 'becoming' (*bhava*). The passage refers to three kinds of spiritual fetters:

i) those binding to the lower shore (i.e. to the sense-desire world: a Non-returner is defined as one who is free of these fetters);
ii) those 'of a kind to take up arising';
iii) those 'of a kind to take up becoming'.

The first fetters are abandoned by one 'going up-stream to Akaniṭṭha', i.e. by the least advanced Non-returner; the first two fetters are abandoned by the *antarā-parinibbāyī* Non-returner, and all three are abandoned by the Arahat. The above distinction between 'becoming' and 'arising' is most instructive. The 'up-stream' Non-returner is clearly not beyond 'arising' in a rebirth, for he has ahead of him several rebirths in the 'pure abodes', ending in Akaniṭṭha. Only the highest kind of Non-returner is beyond such 'arising' (*uppatti-*). He is not an Arahat, though: one who has destroyed fetters leading to 'becoming'. As an Arahat is one who has attained *nibbāna* in his present life, even up to the moment of death (Para.6.22), the highest Non-returner must attain *nibbāna after* his death but *before* 'arising' in any rebirth, this period being called 'becoming'.[14]

(6.25) It can thus be seen that the 'early Suttas' did accept a between-lives state, known as 'becoming',[15] in which it is possible for a Non-returner to attain *nibbāna*. An Arahat, though, attains *nibbāna* in life, so as not to enter 'becoming', while most beings pass through it and go on to arise in a rebirth.

THE NATURE OF THE INTERMEDIARY EXISTENCE

(6.26) It can be seen that an intermediary existence would act as a transition between often disparate forms of rebirth. It would thus be both a vehicle for transferring the continuity of character and also a time for the necessary re-adjustment.[16] The similes 1a–c. in Para 6.23 indicate that it consists of three successive phases, and Para.6.15 provides terms which must be seen as names for these phases: 'inclination', 'coming and going' and 'falling away and arising'.

(6.27) Among the powers attributed to the Buddha and some Arahats is that of the knowledge of how living beings are reborn: knowledge of their 'coming and going and falling away and arising' (D.I.162). At D.I.83, knowledge of 'falling away and arising' is likened to a man seeing that 'these men enter (*pavisanti*) a house, these men leave (*nikkhamanti*) it, these men wander the carriage-road track, and these are sat in the midst where four roads meet'. Here, of course, the language of 'entering' and 'leaving' is reminiscent of D.II.334 (Para 6.7), on the 'life-principle' of a dead person. The simile shows that the three phases of 'becoming' are seen as like leaving a house, wandering about on a road, and then sitting down 'in the midst where four roads meet'. It is worth noting, here, that S.IV.194–95 likens a person's body to a border-town and his discernment to the 'Lord' of such a town, he being sat 'in the midst, where four roads meet' (representing the four physical elements). The becoming seated 'in the midst . . .' of D.I.83, then, represents discernment coming to be established in a new personality, after wandering in search of 'it'. Another simile for knowledge of beings' rebirths likens it to the knowledge of a man standing between two houses, who would 'see men entering a house and leaving it, and going back and forth and wandering across' (M.I.279). This simile emphasizes the mid-stage of becoming as one of wandering and wavering, indeed one of *coming and going*. Similarly M.I.261 (Para 6.13) refers to beings 'seeking to be (*sambhavesīnaṃ*)', who must clearly be those in the intermediary existence.[17]

(6.28) It would thus seem reasonable to see the three stages of this existence as:

i) 'inclination': leaving the body with a desire for a further rebirth, like a man leaving a house, or a bit flying off a hot, beaten piece of iron;
ii) 'coming and going': wandering back and forth *seeking* a rebirth, like a man wandering on a road or between houses, or a hot iron bit that flies up in the air;
iii) 'falling away and arising': falling from one's previous state, one's previous identity, into a new rebirth, like a man settling down in square or entering a house; or a hot iron bit falling and cutting into the earth.

As shown in Para 6.19, the whole between-lives state is likened to that of a leaping flame driven and fuelled by the wind, representing craving. That is, craving provides the impetus and energy to seek another rebirth, and the intermediary existence is flavoured by such craving. As in Para 6.16, craving is the 'moisture' for becoming, and discernment is its 'seed', so that discernment, will and aspiration come to be 'supported' in another rebirth.

(6.29) The between-lives state need not be seen as a what we call a 'fully conscious' state. D.II.334 (Para 6.7) talks of the life-principle as leaving a person either in dreaming or death. Other passages show that the 'early Suttas' talked of going to sleep and dying in similar ways:

i) D.I.333–34 uses the expression 'gone to one's day-bed (*diva-seyyaṃ*)' for taking a siesta, while Sn.29 says 'I go no more to a womb-bed (*gabbha-seyyaṃ*)' in the sense of 'I will not be reborn'.
ii) '*Okkamati*' is used both of the 'descent' of discernment into the womb at conception (Para 6.9) and also of 'falling' into sleep (Vin.I.15).

(6.30) As will be argued in chapter 10, the discernment found in (deep) sleep and at the death-moment is seen, in the Theravāda school, as of a kind which is radiantly 'brightly shining' (*pabhassara*). This makes sense, from the Theravāda perspective, of the experience of a radiant light which the 'Near-death Experience' literature says is reported by many people after they are resuscitated after nearly dying. It also makes sense of the reference in the *Bardo Thötröl* ('Tibetan Book of the Dead') to people confronting a pure white light in the intermediary existence: in the first of the three stages of this, the mind is said to be in an unconscious and luminous state which is somehow equated with Amitābha, 'Infinite Radiance', Buddha (Freemantle and Trungpa, 1978: 37). Such ideas also seem to connect with the idea, in other Mahāyāna Buddhist texts, that this Buddha will come to meet his devotees at death.

(6.31) Returning to the 'early Suttas', then, they see the between-lives state of becoming as entered when, fuelled by craving for rebirth, discernment, the main process comprising the life-principle, leaves the body. In a dream-like existence, it then wanders about seeking a new life, kept going by craving and accompanied by will and aspiration. On finding a new life, it falls into the womb (in the case of rebirths involving this), and sets off the production of a new mind-and-body, which had been craved for. This all takes place, of course, within the parameters set by karma, the 'field' in which the 'seed' of discernment grows (Para 6.16). As for the duration of such an intermediary existence, the opinions cited in later texts is that of a week or more (Kvu.A.106–07) or: as long as it takes to unite the conditions for a new birth; seven days, seven weeks; very quickly (L'AK.II.48–9).

THE *GANDHABBA*: SPIRIT-BEING OF THE INTERMEDIARY EXISTENCE

(6.32) Further light is shed on the intermediary existence by examining the nature and role of the *gandhabba*. This is referred to at M.I.265–66, which is cited by Sammītyas and Sarvāstivādins in support of the intermediary existence: for they equate the *gandharva* (Sanskrit equivalent of Pāli *gandhabba*) with this.[18] In other contexts, the *gandhabbas* are seen as the lowest kind of god (D.II.212), as 'going through the air' (A.II.39), and as living on the odour (*gandha*) of roots, heart-wood, pith, sap, leaves and flowers (S.III.250).[19] At the M.I.265–66 passage, the following is said:

> Monks, it is on the conjunction of three things that there is descent of the embryo (*gabbhass-āvakkanti*) . . . if, monks, there is, here, a coitus of the parents, and it is the mother's season, and a *gandhabba* is present, it is on the conjunction of these things that there is descent of the embryo.[20]

This passage clearly deals with how conception takes place. The Theravādin commentary on it says: ' "*Gandhabba*" is the being going there. "Is present" it is not that he remains in the proximity observing the coitus of the parents, but what is implied is that a certain being is having rebirth in that situation, being driven by the mechanism of karma' (M.A.II.310). This, though, does little to lessen the text's impression of a fully-fledged (between-lives) being as needing to be present for conception to take place. In a Freudian-sounding passage, Vasubandhu gives the Sarvāstivādin view, which *does* see a being as observing the coitus of his future parents: a male is sexually attracted to his future mother, and jealous of the father, while a female is attracted to the father, and jealous of the mother (L'AK.II.50–1).

(6.33) It is notable that discernment-terminology is not used in the M.I.265–66 passage, as it is in the D.II.62–3 passage on the 'descent' of discernment into the womb (Para.6.9). M.I.265–66 is a continuation from the Buddha's rebuke of Sāti's ideas on discernment (Para 6.13), and follows the rejection of speculations on an unchanging 'I' linking past, present and future. This suggests that the passage was phrased in such a way as to avoid any impression that discernment, alone and unaided, links different lives together. The between-lives discernment is not an independent entity, a Self, but part of a kind of being, a *gandhabba*. When this discernment descends into a womb, it does not do so alone, but as part of an 'embryo'. This terminology of '*gandhabba*' and 'embryo' must be seen as both exact and deliberate: a passage on a misconception about discernment and rebirth is hardly the place for 'loose' or inexact language. As part of a *gandhabba* or of an 'embryo', the between-lives discernment must, clearly, be dependent on other factors which compose these, and not be a Self which depends only on itself. The Sarvāstivādins, in fact, saw the intermediary existence, i.e. *gandhabba*, as having the five personality-factors (L'AK.II.32), which clearly follows from a statement at S.III.55, that one cannot 'show forth the coming or going or falling away and arising . . . of discernment' apart from the the four other personality-factors.

(6.34) The statement that the four nutriments are for 'the assistance of those seeking to be' (M.I.261) also shows that the between-lives *gandhabba* must have some sort of body; for otherwise it would need no 'material/food-nutriment'. Now this nutriment can be 'gross' or 'subtle (*sukhumo*)' (M.I.261). For an 'odour' eating *gandhabba*, it will surely be of a subtle kind [21]: thus its 'body' will be a 'subtle' one. Indeed, the Sarvāstivādins (L'AK.II.122) and Sammitīyas saw a being in the intermediary existence as having a 'mind-made' body, with the latter saying that this was 'so subtle and delicate that when it is on the ground, it would not (appear) different from that' (SNS.200).[22] As it has been seen that the mind-made body and discernment are regarded as key aspects of the life-principle, and that the life-principle leaves the body at death (Paras.6.5–7), such an idea seems plausible.

(6.35) Just as the life-principle has been seen as a kind of 'spirit' (Para.6.11), so may the between-lives *gandhabba*. This is because of:

i) the subtle nature of the *gandhabba*;
ii) its being the carry-over from a dead person, after the discernment life-principle has 'left' the body;
iii) its feeding on odour, i.e. on that which is known through the nose: through which one also breathes in and out, in-spires and ex-pires (dies!);
iv) its moving through the air (*viha-*);
v) the parallel of the between-lives state to the *wind* (*vāta*)-blown fire;
vi) the parallel of discernment, the main component of the between-lives state and the life-principle, to air or wind (Para.6.11).

The English word 'spirit', meaning the life-breath of a person, neatly encompasses these various notions.

(6.36) While it has been seen that the later Theravādin orthodox view does not accept an intermediary existence in which the *gandhabba*-spirit exists, it is notable that such an idea is present in 'popular' Buddhism of Theravāda lands. As reported by Melford Spiro, the Burmese believe that a 'butterfly spirit (*leikpya*)' leaves the body at death and needs the broken-off branch of a tree (*gandhabba*s live on the odour of such things!) on which to rest for a week. [23]

(6.37) The *gandhabba*-spirit, of course, is not-Self: not an eternal Self or eternal soul. Scepticism on the notion of a *gandhabba* as not-Self, however, has been expressed by John Garrett Jones. He feels that the Buddha wanted to 'both have his cake and eat it' in accepting rebirth which necessitates some 'pseudo-self' to be reborn and his saying that there is 'no *ātman* to be reborn'(1979: 150 & 151). The *gandhabba* is, for him, such a 'pseudo-self', on which he says: 'I can see no way, however, of reconciling the belief in a surviving *gandhabba* with the much more rigorous doctrine of the *khandhas*' (i.e. of the personality-factors as not-Self; p. 202). As has been seen, though, the *gandhabba* is also composed of personality-factors, and this implies the mutual dependence of such components, and thus their not being a Self. The *gandhabba* is not a '*pseudo*-self', but can be seen as a genuine empirical 'self', as found between-lives. It is, though, no metaphysical Self: all its components are inevitably impermanent, *dukkha* and not-Self.

(6.38) Karel Werner is thus right to criticize the popular contrast which sees Hinduism as teaching a 'transmigrating personality', taken as the eternal *ātman* or Self, and Buddhism as denying this (1988: 94). Even for Hinduism, the 'transmigrating personality' is of a changeable, composite nature, the 'subtle (*sūkṣma*-)' or 'characteristic (*liṅga*-)' body (*śarīra*), and is not the eternal Self, which only underlies it (1988: 84). For Buddhism, there is a kind of 'transmigrating personality' (or, rather, a transmigrating process-cluster), the life-principle or *gandhabba*-spirit; but it has nothing to do with a supposed unchanging Self, for which Buddhism finds no evidence. Werner's suggestion that it is an empty 'personality structure' also seems inappropriate (Para.4.17). Theravāda wariness against accepting a between-lives state, and a being existing in it, may well have been because such a being might be construed as the 'person' of the Personalists (Para 1.36). As the Personalists seem to have equated such a 'person' with the life-principle, which was also easily mistaken for a Self, the Theravādins were also very wary about this term. The life-principle of the 'early Suttas', however, is not-Self, and, though it is not the same as or totally different from the 'mortal body', it is the same as processes such as discernment, vitality, heat and the mind-made body. It thus is unlike the Personalists' 'person', which was seen as 'not the same as or different from' the *personality-factors*, both bodily and mental. For the 'early Suttas', a 'person' is a web of interacting processes, both in life and between lives; it is not something 'neither the same as or different from' these that owns them and acts through them. It is notable, though, that the best evidence for acceptance of a between-lives state is in the *Aṅguttara Nikāya*, and that the term 'person' (*puggala*) occurs frequently in this. It is possible that the Personalist view grew up among monks specialising in reciting this *Nikāya* (or its close parallel, the *Ekottara Āgama*), partly because they misconstrued the nature of the between-lives state.

Part II

SAṂSĀRIC AND NIBBĀNIC DISCERNMENT

7

THE CENTRALITY OF DISCERNMENT

Insofar only can one be born . . . that is to say the sentient body with discernment (D.II.63–4).

(7.1) Part I has shown that, in the 'early Suttas', no metaphysical Self is accepted, but that *citta* (mind/heart) is often seen as 'self' in an empirical sense (Para.1. 9), and can indeed be a major aspect of the 'developed self' of the Arahat (ch.3). It has also shown that discernment (*viññāṇa*) is a key aspect of the 'life-principle', and the central aspect of the process of becoming that links rebirths (ch.6). Part II aims to explore the central role of *viññāṇa* and *citta* within a person, and to examine their nature. It also aims to show that, not only are they central to understanding the nature of an unliberated person, still entrapped in the round of rebirths (*saṃsāra*), but that they, or more specifically discernment, are the key to understanding the nature of *nibbāna*, both within the lifetime of the liberated person and beyond his or her death.

THE NATURE AND CENTRALITY OF *CITTA*

(7.2) The term '*citta*' originated as the past participle of the verb '*cinteti*'/'*ceteti*', which means 'thinks on in a directed way', or simply 'thinks on', 'thinks', 'intends' or 'wills'. From the same root as this verb comes '*cetanā*', 'will' or 'volition', and it is *cetanā* which is usually referred to as that which '*ceteti*' (e.g. A.III.415). *Citta*, then, is that which has been acted on by the activity of willing or directed thought. In the 'early Suttas' it can mean, firstly, a thought (S.V.418); in this, it is quite close to the meaning of '*vitakka*', a 'directed thought': for to read someone's *citta* is to intuit which *vitakka* they will think next (D.III.103–04). Secondly, *citta* can mean a train of thought (S.I.178). A more general meaning, though, is that of a total 'mind-set', a way in which thought and emotion have been deployed towards a certain end or purpose, or with respect to certain concerns:

a 'frame of mind'. 'Mentality' is a possible rendering for this third sense, though this is normally seen as referring to a long-lasting disposition, whereas *citta* can be seen as very changeable, as can a 'mind-set' or 'frame of mind'.

(7.3) *Citta* as an applied 'mind-set' is seen as the third of the four 'bases of success' (*iddhi-pāda*s), which are said to be concentration of desire, of energy, of *citta*, and of investigation (e.g. S.V.268–69). By using these, success in some venture, even in psychic power, can be attained: by an approach in which the dominant state is either desire focussed on the goal, energy directed at it, the focussing of one's whole mind-set on it, or careful investigation of it. *Citta*, as a 'frame of mind' is that which can be 'contracted' (i.e. unworkable), 'distracted', 'grown great', 'composed', or the opposite of such qualities (M.I.59). It can be 'deranged' in one who is mad (S.I.126), and is different in a man and a woman (D.II.271). As a mind-set or frame of mind, it can be dominated by a certain emotion, so as to be 'terrified' (S.I.53), 'astonished' (S.I.178) or 'tranquil' (A.IV.209). It can be 'taken hold of' by pleasant or unpleasant impressions (M.I.423). It can also be that to which a host of emotionally charged states pertain: malevolence, envy, treachery and conceit, and other spiritual hindrances such as drowsiness, agitation, or vacillation (M.I.36). It may also be free of such states (M.I.59), so there is ever the need to develop and purify it: 'For a long time this *citta* has been defiled by attachment, hatred and delusion. By defilement of *citta*, beings are defiled; by purity of *citta*, beings are purified' (S.III.152). Here *citta* is spoken of not as a specific mind-set, but as mind-set in general, in which case it comes close to meaning the seat of the emotions, the 'heart'.

(7.4) As a person's emotional centre, *citta* can be equated with a person as a whole: 'I am burning (*ḍayhāmi*) with desire and attachment, my *citta* is consumed (*pari-ḍayhati*)' (S.I.188). Nevertheless, as the dominating 'set' of a person's mind, *citta* can be out of tune with some of his desires or aspirations. It can go off with a will of its own (Dhp.36) and bring a person to ruin if it is not tamed, so as to be 'set up' in a more stable way, or in relation to more wholesome objects. In this respect, *citta* can be spoken of as if it is another person, a constant companion who can help or hinder one. At Thag.1107–42, the monk Tāḷpuṭa addresses his *citta*: while it has urged him on in a wholesome way (1107, 1113–20, 1124), it also wanders as it wishes (1130), leads to hell (1112), and keeps a person within *saṃsāra* (1126). People under Māra's control are equally 'your servants, *citta*' (1145). The monk thus resolves: 'I shall not do your bidding now' (1122), such that 'I am no longer under your control, *citta*' (1134). That is, he is no longer at the mercy of his whims, moods, emotions, and passing fancies. A monk should control his *citta*, not be controlled *by* it (M.I.214). Thus, when a man says to the Buddha 'obedient is my wife . . . long has she been a loving mate', he replies 'obedient is my *citta* . . . long has it been thoroughly developed and well tamed' (Sn.22–3). As it has been shown that the 'early Suttas' accept no metaphysical Self and no 'owner' of the factors of personality, such passages must simply mean that *citta* is seen as the ownerless driving focus of mind or personality, which may or may not fit in with a person's higher aspirations, and which may lead a person astray or, when properly controlled, directed and integrated, ennoble him. It is, above all, by developing skill in meditative concentration (*samādhi*), which brings mental calm and clarity, that someone may 'make *citta* turn according to' his wishes (A.IV.34).

(7.5) *Citta* is indeed influential: 'the world is led by *citta*' (A.II.177). The reason that a person's 'mind-set' or 'frame of mind' is so powerful is that, once is has been 'set up', it carries on with a will of its own, co-ordinating and operating other aspects of mind. It may 'feel' (S.IV.73) and it may also 'understand' (A.I.9). Indeed it is said 'cognition and feeling: these are mental (*cetasikā*) qualities, dependent on *citta*, therefore cognition and feeling is (each) a *citta*-activity (-*saṅkhāro*)' (M.I.301). Most importantly, *citta* becomes the driving force behind the activity of willing or wilful thought (*ceteti*), the very thing which 'set it up' in the first place. Thus S.III.151–52 says that a painting is 'thought out (*cintitaṃ*)' by *citta* and that, just as a painter fashions the form of a man or woman, *citta* 'produces and reproduces' the five personality-factors in life after life. In this it is like karma, equivalent to *cetanā*, or willing (Para.4.4). In the commentaries, it is clearly said, 'By "*citta*" is meant that which "thinks on (*cinteti*) an object (*ārammaṇaṃ*)", "it discerns (*vijānāti*)" ' (Asl.63).

(7.6) The last quote indicates that *citta* is close to *viññāṇa*, 'discernment', in meaning. In the 'early Suttas', they are sometimes used as synonyms (e.g. S.II.95).[1] Moreover, the 'arising' of *citta* is said to be conditioned by the arising of mind-and-body (*nāma-rūpa*) (S.V.184), just as the arising of discernment is said to be (S.III.60–1). It can be seen from the above discussion, though, that while *citta* and discernment are the same as to content, *citta* is discernment as 'deployed' in a certain way, with various accompaniments. It is the mind-*set*; though it has a great purity and potential which may be unlocked by meditative training, as will be seen in chapter 10.

(7.7) R.Johansson, in his detailed studies of *citta* in the Suttas, sees it as 'the organizing centre, the conscious core of personality' (1969: 131), 'the personal core of purposeful consistency, some sort of super-ordinated organising agency' (1965: 177–78) , 'a conscious centre for activity, purposiveness, continuity and emotionality' (1965: 179), '*the empirical functioning self*' (1969: 30; italics in original). Much of this is acceptable, but Johansson neglects the aspect of *citta* as *itself* 'set up', conditioned and influenced. It is not only active, but also acted upon, which explains its changeable nature: 'the flickering fickle *citta*, difficult to guard, difficult to control' (Dhp.33). It is a fluctuating and ever-changing focus for the co-ordinating of mental states. As much as being the 'empirical functioning self', it is the 'empirical, functioning *selves*' of a person, for there are many competing mind-sets. Thus M.II.27 asks, 'Which *citta*?, for *citta* is manifold, various, diverse', and the commentaries see it as 'variegated according to circumstances' (Asl.63). Generally speaking, though, a person will operate with a limited repertoire of fickle mind-sets, and some will occur regularly. They can thus help account for the persistence of character-traits as outlined in chapter 4, giving a relative 'purposeful consistency' to a person. While the mind-sets are in control of personality, though, they are not in control of themselves, but fluctuate and alternate amongst themselves; there is thus a need for the meditative integration of personality, to provide a greater, more wholesome, consistency.

(7.8) Johansson certainly goes too far in seeing the personality-factors (including discernment) as 'outside *citta*', with *citta* as the 'basis carrying' them and the links of Conditioned Arising (1979: 161–62). As *citta* is said to be itself dependent on one of these links, mind-and-body, this is not possible. In support of his view, Johansson cites S.III.45, which describes the process of enlightenment in terms of *citta* becoming detached from (i.e. not grasping at) the personality-factors. This does not prove his point, though, as S.III.55 says much the same of discernment, one of the personality-factors. If discernment or *citta* may come, through non-grasping, to transcend the personality-factors (see ch.12), it is normally one of these very personality-factors. In the 'early Sutta' analyses of personality, *citta* may not occur among the lists of components, such as the five personality-factors, or twelve links of Conditioned Arising. This is not because it is some underlying 'basis' of these, but because it is *equivalent to* one of these components, namely discernment, in its aspect as deployed, directed and directing in various ways.

(7.9) In the 'early Suttas', then, *citta* may mean a 'thought', 'train of thought', 'mind-set' or 'heart'. In the latter two meanings, it represents the dynamic, fluctuating focus of personality. Conditioned by mind-and-body, particularly by volition, it becomes the co-ordinating, guiding, creative focus of mind, marshalling and integrating other aspects of mind, including volition itself, in an ongoing process of mutual interaction and change. In this process, it can become tainted by manifold unwholesome emotions, particularly if 'set up' with respect to unwholesome objects or constantly 'set up' with respect to different objects, so as to be scattered, diffuse and unintegrated. Thus the need for meditative integration and calming of *citta*.

(7.10) In the Abhidhamma, *citta* is, as in the Suttas, equivalent in content to discernment. It is an umbrella-term for any of the six sense-discernments (visual-, aural- etc.) or mind-organ-element (*mano-dhātu*) (Dhs.1187), as is the discernment personality-factor (Vibh.54). The other mental states, namely the personality-factors of feeling, cognition and constructing activities, are known as *cetasika*s, or 'mental qualities' (Dhs.1189). These are said to be 'associated with *citta* and with *citta* as origination' (Dhs.1524), 'co-existent' with *citta* (Dhs.1520) and to 'turn over' with *citta* (Dhs.1522). That is, they are closely mixed with, originated by, last as long as, and work together with the *citta* that they accompany. Vism.477 adds that discernment, i.e. *citta*, 'dominates' them.

(7.11) The *citta* which sustains its accompanying 'qualities', however, is no unchanging underlying substance, for the Abhidhamma views the mind as a stream consisting of one momentary *citta*-with-*cetasika*s followed by another. This is seen by the fact that when any of the seven types of *citta* are present, the others are absent (e.g. Dhs.441, 467, 496). Kvu.458 also specifically refers to 'one moment of *citta*'. In the *Dhammasaṅgaṇi*, while *citta* is said to be one *dhamma* – one 'basic pattern' or 'basic process' – it is differentiated into eighty-nine kinds, principally by the different 'mental qualities' that accompany it at any moment. Thus, while these qualities are dependent on *citta*, it is they which determine (or indicate) what type of *citta* is occurring. Thus Ñāṇamoli says that *citta*, 'when used technically, refers to a momentary type-situation considered as *viññāṇa* in relation to a the tone of its concomitant feeling, perception and formations'.[2] Apart from the Abhidhamma emphasis on a moment-by-moment analysis, this meaning of *citta* is much the same as in the Suttas, concerning *citta* as mind-set or heart.

A PERSON AS DISCERNMENT AND SENTIENT BODY

(7.12) In the 'early Suttas', not only *citta*, but also discernment is seen as the central focus of personality. This is quite clearly seen at S.IV.194–95, which gives a parable along with its explanation. There is a border town (meaning the 'body' (*kāya*)), with six gates (meaning the six senses), and a wise warder of the gates (meaning mindfulness). Pairs of swift messengers (meaning meditative calm and insight) come from each of the four directions, and are directed by the warder of the gates to the 'lord of the town' (meaning discernment) who sits 'in the midst, where four roads meet' (meaning the physical four 'great elements'). Each of the messengers goes to the lord and delivers the 'message of truth' (meaning *nibbāna*). This passage shows discernment to be 'lord' of the 'town' of the 'body', as the central process within a person, and even to be that which comes to know *nibbāna*.

(7.13) A person, then, is essentially discernment and *kāya*: 'body' or, literally, 'collection' or 'group'. Such a two-fold analysis is also seen in the common phrase 'the discernment-endowed body (*sa-viññāṇako kāyo*)', which at S.III.80 seems equivalent to the five personality-factors internal to a particular person [3]. This could be interpreted in two ways:

i) 'discernment' refers to all four non-physical personality-factors, and *kāya* is equivalent' to 'material form', the remaining factor, so as to mean simply the *physical* body;
ii) 'discernment' refers only to the discernment personality-factor, and *kāya* is the 'body' comprising the other four grouped together.

The description of the 'body' in the above parable is the same as at D.I.76–7 (Para.6.5), which gives a very physical-sounding description of 'body'-as-opposed-to-discernment. This, then, suggests interpretation i). However, the parable also says that the 'town' of the body has 'six gates', which thus means that it includes the mind-organ. This is not equated with the brain, as it is not seen as part of 'material form'.[4] 'Body', then, can include mental processes. Indeed, the 'body' endowed with 'vitality, heat and discernment' can both see visible forms with the eye and discern mental objects with the mind-organ (D.II.337–38). The 'body' is 'covered with ignorance' (Thag.572), but it is also possible for a person to 'see Dhamma with his body' (Dhp.259). These passages indicate the correctness of interpretation ii). This is reinforced by S.II.23–4:

> For a fool or a wise man, hindered by ignorance and fettered by craving, thus is this body (*kāyo*) received. There is just this body and external mind-and-body (*nāma-rūpa-*). Conditioned by this pair is the pair stimulation (and) just six sense-spheres, touched by which a fool or wise man experiences pleasure and pain.

This is clearly a version of the Conditioned Arising sequence . . . mind-and-body → six sense-spheres → stimulation → feeling. . . . In this version, the mind-and-body (*nāma-rūpa*) link is referred to as 'this *kāya* and external *nāma-rūpa*'. Here '*kāya*' must refer to 'internal' *nāma-rūpa*, for Sn.530 refers to both 'internal' and 'external' *nāma-rūpa*. Thus 'body' (*kāya*) here means the mind-and-body of a particular person, as opposed to mind-and-body (or meaningful forms) external to him.[5] Consequently, *kāya* can mean more than the physical body. Indeed D.II.62, on *nāma-rūpa*, refers to the 'mind-group' (*nāma-kāya*) and 'body-group' (*rūpa-kāya*).[6] As equivalent to *nāma-rūpa*, *kāya* seems to be the '*sentient* body'.

(7.14) The *nāma-rūpa* to which it is equivalent is defined, in the 'early Suttas' thus: 'Feeling, cognition, volition, stimulation and attention (*manasikāro*): this is called *nāma*; the four great elements and the material form (*rūpaṃ*) derived from these: this is called *rūpa*' (S.II.3–4). Here, *nāma*, literally 'name', refers to those mental states which are particularly associated with sensitivity to and reaction to objects of the physical senses and the mind-organ. As Vism.558 explains, using a pun, 'it is "*nāma*" because of bending (*namanato*) towards objects'. *Nāma-rūpa*, then, is perhaps well translated as the 'sentient body'.[7] In the Abhidhamma (e.g. Dhs.), the first four components of *nāma* are, with 'one-pointedness of *citta*' and 'life-faculty', mental qualities which *always* accompany *citta*, while Miln.56 adds 'attention' to these as states 'conascent' with any form of discernment. That is, *nāma* refers to those non-physical states of a person, apart from discernment, which are always present, thus comprising basic sentience. The Abhidhamma actually defines *nāma*, in the *nāma-rūpa* link, as the personality-factors of feeling, cognition and the constructing activities (Vibh.136). This is appropriate to the Sutta view as volition is the chief constructing activity (S.III.60), and stimulation and attention can easily be seen as others. *Nāma-rūpa*, then, is the 'sentient body' comprised of the personality-factors other than discernment[8]: the link which conditions it in the Conditioned Arising sequence.

(7.15) For the 'early Suttas', then, the most important dividing line within personality was not that between the non-physical (*arūpa*) and the physical, but between discernment and the rest of personality, mental and physical: the 'sentient body' (*kāya* or *nāma-rūpa*), of which discernment is seen as the 'lord'. The basic ingredients from which personality is generated, though, are the 'six elements': discernment, space, and the 'four great elements' (solidity, cohesion, heat and motion). As is said at A.I.176, 'Derivative upon the six elements, monks, is descent of the embryo (i.e. conception); descent being, there is the sentient body (*nāma-rūpa-*); from the sentient body as condition is the sixfold sense-sphere. . . .' This is clearly a version of the Conditioned Arising sequence on the development of new sentient body in the womb, due to the entry of discernment there (see Para.6.9). In this process, the full living body (*rūpa*) develops, so as to include 'derived' matter (such as the sensitive part of the eye, Dhs.596) in addition to the four basic elements, and *nāma* is a new production, due to the presence of discernment. This derivation of personality from the six elements is probably also alluded to in the parable at Para.7.12, where the 'town' of the sentient body has discernment and the four great elements at its centre, just as a town might develop around a cross-roads or square 'in the middle, where four roads meet'.

(7.16) The components of sentiency (*nāma*), produced due to the presence of discernment, are seen as intimately mingled with it, just as the Abhidhamma came to see the 'mental qualities' as closely allied to *citta* (Para.7.10). At M.I.293, it is said that feeling, cognition and discernment are 'associated, not dissociated, and it is not possible to lay down a diversity [of objects] between these states, having analysed them again and again. Your reverence, what one feels one cognizes, what one cognizes one discerns (*vijānāti*)'. Indeed, M.I.301 sees feeling and cognition as each a '*citta*-activity (*-saṅkhāro*)', and

Miln.64 says that one cannot 'lay down a diversity' between stimulation, feeling, cognition, volition and discernment, 'the nature of which is to arise together', as they are like the acidity, saltiness and bitterness of a well made soup: hard to distinguish separately. Miln.87 also says that the Buddha's analysis of their blended mix into its components is like someone tasting a handful of sea-water and knowing which rivers the water came from.

THE VORTICAL INTERPLAY OF DISCERNMENT AND THE SENTIENT BODY

(7.17) Given that a person is comprised of discernment and the 'sentient body' (*nāma-rūpa*), it is not surprising to learn that the whole process of *saṃsāra,* the conditioned realm of life and lives, is seen as encompassed in the vortex-like mutual interaction of these two:

> Ānanda, insofar only can one be born, or grow old, or die, or fall away, or arise; insofar only is there any pathway for verbal designation, or for explanation of words, or for concepts; insofar only is there any sphere of wisdom; insofar only does the round [of *saṃsāra*] turn for there to be disclosure in the present state [i.e. existence in this life]: that is to say, the sentient body with discernment (D.II.63–4).[9]
>
> Indeed, this discernment turns back round onto the sentient body, it does not go beyond. Insofar only can one be born, or grow old, or die, or fall away, or arise: that is to say, [from the extent that] discernment is conditioned by the sentient body, the sentient body is conditioned by discernment, the sixfold sense-sphere is conditioned by the sentient body . . . [and so on as in the standard Conditioned Arising sequence]
>
> (D.II.32 and S.II.104).

These passages see the process of interaction as producing and encompassing birth and development in the present life, rebirth, the possibility of of describing things in words and concepts, and of analysing them through wisdom. In the first passage, the processes of birth, ageing, death, etc. would seem to be especially based on discernment (see S. III.54–5 in Para.6.15); the 'pathway' for words etc. and wisdom would seem to be based on sentiency – *nāma*, literally 'name' –, and appearance in this life would seem to be based on *rūpa*, the body or material form.

(7.18) At its simplest, the nature of this interplay is that the sentient body (*nāma-rūpa/kāya*) can only move and sense things when it is enlivened and sensitized by 'vitality, heat and discernment' (Para.6.10). On the other hand, discernment, as it arises conditioned by sense-organ and sense-object (Para.6.13), needs a sentient body, endowed with sense-organs, for it to occur as discernment *of* anything. It is apparent, moreover, that the four personality-factors comprising the sentient body are seen as focusses of attachment which discernment clings to as a familiar 'home'. At S.III.9–10, Mahā Kaccāna explains that each of them is an 'element (*dhātu*)' which is the 'home' of discernment, with discernment as a 'home-haunter' by being 'bound by attachment' to them. One is a 'home-abandoner', though, when one is a *tathāgata*, who has, with respect to all *five* personality-factors (including discernment), completely abandoned all desire, attachment, craving, 'graspings by approach (*upāyupādānā*) which are latent tendencies to [view]-adherence, [stubborn] insistings of *citta*'. This passage implicitly encourages the monk, one who has 'gone forth from home into homelessness', to practice 'homelessness' in a more radical fashion, like the one who 'dwells alone' in Para.3.9. In this home-abandoning, discernment is to abandon even the normal process of discernment, which is associated with the sentient body 'home'.

(7.19) The way in which the four components of this are 'home' is illustrated at D.III.228, which describes them as four 'maintenances' or 'stations' (*ṭhitis*) of discernment, explaining:

> Friends, as an approach to material form, a persisting discernment would persist; with material form as object (*-ārammanaṃ*), with material form as support (*-patiṭṭhaṃ*), seeking enjoyment, it comes to growth, increase and abundance [and likewise for feeling, cognition and the constructing activities].

That is, discernment is maintained in existence, and flourishes (leading to more rebirth and suffering etc.) when it 'approaches' the other personality-factors seeking enjoyment, and comes to be supported on them as its objects. Its 'turning back round onto' them as 'home' seems to be largely through taking them as 'Self', as shown by S.III.133. Here Channa's *citta* does not 'spring up' for *nibbāna* on being told that everything is not-Self; rather, 'grasping arises and thinking (*mānasam*) turns back round: "Then who, therefore, is my

Self?" '. As will be seen in chapters 11 and 12, this process is one which can be stopped, leading to the liberation of discernment: the 'lord' of the sentient body which receives (and accepts) the 'message of truth' (Para.7.12).

(7.20) In sum, personality is seen by the 'early Suttas', as a process centred on discernment, or, as it is known when deployed in particular ways, *citta*: mind-set or heart. Conditioned by the six elements – discernment, space and the four material elements –, a new sentient body develops in the womb, with the ingredients of sentiency (*nāma*) blending with discernment. Discernment or *citta* engenders, enlivens and directs the processes of the sentient body, and it in turn is maintained in existence by its dependence on sense-organs and its attachment to the factors of its sentient body 'home', which become its supporting objects. From this vortex of interaction is spun out the conditioned world of life and lives, and the concepts we use to talk about these. In the next chapter, the details of this interaction will be probed and analysed. Later chapters (11 and 12) will focus on its *nibbānic* undoing, after the full nature of discernment has been analysed (9 and 10).

8

DISCERNMENT AND CONDITIONED ARISING

When the object is, there is a support for discernment (S.II.66).

(8.1) In the last chapter, it was shown that the 'early Suttas' saw personality as an interplay between discernment and the sentient body (*nāma-rūpa*/*kāya*); but only a preliminary analysis of the nature of the interaction was given. This chapter will explore this further, so as to better understand the roles and functions of discernment within personality. In order to do this, attention will largely be focussed on the role of discernment in the Conditioned Arising sequence. Part of the standard version of this runs: . . . constructing activities (*saṅkhāras*) → discernment → the sentient body (*nāma-rūpa*) → . . . . There is also a version (e.g. at D.II.63) which runs: . . . *nāma-rūpa* → discernment → *nāma-rūpa* . . . . Both these versions will be explored, to show how they describe two complementary aspects of the conditioning of discernment. The analysis will also show how the whole sequence of Conditioned Arising can be seen *both* as a process spanning more than one life, *and* as the continuous conditioned arising and re-arising of the components of personality during one life. This will prepare the way for chapter 11, which concerns *nibbāna* as the stopping of all these components, during life.

THE NATURE OF THE CONSTRUCTING ACTIVITIES

(8.2) To explore how the constructing activities condition discernment, it is first necessary to understand their nature. The word '*saṅkhāra*' itself is derived from '*saṃ*-' (together) + '*kṛ*' (to do) + '*a*' (denoting an agent or action noun), that is 'putting-together activity', or 'constructing activity'. The term is sometimes given the prefix '*abhi*-', which has the sense of mastery, as in over-coming

(PED.61), but this adds little extra meaning. Either word means activity which is combining, constructing, coordinating, synthesizing, arranging, organizing, forming, preparing. It is also dynamically motivating, as shown at A.I.111, where '*abhisaṅkhāra*' is used to refer to the momentum which keeps a free-rolling wheel turning for a while. The constructing activities occur both in the list of the twelve 'links' (*nidāna*s) of Conditioned Arising and that of the five personality-factors. As a personality-factor, they are 'the six collections of volition (*cetanā-kāyā*): will (*-sañcetanā*) for sights, will for sounds, for smells, for tastes, for touchables, and for mental objects' (S.III.60). As a link, they are said to be the three 'constructing activities' (*saṅkhāra*s): of body (*kāya-*), of speech and of mind (*citta-*) (S.II.4), the three 'doors' of action. S.II.39–40 sees these three 'constructing activities' as equivalent to bodily, verbal and mental will (*-sañcetanā*). D.III.217 also talks of the 'three *saṅkhāra*s' as 'goodness-(*puñña-*)', 'badness-(*apuñña-*)', and 'imperturbable- (*āneñja-*)' *abhisaṅkhāra*s. The 'constructing activities' link, then, is comprised of the activities of will in their aspect as that which leads to actions and the generation of karmic results, which *puñña-* etc. lead to. It refers to the endeavouring, reaching-out aspect of mind, and so is seen, at Ps.I.52, to consist of 'strivings' (*āyuhanā*).

(8.3) Will or volition (*cetanā*) seems to be the central constructing activity. In the Suttas, this is seen as equivalent to karma: 'I say *cetanā* is karma; having willed, one performs an action by body, speech or mind' (A.III.415). That is, it is that which initiates action. In the Abhidhamma, it is described thus

> It wills, thus it is volition; 'it collects' is the meaning. Its characteristic is the state of volition. Its function is to strive. It is manifested as co-ordination. It accomplishes its own and other's functions, as a senior pupil, a head carpenter etc. do. But it is evident when it occurs in marshalling of associated states in connection with urgent work, remembering and so on.
>
> (Vibh. 463)

The commentaries liken it to a cultivator directing strong men at harvest time, or a coordinating chief disciple or general, who incites others by acting themselves (Asl.111). In such a role, *cetanā* seems quite close to *citta*, as discussed in the last chapter.[1]

(8.4) The moulding, fabricating nature of the 'constructing activities' is clearly shown in one definition of them as a personality-factor:

> 'They construct a constructed phenomenon (*saṅkhataṃ*) *abhisaṅkharonti*)', monks, therefore they are called 'constructing activities'. What constructed phenomenon do they construct? Material form is a constructed phenomenon that they construct into the state of material form (*rūpattāya*). Feeling is a constructed phenomenon that they construct into a state of feeling. Cognition. . . . The constructing activities. . . . Discernment is a constructed phenomenon that they construct into what is meant by discernment (*viññāṇatthāya*). (S.III.87)

The commentary (S.A.II.292) links this process to that of cooking, and says 'thus coming together by conditions, it is "constructed" by the state of being made'. That is, the constructing activities co-ordinate the conditioning factors which bring forth each personality-factor: including the constructing activities themselves. The significance of the difference in wording, '*into what is meant by*', in the case of discernment, will be picked up in chapter 12.

THE CONDITIONING OF DISCERNMENT BY THE CONSTRUCTING ACTIVITIES

(8.5) As a standard feature of the Conditioned Arising sequence, it is said: 'discernment is from the constructing activities as condition'. Perhaps the most detailed passage on how this occurs is at S.II.66:

> That which one wills (*ceteti*) and that which one plans (*pakappeti*), and that for which one has a latent tendency (*anuseti*): this is an object (*ārammaṇam*) for the maintenance (*ṭhitiyā*) of discernment; when the object is, there is a support (*patiṭṭhā*) for discernment. When discernment is supported (*patiṭṭhite*) and growing, there is descent of the sentient body (*nāma-rūpassa*) [thus follow the remaining links of Conditioned Arising].

Exactly the same is said to happen even if one just plans and has a latent tendency, or just has a latent tendency. The latter thus appears to be seen as the most deep-seated and stubborn constructing activity;

one which possibly underlies the operation of all the rest, as an unconscious disposition. This passage shows that the constructing activities condition discernment by giving it a certain direction, so that it turns towards a certain object,[2] or kinds of objects on which to 'settle'.[3] It provides it with a supporting and maintaining object, so that it is discernment *of* something. The object is an 'opportunity' (another meaning of *ārammaṇa* [4]) for discernment to continue to arise, a focus of preoccupation, in which there has been volitional energy invested, where discernment turns for its sustenance and continuation. A similar point seems to be made at M.I.115, which says: 'whatever one ponders and reflects on much [e.g. sense-pleasures], towards that is the inclination of the heart (*nati hoti cetaso*).

(8.6) Now in the classical Theravāda interpretation of Conditioned Arising (e.g. Vism.528), the discernment 'link' pertains to the start of a rebirth, with its conditioning factor, the constructing activities, occurring in the previous one. Is this the only natural explanation of the 'early Sutta' material? It fits some passages. Para.6.9 shows that this 'link' can refer to discernment at conception, the start of a new life. Moreover, S.V.449 speaks of those affected by spiritual ignorance as 'constructing (*abhisaṅkharonti*)' constructing activities conducive to birth, so that they 'fall down the precipice of birth', while M.III.99–100 speaks of a virtuous person as fixing his *citta* on the thought of rebirth as a rich noble, such that these 'constructing activities' conduce to such a rebirth. Likewise, the word 'supported' (*patiṭṭhitā*), as at S.II.66, is sometimes used in a rebirth context. It is said that 'good actions (*puññāni*) are, in the world beyond, a support (*patiṭṭhā*) for living beings' (S.I.18); and the evil *Māra* is said to search, after the death of a monk, for where his discernment is 'supported' (S.I.122).

(8.7) Nevertheless, the 'early Suttas' also contain material which shows that the constructing activities → discernment conditioning can take place within one life. This seems allowed for by the idea that the fruitions of karma, i.e. of volition, do not only occur in future lives. Indeed, the 'supporting' of discernment does not only relate to a future life. At D.III.105, it is said that a person 'comprehended a person's stream (*-sotaṃ*) of discernment not broken into two, supported in this world and supported in a world beyond'. That is, an (unenlightened) person's discernment is seen as supported both in a future world after death, and also in the present world in which he lives. One can say that it is sustained in both by the constructing activities that a person generates. Indeed, at S.II.65 there is a passage which is the same as S.II.66 (Para.8.5) except that it moves from discernment being 'supported and growing' to there being rebirth *in the future*.

(8.8) Another important passage which parallels S.II.66 is found at S.III.54–5. This is in fact a very rich passage, and will be referred to a number of times in this work, in several contexts. It will thus be given here in full, though a full analysis of it will not be given here. The Buddha starts by giving a parable. He refers to five 'species of seeds': 'root-seed' (*mūla-bīja*), 'trunk-seed' (*khandha-bīja*), 'seed from a shoot' (*agga-bīja*), 'seed from a joint' (*phalu-bīja*), and 'grain-seed' (*bīja-bīja*). If these seeds are 'capable of sprouting' *and* 'happily planted' *and* have earth and water, they 'will come to growth, increase and abundance'. The Buddha then explains that the 'earth-element' stands for the four 'maintenances (*-ṭhitiyo*) of discernment', which Para. 7.19 has shown to be the first four personality-factors, or the 'sentient-body' (*nāma-rūpa*). The 'water-element' stands for 'delight and attachment', and the five seeds stand for 'discernment with-nutriment (*viññāṇaṃ sāhāraṃ*)'. The Buddha then continues:

> As an approach to material form, monks, a persisting (*tiṭṭhamānaṃ*) discernment would persist; with material form as object (*-ārammāṇaṃ*), with material form as support (*-patiṭṭhaṃ*), seeking means of enjoyment, it would come to growth, increase and abundance. As an approach to feeling. . . As an approach to cognition. . . . As an approach to the constructing activities . . . abundance.
>
> Were one to say this, monks: 'Apart from material form, apart from feeling, from cognition, and from the constructing activities, I will show forth the coming or going or falling away or arising, or the growth, increase and abundance of discernment' that is not possible.
>
> If attachment (*rāgo*) for the element of material form, monks, is abandoned by a monk, by that abandonment of attachment (its) object is cut off, and there is no support for discernment. So also for the elements of feeling, cognition, the constructing activities and discernment. That unsupported (*apatiṭṭhitaṃ*) discernment has no increase, and is without constructing activities (*anabhisaṅkhārañ*), released (*vimuttaṃ*); by (its) release it is steadfast (*ṭhitaṃ*); by (its) steadfastness it is content; by (its) contentment it is not disturbed; not being disturbed it just by

itself (or: he just by himself) attains *nibbāna* (*parinibbāyati*). It/he comprehends: 'Destroyed is birth . . .'

(cf. Para.7.19).

(8.9) This talks of 'object' and 'support' and alludes to constructing activities (here, *abhisaṅkhāra*s) as accompanying discernment (if there is still attachment). It is clearly, then, referring to the same situation as S.II.66 (Para.8.5), on the conditioning of discernment by the constructing activities. It shows that the objects which the constructing activities direct discernment onto, so as to 'persist' with a 'maintenance', are the components of the 'sentient body': the first four personality-factors which are the 'maintenances of discernment'. It is by the constructing activities directing discernment to 'approach' one or other of these that it gets an object for its maintenance (S.II.66). Seeking 'enjoyment' there, it thus proliferates and grows: this must surely mean that diverse thoughts arise, directed towards such an object of attachment.

(8.10) Now, while S.III.54–5 goes on to talk of 'supported', 'growing' discernment as getting involved in 'arising', or rebirth, it is clear from Para.8.7 that such discernment is something which occurs in this life before spilling over into another one. Moreover, it is also significant that S.III.54–5 goes on to talk of someone attaining *nibbāna* in life, indicated by the use of the formula 'destroyed is birth . . .', which is a standard formula used by persons on attaining Arahatship. This event pertains to someone whose discernment is 'unsupported' during their present life: so discernment being 'supported' must also pertain to this life. Thus, again, the constructing activities conditioning discernment by giving it a 'support' can be those of the present life, not only those those of a past life.

THE CONDITIONING OF DISCERNMENT BY *NĀMA-RŪPA*

(8.11) While the standard version of Conditioned Arising has discernment conditioned by the constructing activities, the above analysis shows that this conditioning process also involves *nāma-rūpa*; for this furnishes the objects onto which discernment is directed by the constructing activities. It is thus not surprising that some versions of Conditioned Arising simply start by saying that discernment is conditioned by *nāma-rūpa* (D.II.32 & 66; S.II.104 & 113). In one such passage, there is the following explanation:

> 'Were discernment to gain no support (*patiṭṭhaṃ*) in *nāma-rūpa*, would there, in the future, be evident the origination of birth, ageing and death, and of the arising of *dukkha*?'. 'There would not, Lord'. 'Therefore, Ānanda, just this is the cause, basis, arising and condition of discernment, that is to say, *nāma-rūpa*' D.II.63.

Now it would seem odd to restrict the 'objects' of discernment to the components of a person's own 'sentient body' (*nāma-rūpa*). Such passages as the above, though, need not be seen as implying this. Para.7.13 shows that *nāma-rūpa* can be both 'internal' to a person and 'external', in the form of objects of the five physical senses and the mind-organ. Such 'external' *nāma-rūpa*s can perhaps be seen as 'meaningful forms'. The way in which discernment is conditioned by both internal and external *nāma-rūpa* is indicated by S.II.73:

> Visual discernment arises conditioned by eye and visual forms; the meeting (*saṅgati-*) of the three is stimulation; conditioned by stimulation is feeling; conditioned by feeling is craving; conditioned by craving is grasping; conditioned by grasping is becoming; conditioned by becoming is birth; conditioned by birth is ageing and death . . . [this is then repeated for the other five sense-channels].

Here is a version of the Conditioned Arising sequence which begins with the six sense-organs and the six sense-objects. Now the discernment 'link' is defined as the six types of discernment, visual-discernment etc. (S.II.4), which arise dependent on these. As the sense-organs are sometimes subsumed into *nāma-rūpa* as the sentient body (ch.7, note 5), this passage can be seen as containing a more detailed statement of how the discernment 'link' is conditioned by *nāma-rūpa*. A person's discernment is conditioned by the sense-organs which are part of his 'sentient body' and also by the 'meaningful forms' that his senses perceive; some of these 'meaningful forms' will also be part of his own 'sentient body': a common focus of preoccupation for living beings. In all of this, the factors which condition discernment are not those of a past life, but part of the normal process of perception during one life.

DISCERNMENT AS CONDITIONED BY ATTENTION

(8.12) Discernment arises, then, conditioned by the sense-organs, and directed by the constructing activities onto some internal or external 'meaningful form' as object. Now while these constructing activities may have occurred in the same life, they may also belong to a previous life. Either way, they must be seen as preceding the discernment that they condition by some time, long or short. How, then, do they act on discernment? The most likely answer is that they do so via *manasikāra*, or 'attention', which is said to be an aspect of *nāma* in the 'sentient body' (Para.7.14). The activity of attention in initiating a perceptual process, thus providing discernment with a specific object, can be shown as follows. A.IV.339 strongly suggests that stimulation (*phassa*) is dependent on attention in the process of perception[5]: 'All *dhamma*s are rooted in desire (*chanda-*), originate from attention, arise from stimulation, their coming together (*-samosaraṇā*) is feeling, their chief state is concentration. . . .' Given that the normal perceptual process runs from stimulation to feeling onwards, this passage indicates that for stimulation to arise, there must already be attention.[6] If 'stimulation' is the meeting of sense-organ, sense-object, and discernment (as in Para.8.11), then 'attention' must be the act of selecting the object that discernment will take, following the lead of previous constructing activities, among which 'desire' must surely be counted.

(8.13) The action of attention is clearly indicated at M.I.190, which also shows that the 'all *dhamma*s' of A.IV.399 are the five personality-factors (as A.A.IV.158 explains). In the passage, Sāriputta says:

> But when, your reverences, the eye which is internal is intact, and external visible forms come within its range, and there is an appropriate (*tajjo*) act of attention (*samannāhāro*) [and only when *all three* conditions are met], then there is thus an appearance (*pātubhāvo*) of an appropriate share of discernment (*viññāṇa-bhāga-*). Whatever is material form in what has thus come to be is included in the group of grasping [personality-factor] of material form [and similarly for the other four personality-factors]. He comprehends thus: 'Thus there is, so it is said, the including, the collecting together (*sannipāto*), the coming together (*samvāyo*) of these five groups of grasping' [the same is then said for the other five sense-channels].

Here 'attention' is indicated by the word '*samannāhāra*', which the commentary (M.A.II.229) explains as '*manasikāra*'; this is appropriate as the two words are synonyms.[7]

(8.14) Two questions remain with respect to the above passage. One is the meaning of all five personality-factors arising in the 'share of discernment'. The other is the question of whether discernment is actually *regenerated* by the meeting of sense-organ, sense-object, and attention, or only *modified* by this, so as to be converted into a particular formThe first question will be dealt with under the next heading, while the second will be dealt with in chapter 10.

THE CONDITIONING OF THE SENTIENT BODY BY DISCERNMENT

(8.15) From D.II.62–3, in Para.6.8, it can be seen that this conditioning is certainly seen as taking place at conception and during gestation. D.II.62–3 continues, though, by saying:

> 'Were discernment to be cut off from one yet young, boy or girl, would the sentient body come to growth, increase and abundance?' 'It would not, Lord'. 'Therefore, Ānanda, this is the cause, basis, arising and condition of the sentient body, that is to say: discernment'.

This shows that discernment conditions the sentient body not only in the womb, but also during life.

(8.16) How, then, is the bodily component (*-rūpa*) of the sentient body conditioned by discernment? Such *rūpa* is defined (S.II.3–4) in the same way as the personality-factor of material form (also *rūpa*) at S.III.59: as the 'four great elements [solidity, cohesion, heat and motion] and the *rūpa* derived from these'. Elsewhere, the *rūpa* personality-factor is defined thus, using a pun: '"It is affected (*ruppatī-ti*)", monks, therefore one says "*rūpa*". Affected by what? Affected by cold, heat, by hunger and thirst, by stimulation by gnats, mosquitoes, wind, sun and snakes'. Now only a physical body which is actually living and sensitive can be affected in such ways. *Rūpa* is not a mere carcase, then, but a form through which pain etc. can arise. While the four 'great elements' are not themselves dependent on discernment, the full living body, including 'derived' *rūpa* such as the sensitive part of sense-organs, can be seen as so dependent. Indeed, Para.6.10 shows that discernment, along with 'vitality' and 'heat', is what enlivens a body. When M.I.190 says that the *rūpa* personality-factor is present in a 'share of discernment' occurring in the perceptual process, then, it means that the body, at any point in time, is sensitized and enlivened by the discernment occurring at that time. Accompanied by discernment, it is a sensitive form, not a mere carcase. It is thus appropriate that M.I.190, just before the quoted passage, actually refers to '*rūpa*' in the sense of a mere structure of flesh and bones. The quoted passage must thus imply that only when such a form has (at least some) intact sense-organs, and is endowed with discernment, can it be seen as a 'group of grasping', or personality-factor. This interpretation accords with commentary, which says, on 'in what has thus come to be': 'of what has come to be along with (*saha-bhūtassa*) visual discernment' (M.A.II.230). Vism617 is even more explicit: 'visual discernment, *together with associated states* (*sampayutta-dhammehi*), dependent on light and caused by attention, is generated because the eye is intact and visible forms come into its range'.

(8.17) While the interpretation of M.I.190 given here accords with both other Sutta material and the commentaries, it is notable that some scholars see things differently. N. Ross Reat has translated '*viññāṇa-bhāga-*' at M.I.190 as '*type* of consciousness' (my emphasis), rather than '*share* of discernment' (1987: 19). He thus sees the personality-factors 'in' this as parts of consciousness/discernment itself, rather than as parts of an accompanying package of states. Accordingly, he sees the *rūpa* personality-factor as simply 'the apparently external, objective content of consciousness' (p.20), i.e. the appearance 'in' it of sense-objects. One of his grounds for this interpretation is his equation of *phassa* ('stimulation') and *samannāhāra* ('act-of-attention'). As stimulation depends on discernment, he thus sees attention and by extension its objects as dependent on and contained 'in' discernment, as well as conditioning it (p.19). However, the two states are not in fact the same, as shown in Paras.8.12–13, and the conditioning is not mutual but linear: attention → discernment → stimulation. . . . It is thus inappropriate to say that discernment in some sense 'contains' the *rūpa* personality-factor. Another problem with Reat's interpretation is that M.I.190 sees this personality-factor as present in a '*bhāga*' of discernment even when it has a purely mental object. For Reat, this must mean that *rūpa*, or material form, is, in this case, discernment's awareness of a purely *mental* object. This seems most implausible. Most importantly, Reat is unable to make sense of the text's reference to *rūpa* as a 'space enclosed by bones and sinews and flesh and skin', seeing this as 'a non-technical use of the term or a corruption in the text', and 'absolutely inappropriate to the context' (p.20). In fact, Reat's view is much like Johansson's interpretation of the dependence of *rūpa* on discernment: 'The body is a collection of observed processes. Without *viññāṇa*, there would be no discernment of our own body i.e. no body processes' (1979: 32). This type of interpretation has already been refuted at Paras. 5.7–9. Reat's reading of M.I.190 is thus not acceptable. The way in which *rūpa* – as part of the sentient body (*nāma-rūpa*) and as a personality-factor – is conditioned by discernment, so as to be part of its '*bhāga*' is that it is *sensitized* and *enlivened* by it. *Rūpa* is neither discernment's awareness of 'physical' objects, nor a mere carcase.

(8.18) How, then, does discernment condition sentiency (the *nāma* component of *nāma-rūpa*)? The key, here, is stimulation; for feeling, cognition and the constructing activities, equivalent to *nāma* (Para 7.14), are said to be dependent on this. This is seen from the fact that the 'arising' of each of them is said to be from the 'arising' of stimulation (S.III.59–60), and also from such passages as S.IV.69: 'Stimulated, monks, one feels, stimulated, one wills, stimulated, one cognises'. Here willing indicates the presence of will (*cetanā*), the primary constructing activity. Accordingly, as the main components of sentiency depend on stimulation (itself part of sentiency), and as stimulation is the 'coming together' of discernment, sense-organ and sense-object, sentiency as a whole depends on discernment.

(8.19) Of course stimulation is itself said to depend on the sentient body, in the standard Conditioned Arising sequence. This must be because the arising of sentiency, dependent on discernment, means that the 'attention' aspect of sentiency can go on to select another object for discernment to arise in relation to. The 'meeting' of discernment with this object (and a sense-organ) is, once more, stimulation. When stimulation thus arises again, the factors of sentiency are once more engendered. There is thus a continuing sequence:

> . . . discernment (+ organ and object) → stimulation → sentiency (including attention) → discernment, which, + organ and object → stimulation → sentiency. . .

Here, there is a constant interplay between discernment and sentiency, with sentiency being continually reproduced, dependent on discernment, via stimulation. The process can perhaps be compared to the ticking over of an engine. Stimulation is like the spark which ignites the petrol, setting off a process which turns the crank (the development of the processes of sentiency), which crank also communicates its motion so as to generate another spark (stimulation depends on sentiency – and its accompanying sensitive body).

(8.20) M.I.190, quoted in Para.8.13, summarises the way in which both aspects of the sentient body – sentiency and the body – are dependent on discernment. The passage asserts that the 'share of discernment' arising from the perceptual process contains all five personality-factors, thus including the sentient body. The factors of sentiency – feeling, cognition and the constructing activities – arise to accompany discernment as they are sparked off by stimulation, while *rūpa* is continually engendered as a truly living, sensitive body, from the presence of the discernment which accompanies it at any particular time.

(8.21) In addition, S.II.23–4 (see Para.7.13) implies that 'external' *nāma-rūpa* is also conditioned by discernment in some way; for in place of *nāma-rūpa* in the normal sequence of Conditioned Arising, it says 'there is just this body and external *nāma-rūpa*'. As argued at Para.7.13, the 'body' here means the 'internal' *nāma-rūpa*, the sentient body. 'External' *nāma-rūpa* must be dependent on discernment in that the presence of discernment allows the awareness of 'forms' with 'names'; not that the bare forms are dependent on discernment. Discernment depends on sense-objects, but not vice versa. Rather, discernment allows sense-input to be given meaning and named. The meeting of sense-organ, sense-object and discernment is stimulation (*phassa*). From this, the sentiency aspect of the sentient body is renewed (Para.8.19), and sense-objects come to have meaning. This is indicated by D.II.62, which says that stimulation has two aspects to it: impact-stimulation (*paṭigha-samphassa*), which depends on the sensitive body (*rūpa*), and designative-stimulation (*adhivacana-samphassa*), which depends on sentiency (*nāma*, literally 'name'). Discernment, then, makes possible the designation, or some form of naming, of sense-objects. It conditions both internal *nāma-rūpa* – the sentient body, or perhaps 'naming form' – and external *nāma-rūpa* – 'named' or 'meaningful' 'forms'.

CONDITIONED ARISING AS AN ANALYSIS OF THE PERCEPTUAL PROCESS

(8.22) The sequence of Conditioned Arising is a rich and multi-faceted analysis of existence, and lies at the heart of the early Buddhist understanding of reality. There is no doubt that it can be seen as describing a process which links rebirths, as seen in chapter 6. In this reading of the sequence, the analysis covers three lives, with new rebirths occurring at the discernment and the 'birth' (*jāti*) links. However, the sequence can also be seen as encompassed in, and explaining, the life-process within one life, in the ongoing interaction of discernment and the sentient body. Indeed, all twelve links of the sequence can be seen as included in these, as already implied by D.II.63–4 (Para.7.17):

i) spiritual ignorance can be seen as equivalent to cognition (*saññā*), and thus part of sentiency. This is shown from Sn.732, part of a set of verses on the links: 'all constructing activities are calmed from the stopping of cognition'. As spiritual ignorance is normally that which conditions the constructing activities, and from whose stopping these stop, cognition here stands in its stead as its equivalent.
ii) the constructing activities are part of sentiency.
iii) discernment is itself discernment, and the sentient body the sentient body.
iv) the sense-spheres can be subsumed within the sentient body, as has been seen.
v) stimulation and feeling are part of sentiency (*nāma*).
vi) craving and grasping are active states which can be seen as forms of constructing activities, as so part of sentiency.
vii) becoming is principally an aspect of the working of discernment (Para.6.15). While chapter 6 saw this as occurring between lives, chapters 9 and 10 will show that it can also refer to discernment between perceptual cycles.
viii) birth and death etc. can be seen as continually happening to discernment and the sentient body, throughout life: this will now be argued.

(8.23) 'Birth', in the Conditioned Arising sequence does refer, in one sense, to the start of a new life, and the definition of 'death', in the sequence, includes 'the laying down of the carcase' (S.II.3), i.e. physical death. 'Birth' and 'death', however, are also seen as occurring from moment to moment. At S.IV.26–7, the various forms of discernment, stimulation and feeling are each said to be 'subject to birth (*jāti-dhammaṃ*)' and 'subject to death'. As these can hardly 'lay down a carcase', their 'death' must be their constant ceasing as part of an ongoing process of arising and ceasing. Indeed S.II.94–5 explicitly says that discernment constantly arises and ceases. S.IV.215 also implies that feelings are constantly born and die. Just as 'warmth is born, heat is produced (*abhinibbattati*)' from the rubbing together of sticks, so feelings are 'born of stimulation . . . depending on the appropriate (*tajjam*) stimulation, the appropriate feelings arise; from the cessation of the appropriate stimulation, the appropriate feelings cease'.[8]

(8.24) Now the arising of the sentient body from discernment is in several passages referred to as the 'descent' (*avakkanti*) of the sentient body (e.g. S.II.66, Para.8.5). Moreover, '*avakkanti*' is equivalent to '*okkanti*', which is part of the definition of 'birth (*jāti*)' in Conditioned Arising: 'That which, of these or these beings, in this or that group, is birth, generation, descent (*okkanti*), production (*abhinibbatti*), appearance (*pātubhāvo*) of the personality-factors, gaining of sense-spheres'. Returning to M.I.190 (Para.8.13), it can be seen that this in fact describes how discernment conditions the repeated 'birth' or 'descent' of the sentient body, in the ongoing perceptual process. This can be argued on several points. Firstly, M.I.190 refers to the 'appearance (*pātubhāvo*)' of a 'share of discernment' which contains all the personality-factors, just as S.II.3 sees 'birth' as the 'appearance of the personality-factors'. Secondly, the 'share of discernment' is said to be '*tajja*'. This was translated above as 'appropriate', but it is derived from '*tad-ja*', and literally means 'that-born'. Thirdly, the 'share of discernment' is described as 'what has thus come to be (*tathā-bhūta-*)'; this suggests, at least, the 'becoming' (*bhava*) which precedes 'birth' in the Conditioned Arising sequence: what has 'come to be' depends, surely, on 'becoming'.

(8.25) The M.I.190 passage is, in fact, followed by one which confirms it as dealing with Conditioned Arising:

> This was said by the Lord, 'Who sees Conditioned Arising sees Dhamma; who sees Dhamma sees Conditioned Arising'. These are conditionally arisen: that is to say the five groups of grasping [the personality-factors]. Whatever among these five

groups of grasping is desire (*chando*), affection, catching at, this is the arising (*-samudayo*) of *dukkha* . . . .

(M.I.191)

This clearly means that M.I.190 concerns the conditioned arising of *dukkha*, in the form of the groups of grasping (*upādāna-kkhandhas*) or personality-factors, which encompass all *dukkha* (Vin.I.10). As Conditioned Arising sees 'this entire mass (*-khandha-*) of *dukkha*' as arising conditioned by 'birth', then this makes it certain that M.I.190 is intended as describing the repeated 'birth' of the personality-factors, as part of the ongoing process of perception. When attention picks out an object, an appropriate discernment is born from that and comes to engender accompanying factors of the sentient body, so that all the personality-factors, equivalent to *dukkha*, 'appear' or are 'born', in a moment-to-moment renewal. Moreover, just as A.IV.339 (Para.8.12) says that desire is the root of 'all *dhamma*s', and implies that it precedes attention, so M.I.191 specifies desire as a root-cause of the personality-factors. Desire, indeed, is closely related to grasping; for M.III.16 sees the 'grasping' in the 'groups of grasping' as 'desire and attachment'. This is appropriate as Conditioned Arising runs: . . . grasping → becoming → birth → ageing etc.: the 'mass of *dukkha*'. That is, from desire/grasping, via the process of 'becoming' and the activity of attention, comes the constant 'birth' of the personality-factors.

(8.26) The sentient body, then, is not only conditioned by discernment at conception and in the womb, but is constantly renewed by the occurrence of discernment. Both are constantly 'born' and 'die' in an interplay which encompasses all twelve links in Conditioned Arising. In this interplay, the constructing activities, in their striving and coordinating, sustain discernment by directing it onto some aspect of the sentient body, or other meaningful forms, as objects. It thus 'turns back round' onto these so as to settle on them as a 'home' (Paras.7.17–19). This directing is done through the medium of grasping desire and subsequent attention, and also dependent on the sense-organs, which are part of the sentient body (*nāma-rūpa*). Once an instance of discernment arises in this way, it sparks off the renewal of sentiency (*nāma*), via stimulation, and continues to enliven the material form (*rūpa*) of the body and keep its sense-organs sensitive to objects, so that the process continues. It also enables sense-objects to become meaningful forms. In due course, death ensues and the flux of discernment, driven by craving, goes through the between-lives phase of becoming, and then falls into a womb so as to help set off the generation of a new sentient body. Thus does the process of life and lives proceed. To continue, it must be sustained by spiritual ignorance, that which conditions the constructing activities. Such ignorance is defined as lack of insight into the Four Holy Truths, on *dukkha* and its ending, that is, lack of insight into the very process of Conditioned Arising. The process, then, can only operate 'in the dark', so to speak: in ignorance of itself. Once spiritual insight replaces ignorance, or ingrained misperception, it can be stopped. Indeed, the whole process is seen as constantly changing and tantamount to *dukkha*, unsatisfactoriness: it is something which needs to be transcended. This is done in the experience of *nibbāna*, which is the 'stopping' of all the links of Conditioned Arising: the subject of chapter 11.

9

DISCERNMENT AND THE PERCEPTUAL PROCESS

By the five sense discernments, one re-discerns no state . . . other than mere falling in (Vibh.321).

(9.1) Given the central importance of discernment (*viññāṇa*) in both the Suttas and Abhidhamma, it is appropriate to probe further into the understanding of this phenomenon in these texts and the commentaries. The most usual context in which discernment is referred to is in the perceptual process, in which it works closely with other states such as cognition (*saññā*). What is discernment seen to contribute to this overall process, what function(s) is it assigned, and what does this tell us about how its nature is viewed?

THE PERCEPTUAL PROCESS IN THE 'EARLY SUTTAS'

(9.2) The 'early Suttas', on numerous occasions, list six types of discernment: literally, eye-discernment, ear-discernment, nose-discernment, tongue-discernment, body-discernment and *mano*-discernment. The '*mano*' of the last of these can loosely be referred to as the 'mind-organ', though a more exact translation would be 'conception', for which the OED gives, as one meaning, 'The action or faculty of conceiving in the mind, or of forming an idea or notion of anything, apprehension, imagination'. While this does not include any reference to memories, which must be among the objects of the 'mind-organ', it is appropriate in other ways. In particular, the word keeps a connection to 'conceives' and 'conceit', just as their Pāli equivalents, '*maññati*' and '*māna*', are linked to '*mano*': the first is from the same root and both are conceptually connected to it (see Paras.1.47 and 5.6). Discernment, then, can be seen to arise in one of six sense-channels: the visual, auditory, nasal, gustatory, tactile, or conceptional 'channels'. The 'early Suttas' give various descriptions of the way in which mental states process and respond to objects in the six sense-channels. A good example is at M.I.111–12:

> Visual-discernment, your reverences, arises conditioned by eye and visual forms; the meeting of the three is stimulation (*phassa*); from stimulation as condition is feeling (*vedanā*); what one feels one cognizes (*sañjānāti*); what one cognizes one applies thought to (*vitakketi*); what one applies thought to one elaborates (*papañceti*); what one elaborates is the origin of the interpretations and reckonings (*-saññā-saṅkhā*) (that come) from elaboration, which assail a man in regard to visual forms discernible (*viññeyyesu*) by the eye, past, future or present [this is then repeated in a parallel way for the other five sense-channels].

Other descriptions are similar as far as cognizing/cognition (*saññā*), and then branch off in different ways. S.II.146–47 gives a sequence in which, for each sense-channel, one process arises conditioned by the one before it in the sequence: sense-object, cognition, purposive thought (*saṅkappa*), stimulation, feeling, desire, fever, search, acquisition. An implied sequence at A.IV.146–47 runs: discernment, stimulation, feeling, cognition, volition, craving, applied thought, examination (*vicāra*).[1] The various states which occur after cognition can all be seen as constructing activities (the *saṅkhāra*s), which the Abhidhamma sees as comprising fifty states, such as stimulation, volition and applied thought (Dhs.62). Both the *saṅkhāra*s as a whole, and the most important of these, volition, are said to arise dependent on stimulation (S.III.60, S.IV.68), just as feeling and cognition are said to. Thus the general order of the perceptual process can be summarised thus:

> discernment → stimulation → feeling → cognition → various constructing activities.

(9.3) In this sequence, discernment only explicitly occurs at the start; yet there are clear indications that this is not the only place it occurs. S.IV.146–47, above, has stimulation occurring part way into the process. As it must also have occurred at its start, to help initiate it, it must be a second occurrence. But as stimulation is the 'meeting' of sense-organ, sense-object and a form of discernment, there must also be a second occurrence of discernment in the process. Indeed,

M.III.279 says that feeling, cognition, the constructing activities *and discernment* all arise from stimulation (which itself needs a prior occurrence of discernment for it to arise). Again, M.I.293 says 'whatever one feels, that one cognizes, whatever one cognizes, that one discerns (*vijānāti*)'. As discernment (*viññāṇa*) is defined as 'it discerns' (S.III.87), this shows that feeling, cognition and discernment are a sequence of states working on the same object.

(9.4) In the Abhidhamma, it is specified that, in each of the six sense-channels, there is a relevant kind of discernment (eg. visual-discernment for a visual form) followed by a series of conceptional-discernments, and accompanying states such as cognition, which process the object (see Appendix). The *Milindapañha* (p.57, 59) also makes clear that, after discernment related to one of the five physical sense-organs arises, conceptional-discernment then arises. While the details of such a system postdate the 'early Suttas', it is clear that the basis of such a system is already present in them. Not only do they indicate a 'second' discernment in each sense-channel, they also show that this must be conceptional-discernment. M.I.295 explains that, while the five physical sense-organs do not 're-partake (*paccanubhonti*)' of the 'pasture and range (*gocara-visayaṃ*)' of each other (ie. the eye cannot see a sound, etc.), conception (*mano*) does so. This is also indicated by M.III.216–17, which describes the eighteen 'ranges (*upavicārā*)' of conception as the six sense-objects inasmuch as they give rise to 'gladness (*somanassa-*)', 'sorrow (*domanassa-*)' or indifference. Indeed, sorrow and gladness are types of feeling (*vedanā*) which *only* arise from conception (S.V.209): the eye, ear, nose and tongue can only, in themselves, give rise to indifferent feeling, with body-sensitivity also giving rise to pleasure and pain. States such as 'search (*pariyesanā*)' and 'examination (*vicāra*)', which occur late on in the perceptual processes outlined in Para.9.2, also imply he activity of conception. This is shown by M.I.135, which lists the objects of discernment as 'whatever is seen, heard, sensed, discerned (*viññataṃ*), reached, searched for, pondered over by conception (*anuvicaritaṃ manasā*) . . . .' Here 'seen, heard, sensed' clearly refer to the objects of the five physical senses, while the rest are the objects of conception and its associated discernment. The 'early Suttas' thus clearly take the view that each type of sense-object is worked over by both an appropriate kind of sense-discernment and also byconceptional-discernment (cf.Para.5.6). This is probably why discernment is defined both as a personality-factor (S.III.61) and as a link of Conditioned Arising

(S.II.4) – as the six *viññāṇa-kāyas*, or 'discernment-collections': those of the five physical senses and of conception. Each of these must refer to a particular sense-discernment, and any conceptional-discernment which works over its object.[2] 'Auditory-discernment-collection', for example, will refer to auditory-discernment and any conceptional-discernment that is involved in processing a sound. The same would apply to the six 'collections' of cognition etc: they are such states as accompany these discernments in processing a particular type of object. What is involved in this processing will be investigated below.

THE NATURE AND FUNCTIONS OF COGNITION (*SAÑÑĀ*)

(9.5) Before probing the nature and functions of discernment, it is useful to do the same for *saññā*, which also plays an important role in the perceptual process. By doing this, the relative contributions of the two to the overall process can be assessed. '*Saññā*' is often translated as 'perception', but this is inappropriate, both because it is only part of the perceptual process and because one can have a *saññā* of a mental object but cannot, in English, be said to 'perceive' such an object. Johansson (1979: 93) and Wayman (1976: 326) both use 'idea' for *saññā*, but while this might cover *saññā* of a mental object, it does not cover *saññā* of a visual form, for example. What is involved simply in seeing can hardly be termed an 'idea'. The word '*sa-ññā*' and its verbal form '*sañ-jānāti*' clearly refer to some kind of knowledge or knowing which is done in an associative, connective, linking (*sa-*) way. An English term which parallels this type of derivation is 'co-gnition', which can, in fact, be seen as an appropriate translation.

(9.6) The *saññā* personality-factor is defined, at S.III.87, as that which 'cognizes (*sañjānāti*)', with various colours being given for what it cognizes. As apprehension of colours does not normally require any act of judgement or ideation, except in a few borderline cases, it seems that 'cognition' operates in a very direct, automatic manner. It can best be seen as that which 'sees' e.g. the colour red *as* red – it can co-gnize it, i.e. know that it is like other similar phenomena, or re-cognize it. That is, it is that mental process which labels, categorizes and classifies sense-objects. This is seen at D.I.93: 'Now just as now, Ambaṭṭha, men see (*sañjānanti*) devils as "devils", so then they saw devils as "black ones"'. *Saññā* is the activity of seeing-as: knowing something through the application of a specific perceptual label. This is then the basis for what one calls something or says about it: 'I say, monks, that *saññā*s result in common expressions; as one cognizes something, so one expresses oneself, "I saw it like this (*evaṃ saññī ahosin*)" ' (A.III.413). A good example of this would be the Wittgensteinian ambiguous duck-rabbit drawing. A particular person will 'see' this as either a duck or a rabbit, though of course with some effort he or she can also 'see' it in the other way. Each type of 'seeing' would be, in early Buddhist language, a different *saññā*. Some might regard this as a 'mental image' (e.g. Johansson, 1979: 193), but this would only really work for the visual sense-channel, not, e.g. for the sound one.

(9.7) The commentarial literature sees several aspects to the meaning of '*saññā*'. Asl.110 sees some *saññā* as recognition of what has been learnt:

> All *saññā*s have the characteristic of cognizing (*sañjanana-*). Of them, that which cognizes by special knowledge has the function of recognition (*paccābhiññāna*, literally re-back-through-knowledge). We may see this procedure when a carpenter again recognizes a piece of wood by the special mark that he has (previously) made on it; when we recognize a man by the sectarian mark on the forehead, which we have noted and say 'he is so and so'; or when a king's treasurer, in charge of the royal wardrobe, having had a label bound on each garment and, being asked to bring a certain one. . . reads the label and brings the garment.

Here, *saññā* is clearly recognition based on first having learnt or assigned the identifying feature of a thing. *Saññā* not only recognizes specific items, but also cognizes general features possessed by a number of items. Asl.110 continues:

> According to another method, *saññā* has the characteristic of cognizing by general inclusion, and the function of making a sign as a condition for cognizing, as woodcutters etc. do in the case of timber etc.

This is suggestive of woodcutters who make a mark on a number of trees, *all* of which are 'to be felled'. The commentarial literature also see an aspect of the meaning of '*saññā*' as 'interpretation':

'It is manifested as the action of interpreting (*abhinivesa-karaṇa-*) by means of a sign apprehended, like the blind who "see" an elephant' (Vism.462). This is clearly an allusion to the story of several blind men who argue over whether an elephant is like a pot, a ploughshare, a pillar etc, on the basis of each feeling only one different part of it (Ud.68–9). That is, *saññā* interprets sense-objects by assigning them to one or other familiar category. This is not necessarily a matter of judgement, but can occur quite automatically in the process of perception.

(9.8) Given that *saññā* includes the interpretation of sense-objects, it can clearly include the mis-interpretation of them. Thus Vism.462 continues, 'Its proximate cause is an objective field in whatever way that appears, like the *saññā* that arises in fawns that see scarecrows as "man!" '. This sense must also be present in the Suttas, for they constantly warn e.g. not to consider the *saññā* of permanence in what is impermanent, ie. *don't* misinterpret. Given that *saññā* can stand in the place of spiritual ignorance in the Conditioned Arising sequence (Para.8.22), taking *saññā* as including 'misinterpretation' seems valid. As seen at M.I.111–12 (Para.9.2), the activity of *saññā* leads on, through applied thought, to 'elaboration' (*papañca*). Elsewhere, the topics of such elaboration are I-centred thoughts on what 'I' am, was or will be (S.IV.202–03), or the views on the state of a *tathāgata* after death (A.IV.68–9). These are also each called a 'conceited imagining (*maññitaṃ*)' and the views are even each called an 'issue of *saññā*'. That is, *saññā* can easily lead on to a host of conceited imaginings and speculations. Thus *saññā* is specified as the source of 'reckonings (that come) from elaboration (*papañca-saṅkhā*)' (Sn.874). As Sn.916 specifies "I am" as the root of such elaboration-reckonings, it can be seen that *saññā* is what introduces this illegitimate idea, through its misinterpretation of reality. Given appropriate guidance, however, *saññā* can come to cognize true features of reality, e.g. recognize impermanence in what is impermanent.

THE ACTIVITY OF 'DISCERNMENT' (*VIÑÑAṆA*)

(9.9) *'Viññāṇa'*, being derived from *'vi'* + *'ñāṇa'*, is a kind of knowledge (*ñāṇa*) which separates (*vi*). As a personality-factor, it is defined as that which *'vijānāti'* : that which 'discerns', 'discriminates' or 'distinguishes' (S.III.87, M.I.292). This is in contrast to *saññā*, which knows by grouping things together, labelling them. This contrast can be seen in terms of the typical objects of these states: colours for *saññā* (S.III.87), but tastes (S.III.87) or feelings (M.I.292) for *viññāṇa*. While colours can usually be immediately identified, tastes and feelings often need careful consideration to properly identify them: discernment and analysis are needed. The commentary on S.III.87 (S.A.II.293) thus says that cognition is explained with respect to *seeing*, as it is commonly known through seizing the 'form and configuration (*ākāra-saṇṭhāna-*)' of an object, while *viññāṇa* is commonly known through seizing the 'separate divisions (*paccatta-bheda-*)' of an object, not its configuration. That is, cognition grasps the general configuration of an object while *viññāṇa* analyses and discriminates its parts or aspects.

(9.10) S.A.II.293–94 and Vism.437 also compare the relative functions of cognition (*saññā*), discernment (*viññāṇa*) and wisdom (*pañña*). All three are states of 'knowing (*janana-*)', but while 'cognition is only the mere cognizing of an object as blue etc.', discernment does this and also 'brings about the penetration of characteristics as impermanent etc.'. Wisdom does both of these but also 'brings about, by endeavouring, the appearance of the Path'. This is then illustrated by similes. Cognition is like a child 'of undeveloped intelligence' who, on seeing some coins, 'knows just their form as figured and ornamented, square or circular', and discernment is like a villager who also knows the coins as valuable. Wisdom, though, also knows whether the coins are genuine or counterfeit, and where and by whom they were made, this being done by carefully testing and assessing the coins. This passage sees cognition, discernment and wisdom, then, as three states of a successively higher order, each of which builds on the work of the previous ones. *Saññā* refers to 'cognition' of sense-objects in the sense of their preliminary classification in terms of concrete characteristics. *Viññāṇa* goes beyond the object as a mere visual form or sound etc. and discerns more abstract general features of the cognized items, such as it being impermanent, or as having value. Given that there are contemplations in which there is *saññā* of impermanence, it is clear that, while unaided *saññā* cannot cognize such things as impermanence, it can do so when aided by discernment: it is like child, as the simile says, in need of adult guidance. As regards wisdom, this is seen to be a more all-round, testing knowledge than discernment, it is that which knows the very *nature* of a thing and not only *certain* aspects or parts. Presumably, it can guide cognition and discernment to cognize and discern what it knows; but it must do the work before they can follow.

(9.11) In the above explanation, it is clear that the discernment referred to cannot be e.g. visual-discernment; for the discernment which is simply aware of a visual field could hardly be aware of something as impermanent etc.. What must be referred to is the conceptional-discernment which follows visual-discernment etc., processing and judging its object. Similarly, when S.III.87 (Para 9.9) talks of discernment as that which discriminates between various tastes, this is likely to be referring to conceptional-discernment, rather than merely to gustatory-discernment, which occurs earlier in the perceptual process. Indeed, it is said that, while the eye 'sees' and the ear 'hears', it is conception that 'discerns (*vijānāti*)' (D.II.338). That is, the activity of discernment is typically done by conception (*mano*). As seen in Para.9.4, conceptional-discernment is part of the 'discernment-collection' relating to each sense-channel.

THE FUNCTIONS OF DISCERNMENT IN THE ABHIDHAMMA 'PROCESS OF *CITTAS*'

(9.12) Why is it, then, that forms of *viññāṇa* other than that arising from conception are said to *be* kinds of *'viññāṇa'*, knowledge which *discerns or discriminates?* To what extent does auditory-*viññāṇa* 'discern', for example? To answer this, it is useful to refer to the detailed model of the perceptual process built up in the Abhidhamma literature. The fully developed version of this theory is found in the commentarial literature, such as Buddhaghosa's *Visuddhimagga*, but most of it is already implicitly found in the Canonical Abhidhamma, especially the *Paṭṭhāna* (see Appendix). The theory views the key aspect of the perceptual process as a series of *citta*s, in the sense of momentary mind-sets. These consist of the forms of discernment related to each of the five physical senses, plus conceptional-discernment and the conception-element (*mano-dhātu*), each performing various functions. In waking consciousness, there is said to be constant alternation between the different *citta*s. As only one of the five-sense discernments can occur at one time, there must be a constant and extremely rapid flickering between the 'sense-doors', with seeing rapidly followed by hearing etc., so that, at the level of conscious experience, it all *seems* simultaneous. It is explained that the resting state of *citta* is called *bhavaṅga*, a state which also occurs in dreamless sleep. During waking consciousness,

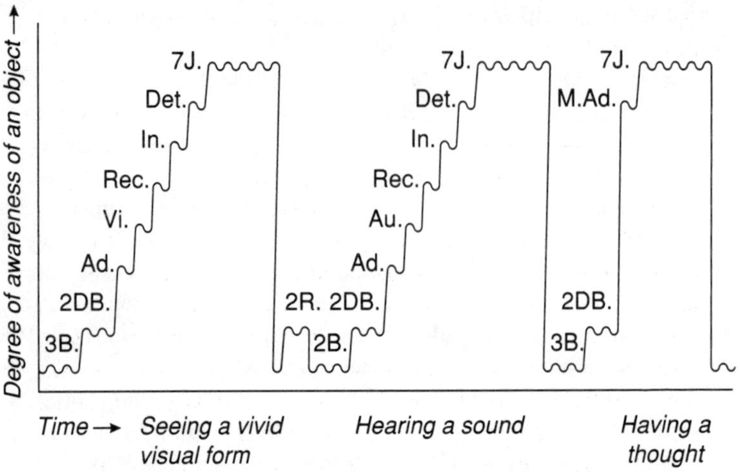

Key

B.	*Bhavaṅga*	Rec.	Receiving
DB.	Disturbance of *bhavaṅga*	In.	Investigation
Ad.	Advertence to a physical sense-object	Det.	Determining
M.Ad.	Advertence to a mental object	J.	*Javana* (Impulsion)
Vi.	Visual-discernment	R.	Registration
Au.	Auditory-discernment		

A number before an abbreviation indicates the number of times a particular type of *citta* occurs successively.

Chart 1 The 'process of *citta*s' in waking consciousnes, according to Abhidhamma theory.

the mind momentarily lapses back into *bhavaṅga citta* after having processed each sense-object. It is then disturbed by another object, so that a moment of conception arises as 'advertence' to the object. If it is a visual object, there is then a moment of visual-discernment, and then a series of conception or conceptional-discernments which assess and determine what the object is, culminating in *javana*, 'impulsion', in which the mind reacts to the perceived object in some way, thus generating karmic results. If the impression of the object is strong, there is a moment or two of 'registration', before the mind again relapses back into the *bhavaṅga* state (Para.A.5). An example of such a sequence is depicted as in chart 1, in which each wave represents a *citta* arising and passing away, to be followed by another, with a different function.[3]

(9.13) The functions of the different *citta*s is illustrated, at Asl.280–01, by an allegory:

> Herein, like many boys playing and sitting in the middle of the road is the occurrence of the *process of citta*s (*vīthi-citta-*); like a coin striking the hand (of one of them) is the object *impinging* on the sensitive surface (of a sense-organ); like the asking (by him) 'What is this?' is the functional conception-element *setting bhavaṅga in motion* after seizing the object; like the saying (by another), 'it is white' is visual-discernment accomplishing the function of *seeing*; like the seizing it firmly together with some dust (by another) is the fruitional conception-element *receiving* the object; like the saying (by another), 'It is a flat, square thing' is the fruitional conceptional-discernment-element *investigating* the object; like the saying (by another), 'this is a *kahāpaṇa* coin' is the functional conceptional-discernment-element determining the object; like the mother making it into some jewelry is *javana experiencing the taste of the object.*[4]

A problem here is that Buddhaghosa also uses a simile of coming to know a coin in his explanation of the differences between cognition, discernment and wisdom (S.A.II.293–94, Para.9.10). Cognition, which knows the colour and shape of a visual object, would seem to provide the same knowledge as do visual-discernment and 'investigating' conceptional-discernment combined. The discernment of S.A.II.293–94, which knows the coin as valuable, would seem to have the same knowledge as 'determining' conceptional-discernment, which recognizes the object as a coin, and perhaps would include aspects of *javana*, in the sense that it knows a coin to be valuable for human use and enjoyment, and thus contains reference to certain potential actions (karmas). On the other hand, one would think that the 'cognition of mental objects' could also recognize a coin.

(9.14) In Abhidhamma theory, each type of *citta* is said to be accompanied by a moment of cognition (and of feeling and certain other mental states). It seems appropriate to say that cognition is dependent, as to what it can cognize, on what the *citta* it accompanies can discern: as seen at Para.7.10, *citta* dominates the states which accompany it. Thus at the moment of visual-discernment arising, cognition can only cognize colour, as this is all this *citta* is aware of; at 'determining', cognition can recognize e.g. 'a *kahāpaṇa*', as this is what this *citta* can discern. An appropriate model here, would be to say that a discernment 'scans' an object's aspects or parts, thus allowing the accompanying cognition to cognize/label/recognize what has thus been scanned. There is then a 'scan' of higher order aspects of an object (e.g. its shape rather than its mere colour), with cognition labelling these, and so on. In all of this, cognition follows after discernment, dependent on its discriminatory power. It is thus appropriate for S.A.II.293–94 to describe cognition, in general, as a lower order process than discernment. Discernment of a higher level, though, builds on the cognition of a lower level of scanning an object: 'whatever one cognizes, that one discerns' (M.I.293). That is, at one level of scanning, there is discernment and a cognition which is dependent on it, then a discernment builds on this cognition for a higher level of scan, accompanied by a higher level of cognition. The difference between the S.A. and Asl. passages is that the latter follows the Abhidhamma approach of giving a detailed moment-by-moment analysis, while the former follows the Sutta approach, which operates more at the level of the normal flow of experience, analysing the different aspects of this. As 'cognition' is in its more characteristic phase when it accompanies a sense-discernment and 'investigating' *citta*, the Sutta approach concentrates on it in these phases; likewise it concentrates on discernment at the phases of 'determining' and *javana*.

THE NATURE OF *VIÑÑĀṆA*

(9.15) The above now allows an answer to the question posed in Para.9.12: in what sense are the forms of *viññāṇa* related to the five physical senses actually forms of *discernment*? From the Abhidhamma, we see Vibh.321 asserting that, for the *viññāṇa* of the five physical senses, there is no 'advertence (*āvajjanā*)' or 'attention (*manasikāro*)'; they do not 're-discern (*paṭivijānāti*)' anything but are the 'mere falling in' to the mere sensory range. That is, visual-*viññāṇa*, for example, arises once 'adverting' *citta* has done its work; while it discerns its object, it does so simply as a visual patch – just colours – without re-discerning it, at a higher level of analysis. As Vibh.A.405 comments, 'Here, visual-*viññāṇa* is the mere seeing, auditory-*viññāṇa* is the mere hearing. . . .' E.R. Sarathchandra, on the basis of these passages, says, 'In the Abhidhamma *viññāṇa* is defined as bare consciousness or sensation as yet undiscriminated by the selective activity of the mind. It is mere awareness of the presence of objects. It does not produce knowledge of any sort' (1958: 25).

He also says that 'In the stage of visual sensation, therefore, a confused mass of matter constitutes the object of vision. This confused mass is as yet undistinguished in shape or colour or any specific qualities because selective attention has not yet distinguished the object in its details' (p.25). In the Suttas, too, he regards *viññāṇa* as 'bare sensation, a kind of anoetic sentience that occurs before the object is completely apprehended' (p.5). Sarathchandra thus denies that visual-*viññāṇa* even knows what colour an object is, or that it is *knowledge* of any sort. Similarly, Professor Conze says that *viññāṇa* is just a 'general awareness of there being an object' (1962: 111), and Nyanatiloka explains that the *viññāṇa* personality-factor (*khandha*) 'furnishes the bare cognition of an object while the other three (*khandha*s) contribute more specific features' (1972: 193).

(9.16) How far are the above interpretations acceptable? Can *viññāṇa* be, or include, something which is neither any kind of knowledge (*ñāṇa*) nor has any discerning or discriminative power (*vi-*) to it, being merely a 'general awareness'? The commentaries do not support such a view. S.A.II.293 says, on '*viññāṇa*' at S.III.87 (Para.9.9), 'As it knows the division into sour etc. by the state of sour etc. distinguished one from another, "therefore it is called *viññāṇa*" '. The passage continues by saying that the individual characteristic of *viññāṇa* is 'discerning (*vijānana-*)'. In the Abhidhamma 'process of *citta*s', it is adverting conception, which precedes e.g. visual-*viññāṇa*, that has a confused mass as its object, for Asl.280–01 (Para.9.13) compares this to a boy who asks 'what is this?'. The same passage likens visual-*viññāṇa* to a boy who says 'It is white', though not to a boy who knows the shape of the object, who parallels 'investigating' *citta* in the allegory. Visual-*viññāṇa* must thus be seen as the 'mere falling in (*abhinipātamattâ-*)' (Vibh.321, Para.9.15) to a visual range consisting of colour areas of indeterminate shape. Given that it is the function of visual-object-cognition (*rūpa-saññā*) to actually recognize and classify such areas in terms of colour concepts (Para.9.6), it must be the function of visual-*viññāṇa* which it accompanies (and on which it is dependent) to discerningly discriminate, distinguish and separate out the various colour-areas. As this is done, cognition works in unison with visual-*viññāṇa*, classifying the areas so divided. As S.A.II.293 says (Para.9.9), *viññāṇa* seizes the 'separate divisions' of an object, while cognition seizes the 'form and configuration'. Clearly, prior to 'investigating' conceptional-*viññāṇa*, cognition cannot cognize an object's 'configuration' or 'shape' in a literal sense, but can know a colour-area as 'shaping up' as 'red', for example.

(9.17) It is to be noted, in fact, that '*abhinipāta*', which is used at Vibh.321 to refer to the five sense-*viññāṇa* 'falling in' to their object-ranges, can also mean 'splitting': *Divyāvadāna* 125 uses the phrase '*satrâbhinipāta-*', 'splitting open or cutting with a knife' (PED.65). Thus visual-*viññāṇa* falls upon/splits up its object, which is an expanse of colour-areas, and its accompanying cognition classifies the areas as 'red', 'green' etc. If there is any ambiguity as to how the colour is to be classified, then, if this is important, it is assessed by one of the conceptional-*viññāṇa*s which follow visual-*viññāṇa* – presumably that which is 'determining' –, working in unison with its accompanying cognition. Thus the *viññāṇa* s of the five senses are a little more than a 'bare awareness': they are such bare awareness of a sensory object being present, plus the knowledge of which sense-modality it belongs to, and the discernment which discriminates the object into its basic parts or aspects. As for conceptional-*viññāṇa*, its degree of awareness and discernment can be of a considerably higher level. Only cognition, though, can label the parts or aspects discerned by its accompanying *viññāṇa*, of whatever level. In this context, it is relevant to point out that the six forms of *viññāṇa* are differentiated by reference to the relevant sense-organ, while the six forms of cognition are differentiated with reference to the relevant sense-object (S.III.59–61): thus eye-*viññāṇa* but visual-object-cognition, etc. That is, *viññāṇa* is the awareness that a particular sense-organ has a 'something' as object, plus a discernment of the parts of this 'something'; cognition is more outward-directed, and gives an interpretation of *what* is known by the sense-organ. In a full perceptual process directed to a visual object, for example, an eye-centred *viññāṇa* is followed by conception-centred ones, with a sequence of cognitions interpreting the same object as it is discerned at a progressively higher level.

(9.18) It is now possible to justify the use of 'discernment' as the most appropriate and usable translation of '*viññāṇa*'. As pointed out by Alex Wayman, the common 'consciousness' is really too vague, as it covers all mental processes.[5] His preferences are for 'perception' (p.326) or 'understanding' (p.332). These, however, can each be seen to cover the combined functions of *viññāṇa* and *saññā*. 'Perception' is also only applicable to the mind's processing of non-mental objects: what, then, of conceptional-*viññāṇa*? 'Understanding' might cover this to a certain extent, but it does not capture the discriminative aspect of *viññāṇa*, and is strained as a translation when applied to the *viññāṇa*s of the five physical senses: minimal 'understanding' operates here. Admittedly, work on artificial intelligence has demonstrated that a kind of 'intelligence' is needed to make sense of visual objects, for example. So one might even call visual-*viññāṇa* 'visual-intelligence'. This, however, has a strange ring, and such intelligence would, again, arise from the combined work of *viññāṇa* and *saññā*. A good rendering is 'discriminative consciousness', as used by I.B. Horner in her translations (e.g. MLS.I.351). This indicates the fact that *viññāṇa* is what 'discriminates' or 'discerns', and also that it is the basic awareness of an object on which is dependent 'cognition' of that object.[6] A disadvantage of 'discriminative consciousness', however, is its cumbersomeness, which tends to lead to it being abbreviated back to the too broad and vague 'consciousness'. 'Discrimination' might stand as a translation, yet its associations are not normally with the process of perception but with such things as 'racial discrimination'. 'Discernment' lacks these disadvantages, has associations with the perceptual process[7] and includes 'distinguishing' or 'separating' as part of its meaning. It also has a verbal form, 'discern', just as '*viññāṇa*' has: '*vijānāti*'. While 'discernment' can mean 'insight, keen perception' (OED), and *viññāṇa* is not always this, S.A.II.293–94 (Para.9.10) shows that it can have insight into such matters as impermanence, though it falls short of the insight of wisdom (*paññā*). Overall, it is the most usable translation which captures the separative aspect of the knowledge which *viññāṇa* is. '*Viññāṇa*', then, is 'discernment' as related to one of the five sense-organs or conception, inasmuch as it is aware of the presence of the object of such an organ and discerns its basic parts or aspects. In the processing of a specific perceptual object, discernment initially operates at a basic level, as a sense-discernment, but following states of conceptional-discernment then develop a more sophisticated awareness.

THE EFFECT OF KARMA ON DISCERNMENT IN THE PERCEPTUAL PROCESS

(9.19) One curious feature of the Abhidhamma view of the perceptual process is that the discernments related to the five physical sense-organs are always said to be the fruition of karma.[8] This might be seen as being because:

a) all the *objects* of such discernments i.e. the whole physical world arise due to karma; or

b) what objects come within the sensing-range of a particular being is determined by his karma.

As regards a), though, *Paṭṭhāna* I.22–3 (CR.27–8) makes clear that only some physical processes are originated from karma; others originate from *citta*, 'nutriment' or 'temperature' (cf. ch.4, note 2). If, on the other hand, b) were the case, it would mean that a person had no freedom of action: he would continually *have* to move to certain places in order to be able to sense the range of phenomena determined by his karma. Such determinism, though, is at odds with A.III.337–38, where the Buddha asserts that a person has an 'element of initiating' whereby he can step forward or back as he wishes: he has 'self-agency (*attakāro*)'. An adapted version of b) is the most plausible explanation. This is that karma affects discernment by determining which of the many phenomena in a person's sensory range are actually *noticed*.[9] This is in line with Paras.8.12–13, where it was shown that a discernment arises dependent on an intact sense-organ, a potential object within the range of the organ, and an appropriate act of attention. It is very plausible to regard such selecting attention as the path by which a sense-discernment becomes a result of karma.[10] In the same room, for example, one person naturally tends to notice certain things which give rise to pleasure, while another tends to notice things which give rise to some displeasure.[11] The difference would be due to their past karma, their past constructing activities, as in the Conditioned Arising sequence. Each person thus perceives the external 'world' in a way which is influenced by their past karma, which contributes to the differences in their internal 'lived worlds' (cf. Para.5.11). Of course, a vivid object such as a sudden noise would *demand* the attention of any person (unless asleep or in deep meditation). It would enter the lived-world of both the pleasant-noticer and unpleasant-noticer (though it may be more, or less, shocking to them and they may mentally respond to it in different ways: with anger or patience). In such a case, karma can only actively determine the kind of external world a being is born into – one where sudden noises are possible! – and the shockability of the mind. Beyond that, karma could only be passively involved: a loud noise would demand attention and bring some of a being's past karma to fruition, thus expending it. The relevant auditory-discernment would still be, technically, a karmic fruit.[12]

(9.20) Another potential problem in this area is that, in the Conditioned Arising sequence, discernment is conditioned by the constructing activities, suggesting that all discernment is the result of karma. In the Abhidhamma, however, only some discernment is described thus. The *Vibhaṅga* sees the discernment 'link' as karmically resultant discernment of any of the six senses (pp.173 and 175–76), but also as karmically active conceptional-discernment (pp.167 and 144) and functional conceptional-discernment and conception (pp.182–84). Even karmically active (wholesome/unwholesome) discernment, though, will be affected by the object 'noticed' due to past constructing activities – thus being indirectly conditioned by these, if not technically a karmic result – as well as being mutually related to the present constructing activities which accompany it.

(9.21) This chapter has analysed the nature of *viññāṇa* as it occurs in the perceptual process: the main context in which the Pāli Canon refers to it. In this context, *viññāṇa* has been shown to be the process of 'discernment' which is aware of and discriminates objects at various levels of sophistication, working in unison with the labelling, interpreting activity of cognition (*saññā*). It arises in a flow of mental states in which karma influences which specific objects are noticed and focussed on. At first, an object is known in a rudimentary way, for example as patches of colour. It is then analysed in more sophisticated ways until the mind fully registers it, determines its nature (correctly or incorrectly), and responds to it, generating more karma. At whatever level of sophistication, *viññāṇa* is the basic awareness of the object as perceived-so-far, and the discerning discrimination of further aspects or parts of it, to be labelled by *saññā*. While the full analysis of the functioning of different forms of discernment is only developed in the Abhidhamma and commentarial literature, the 'early Suttas' contain strong support for this kind of development. They talk of a 'discernment-collection' processing each type of sense-object, and clearly imply that this includes conceptional-discernment as well as the relevant kind of sense-discernment. As seen in Para.8.23, the 'early Suttas' also imply that discernment is subject to constant 'birth' and 'death', or momentary change, a view which is also a key ingredient of the Abhidhamma account of the perceptual process. As the Appendix shows, the commentaries add only a few details to the account given in the Canonical Abhidhamma. The present chapter shows that while the Abhidhamma focusses on a moment-by-moment analysis, the Sutta approach more often gives an analysis which discusses processes as they are experienced over longer time-segments. Both approaches show, though, that the *viññāṇa* which lies at the centre of the whole dynamic matrix of personality is the process of discerning, discriminating, analytical awareness. It is a form of awareness which does not actively classify, interpret or label objects, but which scans or probes in such a way as to make this possible, and also utilises the result of such labelling.

10

BHAVAṄGA AND THE BRIGHTLY SHINING MIND

This mind is brightly shining, but it is defiled by defilements which arrive (A.I.10).

(10.1) The last chapter concentrated on discernment (*viññāṇa*) or *citta* as it functions in the process of perception. This chapter will begin by investigating the Abhidhamma concept of *bhavaṅga*, the resting state of discernment/*citta* which occurs between perceptual cycles.[1] Does the world-view of the 'early Suttas' allow the possibility of such a state, or indeed contain support for it? What is the nature of *bhavaṅga* and what range of roles is assigned to it? To assist in understanding the concept of *bhavaṅga*, the second part of the chapter will investigate the 'brightly shining' (*pabhassara*) *citta*, which came to be identified with *bhavaṅga*. This radiant *citta* will also be examined for the light it sheds on the early Buddhist view of human potential.

IS THE *BHAVAṄGA* CONCEPT RULED OUT BY THE 'EARLY SUTTA' WORLD-VIEW'?

(10.2) The crucial feature of *bhavaṅga* is that it is seen to be a form of discernment other than those which occur in the six sense-channels. It may be asked, though, whether a passage at M.I.259–60 rules out such a concept. Here, the Buddha says to the monk Sāti, who believes in an unchanging, unitary discernment (Para.6.13):

> '. . . has not discernment as arisen from conditions been spoken of in many a figure by me, saying: apart from conditions, there is no origination of discernment? . . . Whatever condition it arises dependent on, through just that discernment gets its name: if discernment arises conditioned by eye and visual forms, it is known as visual-discernment [and likewise for its arising from

> the other five sense-organs and sense-objects]. Monks, just as, whatever condition a fire burns dependent on, through just that it gets its name: if it burns dependent upon sticks, it is known as a stick-fire; . . . Even so . . . Do you see monks, "this has come to be" '. 'Yes, Lord'. 'Do you see, monks, "the origination of that nutriment (*-āhāra-*)"?'. 'Yes, Lord'. 'Do you see, monks, "from the stopping of that nutriment, that which has come to be is subject to stopping"?' 'Yes, Lord'.

This passage might be seen as implying that, just as there is no latent, non-burning form of fire, so there is no latent form of discernment, apart from its six forms arising dependent on a sense-organ and sense-object.

(10.3) We should not take our own ideas on the nature of of fire, though, as those of the Indian cultural background against which the Buddha's hearers would have understood the above simile. In this culture, fire *was* seen as having a latent form. F.O. Schrader has pointed out the relevance of Upaniṣadic ideas of fire to Buddhist similes, asserting that such ideas illustrate 'the common Indian view . . . since the oldest times' (1904–05: 167). *Śvetāśvatara Upaniṣad* I.13 talks of 'the form of fire when gone to its source (*yoni-gatasya*) is not seen and yet its seed is not destroyed'. As pointed out by Schrader (p.167), *Śvetāśvatara Upaniṣad* IV.19 speaks of the God Maheśvara as 'a fire, the fuel of which has been consumed'. He attaches special importance to *Maitrī Upaniṣad* VI.34.1 as 'it shows the image in question in connection with the Yoga philosophy which is known to have influenced the Buddha more than any other system' (p.167–68). His translation of this runs: 'As fire from want of fuel comes to rest (*upasāmyati*) in its own place of birth, so, through the cessation of its motions, the thinking principle (*cittaṃ*) comes to rest in its own birth-place'. Thus, for the *Upaniṣads,* a quenched fire still exists in its source in a quiescent, latent form. It is notable, here, that such ideas are not given as substantive teachings, but as *similes* used to illustrate other ideas. For an idea to be used as an illustrative simile shows that it must have been an accepted commonplace of the day.

(10.4) In the Pāli Suttas, an allusion to this idea of fire is seen at M.I.240. This says that by rubbing a fire-stick, one 'could produce fire, make manifest heat'. That is, the production of fire is spoken of as the making manifest of something already there, for 'heat (*tejo*)' is one of the four elements which are always present in, e.g.

a log of wood (A.III.340–41). In the *Milindapañha*, the heat element is referred to as 'fire (*aggi*)' and it is said that, unlike the other three elements, but like everything born of seeds, fire is 'born of a root-cause (*hetujāni*)' (p.271). That is, that fire springs from its source in a way parallelling the arising of plants from seeds. At Miln.73, moreover, it is said that 'when the flame of a great mass of fire has gone out (*atham-gatā*) . . . it has gone beyond designation (*appaññattim gatā*)', this being a simile for the state of the Buddha after his death: he exists, but cannot be pointed to as here or there. This, like the *Upaniṣads*, takes for granted a quiescent, non-burning form of fire, latent in fuel and still existing after a fire has gone out. This supports R.H. Robinson's assertion that people in the Indian tradition took fire as 'an indestructible element latent in every bright or warm thing, but especially in fuel. It alternates between manifestation and "going home" to its occult source' (1970: 38–9).[2]

(10.5) The fire simile of M.I.259–60, then, is to be understood against the background of such ideas. This means that the text does not rule out a latent form of discernment, but indirectly alludes to it: just as different and changing forms of fire arise from the latent form of fire dependent on certain fuels, so different and changing sorts of discernment arise from a latent source dependent on certain sense-organs and sense-objects.

'EARLY SUTTA' EVIDENCE FOR A *BHAVAṄGA*-TYPE STATE

(10.6) A good source-text, here, is S.III.54–5, quoted in Para.8.8. This gives an allegory in which 'discernment with-nutriment (*viññāṇaṃ sāhāraṃ*)' corresponds to five species of seeds. It is clear that the standard four kinds of nutriment are here being referred to – those of (physical) food, stimulation (*phassa*), conceptional-volition and discernment – as this is the only apparent way of making up the number *five*, along with discernment itself. Moreover the *names* of the seeds can be seen to correspond to those of the nutriments:

i) The *khandha* (trunk) seed corresponds to the discernment 'nutriment', as this is the only nutriment which is also a *khandha* ('group' or personality-factor).
ii) The *phalu* (joint) seed corresponds to the *phassa* (literally

'contact') nutriment, from the common aspect of 'coming together' in the meaning of the two words.

iii) The *bīja* (seed/grain) seed can be seen to correspond to the nutriment of food, for such nutriment often consists of seeds or grain, and while a grain- or seed-seed is 'seed' (*bīja*) in the most obvious sense, food nutriment is 'nutriment' in the most obvious sense.

iv) The ordering of the five seeds is changed from the sequence normally used in referring to them, e.g. at D.III.47. This must be so that the ordering corresponds to the order of the nutriments: thus the *agga* seed would correspond to the conceptional-volition nutriment.

This, then, leaves the first, 'root (*mūla-*)', seed to correspond to discernment itself. Thus:

The five sorts of seed		*'Discernment with-nutriment'*
root-seed	:	discernment
trunk (*khandha-*) seed	:	discernment-nutriment
seed from a shoot (*agga-*)	:	conceptional-volition-nutriment
seed from a joint (*phalu-*)	:	stimulation-nutriment
grain-seed	:	food-nutriment.

(10.7) The significance of the above is that it shows that the 'early Suttas' accepted a form of discernment which is not the same as the discernment-nutriment. What, though, does the latter refer to? As a 'nutriment', it is what sustains beings in existence, part of their physical and mental food. In this role, though, it is no different from the discernment which is part of the Conditioned Arising sequence, for S.II.13 has a sequence: discernment-nutriment → future rebirth → the six sense-spheres → stimulation. Here, discernment-nutriment fulfils the role of the discernment causal 'link' (*nidāna*). The latter is itself defined as the six discernment-collections (S.II.4), which, from Para.9.4 can be seen to be the forms of discernment which occur in each of the six sense-channels. Discernment-nutriment must thus be equivalent to these, with the root-like discernment of S.III.54–5 being a form which does not occur in the processing of sensory or mental objects, just as *bhavaṅga* does not. The root-like nature of this discernment would also make it like *bhavaṅga*, for this not only precedes but also makes possible the 'process of *citta*s' which arise in the sensory channels: it is itself like a root from which they grow. Indeed, Bareau reports that the Mahāsāṅghika school believed in a *bhavaṅga*-like state which they referred to as root-(*mūla*-) discernment: it acts as the support (*āśraya*) for visual-discernment etc. as the root of a tree sustains the leaves etc. (1955: 72).[3]

(10.8) An analysis of M.I.190 (quoted at Para.8.13) also shows that it implies a *bhavaṅga*-like state. This it does in two ways. Firstly, it refers to an act-of-attention as among the conditions for the arising of a 'share' of discernment at the start of a perceptual process. This implies the existence of a mind ready-to-attend, i.e. some prior state of discernment, conception or *citta*. Secondly, Paras.8.24–5 have already shown that M.I.190 concerns a portion of the Conditioned Arising sequence, with the 'appearance' of the 'share' of discernment at the start of a perceptual process as a kind of 'birth'. As birth is conditioned by 'becoming (*bhava*)' in the standard sequence, and as M.I.190 even alludes to 'becoming', this indicates that the start of a perceptual process is dependent on a prior state of 'becoming'. As, in later theory, *bhavaṅga* also occurs immediately prior to the start of a perceptual process, and as it is also clearly connected to *bhava*/becoming, then M.I.190 seems to indicate the acceptance of a *bhavaṅga*-like state, called, in Sutta-terminology, '*bhava*'. Each time the mind attends to a new object, and there is the 'birth' of discernment and accompanying personality-factors, a necessary condition is a preceding state of 'becoming' or a mind ready-to-attend.

(10.9) Of course, the Conditioned Arising sequence's usual application is to the process of rebirth, not to the process of perception. In this more usual application, 'becoming' refers to the transition between lives, as argued at Paras.6.24–28. Is it plausible to see the one 'becoming' as referring to *both* a *bhavaṅga*-like state *and* to the transition between rebirths? These seem rather disparate. Yet the developed theory of *bhavaṅga* shows a connection. The 'early Suttas' saw dying and going to sleep as parallel states (Para.6.29), with (dreamless) sleep being seen, in the *Milindapañha* (pp.299–300), as a state of uninterrupted *bhavaṅga*. The Abhidhamma sees this as also occurring between perceptual cycles. So the transition from life-to-life is like the day-to-day transition that is sleep, which in turn is like the transition from perceptual-process-to-perceptual-process. A potential problem, here, is that the 'early Suttas' define 'becoming' as sense-desire-becoming, (pure)-form-becoming and formless-becoming (S.II.3), i.e. becoming as related to the three levels which rebirths are classified under. Does the use of these terms preclude 'becoming' being a *bhavaṅga*-like state? Not so, for the later theory sees the *bhavaṅga* state occurring between perceptual cycles as itself varying in type according to the type of rebirth the being is in (Para.A.7).

(10.10) It can thus be seen that the 'early Suttas' allude to a *bhavaṅga*-like state: as a form of discernment which is like the latent form of fire from which the various visible forms of fire spring; as a 'root'-discernment different from the forms occurring in the processing of sense-objects; as a state of mind prior to attention, and as the 'becoming' which conditions the 'birth' of discernment in the perceptual process. That is, a number of the key ideas which later crystallised into the concept of *bhavaṅga* were already present in the 'early Suttas'. It is inappropriate, then, to see the later theory as a kind of alien addition – an attempt to smuggle a Self-like state back into Buddhism –, as some have held. In any case, given that *bhavaṅga* only exists between perceptual cycles, it is hardly a candidate for being a permanent Self.

THE MEANING OF '*BHAVAṄGA*'

(10.11) What, then, is the best translation of '*bhavaṅga*'? Given that it has been argued that the term corresponds to one sense of 'becoming' in the Suttas, it might be appropriate to derive it from '*bhavaṅgya*', thus making it mean 'becomingness'.[4] Such a derivation is not favoured by the commentaries, though. D.A.I.194, on *bhavaṅga* as occurring between perceptual cycles, explains, 'There *bhavaṅga* occurs accomplishing the function of being the characteristic factor (*aṅga-*) of arising-(*uppatti*)-becoming'. Now as the Theravāda tradition came to rule out a between-lives state (though chapter 6 has shown it was accepted by the composers of the 'early Suttas'), 'becoming' was not seen as pertaining to such a state. Rather, it was explained as 'arising (*uppatti-*) becoming' the state of existence in a rebirth and 'karma-becoming', the karmic activity which leads to rebirth (Vibh.137, Vism.571). Thus the above explanation of *bhavaṅga* sees it as the 'characteristic factor' of life other than in its active karmic phase [5]. An alternative rendering of '*-aṅga*' would be to follow the *Abhidhammattha-Vibhārani*, a late text, and take it as equivalent to '*karāṇa*', 'foundation', 'condition' or 'reason'.[6] *Bhavaṅga* would thus be the 'foundation' of such life. As to what it is comprised of, Buddhaghosa sees it as a form of discernment, *citta* or conception, and the *Vimuttimagga* defines *bhavaṅga* as 'the consciousness-faculty of becoming'.[7] It does not occur alone, though, but is accompanied, for example, by feeling (Pt.I.411; CR.461).

(10.12) The literal 'characteristic factor of becoming' or 'foundation of becoming' convey little of *bhavaṅga*'s nature, though. What of other non-literal translations which better capture this? K.N. Jayatilleke uses 'dynamic unconscious' (1975: 226) and E.R. Sarathchandra uses 'unconscious continuum' (1958: 49). One cannot see *bhavaṅga* as 'unconscious', however, for although it occurs in dreamless sleep, it is seen as having an object (Para.A.7), and as being a form of discernment or *citta*. In any case, it is not seen as a compartment of the mind which co-exists with other forms of consciousness or discernment, as is the Freudian 'unconscious'. Again, it is not a seat of motivation, as is Freud's 'unconscious' (Collins, 1982: 243–44), nor a 'dark' place, a seething Id, for Miln.299–300 compares it to the radiance of the sun. The 'dynamic' and 'continuum' aspects of the above translations are appropriate, though. S.Z. Aung and C.A.F. Rhys Davids use 'subliminal consciousness' (1910: 27 & 266), but this would most accurately describe the 'disturbance of *bhavaṅga*' which occurs just before 'advertence'. As indicated by the term 'subliminal', discernment/consciousness is then 'below the threshold' of full awareness but still directed to one of the six sense-organs in a minimal way. As *bhavaṅga* occurs in dreamless sleep, though, *it* is not directed to any sense-organ, though it does have an object. H. Saddhatissa's 'infra-consciousness' (1970: 42) avoids some of the inappropriate connotations of 'subliminal consciousness', but itself has such connotations. 'Infra-' means both 'below' and 'less than'; as will be seen, *bhavaṅga* is in no way an inferior state, as it is naturally pure and radiant. Ñāṇamoli's 'life continuum'[8] captures the dynamic aspect of *bhavaṅga* and its nature as a key factor, or foundation, of the process of life. A qualification which is usefully added to this is 'latent', for this suggests a state which is present in a somewhat passive form, and which is replaced by the more active forms of discernment or *citta* that arise following advertence. *Bhavaṅga*-discernment is thus 'latent life-continuum discernment', the resting ground-state of discernment which is not turned towards the senses but has, as object, what was on the mind in the moments immediately preceding the end of the previous life (Para.A.7). It is accompanied by feeling and acts as the foundation for the process of non-karmically-active life, of which it is the characteristic factor: the state it returns to when not doing anything else. Asl.279, in fact, compares *bhavaṅga* to a spider sleeping at the centre of its web, with the process of *citta*s likened to the spider passing along its web to devour an insect caught in it. As such, *bhavaṅga* clearly has features in common with the *ālaya-vijñāna* of the Mahāyāna Yogācāra school, for this is also a form of discernment, as an underlying mental continuum, which is literally a 'home' (a natural resting place) or 'roosting place'. *Bhavaṅga citta* is also the natural, unencumbered state of *citta*, for Kvu.615 calls the *citta* of the very last moment of a person's life – i.e. *bhavaṅga-citta* in the form of 'falling away' *citta* (Para.A.7) – the 'natural (*pakati-*)' *citta*.

THE ROLES OF *BHAVAṄGA*

(10.13) The role of *bhavaṅga* in the perceptual process has already been described at Para.9.12. What of its role in sleep, which has only been mentioned in passing so far? Miln.299–300, which discusses this, explains that in order to 'see' a dream, one's *citta* must be 'functioning', which it is not when one has 'entered *bhavaṅga*'. Only in the interval between wakefulness and (deep) sleep, when one is drowsy and have not reached the state of *bhavaṅga* in deep, dreamless sleep, does one 'see' a dream. Such dreaming 'monkey sleep' ends when there is 'going to *bhavaṅga*'. As Vism.458 says, the 'continuity (*santāna-*)' of *bhavaṅga-citta*s goes on occurring endlessly in 'dreamless sleep', like the 'current of a river'.

(10.14) A.A.III.317 (on A.III.240) explains that the *citta*s of dreaming, unlike *bhavaṅga*, are associated with attachment and other defilements. Nevertheless, the karmically active *javana* state seems not to occur fully in dreams, for A.A.III.317 continues (after quoting Miln.299–300):

> as indeed, the sleep of a monkey is quick to change (*lahu-parivattā*), thus such (dreaming) sleep is quick to change due to the repeated state of confusion of wholesome etc. *citta*s (and) is, in its occurrence, a repeated moving out from *bhavaṅga*.

This must mean that the full complement of seven *javana citta*s does not occur, so that there is a particularly rapid flicking between *bhavaṅga* and *javana*, the karmically active state. In dreaming, unlike *bhavaṅga*, the objects consist of 'the sign of visible forms etc.' (A.A.III.317), though the type of *citta* involved in dreaming is not any of the forms of discernment related to the five senses, or the

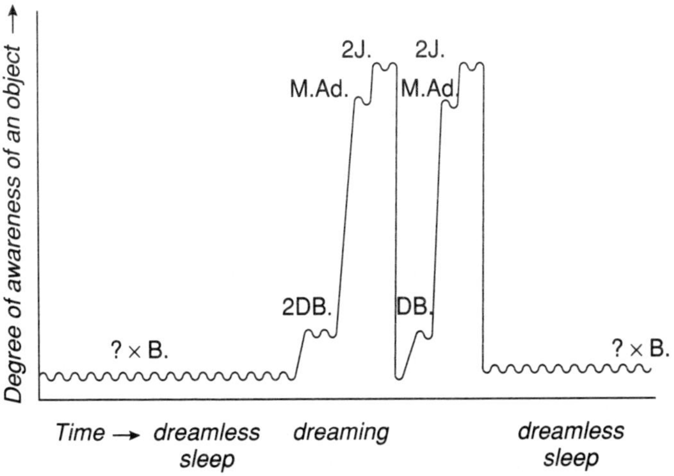

Chart 2 The *citta*-sequence in sleep. Key as at Para.9.12.

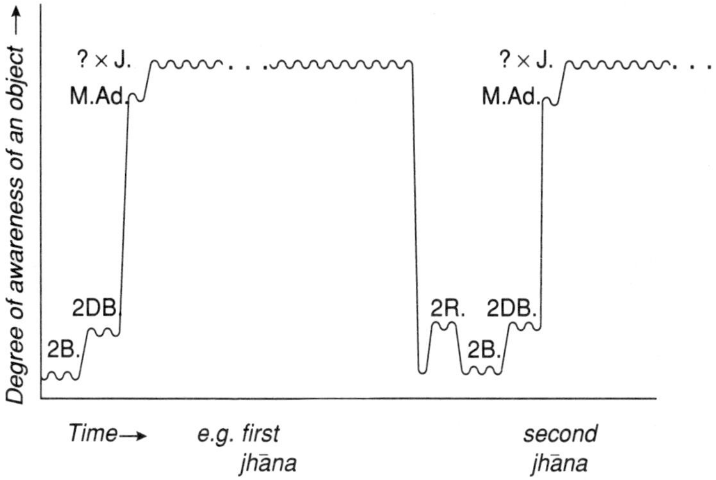

Chart 3 The *citta*-sequence in meditative *jhānas*. Key as at Para.9.12.

following state of conception-element (Vibh.322). It is thus a form of conceptional-discernment, arising in the mental sense-channel. As the normal *citta*-sequence relating to this channel is: *bhavaṅga*, two 'disturbances' of *bhavaṅga*, advertence, seven *javanas*, then return to *bhavaṅga* (Para.A.5), the sequence in dreaming thus becomes one which rapidly alternates between *bhavaṅga* (or its disturbance), advertence, and *javana*, as in chart 2. In normal waking consciousness, the mind is more active, such that more *javana citta*s occur (Para.9.12), yet the *bhavaṅga* state, typical of deep sleep, also occurs. This is not the case, though, when the mind attains the meditative states known as the *jhāna*s: deeply calm lucid trances, based on strong concentration and mindfulness. Here, wholesome *javana citta*s alone occur for hours, with no *bhavaṅga*. *Jhāna* is thus pure *javana*, with the mind in a state which is more awake and (calmly) active than in normal waking consciousness, as in chart 3. Only when there is a change from one *jhāna* to another is *bhavaṅga* entered (Vism.126), so that it again acts as a natural transition-state.

(10.15) In the meditative state of the 'cessation of cognition and feeling', also known as the 'attainment of cessation (*nirodha-samāpatti*)', however, the situation is different. In the developed Theravāda theory, it is said that, in this state, a person is '*citta*-less' (Vism.708), with even *bhavaṅga-citta* 'ceased' (*niruddha*) (Asl.283). This position is the same as taken in the Canonical Abhidhamma, which says that neither *citta* nor wisdom exist in cessation (Kvu.519). The *Milindapañha* passage on *bhavaṅga* is rather more open-ended, for it says that, for a living person, *citta* is not 'functioning (*appavattaṃ*)' in one of two circumstances: 'when it has become drowsy and entered *bhavaṅga*; and . . . when it has attained cessation' (Miln.300). As this sees *citta* as not 'functioning' when *bhavaṅga* occurs, such a 'non-functioning' *citta could* also occur in cessation.

(10.16) The evidence from the 'early Suttas' as regards whether a residual *citta* exists in cessation is as follows. At M.I.296, a comparison is made between a dead body and a person in the state of cessation. In the first case, the body is without 'vitality, heat and discernment', being like a 'mind-less (*acetanan*)' log of wood, and the five sense-faculties are 'broken asunder'. In the second case, 'vitality' and 'heat' are not destroyed and the sense-faculties are 'purified'. The avoidance of saying that discernment is present in cessation is clearly deliberate. The passage also says that one in cessation is without 'bodily-activities', 'vocal-activities' and '*citta*-activities'. M.I.301 sees these as, respectively, breathing, applied and investigative thought, and cognition and feeling. Cognition and feeling are said to be 'bound to *citta*' just as breathing is 'bound to the body', while speech follows after applied and investigative thought. Now, while speech is impossible without these speech-activities, the body (*kāya*) does not cease when breathing ceases, as it does temporarily in cessation and even the fourth *jhāna* (Vism.275). It is left unspecified whether *citta* can exist without its activities, like the body, or not, like speech. Several passages, e.g. M.I.175 and A.IV.454, describe a monk who 'enters on and abides in the cessation of cognition and feeling; and having seen by wisdom, his cankers are utterly destroyed'. This describes the attainment of Arahatship either in or *immediately after* the state of cessation. If the former is meant, then wisdom (*paññā*) can be present in cessation; if this is so, then so can discernment, for whatever is the object of wisdom is also known by discernment (M.I.292). Kvu.519, though, as seen above, denies that wisdom is present in cessation.

(10.17) The early texts, then, are not without some ambiguity on the issue of whether any kind of *citta* is present in cessation. It is not surprising, then, that the different schools had different opinions on this matter. Bareau reports that the Sarvāstivādin Vaibhāṣikas denied any *citta* in cessation, while it was accepted by the Sautrāntikas, Dārstāntikas, the Vibhajyavādins – who are almost identical to the Theravādins – and even by the Theravādins themselves.[9]

(10.18) Paul Griffiths (1987) has made a detailed study of different schools' views on the issue. He regards the developed Theravādin view, of a *citta*-less cessation, as being inconsistent with other Theravādin views. This is because he sees Theravāda as holding to a 'dualism' in which mental events never directly arise from physical ones (p.37). In the case of the resumption of *citta* after a *citta*-less cessation, however, such *citta* must be conditioned by a purely physical, *citta*-less body. In fact, Theravādin Abhidhamma is not so dualistic as Griffiths claims. While conception and conceptional-discernment normally arise conditioned by other mental states, they also have an unspecified form of matter (*rūpa*) as 'support condition' and 'basis' (Pt.I.5; CR.I.6; Pt.I.72; CR.80). It seems a small extension of explicit Theravādin doctrine to say that it is from this physical basis, unaided by mental states, that *citta* resumes on emergence from cessation.[10]

(10.19) It can thus be seen that the theory of *bhavaṅga* and the process of *citta*s sees dreamless sleep as pure *bhavaṅga*; dreaming sleep as an extremely rapid alteration between *bhavaṅga*, advertence and karmically active *javana* (impulsion); waking consciousness as a less rapid alteration between *bhavaṅga* and the other forms of *citta*; and *jhāna* as pure *javana*. While *bhavaṅga* is a plausible candidate for a form of *citta* present in cessation, this is denied. At all other times, however, *bhavaṅga* plays a crucial role in preserving the continuity of a person's mental life. It is the latent life-continuum which is the ground-state returned to by discernment when not actively processing objects through the six sense-channels. As such a ground-state, it also acts as a natural transition phase: from perceptual cycle to perceptual cycle, from day to day (through sleep), from *jhāna* to *jhāna*, and from life to life (through its occurrence as 'relinking (*paṭisandhi*)' *citta*, at the moment of conception).

THE BRIGHTLY SHINING *CITTA*

(10.20) To add to the above discussion of *bhavaṅga*, the 'brightly shining' (*pabhassara*) *citta* which the commentaries identify it with (A.A.I.60) will now be investigated. The 'brightly shining' mind is a mysterious form of *citta* often alluded to in the living Theravādin tradition,[11] and also the basis for Mahāyāna talk of the 'Buddha-nature', or enlightenment-potential, in all beings. Its treatment in the early texts has been little discussed, however. By examining it alongside *bhavaṅga*, it is hoped that there will be a mutual illumination between these two important concepts.

(10.21) The key 'early Sutta' reference for the 'brightly shining' *citta* consists of two Suttas found at A.I.8–10 and 10–11. The first, called 'The *citta* directed and uncovered section', develops as follows:

i) Just as the spike of bearded wheat will pierce the hand and draw blood, provided that it is well directed, so the *citta* will pierce spiritual ignorance, draw knowledge, and realize *nibbāna* provided it is well directed.
ii) A person whose *citta* is corrupt and turbid will be reborn in a hellish realm (of tortured consciousness), and cannot understand what is for the true welfare of himself or others, nor realize 'the states surpassing those of (ordinary) humans, the excellent knowledge-and-vision (*-ñāṇa-dassana-*) befitting the holy ones (*ariya-*)': the states of deep calm and liberating insight that are the fruit of spiritual practice. One whose *citta* is 'translucent (*pasanna-*)' and unturbid, however, will be reborn in a heavenly rebirth, and be able to realize such things, just as a person with

good eye-sight is able to look into a clear and undisturbed pool, unmuddied and uncovered by froth, and see 'the oysters and the shells, the pebbles and the gravel as they lie, or the shoals of fish that dart about'.[12]

iii) 'I know of no other single process which, thus developed and made much of, is pliable (*mudu*) and workable (*kammaññaṅ*) as is this *citta*. Monks, the *citta* which is thus developed and made much of [through meditation] is pliable and workable. Monks, I know of no other single process so quick to change (*lahu-parivattaṃ*[13]) as is this *citta* . . .'

iv) Monks, this *citta* is brightly shining (*pabhassaram*), but it is defiled (*upakkiliṭṭhan*) by defilements which arrive (*āgantukehi upakkilesehi*[14]). Monks, this *citta* is brightly shining, but it is freed (*vipamuttan*) from defilements which arrive'.

This clearly indicates the existence of a radiant *citta* which exists whether or not it is 'corrupt' and 'defiled' or 'translucent' and 'freed from defilements'. Even the corrupt person destined for hell thus has a 'brightly shining' *citta* 'covered', so to speak, by the defilements which obscure it. This expresses a very positive view of human nature and, indeed, of the nature of all beings. Buddhaghosa refers to this radiant *citta* as the 'naturally pure (*pakati-parisuddhaṃ*) *bhavaṅga-citta*' (A.A.I.61).

(10.22) In line with this, the following Sutta (A.I.10–11) implies that lovingkindness (*mettā*) is a quality of the brightly shining *citta*. The passage refers to knowledge of this *citta* as leading a person to meditatively develop their *citta*, and then immediately says that the development of lovingkindness-*citta*, for however little time, is always of great benefit. This implies that the brightly shining *citta*, which is always there to be 'uncovered', is already endowed with lovingkindness, providing a sound basis for any conscious development of this quality. Accordingly, it is said that the liberation of mind by lovingkindness 'shines (*bhāsate*) and glows and radiates' and is like the radiance (*pabhā*) of the moon (It.19–20).

(10.23) What, though, are the 'defilements' (*upakkilesas*) which cover and defile the radiant *citta*? The commentary (A.A.I.60) says 'attachment (*rāga*) etc.', i.e. attachment, hatred and delusion, while M.I.91 speaks of greed, hatred and delusion as *upakkilesas* of *citta*. S.III.23–24 lists the *upakkilesas* as desire-and-attachment (*chanda-rāga*) for a comprehensive range of mental and physical states; abandoning such defilements allows the *citta* to be 'workable (*kammaniyaṃ*) with respect to the states to be experienced by higher knowledge (*abhiññā*)'. Other texts refer to different sets of *upakkilesa*s of *citta*. M.III.157–61 lists vacillation, non-attention, dullness-and-drowsiness, consternation, elation, distress, too much or too little energy, longing, cognition of diversity, and being too intent on visible forms. Free of these, the *jhāna*s can be developed, then liberating insight attained. M.I.36–7 lists, as defilements of *citta* which lead to a bad rebirth: greed and covetousness, ill-will, anger, malice, hypocrisy, spite, envy, stinginess, deceit, treachery, obstinacy, impetuousness, conceit, arrogance, pride, heedlessness. S.V.92–3, on the other hand, reduces such long lists to that of the five hindrances: sense-desire, ill-will, dullness-and-drowsiness, restlessness-and-worry, and vacillation:

> there are these five defilements of *citta*. Defiled by these defilements, *citta* is not pliable (*mudu*) nor is it workable (*kammaniyam*), nor is it brightly shining (*pabhassaram*) . . . nor perfectly concentrated for the destruction of the cankers [i.e. for Arahatship[15]]'.

The parallel of wording, here, to the A.I.8–10 passage ('defilements . . . pliable . . . workable . . . brightly shining') is obvious, and shows the close relationship of the two passages.[16] S.V.92–3 also compares the defilements of *citta* to impurities in gold ore, an interesting image implying that, just as gold does not manifest its intrinsic radiance when mixed with impurities, so the intrinsic radiance of *citta* is not apparent when it is defiled by the hindrances – or by the other defilements listed above. A.I.253–55 also gives a simile of a gold-refining, parallelling this with the process of meditative development. The gold-ore must be washed three times, to get rid of the gross, moderate and fine defilements (*upakkilesa*s). This parallels a monk getting rid of the following defilements: bad conduct of deed, word and thought; thoughts of sense-desires, ill-will or cruelty; and reflections on his relatives, district or reputation. A gold-refiner must then properly smelt the gold, till it is fully free of dross; only then will it be 'pliable, workable, brightly shining, no longer brittle', and ready to be made into various ornaments. Just so, a monk must not only to get rid of the defilements specified above, but also of 'thinking about mental objects', before he attains one-pointedness of *citta*, a peaceful state of meditative concentration. He may then realize whichever higher knowledge (*abhiññā*)[17] he wishes.

FREEDOM FROM DEFILEMENTS

(10.24) In what state, then, is the 'gold' of the radiant *citta* when it is free of obscuring defilements? Such a defilement-free state is described in a common passage (e.g. D.I.76) on someone who has attained the fourth *jhāna*:

> With his *citta* thus serene, purified, cleansed, without blemish, with defilements gone, become pliable, workable (*vigat-ûpakkilese mudu-bhūte kammaniye*), firm and imperturbable, he applies and bends down his *citta* for [various knowledge-and-visions (*ñāṇa-dassanas*), the six higher knowledges (*abhiññās*) and the destruction of the cankers are then listed].

As at A.I.8–10, there is here a language of purity and reference to pliability, workability, lack of defilements, and knowledge-and-vision. The passage refers to a *jhāna*, a state developed by calming (*samatha*) meditation, using deep concentration, though the passage also implies the development of insight (*vipassanā*) meditation too. This is because insight (M.I.494) and wisdom (*paññā*) (A.III.26–7) are needed for the development of the higher knowledges, and knowledge-and-visions are classified as requiring wisdom, not just concentration (D.I.207–08). A.I.61 shows that calming suspends the defilement which is attachment, while insight suspends the defilement which is ignorance (*avijjā*), so as to develop wisdom (*paññā*). The commentary on A.I.8–10, in fact (A.A.I.59), sees the 'developed' *citta* as developed by repeated calm-and-insight, and says 'the fourth *jhāna* as a basis for the higher knowledges is extremely pliable and workable'. Another meditative state where the *citta* is pliable, workable, and poised for the higher knowledges is emergence from the 'cessation of cognition and feeling' (A.IV.421). This, too, requires a combination of calm and insight.

(10.25) Another route to a defilement-free *citta* is described at D.I.110. Here the Buddha gives someone a step-by-step discourse: 'talk on giving, moral virtue, heavenly rebirth, showing the disadvantage, degradation and stain (*saṃkilesaṃ*) of sense-desires, and the advantage of non-sensuality', such that his listener's *citta* is 'ready' and 'pliable', without hindrances, and 'translucent (*pasanna-*)'. He goes on to teach the four Holy Truths, so that his listener attains the 'Dhamma-eye', i.e. attain Stream-entry, the first glimpse of *nibbāna*. In this 'ready' state, then, the *citta* is poised for a break-through, as it is in the fourth *jhāna* or after cessation, when ready for the higher knowledges. The feature in common between these three states is being without the hindrances – ie. at least 'access' concentration, in later meditative terminology – and being intently open to the truth, be this in the form of the higher knowledges or Stream-entry.

THE SHINING *CITTA* AND *BHAVAṄGA*

(10.26) The equation of *bhavaṅga* with the radiant *citta* is directly asserted in the commentaries, and is also implicit in a relatively late portion of the *Milindapañha*, which applies metaphors of radiance to *bhavaṅga* (pp.299–300). This is seen from two similes it uses to illustrate the state of dreamless sleep, which is an uninterrupted stream of *bhavaṅga*:

i) the 'radiance (*pabhā*)' and rays (= *citta*) of the sun (= the mortal body) always exist, but may be obscured by fog (= drowsiness) so that there is no light (= the non-functioning of *citta*).
ii) when there is dense darkness (= drowsiness) and there is no 'illumination (*appabhāse*)', no shadow is seen even of a well burnished mirror (= the mortal body), for light (= *citta*) is lacking.

These similes indicate that, while the normal functioning of *citta* is like light, which may get cut off, the *bhavaṅga citta* of dreamless sleep has a radiance which exists whether or not it is obscured.[18]

(10.27) How, then, is *bhavaṅga* related to the the radiant *citta* free of defilements? When the mind is still in *jhāna*, there is said to be a series of *javana citta*s, with no *bhavaṅga citta*s intervening (Para.10.14). To develop the higher knowledges, however, *jhāna* must be left, so that there is again *bhavaṅga* before adverting to an appropriate object (Vism.394, 408). During the course of experiencing the first five higher knowledges, *javana* lasts for only a single moment in each perceptual cycle – this compares to the seven moments in normal consciousness –, before being followed by *bhavaṅga* (Vism.139). There is thus an extremely rapid alternation between *bhavaṅga* and *javana*. This feature of the later theory accords with the A.I.10 description of the developed *citta* as supremely 'quick to change'. The commentarial view of the undefiled state of the radiant *citta* is, then, that it is one where there is a very rapid flickering between the radiant *citta*, i.e. *bhavaṅga*, and undefiled moments of *javana*. *Javana* is the karmically active state in which defilements 'arrive' (A.A.I.60) like visitors arriving at a house (D.A.I.195). The *bhavaṅga* state which precedes *javana*, however, is naturally pure and undefiled.

(10.28) The Sutta at A.I.10–11 is also given a very plausible interpretation in terms of the theory of *bhavaṅga* and the process of *cittas*. After referring to the radiant *citta*, and recommending the practice of lovingkindness, it says:

> Monks, whatever states are unwholesome, have a part in unwholesomeness, are on the side of unwholesomeness, all those have conception as their forerunner (*mano-pubbaṅgamā*). Conception arises first, the unwholesome processes after [there is then a parallel passage on wholesome states].

The Sutta then ends by saying that 'heedlessness (*pamādo*)' – lack of mindfulness – and 'indolence (*kosajjaṃ*)' have the greatest power to lead to unwholesome states and undermine wholesome ones, while heedfulness does the opposite. The quoted portion is close to the famous opening verse of the *Dhammapada*:

> 'Conception is the forerunner of (all) processes (*dhammā*)
> Conception is chief, they are made by conception . . .'

The later theory makes sense of such passages as follows. After *bhavaṅga* comes adverting conception-element. If the adverting is done in a heedless, negligent way, with unmethodical attention, then unwholesome states will arise at *javana*.[19] Accordingly, *Paṭṭhāna* I.449 (CR.511) says that advertence is 'without stains (*asankiliṭṭa-*) but staining' and Asl.277–78 says 'when adverting and determining are done wisely and methodically, *javana* is unlikely to be unwholesome'. This shows that the way the mind adverts to, or attends to objects, at the very start of a perceptual process, is the key to whether unwholesome or wholesome states will follow. Indeed, the term for 'attention', '*manasikāra*', literally means 'work-of-*mano*', 'activity of conception', and from Para.1.47 it is apparent that the 'early Suttas' saw the 'I am' conceit, a crucial defilement, as arising once conception is 'touched by feeling born of stimulation by spiritual ignorance' (S.III.46). While the shining *bhavaṅga* is naturally pure, advertence is morally neutral but can tip the balance either to the wholesome or wholesome. Thus the Suttas' constant emphasis on methodical or systematic attention, *yoniso manasikāra,* and the avoidance of its opposite. Unmethodical attention refers to such things as latching on the attractive or unpleasant features of things, thus giving rise to sense-desire or ill-will (the first two hindrances). A.V.113–14 makes clear that unmethodical attention triggers a series of states: lack of mindfulness and clear comprehension → non-restraint of the sense-faculties (being uncircumspect about how one responds to sense-objects) → misconduct of body, speech and mind → the five hindrances → spiritual ignorance. That is, once conception attends to things in inappropriate ways, a train of unwholesome results is set in motion.

(10.29) A.I.11 also emphasizes 'indolence' as a key factor in the arising of unwholesome states. Closely related to this is 'dullness and drowsiness' (*thīna-middha*), the third hindrance. The *Milindapañha* passage on the radiant *bhavaṅga* sees the onset of drowsiness as: 'the shrouding and enveloping of the (mental) body, a weakness, a stupidity, an unworkableness of the (mental) body'. The Abhidhamma sees drowsiness as 'indisposition, unworkableness, a shrouding, an enveloping, a barricading within of the (mental) body . . . sleep' (Dhs.1157), with the commentaries seeing this 'body' (*kāya*) as feeling, cognition and the constructing activities (Asl.378). Drowsiness thus makes the accompaniments of *citta* sluggish, weak and unworkable, though the radiant *citta* still remains. 'Dullness', on the other hand, is a quality of *citta*, being its 'indisposition, unworkability, . . . stickiness . . . a stiffening, a rigidity of *citta*' (Dhs.1156). Among the defilements of *citta*, 'dullness and drowsiness' is the one which *most* hinders the suspension of the other defilements, thus preventing the radiance of the brightly shining *citta* pervading the whole mind. This is seen from the fact that the contemplation which overcomes this hindrance, the 'cognition of light' (A.IV.86), leads to a state where 'with an open *citta* which is not overgrown, one develops a radiant (*sappabhāsaṃ*) *citta*', a state which is also conducive to knowledge-and-vision (D.III.222–23). It is by developing such a bright, open *citta*, moreover, that the 'bases of success' (*iddhi-pada*s) are developed (S.V.277), which thus enable a person to experience the higher knowledges (S.V.280–81), preparation for which frees the *citta* of defilements. The way to prevent the purity and radiance of *bhavaṅga* from being defiled at *javana*, then, is to to have heedful, methodical attention, which is wide awake and free from dullness and drowsiness.

(10.30) The emphasis on overcoming sleepiness is particularly appropriate; for the mind functions in a parallel way in dreaming and in experiencing the higher knowledges, when the *citta* is free of defilements. In both cases, there is a very rapid alternation between *bhavaṅga* and *javana* (Paras.10.14 and 27), the mind being 'quick to change' in both. The difference lies in the fact that, in dreaming, wholesome *citta*s are 'confused', due to the debilitating effect of dullness-and-drowsiness. In the higher knowledges, the full radiance of *bhavaṅga* is uncovered, and can empower the *javana citta*s with the ability to develop paranormal powers. The theory of *bhavaṅga* and the 'process of *citta*s', then, dovetails well with the 'early Sutta' material on the brightly shining *citta*. *Bhavaṅga* is the mind's naturally pure state, but one which is normally inaccessible, as it mainly occurs during deep sleep. To unlock the power of this natural purity, the mind must be fully 'woken up' by meditative development, so that its radiant potential may be fully activated.

THE ARAHAT'S EVER-SHINING *CITTA*

(10.31) The state of *citta* in which it is free of defilements and poised for the higher knowledges is compared to a brim-full water pot, which will spill water as soon as it is rocked (A.III.27–8). The *citta* is thus set to overspill its normal boundaries. Having been developed to this state by the narrowing down of focus to meditative one-pointedness, it can then 'expand' in the six higher knowledges. In these, it:

i) enables a person to overcome the restrictions of normal physical laws by the exercise of psychic powers *(iddhis)* such as flying;
ii) overcomes the barrier of space by hearing sounds at a great distance by the 'divine ear';
iii) overcomes the self-other barrier by reading the *citta* of other beings;
iv) overcomes the barrier of time by remembering past lives;
v) overcomes the self-other barrier, and the barrier of death, by observing the rebirth of other beings, in accordance with their karma;
vi) overcomes the barriers of spiritual ignorance, conceit and craving, destroying the cankers (*āsava*s), the most deep-rooted limitations of *citta*, and so experience *nibbāna*, the unconditioned which is beyond the barrier of conditioned existence, beyond *all* limitations.

(10.32) Prior to the development of the last higher knowledge, however, the brightly shining *citta* may be temporarily free of all defilements and yet unenlightened, still affected by the cankers or 'influxes', which might be seen as festering sores on the mind, leaching off its energy. Temporary freedom from the defilements is simply an ideal opportunity for their complete destruction, but is not the same as this. Only the Arahat has destroyed the cankers and is permanently free of the defilements (except perhaps drowsiness, during sleep). He or she has 'six-factored equanimity': 'non-abandonment of the natural state of purity (*parisuddha-pakata-bhāvā*) when desirable or undesirable objects of six kinds come into focus in the six (sense-) doors' (Vism.160). That is, the natural radiance of the brightly shining *citta* is never obscured by the defilements, which otherwise 'arrive' when the mind mishandles its transactions with objects of the five senses and of conceit-prone conception. *Bhavaṅga*, the 'latent life-continuum' which is the naturally pure and radiant resting state of discernment, having been known through meditative development, now retains its integrity, no longer prone to obscuration by defilements. Whether or not the Arahat has utilized the power of his or her mind to develop the first five higher knowledges, he has the key one, which enables him to remain in the natural purity of the mind's resting state. He has attained an 'awakening' (*bodhi*) in which the pure state of the mind in dreamless sleep shines through all consciousness. The *nibbāna* which he or she experiences, though, cannot be the same as the brightly shining *citta*, for even when this is temporarily free of defilements, *nibbāna* is still to be attained. Nevertheless, for the Theravāda, it is, as *bhavaṅga*, aware of the object of mind at the time of the last death (Para.A.7), which must imply that it has an awareness of the impermanence and suffering of limited, conditioned existence.

THE SHINING *CITTA* AND THE BUDDHA-NATURE

(10.33) Other than the Theravāda, a number of the pre-Mahāyāna schools made reference to the radiant *citta*. The Vibhajyavādins, who were close to or identical with the Theravādins, held that the fundamental or root-nature (*mūla-bhāva*) of *citta* was brightly shining (Skt. *prabhāsvara*; Bareau, 1955: 175), while the Mahāsāṅghikas said the same of the 'own-nature' (*svabhāva*) of *citta* (Bareau, 1955: 67-8), and the Dharmaguptakas said this of the 'nature' (*bhāva*) of *citta* (Bareau, 1955: 194). The Sarvāstivādin Vaibhāṣikas, however, disagreed (Bareau, 1955: 147). In the Mahāyāna, the concept became one of great importance. The *Aṣṭasāhasrikā* Perfection of Wisdom Sutra, a text from around the first centuries BC or AD, identifies it with the compassion-based 'thought of awakening' (*bodhi-citta*), the aspiration to attain Buddhahood, for the sake of liberating all beings. Of this it says, 'that *citta* is no *citta*, since it is by nature brightly shining (*taccittam-acittam: prakṛtiścittasya prabhāsvāra*)' (Vaidya, 1960: 3, cf. Conze, 1973: 84). Here, the link with compassion tallies with the 'early Sutta' linking of the lovingkindness to the radiant *citta* (Para.10.22). The unusual nature of this *citta* is here signalled by it being termed a non-*citta citta*. The connection to *bodhi*, awakening or enlightenment, is also found in the 'early Suttas', if not quite in the same way. Arahatship is, of course, a kind of *bodhi*, and the seven 'factors of *bodhi*', which conduce to liberation, are developed by a *citta* which is without defilements (S.V.93), i.e. with its radiance uncovered.

(10.34) The uncovered brightly shining *citta* is thus the ideal springboard from which to attain awakening, such that it can be seen as a kind of enlightenment-potential. Appropriately, one strand of Mahāyāna thought identifies the brightly shining *citta* with the *tathāgata-garbha*: the Buddha-embryo, or Buddha-potential which is the Buddha-nature (*Buddha-dhātu*) present in all beings. Indeed, it is awareness of this which prompts the arising of the 'thought of awakening'. The *Laṅkāvatāra Sūtra* (p.77) says of the *tathāgata-garbha* that it is 'by nature brightly shining and pure (*prakṛti-prabhāsvara-viśuddy-*), originally pure (*-ādi-viśuddha*)'. It is 'naturally pure (*prakṛti-pariśuddho*) but it appears impure as it is defiled by stains which arrive' and is 'enveloped in the garments of personality-factors, (sensory) elements and sense-spheres, and soiled with the dirt of attachment, hatred, delusion and imagining (*-parikalpa*)' [20]. As discernment is a personality-factor, and is generally equivalent to *citta*, this implies that the *tathāgata-garbha* is not a normal kind of '*citta*', just as the *bodhi-citta* is not.

(10.35) The *Śrīmāla-devī Siṃhanāda Sūtra* sees the Buddha-potential as that which aspires for *nirvāṇa* (Paul, 1980: ch.13), while the *Ratnagotra-vibhāga* sees is as replete with the qualities of Buddhahood (vv.51, 84). It is both 'since beginningless time naturally present' and 'perfected through proper cultivation' (v.149). It is already present, 'the immaculate true nature to which nothing need be added and from which nothing need be taken' (v.113). Yet it has to be separated from accompanying impurities, just as gold-ore has to be refined so as to bring out and manifest the intrinsic purity of gold (v.47). Its relation to the defilements is much as in Theravāda thought. The *Ratnagotra-vibhāga* says that karma and the defilements are based on unmethodical attention, that this is based on 'the mind's purity', yet it also says that this 'true nature of mind' is itself without further basis (vv.56–7): a step beyond the Theravāda view. In fact, in Tathāgata-garbha thought, the Buddha-potential becomes the basis of all existence. The *Laṅkāvātara Sūtra* says that it 'holds within it the cause for both good and evil, and by it all forms of existence are produced. Like and actor it takes on a variety of forms . . .' (p.220). The *Ratnagotra-vibhāga* equates it with the subject of the following verse:

> The Realm (*dhātu*) is without beginning in time,
> It is the common basis (*āśraya*) of all states.
> Because it exists, there also exist
> All places of rebirth and full attainment of *nirvāṇa*
> (Holmes & Holmes, 1985: 72–3).

In the *Laṅkāvatāra Sūtra*, the Buddha-potential is actually seen as eternal and permanent but, while it may seem like a metaphysical Self (*ātman*), or eternal creator, it is not so, for it is the same as emptiness (p.778), i.e. lack of inherent Self-nature. The *Laṅkāvatāra Sūtra* (p.221) also equates it with the *ālaya-vijñāna* or 'home-discernment' of Yogācārin thought. This is a similar concept to that of the Theravādin *bhavaṅga citta*, being part of a system which also includes conception (*manas*) and the six forms of sense-discernments (see Harvey, 1990: 107–09). As in Theravāda thought, it is conception which is the agent of generating defilements. Unlike *bhavaṅga*, though, the *ālaya* is seen as projecting out of itself the apparently external objects which are taken by the sense-discernments. The Theravāda view, here, is simply that past karma affects which objects are *noticed*, and conception and cognition then interpret and misinterpret these objects.

(10.36) It can thus be seen that the Buddha-potential, a key concept of the Mahāyāna, which became particularly central in Zen Buddhism, has links to both the 'early Suttas' and to the later Theravāda. While the Mahāyāna makes more explicit use of this type of concept, analogues to it are found in the early texts and the scholastic Theravāda tradition. The radiant *citta* as an enlightenment-potential is also a part of the living Theravāda meditation tradition.

THE SHINING *CITTA* AND THE REALM OF REBIRTHS

(10.37) If the radiant *citta* is the basis for attaining enlightenment, what of its relation to *saṃsāra*, the round of rebirths? In the 'early Suttas' it is clearly seen that it is covered with different degrees of defilements in different levels of rebirth, so that its radiance is apparent to different degrees in beings of these levels. This is made particularly clear by examining the heavenly rebirths. The gods of the six lower heavens, of the sense-desire realm, are known as *deva*s, a term which derives from an Indo-European root meaning 'to shine' (PED.329). Radiance is particularly associated with the higher gods, though, those of the realm of (pure) form. Important types of these gods are the 'Brightly Radiant' (*Ābhassara*) and 'Utterly Shining' (*Subhakiṇṇa*) gods (e.g. D.II.69). Rebirth as an Ābhassara god comes from the development of a *citta* of lovingkindness (It.15), a quality associated with the brightly shining *citta*. It also comes from the prior attainment of the second *jhāna*, with the third *jhāna* leading to rebirth as a Subhakiṇṇa god (Vibh.424–25). Such gods can thus be seen to have *citta*s whose purity and brilliance corresponds to that of *citta* in *jhāna*, which is relatively undefiled by defilements. Indeed D.I.247 says that a Brahmā god – who corresponds to the first *jhāna* (Vibh.424) – has a *citta* which is 'unstained (*asaṃkiliṭṭha-*)' (if not wholly undefiled).

(10.38) The *Aggañña Sutta*, at D.III.84–5, shows further links between the the Ābhassara gods and the radiant *citta*. Speaking of a time when a past physical world came to an end, it says that beings were then mostly reborn as Ābhassara gods. As such, they were 'mind-made (*manomayā*), feeding on joy (*pīti-*), shining in themselves (*sayam-pabhā*), traversing the air, continuing in lustre (*subha-ṭṭhayino*)'. After a very long time, the physical world started to re-evolve and the Ābhassara gods mostly died and were reborn here, though they were still 'mind-made' etc. The Sutta then goes on to say how humans gradually developed from these beings through a long period of moral decline. The qualities of these Ābhassara gods and early proto-humans are strongly linked to radiance. Even the *jhānic* joy that they feed on is compared to a flame which is 'brightly shining' (*pabhassara*) (M.II.203–04), and the development of the 'mind-made' body which they have is normally said to require a meditation where the (mental) body is made more *pabhassara* (S.V.283). As 'evolution' proceeds, however, this level of radiant purity, corresponding to that of the second *jhāna*, comes to be gradually obscured as the defilements increase. In this way, the various types of beings develop, according to the level of defilement of their *citta*s. This is shown by S.III.151, where the Buddha refers to the incalculable length of the round of rebirths, due to grasping at the personality-factors:

> Accordingly, monks, one must repeatedly regard one's own *citta* thus: 'For a long, long time this *citta* has been stained (*saṃkiliṭṭham*) by attachment, hatred and delusion'. By stain of *citta*, monks, beings are stained. By purity (*-vodānā*) of *citta* beings are purified.

The Sutta continues by saying that the diverse creatures of the animal world are 'thought out (*cittatā*) by *citta*'. Just as the *Aggañña Sutta* sees humans as deriving from beings whose radiant *citta* gets gradually defiled, so this implies that animal rebirths are developed from having a strongly stained *citta*.

(10.39) The above suggests the following role for the brightly shining *citta*. It is a kind of basic *citta* whose purity is normally obscured by defilements and stains such that it is subject to various forms of rebirth, good and bad. In bad rebirths, it is heavily defiled, but in good rebirths, such as those of the pure form gods, it is only lightly defiled and exhibits much of its its natural brilliance.[21] At the purest phase normally taking place in a world-cycle, most beings are Ābhassara gods, with their *citta* in a pure state corresponding to that of the second *jhāna*. As the world-process proceeds, beings then decline in morality and their lightly defiled radiant *citta*s get progressively obscured by increasing defilements. Nevertheless, through meditation, these obscurations can be gradually removed. When all the defilements – the five hindrances, attachment, hatred and delusion, and spiritual ignorance – are suspended, the natural radiance of *citta* is wholly uncovered and it is poised for the higher knowledges, the last of which ensures that *citta* is never more defiled.

(10.40) This chapter has thus shown that the 'early Suttas' allude to a state akin to the later Theravādin concept of *bhavaṅga*: a latent form of discernment which lies at the root of the six forms of sense-discernment. The developed concept of *bhavaṅga* sees it as the latent life-continuum which is the 'natural' ground-state or resting-state of *citta*. In dreamless sleep, moments of such a natural *citta* occur in an uninterrupted stream; in waking consciousness, there is an alternation between it and more active forms of discernment directed to sense-objects; in meditative *jhāna*, it is absent, as there are only very pure *javana* discernments. In dreaming sleep, drowsiness means that there is a very rapid alternation between *bhavaṅga* and weak *javana*; while in the activation of the higher knowledges, there is likewise a very rapid alternation, but in a context where the power inherent in *bhavaṅga* leads to overcoming a variety of barriers through potent *javana*. *Bhavaṅga* is very plausibly equated with the 'brightly shining' *citta* which exists in all beings, but is usually defiled by defilements which arise from unmethodical attention in the mind's dealing with objects. Such defilements – the five hindrances etc. – are temporarily suspended when the mind is poised for a spiritual break-through – Stream-entry or the development of the higher knowledges – while the Arahat's radiant mind is forever free of them. Just as the latent life-continuum is the transition-state between perceptual cycles, between periods of waking consciousness, between lives, and between *jhāna*s, so it is, as the brightly shining *citta*, the ideal transition-state into liberating knowledge. The radiant *citta* which is the latent life-continuum has loving kindness implicit within it and also has an implicit awareness of impermanence, its object being that taken by the mind just prior to the end of the prior rebirth. Mahāyāna ideas on the 'brightly shining' *bodhicitta* and *tathāgata-garbha* are more elaborated forms of this strand of Buddhist thought concerning a compassionate wisdom-potential within beings. In the 'early Suttas', the naturally radiant *citta* can be seen as relatively heavily or lightly obscured in the different forms of rebirth; but it remains throughout a pure basis for spiritual growth. This potential may be brought to fruition once conception (*mano*) overcomes unmethodical attention, so as to stop mishandling sense-objects and thus strengthening the defilements. The resting state of the mind is naturally pure, and is the transition-state between various consciousness-situations. With consistent methodical attention, the long-overlooked 'door to the deathless' may be opened, and a transition to the unconditioned accomplished.

11

NIBBĀNA AS THE TIMELESS 'STOPPING' OF THE ENTIRE PERSONALITY

. . . the stopping of *dukkha* states . . . bliss (It.37–8).

(11.1) If the 'brightly shining' *citta* offers a basis for the attainment of the unconditioned, *nibbāna*, what do the 'early Suttas' have to say on this religious ultimate? As the early texts focus on the path leading to the experience/realization of *nibbāna*, they are sparing in their accounts of *nibbāna* itself. Nevertheless, if what *is* said on it is carefully examined and pieced together, an interesting picture emerges. This is that *nibbāna* during life is, contrary to the generally accepted interpretation,[1] not the ever-present liberated state of the Arahat, but a transcendent experience in which all temporal phenomena drop away. Here, the personality-factors are (temporarily) subject to *nirodha* or 'stopping', a prelude to their final stopping at the death of an Arahat.

(11.2) The key passage on *nibbāna* in life and beyond death is at It.38–9. Here the Buddha distinguishes two 'elements' of *nibbāna* (*nibbāna-dhātu*s): that 'with remainder of *upādi* (*sa-upādi-sesā*)' and that 'without remainder of *upādi* (*an-upādi-sesā*)'. Both relate to an Arahat:

> Herein, monks, a monk is an Arahat with cankers destroyed (*khīnāsavo*), who has lived the life, laid down the burden, attained his own goal, the fetter (relating to) becoming utterly destroyed (cf. Para.6.24), released by perfect gnosis (*sammad-aññā-vimutto*).

On 'with remainder' *nibbāna*, it is said:

> In him the five (sense-) faculties still remain, through which, as they have not departed, he undergoes the pleasant and the unpleasant, he experiences happiness and suffering (*-dukkhaṃ*).

> In him, that which is the destruction (*-kkhayo*) of attachment, hatred and delusion, this is called, monks, the element of *nibbāna* with remainder of *upādi*.

The verse section, after the above prose, adds that this 'element' is 'here in this visible world (*idha diṭṭha-dhammikā*)' and is the 'destruction of the conduit of becoming (*bhava-netti-saṅkhayā* [2])', i.e. the destruction of 'craving for becoming' (D.II.90) or of 'desire, attachment, delight, and craving' for any of the personality-factors (S.III.190–91). On 'without remainder' *nibbāna*, it is said, after describing the Arahat's state as above:

> Here itself, monks, all that is experienced, with no delight for him, will become cool; this is called, monks, the element of *nibbāna* without remainder of *upādi*.

The following verses add that this 'belongs to the future, wherein becomings stop altogether (*nirujjhanti bhavāni sabbaso*)'. A final verse then seems to return to talking of the former 'element':

> Whoever, from gnosis of this unconstructed state (*padaṃ asaṅkhataṃ*)
> With *citta*s released, from destruction of the conduit of becoming,
> They, having attainment of Dhamma-essence (*dhamma-sārādhigamā*), are delighting in destruction (*khaye*) (cf.S.V.402).
> Those who are such (*tādino*) have abandoned all becomings.

THE *NIBBĀNA*-ELEMENT WITHOUT REMAINDER OF *UPĀDI*

(11.3) This 'element' clearly refers to *nibbāna* as it is entered at the death of the Arahat, for it pertains to the future when there is absolutely no 'becoming', and experiences have 'become cool'. Peter Masefield, has argued, however, that this *nibbāna* is during the life of the Arahat and that It.38–9 has become garbled in transmission (1979: 219). This can be disproved by reference to passages of parallel wording. S.II.83, for example, says that the Arahat knows that, when he dies, 'here itself *all that is experienced, with no delight for him, will become cool*, and relics (*sarīrāni*) will be left over' (see also D.III.135).

(11.4) What, though, is the '*upādi*' that the second *nibbāna* is without? The word only appears in compounds and appears to be a contracted form. At A.IV.75–9, the living Arahat is said to be without *upādi*, '*an-upādi-seso*', while lesser saints such as Non-returners still have *upādi*, being '*sa-upādi-seso*'. Here '*upādi*' must clearly be equivalent to '*upādāna*', 'grasping', for only the Arahat is completely free of this. But this cannot be the meaning of '*upādi*' at It.38–9, which is concerned only with Arahats, and where the terms '*sa*-' and '*an-upādi-sesa*' are applied to *nibbāna*, not to a person. Here, '*upādi*' is most likely to be a equivalent to '*upādiṇṇa*', meaning the 'grasped at', i.e. the personality-factors 'grasped at' by past craving (see Para.4.16). This is how the commentaries take the term. S.A.II.81, on S.II.83 (last Para.) says, 'from the break-up of the personality-factors which are grasped at (*upādiṇṇaka*-), he attains *nibbāna* in the element of *nibbāna* without remainder of *upādi*'. It.A.I.165, on It. 38–9, says, ' "There, with craving etc. having the nature of fruit he grasps", (thus) *upādi*, which is the five-fold personality-factors'. That is, while the living Arahat does not actively grasp, he or she still has the personality-factors resulting from past grasping.

NIBBĀNA DURING LIFE AS NOT EVER-PRESENT IN THE ARAHAT

(11.5) The above clearly means that *nibbāna* '*with* remainder of *upādi*' relates to the living Arahat. Does this 'destruction (*-kkhayo*) of attachment, hatred and delusion' refer, though, to the Arahat's perpetual destroy*ed* state of attachment etc., or to the experience/event *which destroys* these? The commentary on It.38–9 seems to support the first alternative, for it explains 'destruction of attachment' as 'the state of being destroyed, non-existence, perpetual non-arising' (It.A.I.166). An examination of the 'early Suttas', though, shows that they support the second alternative. Action nouns are frequently used in talking about *nibbāna* during life, suggesting that it is, in one sense, a kind of 'event' and not an ever-present state of the Arahat. It.88 and A.III.35 refer to, 'the subdu*ing* of intoxicating pride, the driv*ing* out of thirst, the uproot*ing* of a settling place, the cutt*ing* off of the round, the destruction (*-kkhayo*) of craving, dispassion (*virāgo*) stopping, *nibbāna*'. In such a context, 'destruction' must have the sense of 'destroy*ing*'. Indeed *nibbāna*, whether during life (Thag.906) or at death (D.II.157) is directly compared to the 'extinction' (also '*nibbāna*') of a lamp: clearly a specific 'event'.

(11.6) The 'destruction of attachment, hatred and delusion' is also given as the definition of *Arahatta*, or Arahat-ness (S.IV.252). One might expect this to refer to the general state of the Arahat, but the way the term is used shows that it actually means the crucial transition which makes a person an Arahat. That is, it is the state in which attachment etc. and the cankers *get destroyed*, so that a person now *is* an Arahat, 'one with cankers destroyed (*khīnāsavo*)'. It is a canker-destroying experience that is the very nature of an Arahat. The correctness of such an interpretation is made clear from the way in which various texts talk of the four grades of holy person: Stream-enterer, Once-returner, Non-returner and Arahat. A.III.272–73 says that selfishness makes it impossible to realize the 'Stream-entry-fruit' (*sotāpatti-phala*) or other fruits including 'Arahatness-fruit' (*arahatta-phala*). Here '*arahatta*' parallels '*sotāpatti*': 'stream-*entry*'. As 'stream-entry' is a term for an *event*, and a Stream-enterer is one who has experienced it, so 'Arahatness' must in some sense be the name of an event, with an Arahat being one who has experienced it. Now the 'Arahatness-fruit' is not a 'fruit' of a previously attained Arahatness; it is the same as it. This is shown by a precisely parallel passage at A.III.273, which puts 'Arahatness' in place of 'Arahatness-fruit.[3] Similarly, A.IV.293 distinguishes the Arahat from one who is 'practising (*paṭipanno*) for Arahatness', just as it distinguishes a Stream-enterer from one 'practising for the realization of Stream-entry-fruit'. That is, Stream-entry and Arahatness are both fruits of prior practice. That they are events to be experienced is indicated by Ps.II.145, which refers to the 'moment of Arahatness-fruit'.

(11.7) Arahatness is not only *like nibbāna* during life in being the destruction of attachment etc., it is the *same* as it, for both are described as the 'highest *dhamma*' (A.III.433 and It.88). This, however, also makes *nibbāna* in life the same as Arahatness-fruit, and thus a 'fruit'. Does this conflict with *nibbāna* during life being described as unconditioned (*asaṅkhata*) (S.IV.362), not dependent on anything? Not according to S.I.173, where the 'deathless' – *nibbāna* – is said to be the 'fruit' of the Buddha's metaphorical 'ploughing'. Nevertheless, that the compilers of the Suttas were not always happy with the unconditioned as a 'fruit' can perhaps be inferred from their often putting 'Arahatness' instead of 'Arahatness-fruit', as has been seen.

(11.8) Perhaps the most crucial argument against seeing *nibbāna* as an ever-present state is that the living Arahat is not wholly beyond *dukkha*, whereas *nibbāna*, as the third Holy Truth, is the 'stopping' (*nirodha*) of *dukkha*, due to an entire 'stopping' of craving. Now *dukkha*, or unsatisfactoriness, is said to be of three types (S.IV.259): unpleasant sensation, the imperfection of something being conditioned, and the suffering arising from change in something that one clings to. The living Arahat is free of the last of these (S.II.274), but he still has the second, for his personality-factors are conditioned and are said, even up to his death, to have been *dukkha* (S.III.112). He also experiences unpleasant sensations, as said at It.38–9 itself. If the living Arahat in his normal state still has some *dukkha*, there are two possibilities as to his relationship with *dukkha*:

i) he has destroyed all causes of *dukkha*, but that he will continue to experience residual *dukkha* until he dies, when the *complete* end of *dukkha* comes.
ii) the *nibbāna* he experiences during life is itself completely beyond all *dukkha*, such that it is a state other than the Arahat's normal one: for in this normal state he is still subject to unpleasant sensations and is comprised of the conditioned personality-factors.

The first possibility is that favoured by the Theravādin commentarial tradition: *nibbāna* in life is 'complete extinction of the defilements' (*kilesa-parinibbāna*), whereas *nibbāna* beyond death is 'complete extinction of the personality-factors' (*khandha-parinibbāna*; Dhp.A.II.163). Such a view is already found in the Canonical commentarial text, the *Niddesa*. In commenting on 'where sentiency and body (*nāmañ ca rūpañ*) stop without remainder: by the stopping of discernment, here, this is stopped' (Sn.1037), Nd.I.245 says that this even applies in the case of Stream-entry. Here sentiency and body which *would* have arisen in the future, other than in a Stream-enterer's seven remaining lives, 'stop'. For one becoming an Arahat, 'sentiency and body which *would* arise (beyond his death), here they stop'. Only in the case of the death of an Arahat do sentiency and body 'stop' completely. This interpretation, though, seems rather artificial: the 'stopping' of something really means that either *some* or all future examples of it do not occur! This view thus implies an odd interpretation of the Four Holy Truths. It makes the third, on the cessation of *dukkha*, more like the fourth, on the *path* to the end of *dukkha*, for it sees cessation as the final thing which *leads* to the *future* end of *dukkha*. In this, it makes '*nirodha*', literally 'cessation' or 'stopping', mean 'cause of future cessation', which is odd. Indeed, if this were the meaning of '*nirodha*' in the third Holy Truth, it would *also* have to apply to the '*nirodha*' of craving, which would then mean that this allowed for some residual craving, until craving finally ended. Yet it is clear that the living Arahat has undergone the complete destruction of craving. He or she must thus have undergone a state where there is *no dukkha*, just as he has *no* craving. The end of either is not an event in the future: *nirodha* means 'cessation' or 'stopping' of what would otherwise exist *now*. Moreover, there is no evidence from the 'early Suttas' that *dukkha*, and the 'sentient body' (*nāma-rūpa*) could 'stop' for anyone but the Arahat.

(11.9) While the Arahat does not continually experience *nibbāna*/Arahatness, he or she is nevertheless very different from a non-Arahat. This is because he has undergone a radical transformation of disposition, in which the cankers, and the very possibility of attachment, hatred and delusion, have been permanently destroyed. He thus lives in the world with a mind undistorted by defilements, but still undergoes physical (not mental) pain, and 'his' conditioned personality-factors still exist. Though these are replete with such wholesome states as mindfulness, concentration and lovingkindness, they are nevertheless conditioned.

THE 'STOPPING' OF THE PERSONALITY-FACTORS DURING LIFE

(11.10) A number of passages in fact show that there is not only *nirodha* of craving during life, but that this also happens to the personality-factors and causal links (*nidanas*). At S.III.58–61, the Buddha applies the schema of the Four Holy Truths to each of the five personality-factors in turn, in terms of their nature, origin, cessation, and the way going to their cessation (the Holy Eightfold Path). He explains that having 'fully come to know (*abbhaññāsim*)' each of the factors in this way, he was enlightened. He then talks of two kinds of people who share this understanding. The first are those 'practising (*paṭipannā*)' '*for* the turning away from (*nibbidāya*)' and '*for* the cessation (*nirodhāya*) of' each personality-factor, and the second are those who '*from* the turning away from (*nibbidā*)' and '*from* the cessation of (*nirodhā*)' [4] of the personality-factors are 'liberated without grasping'. The former are clearly Stream-enterers and other saints established on the Holy Eightfold Path by insight into the Four Holy Truths: they are still 'practising (*paṭipannā*)', i.e. still on the *paṭipadā*, the term used here and elsewhere for the 'path' or 'way'. The second type of person, those 'liberated without grasping', having completed the path, must be Arahats. As 'turning away' and ending grasping are attained during life, they must be living Arahats, like the living Buddha who shares their attainment. They are thus said, during life, to have already experienced the cessation of their personality-factors. Indeed S.I.62, in applying the Four Holy Truths schema to the 'world' (*loka*), says that this ceases 'in this fathom-long carcase'.

(11.11) S.II.106 likewise applies the Four Holy Truths schema to each of the causal-links, and says that the Buddha has 'fully come to know' their cessation. Sn.726 ff., in discussing various links which each cause *dukkha*, describes how there is no 'origination (*sambhavo*)' of *dukkha* – i.e. there is *nibbāna* – when the links are inoperative. Thus:

> All constructing activities are calmed (*sabba-saṅkhāra-samathā*) from the stopping (*uparodhanā*) of cognition. Thus is the destruction of *dukkha*. (v.732) . . . by *nirodha* of discernment, there is no origination of *dukkha*. The monk, from the tranquillising (*-upasamā*) of discernment, without hunger, attains *nibbāna* (*nicchāto parinibbuto*) (vv. 734–35) . . . The monk, from the destruction (*khayā*) of feelings, is without hunger, attains *nibbāna* (v.739).

These verses clearly refer to a state during life, as the phrase 'without hunger, attains *nibbāna*' is often applied to the still living Arahat.[5] It is thus clear that the causal links, as well as the personality-factors 'stop' during life, this being tantamount to *nibbāna*.

(11.12) Here, an objection might be raised. If feelings (*vedanā*) (i.e. pleasant, unpleasant and neutral sensations) are destroyed in *nibbāna* during life, what is to be made of the reference, at Para.11.2, to the living Arahat as still experiencing feelings, in the specific context of *nibbāna* 'with remainder of the grasped at'? The point must be that the 'grasped at' personality-factors, including feelings, must be *associated with nibbāna* during life, even though they undergo cessation in the actual experience of *nibbāna*. As the 'grasped at' personality-factors recur once the experience is left, they can be said to be associated with *nibbāna* in life, whereas *nibbāna* at death is entirely beyond them. In the Conditioned Arising sequence, feeling depends on stimulation, which depends on the six sense-faculties. At S.IV.98, the Buddha, in talking of the cessation (*nirodha*) of these, describes a state where each of the six sense-organs 'stops (*nirujjhati*)' and cognition of its sense-object 'fades (*virajjati*)', this being a state 'to be known', which surely implies a feeling-transcending state known during life. The commentarial view, that *nibbāna* 'with remainder of the grasped at' exists simultaneous with the personality-factors (Vism.508) can thus be seen to be out of tune with the outlook of the 'early Suttas'.

NIBBĀNIC 'STOPPING' AND *NIRODHA-SAMĀPATTI*

(11.13) If *nibbāna* is a stopping of the personality-factors during life, is this simply the same as the 'cessation of cognition and feeling', also known as the 'cessation-attainment' (*nirodha-samāpatti*) (see Paras.10.15–18)? One passage which might be taken to mean that *nibbāna* during life is cessation-attainment, is A.IV.454. This says, with respect to dwelling in each of the four meditative states of *jhāna*, and the four further 'formless' mystical spheres: 'thus far, sir, with a qualification (*pariyāyena*) has *nibbāna* in this visible world (*diṭṭha-dhamma-*) been spoken of by the Lord'. In speaking of cessation, though, the state reached via, but beyond these lesser attainments, it is said: 'attaining the cessation of cognition and feeling, he dwells therein, and having seen by wisdom, the cankers are completely destroyed. Thus far, sir, without qualification has *nibbāna* in this visible world been spoken of by the Lord'. This passage, though, does not show that 'attainment of cessation' is '*nibbāna* in this visible world', but that the destruction of the cankers is. It is just that this occurs, in this passage, in (or immediately after?) the cessation-attainment.

(11.14) The problem with equating cessation-attainment with nibbānic cessation is twofold: a) *nibbāna* is often said to be attained from states other than cessation-attainment, and b), people can reach cessation-attainment and yet *not* attain *nibbāna*. As regards a), M.I.477 makes clear that while some Arahats had attained the 'deliverances (*vimokhā*)' – which include cessation-attainment (D.II.70–1) – others had not. As regards b), A.III.194 says of a person entering and then emerging from the cessation of cognition and feeling, 'if in this visible world he does not attain gnosis (*aññā*), transcending the god-community that feed on food-nutriment, he would arise in a mind-made body'. Here, 'gnosis' is the realization of *nibbāna*, from It.38–9, while the second possibility relates to someone, probably a Non-returner is meant, who is still subject to rebirth. An Arahat is one who has fully realized the third Holy Truth, the full cessation of *dukkha*. This is attained by *all* Arahats and by no-one who is *not* an Arahat: it cannot, then, be the same as cessation of cognition and feeling, though this is a common route to it.

RE-ENTRY TO THE STATE OF 'STOPPING'

(11.15) The 'stopping' which is *nibbāna* is not only experienced at the point at which a person becomes an Arahat, but can, it seems, be periodically re-entered by him. In the commentaries there is the idea that Arahatness-fruit can be re-entered and dwelt in for a certain time 'for the purpose of dwelling in bliss in this visible world' (Vism.700) [6]. This idea, which from Paras.11.6–7 would be the same as a re-entry into the *nibbānic* experience, also seems to be indicated in the 'early Suttas'. S.III.168 says that if an Arahat were to 'methodically attend' to the personality-factors as impermanent, *dukkha* and not-Self, this would conduce to his 'dwelling in bliss in this visible world'. Now A.IV.111 says that the four *jhāna*s are forms of 'dwelling in bliss in this visible world' and are for 'pleasant dwelling (*phāsu-vihārāya*)'. On page 119 of the same text, five 'pleasant dwellings' are then listed: the four *jhāna*s and the state of one who 'having himself, in this visible world, experienced by higher knowledge the cankerless liberation of mind, the liberation by wisdom from the destruction of the cankers, enters and dwells (there)'.[7] This clearly seems to imply that the Arahat may re-enter and dwell in the state that first made him an Arahat, experiencing *nibbāna*, the 'highest bliss' (Dhp.203).

(11.16) The Buddha is said to have re-entered his enlightenment experience on at least six occasions. At Ud.1, it is said that, 'when recently fully awakened', he sat in one posture for seven days in meditation, in which he 'experienced the bliss of freedom (*vimutti-sukhaṃ paṭisaṃvedī*)'. Vin.I.1–4 describes him then repeating this experience for three more weeks at different locations. At S.V.12–14, he is said to have spent two periods alone, for half a month and three months. After these, he says that he had 'been dwelling partly in the same manner as when recently fully awakened'. He goes on to say that he knew the 'experience (*vedayitaṃ*)' which came from each of the factors of the Holy Eightfold Path and also from their opposites. He also says that when desire (*chanda*), applied thought (*vitakka*) and cognition (*saññā*) are 'suppressed (*vūpasanto*)', there is an 'experience'. Again, this is clearly not the 'cessation of cognition and feeling (*-vedayita*)', for this lacks *vedayita*. Nor is it any normal state or *jhāna* or formless state, for cognition operates in all of these (even in the sphere of neither-cognition-*nor-non-cognition*). It is not even the 'signless' (*animitta*) state which knows but does not yet enter *nibbāna* (see below Paras.11.25ff.), for cognition exists in this. This state of 'experiencing the bliss of freedom' is thus likely to be an experience of blissful *nibbānic* 'stopping'. The length of time spent in this state was probably not normally measured in days, as these experiences of the Buddha were. Particularly in the case of a person's first attainment of *nibbāna*, for example when listening to a discourse, it may have only lasted a few seconds.

NIBBĀNA DURING LIFE AS 'UNBORN', 'UNCONSTRUCTED' AND 'DEATHLESS'

(11.17) If *nibbāna* during life is a temporary stopping of all the personality-factors, and is not ever-present in the Arahat, in what sense can it be seen as the 'unconditioned/unconstructed' (*asaṅkhata*) or the 'stable' (*dhuva*), 'deathless' (*amata*) etc, as it certainly is (S.IV.362, 370). To decide this, it is necessary to examine the meaning of such terms. This will, in turn, allow greater insight into the nature of *nibbānic* 'stopping'.

(11.18) One well-known passage on *nibbāna*, Ud.80–1, says:

> Monks, there exists the unborn (*ajātaṃ*), unbecome, unmade, unconstructed. Monks, if that unborn . . . were not, there would not be apparent the leaving behind (*nissaraṇaṃ*), here, of the born, become, made, constructed.

It.37–8, in explaining this, says that the 'leaving behind' of the 'born, become, arisen (*samuppannaṃ*), made, constructed, unstable' is:

> the real (*santaṃ*), beyond the sphere of reason, stable, unborn, un-arisen (*asamuppanaṃ*), the sorrowless, stainless state, the stopping (*nirodho*) of *dukkha*-states, the tranquillising (*-ūpasamo*) of constructing activities, bliss.

Again, D.III.275 says:

> whatever is become, constructed, arisen from conditions (*paṭicca-samuppannaṃ*), the leaving behind of that is stopping (*nirodho*).

These passages make clear that *nibbāna* is 'unborn' and 'unconstructed' etc. in being the stopping of all those ephemeral, *dukkha*, constructed processes which arise through the process of Conditioned Arising (*paṭicca-samuppāda*). It is a transcendent experience in which nothing which is conditioned, constructed or 'born' (subject to time) is present.[8]

(11.19) *Nibbāna*'s quality as 'unborn' is, specifically, due to the fact that it is the stopping of the causal-link known as 'birth' (*jāti*). Paras. 8.23–5 show that this link occurs not only at the start of a life, at conception, but also at the start of each perceptual cycle, in which the personality-factors are constantly re-generated. As is stated at Ps.II.241, *nibbāna* is 'unborn' as it is the stopping of the five personality-factors, which are to be seen as 'subject to birth'. As the personality-factors arising from the perceptual process are also said to be 'become' (Paras.8.24–5), *nibbāna*, as their transcending, is likewise 'unbecome'.

(11.20) *Nibbāna* is 'unmade' (*akata*) as it is the stopping of the constructing activities: 'knowing the destruction of the constructing activities, be, O Brahmin, a knower of the unmade' (Dhp.383). That is, *nibbāna* is not anything that is put together or compounded, it is *sui generis*, unitary and beyond all conditioning. It is thus likewise 'unconstructed'. As is made clear from It.37–8, in the last Para., it is 'unconstructed' because it is the 'tranquillizing of the constructing activities [9]'. This transcending, or 'leaving behind' of the construct*ed* through the cessation of the construct*ing* is partially illuminated from a passage at S.III.87, quoted at Para.8.4. This explains that each personality-factor is a constructed (*saṅkhata*) phenomenon which is arranged or synthesized into the state of itself [10] by the personality-factor known as the constructing activities. When this, as a factor or causal-link, is tranquillized to the point of stopping, constructed phenomena will no longer be generated, and only the 'unconstructed' will remain. This will be 'unconstructed' (*asaṅkhata*) in that it is free from *saṅkhāra*s in the sense of either 'construct*ing* activities' or 'construct*ed* states'.[11]

(11.21) The stopping of constructing activities is described at

Miln.325–26. This explains how someone comes to realize *nibbāna*:

> He who, sire, is practising rightly, masters the functioning (*pavattaṃ*) of the constructing activities; on mastering their functioning, he sees birth there, he sees ageing, he sees disease, he sees death . . .'.

That is, he realizes that the process of putting together only produces something that will later fall apart. The meditator thus 'turns away (*nibbindati*)' from the activities, seeing their functioning as dangerous and 'of much *dukkha*', and thinks:

> if only one could attain non-functioning (*appavattaṃ*) – that is the real, that is the excellent, that is to say the calming of all constructing activities (*sabba-saṅkhāra-samatho*) . . . stopping, *nibbāna*.

His *citta* thus 'leaps forward to non-functioning' and he joyfully thinks, 'I have obtained leaving behind'. This is then summed up by saying:

> by repeated attention, his *citta*, transcending functioning, enters on non-functioning. If he obtains non-functioning, sire, while practising rightly, he is said to realize *nibbāna*.

This very clearly sees the transcending of *dukkha*, during life, as a state where the constructing activities are transcended, and that this is 'stopping, *nibbāna*'. Admittedly, the *Milindapañha* may here be referring to the cessation of cognition and feeling, for at Miln.300 (see Para.10.15) it is said that the two occasions when *citta* is 'not functioning' is in the *bhavaṅga* state of dreamless sleep, and in cessation-attainment. Nevertheless, this reference to the 'non-functioning' of *citta* may not be the same as Miln.325–26 means by the 'non-functioning' of the *constructing activities*.

(11.22) If *nibbāna* during life is 'stable', 'deathless' and 'permanent', how can it be something that is not ever present in the Arahat? The answer to this is provided by a short discourse at S.III.24–5, on '*nirodha*':

> Material form, Ānanda, is impermanent, constructed, arisen from conditions, of the nature of (*-dhammam*) destruction,

> falling away (*vaya-*), fading (*virāga-*), stopping (*nirodha-*). From the stopping of this there is said to be 'stopping' [this is then repeated for each of the other four personality-factors].

The meaning of this is illustrated by parallel passages at S.IV.26–8, on the eighteen sensory 'elements' and the forms of stimulation and feeling arising from them. Each of these items is said to be 'of the nature of' 'birth', 'destruction', 'falling away', 'ageing', 'death', 'arising (*samudaya-*)' and 'stopping'. As shown at Para.8.23, this must refer to the fact that they constantly arise and cease. From this, it can be seen that the *nirodha* of S.III.24–5 is the stopping of the normal process of the constant arising-and-falling of the conditioned processes which comprise the personality-factors and elements. It is the stopping, or arresting, of the process in which particular instances of, say, feeling, arise and cease. As the stopping of such an unstable process, it is clearly 'stable', and though not ever-present in the Arahat, can be seen as 'permanent' (*nicca*) and 'deathless', as it is the stopping of all that is impermanent and subject to constant 'death'. This is clearly seen at Ps.II.238, quoted in Para.2.13: *nibbana* is permanent because it is the stopping of the personality-factors which are impermanent, and is 'deathless' (p.241) as it is the stopping of the personality-factors which are 'of a nature to die'. It can also be said that *nibbāna* in life is 'permanent' in the sense that it can be re-entered by the Arahat at any time – he does not 'fall away' from it – and is finally entered at death.

(11.23) It is notable that the 'early Suttas' do not actually say that *nibbāna* is 'eternal' (*sassata*), for it cannot be seen as lasting forever *in time*. Rather, it is 'timeless (*akāliko*)' (A.I.158), and, as later texts say, neither past, present nor future (Dhs.1416, Miln.270). While, from the outside, someone's attainment of it is an event in time, from within, it is beyond the flow of changing temporal events. If *nibbāna* is to be called 'eternal', as it is at Kvu.121, this must be because it is *beyond* time. The Arahat's full experience of *nibbāna*, as a state in which the personality-factors temporarily stop, might be seen as his 'participating in' this timeless reality. What such a state entails will be investigated in the next chapter.

NIBBĀNA AS A TIMELESS OBJECT OF INSIGHT

(11.24) The timeless *nibbāna* which is periodically participated in by the Arahat can also be perceived, but not entered, by lesser grades of saint. Such experiential knowledge of the existence and nature of *nibbāna* is first attained by the Stream-enterer, one who gains insight into the Four Holy Truths. A standard passage on Stream-entry goes:

> the Dhamma-eye, dustless, stainless arose to him that: whatever is of the nature to arise (*samudaya-dhammaṃ*), all that is of the nature to stop (*nirodha-dhammaṃ*). Then . . . as one who had seen Dhamma, attained to Dhamma, known Dhamma, plunged into Dhamma . . . (M.I.380).

This realization, often the stimulus to ordination in the early texts, is said to be where a person sees 'the stainless Dhamma, *nibbāna*, the unshaken state' (Thig.97). This 'seeing' is a seeing of the 'difficult to see' Dhamma fully known by the Buddha at his enlightenment, namely Conditioned Arising and *nibbāna* (M.I.167). For the Stream-enterer, insight into phenomena as 'of the nature to arise' can be seen as knowledge of Conditioned Arising, and insight into them as 'of the nature to stop' can be seen as knowledge of *nibbāna*, the stopping of all the links of Conditioned Arising (S.II.70). At S.II.118, the monk Nārada says that he has direct knowledge of Conditioned Arising, and says that ' "the stopping of becoming, *nibbāna*" is well-seen by me as it really is, by perfect wisdom, but I am not an Arahat, with cankers destroyed'. He then compares this to a thirsty man looking down a rope-less well at water that he is unable to drink. Nārada is clearly at least a Stream-enterer, but he cannot fully experience the *nibbāna* that he has seen as a distant object. Indeed, if one 'focuses *citta* on the deathless element' as 'This is the real . . . stopping, *nibbāna*', one *may* become an Arahat, but then one may only become a Non-returner (M.I.435–36). That is, experiential knowledge of *nibbāna* does not necessarily entail the full realisation of it.

(11.25) A state of high insight which has *nibbāna* as its object is the 'signless concentration' (*animitta-samādhi*), an advanced meditative state which, as 'constructed' (M.III.108), is not itself the same as the Arahat's full experience of *nibbāna* (A.IV.78). It is part of the Holy Eightfold Path (S.IV.360) which is itself simply the best of all constructed states (A.II.34). A number of different states can be seen as partially 'signless', but the one which is fully so is that which takes *nibbāna* as its object (Harvey, 1986). At M.I.296, the signless 'freedom of mind' (*ceto-vimutti*) is said to be attained when there is no attention paid to 'signs' (*nimitta*s) but attention is paid to the 'signless-element', which is clearly *nibbāna* (Ps.I.91). As regards the meaning of 'sign', in the Suttas it is taken to mean 'a delimited object of attention that may, or should be taken as indicating something beyond itself or the general features of that to which it belongs' (Harvey, 1986: 33). As the term is applied in the context of spiritual training, it can be used to refer to: the delusive appearance of phenomena as permanent, non-*dukkha* or as Self; sense-objects as targets of perception and as indicating particular features of the world; and mental images which arise in Calming (*samatha*) meditation, as a reflex of the mind's concentration eg. on a disc of earth, and the focus of further meditation (Harvey, 1986: 36).

(11.26) In the *Nissāya-vagga* of the *Aṅguttara Nikāya*, A.V. 318–26, are a number of passages which are clearly on the 'signless' apprehension of *nibbāna*. At A.V.321–22, Ānanda asks the Buddha:

> May it be, venerable sir, that a monk's acquiring of concentration may be of such a sort that he does not attend to the eye or visual forms . . . to body or touchables; though he does not attend to solidity (*paṭhaviṃ*, lit. 'earth'), cohesion, heat or motion; to the spheres of infinite space, or of infinite discernment, or of nothingness, or of neither cognition-nor-non-cognition; though he does not attend to this world, or a world beyond; to whatever is seen, heard, sensed, discerned, attained, sought after, thought round by mind: and yet he *does* attend?

To this, the Buddha replies that there is such a meditative concentration, in which a monk attends: 'This is the real . . . stopping, *nibbāna*'. This is clearly a case of turning the mind away from all 'signs' – the five physical sense-organs and their objects, the four physical elements (perhaps here as objects of *jhāna*), the four formless mystical states, any world, any object of the six senses – and turning the mind to *nibbāna*, which is beyond all such 'signs'. The movement towards the signless meditation can be seen as one of a progressive emptying, in which signs of both gross and subtle phenomena are gradually transcended. This can be seen from a parallel passage at M.III.104–09. Here, a monk is said to progressively 'attend to the perception' of human beings, a village, the forest, earth, each of the four formless states, and the signless-concentration, with each of the perceptions being 'empty' (*suñño*) of the previous ones.

(11.27) A *Nissāya-vagga* passage at A.V.318–19 indicates that the transcending of perceptual 'signs' is not simply a question of turning the mind away from them, but more a 'seeing through' them, so that they dissolve in the light of insight, allowing 'sight' of the signless *nibbāna*. In the passage, Ānanda asks the Buddha:

> May it be, venerable sir, that a monk's acquiring of concentration is of such a sort that in solidity he is not cognizant of solidity (*paṭhaviyaṃ paṭhavī-saññī*) . . . [this formula is then repeated for each of the remaining items at A.V.321–22, as in last Para.] . . . and yet he is cognizant (*saññī*)?

The Buddha replies that such a concentration exists, where a monk has the cognition: 'This is the real . . . stopping, *nibbāna*'. Here, even when applying the mind to various items, they are not perceived, as such: *in* solidity, no solidity is cognized. The commentary [12] explains 'having made solidity his object (*ārammaṇaṃ*), he would not be cognizant with the arisen cognition "solidity"'. Solidity is perceived, as it were, as empty of 'solidity': *saññā* – 'cognition' or 'interpretation', that which classifies or labels experience – does not latch onto a 'sign' as a basis for seeing solidity *as* solidity. Rather, the mind perceives the signless *nibbāna*.

(11.28) Another related passage illustrates this process. At A.V.324–26, the Buddha describes a monk who 'meditates (*jhāyati*)' in such a way that his meditation is not dependent on any of the phenomena listed at A.IV.321–22, and yet he *does* meditate. This suggests that the signless concentration is again being referred to. The way the monk meditates, here is such that 'in solidity, the cognition of solidity is *vibhūta*'. Now '*vibhūta*' can mean 'made clear' or 'destroyed', with the commentary (A.A.V.80) preferring the former:

> arisen cognition of four-fold or five-fold *jhāna*, with solidity as object, is *vibhūta*, unconcealed (*pākaṭā*) . . . here it is born *vibhūta* from the state of being seen as impermanent, *dukkha* and not-Self by means of insight.

What this means is shown by the *Paṭisambhidāmagga*, in its discussion of the signless, 'undirected' (*appaṇihita*) and 'emptiness' (*suññatā*) liberations. This explains that insight into impermanence leads to the first, insight into *dukkha* leads to the second, and insight into not-Self leads to the third (Ps.II.58). Nevertheless, if any of these liberations is developed in a sustained way, the others naturally develop (Ps.II.59). In the signless liberation, constructed phenomena are seen as 'limited and circumscribed (*pariccheda-parivaṭṭumato*)' (Ps.II.48) by their ephemeral nature. The move towards the signless apprehension of *nibbāna* could thus be seen as follows. When the mind thoroughly contemplates any condition phenomenon, such as solidity, as impermanent, it overcomes the 'sign' of permanence etc. so as to perceive merely a stream of changing sense-objects not 'indicative' of anything beyond themselves. Beyond this, it transcends even perceiving the sign of sense-objects. It 'sees through' these, no longer registering *what* has been the object of contemplation. This is because, having so developed the perception of the perpetual (arising and) cessation of such objects, it naturally turns away from this wearisome flux towards *nibbāna*, which is beyond all arising and ceasing (see Harvey, 1986: 43–4).

(11.29) *Nibbāna* as itself 'signless', 'undirected' and 'emptiness' (Ps.I.91–2) can be understood in the following way. It is 'signless' as it is devoid of signs indicative of anything graspable; it is the profound realm which is beyond all particular and limited phenomena, which are all subject to constant change. It is 'undirected' in that it lies beyond goal-directedness concerning conditioned phenomena, which are all *dukkha*: it is what is known when there is letting go of all these. It is 'emptiness' or 'void' in being free of all 'misinterpretation' (*abhinivesa*) of phenomena as 'Self' or 'permanent' etc. (Ps.II.67–8). Its nature is illustrated by the discussion of the emptiness 'freedom of mind' at M.I.297–98. This state concerns contemplation of phenomena as 'empty' (*suñña*) of Self, and its highest form, the Arahat's 'unshakeable freedom of mind', is empty of attachment, hatred and delusion. *Nibbāna* can thus be seen to be void of any ground for notions of 'I' – these can only arise from grasping at the personality-factors (Para.1.31) – and is devoid of attachment etc.

(11.30) The apprehension of *nibbāna* as a signless emptiness by 'seeing through' empty phenomena is of course reminiscent of the Mahāyāna Madhyamaka school's view: of *nibbāna* and the conditioned world being non-different, both being equally 'emptiness' (*śūnyatā*). Hints in this direction are in fact contained in the *Paṭisambhidāmagga*. This asserts that the Four Holy Truths are known by 'a single knowledge (*ekena ñāṇena*)', for they are 'one' in their nature as being true (or 'thus': *tatha*) and being not-Self (Ps.II.105). This suggests that *dukkha* (the first Truth), is known at the same time as *nibbāna*, the cessation of *dukkha* (the third Truth). This could be taken to imply that they are the same thing, but seen in different ways. The Pāli Canon contains no further hint in this direction, though. In any case, the above Madhyamaka-like perspective is only an *approach* to becoming an Arahat and attaining the full experience of *nibbānic* 'stopping', for it has been seen that the signless state is 'constructed' (Para.11.25), albeit at a very subtle level. To fully realize *nibbāna*, the unconstructed state, even the signless meditation must be transcended. Once *nibbāna* is attained, the Arahat may, at a later time, either fully participate in it again, or simply take this timeless, signless realm as the object of his attention. Thus it is said that an Arahat's 'field of action (*gocaro*) is emptiness and signless liberation' (Dhp.92).

(11.31) This chapter has thus shown that *nibbāna* during life is a transcendent, timeless experience which totally destroys attachment, hatred and delusion. Being what makes the Arahat an Arahat, it is also 'Arahatness'. It is a state in which all the personality-factors and causal links 'stop', but it is not the same as the 'cessation of cognition and feeling'. Being beyond all conditioned, constructed phenomena, with their constant arising and ceasing, it is unconditioned, unborn, and deathless. It is not experienced by the Arahat all the time, but he or she can periodically re-experience it before entering it for a final time at death. Being unconstructed, *nibbāna* is uncompounded, not consisting of any parts: so *nibbāna* in life and beyond death are not different *nibbāna*s, but the same state experienced in different contexts. *Nibbāna* can also be experienced in a more indirect way, as when a Stream-enterer gains insight into it. This knowledge-at-a-distance of it is often attained in a 'signless' state, where the mind attends to constructed phenomena in such a way that their insignificant, ephemeral nature allows the deathless, unconstructed realm beyond them to be seen. While the Arahat is able to fully participate in this signless realm of emptiness, by stopping his personality-factors, he may also simply take it as the object of a reviewing knowledge. *Nibbāna*, then, is a timeless realm which is first glimpsed at Stream-entry, periodically participated in, and also reviewed, by the Arahat, and entered once and for all at the Arahat's death.

12

NIBBĀNA AS A TRANSFORMED STATE OF DISCERNMENT

Discernment, non-manifestive, infinite, shining in every respect . . . (M.I.329–30).

(12.1) Having shown that the 'early Suttas' see *nibbāna*, even during life, as a state where all the personality-factors 'stop', this chapter will probe more deeply into what is said of this state. In particular, it will seek to show that, just as discernment (*viññāṇa*) is seen as the central factor in the normal unliberated state, (Chs.7–8), so it is that a form of discernment is regarded as attaining and actually *being nibbāna*. The importance of this is that it counteracts any impression that nibbānic stopping is viewed as merely a blank nothing. It shows, to some extent, what *nibbāna* positively *is*, and by so doing explains the link between a person, comprised of *dukkha* states, and *nibbāna*, which is the complete cessation of *dukkha* states.

(12.2) Rune Johansson's *The Psychology of Nirvana* has already argued that the *nibbāna* of the Pāli Suttas can be understood as a transformed state of *citta*. The arguments that he develops, though, are not in themselves very persuasive. This is largely due to that fact that '*citta*' is not a term of very precise usage in the Suttas. Consequently, passages suggesting that *citta* is what attains *nibbāna*, or that a form of *citta* 'is' *nibbāna*, might be put down to the use of 'loose' or 'conventional' language, if one so wishes. *Viññāṇa*', however, is a much more closely defined and exactly used term. Sutta passages linking it to *nibbāna* therefore need to be treated with careful attention – which has so far been done by others in only a preliminary way.[1] This chapter will thus focus on such passages, in preference to those concerning *citta*, which Johansson has investigated.

NIBBĀNA AS A FORM OF DISCERNMENT

(12.3) Two parallel passages are among those which are crucial in developing the argument of this chapter. These will first be quoted, and then analysed. At D.I.221–23, a monk goes to various types of gods, and finally to a Brahmā, seeking the answer to a question. The Brahmā boastfully claims that he is the creator of the world, and his attendant gods claim that he knows everything. Nevertheless, he cannot answer the monk's question, and shamefacedly says that he should really be asking the Buddha. The monk's question is:

> Where, now, sir, do these four great elements (*mahābhūtā*) stop (*nirujjhanti*) without remainder, that is to say the elements of solidity, cohesion, heat and motion? (p.221).

This question is first rephrased by the Buddha, so that it asks where the four elements 'have no footing' and the *sentient body* (*nāma-rūpa*) stops:

> Where do solidity, cohesion, heat and motion have no footing (*na gādhati*)?
> Where do long and short, course and fine, foul and lovely (have no footing)?
> Where are sentiency and body stopped without remainder (*nāmañ ca rupañ ca asesaṃ uparujjhatīti* [2])?

After thus rephrasing the question, the Buddha answers it:

> Discernment, non-manifestive, infinite, accessible from all round (*viññāṇaṃ anidassanaṃ anantaṃ sabbato pahaṃ*).
> – Here it is that solidity, cohesion, heat and motion have no footing,
> Here long and short, coarse and fine, foul and lovely (have no footing),
> Here sentiency and body are stopped without remainder.
> – With the stopping (*nirodhena*) of discernment, here, this is stopped (p.223).

(12.4) The second passage to be examined is at M.I.328–30. Here again, a Brahmā figures, as the Buddha is speaking to Baka the

Brahmā. As in the first passage, the Brahmā thinks he created the world, though he is more persistent in thinking that he knows more than the Buddha. The Buddha points out that, influential though Baka may be, holding sway 'as far as sun and moon revolve in their course', he is ignorant of such things as the kind of divine beings who are superior to him. The Buddha then continues:

> I, Brahmā, intuitively knowing solidity as solidity, to that extent knowing that which is not reached (*ananubhūtaṃ*) by the solidness of solidity, do not think: ('I' am) solidity, ('I' am) in solidity, ('I' am different) from solidity, I do not think 'solidity is mine', I do not salute solidity.

This is then repeated for the three other physical elements, creatures, gods, Pajāpati, Brahmā, four other types of divine beings, and the 'all (*sabbaṃ*)'. Baka then replies, 'if it is not reached by the allness of the all, take care lest it be vain, take care lest it be empty (*tucchakam*)'. That is, 'what in heaven or on earth could such a thing be?: there *is* nothing beyond "all"!'. To this the Buddha[3] replies:

> Discernment, non-manifestive, infinite, shining in every respect (*viññāṇaṃ anidassanaṃ anantaṃ sabbato-pabhaṃ*) that is not reached by the solidness of solidity . . . by the allness of the all' (p.329–30).

(12.5) Clearly these two passages are referring to the same state, the very same type of discernment, from the parallels in both wording and contexts. If these passages are to be used to link discernment to *nibbāna*, though, it must be shown that they are about *nibbāna*, as the commentaries, at least, specify (D.A.II.393–94 & M.A.II.412). A state where the sentient body stops and which is beyond the knowledge of even a Brahmā is certainly likely to be *nibbāna*. Moreover, 'the non-manifestive (*anidassanaṃ*)' is a term for *nibbāna* (in life): the destruction of attachment etc. (S.IV.370–71). A further confirmation comes from M.I.1–4. Here, it is said that it is only an Arahat that, from 'intuitively knowing' the very items listed at M.I.329–30, does not 'conceive (*maññati*)', '("I" am) solidity, ("I" am) in solidity, ("I" am different) from solidity, I do not think "solidity is mine", I do not salute solidity', and likewise for the other items. Moreover, this passage adds *nibbāna* as a further item which the Arahat has no conceits on. As what comes after 'the all' at M.I.4, *nibbāna* must therefore be what lies beyond 'the allness of the all' at M.I.329–30. Indeed, S.IV.23 says that one who does not conceive on the all, as above, is without grasping, and attains *nibbāna*. A final point is that 'the all' – the eighteen elements and states discernible by the six forms of discernment – is equivalent to *dukkha* (S.IV.39). What lies beyond the 'allness of the all' must thus be *nibbāna*, the cessation of *dukkha*. The passages at D.I.223 and M.I.329–30, then, clearly are intended as descriptions of *nibbāna* – in life, and probably beyond death, also.

(12.6) D.I.223 and M.I.329–30 therefore clearly say that *nibbāna* is a type of discernment – precisely what type will be investigated below. The commentary, D.A.II.393–94, tries to avoid this obvious conclusion by saying the '*viññāṇaṃ*', "discernment', means '*viññāṇitabban*', 'to be discerned'. That is, while admitting that *nibbāna* is meant, it takes it purely as an *object* of discernment, rather than as an actual *form* of discernment. But while *nibbāna can* simply be an *object* of discernment, as it is in the signless concentration (Para.11.26), the above passages clearly say that it itself *is* a form of discernment.

NIBBĀNIC DISCERNMENT AS 'STOPPED', 'OBJECTLESS' AND 'UNSUPPORTED'

(12.7) What kind of discernment is *nibbāna*, then? Among other things, it is said to be one which has undergone 'stopping'. This is clear from the fact that the first and last lines of the D.I.223 passage form a single answer to the question previously posed: the 'non-manifestive' discernment is also a 'stopped' discernment. As seen in the last chapter, the stopping of all the links of Conditioned Arising can take place during life. As the whole process of Conditioned Arising is spun out from the interaction of discernment and *nāma-rūpa* (Para.7.17), it is to be expected that *nibbāna*, the stopping of all the links, will be where *nāma-rūpa* stops due to the stopping of discernment, as at D.I.223. The importance of this stopping is highlighted by A.I.236, on *nibbāna* during life: 'To him who is released in the destruction of craving by the stopping of discernment (*viññāṇassa nirodhena*), the liberation of mind is like the extinction (*nibbānaṃ*) of a lamp'.[4]

(12.8) Does discernment simply cease to exist when it is 'stopped', though? This is not the view of the 'early Suttas'. This can be seen both from the fact that it has qualities – it is 'non-manifestive, infinite' – and from other independent evidence. This evidence in turn reveals more about the nibbānic discernment. The 'stopped' form of discernment is described at S.II.66 (cf. Para.8.5):

> Since, monks, one does not will, or plan, or have a latent tendency: this is not an object (*ārammaṇam*) for the maintenance (*ṭhitiyā*) of discernment; when there is no object, there is no support (*patiṭṭhā*) for discernment. So when discernment is unsupported (*appatiṭṭhite*) and not growing, there is no descent of the sentient body (*nāmarūpassa avakkanti*). From the stopping of the sentient body is the stopping of the sixfold sense-sphere [and thus the stopping of all the remaining causal links, all *dukkha*].

This clearly describes how the stopping of the constructing activities leads to the stopping of discernment, and thence of all the other causal links. It thus shows that 'stopped' discernment is that which lacks any 'object' or 'support'. Now such an 'unsupported' discernment is compared, at S.II.103, to a sunbeam which would 'settle (*patiṭṭhitā*)' on whatever was in its path, but in the absence of any such thing, it would be 'without any settling place (*appatiṭṭhitā*)'. As such a non-settling sunbeam is not non-existent, then neither is the 'unsupported', 'objectless' 'stopped' discernment to which it is compared.

(12.9) That this form of discernment is *nibbāna* is reinforced by S.III.54–5 (cf.45–6), quoted at Para.8.8. This shows that it is such 'unsupported' discernment, whose 'object is cut off', and which is 'without constructing activities' that is 'released' and 'attains *nibbāna*', clearly meaning *nibbāna* during life.

(12.10) Nibbānic discernment is again alluded to at S.I.1, which describes how the Buddha 'crossed the flood', i.e. attained *nibbāna*, when he was 'unsupported':

> When I, friend, am supported (*santiṭṭhāmi*), then I sink down; when I strive (*āyūhāmi*), then I am whirled about. Thus, friend, without support, unstriving (*appatiṭṭham anāyūham*), I crossed the flood.

This clearly alludes to the above 'unsupported' state free of constructing activities: at Ps.I.52, these are explained as 'strivings (*āyuhānā*)'. The paradoxical nature of the Buddha's statement: he sunk in the flood only when he had a support to depend on, is underlined by S.I.53, where the Buddha is asked:

> How does one cross the flood, not giving way day and night; in the deep which has no support (*appatiṭṭhe. . . gambhīre*), nothing to hang on to (*anālambe*), who would not sink?

Here, a paradoxical answer is not given, but the description of the 'deep' is interesting. S.I.1 and 53 together suggest that, though discernment is normally accompanied by 'strivings' – constructing activities –, and has a 'support' and something to 'hang on' to as object (*ālamba* is from the same root as *ārammaṇa*), these are in fact unreliable and weigh it down: only by dispensing with constructing activities and all hindering 'supports' can discernment freely swim in the 'deep' to safety.

UDĀNA 80 AS A DESCRIPTION OF NIBBĀNIC DISCERNMENT

(12.11) Perhaps the most well-known description of *nibbāna* is that given at Ud.80, which largely consists of a string of negations. This is often used to show that *nibbāna* is indescribably in any positive terms. The above analysis, however, enables a clear item-by-item interpretation of the passage as a description of the state of objectless, unsupported discernment. The passage runs as follows:

> There exists (*atthi*), monks, that sphere where there is neither solidity, cohesion, heat, nor motion; nor the spheres of infinite space, infinite discernment, nothingness, or neither-cognition-nor-non-cognition; neither this world, nor a world beyond, nor both, nor sun-and-moon; there, monks, I say there is no coming (*āgatiṃ*), nor going (*gatiṃ*), nor maintenance (*ṭhitiṃ*), nor falling away (*cutiṃ*), nor arising (*upapattiṃ*); that, surely, is without support, non-functioning, objectless (*appatiṭṭhaṃ appavattaṃ anārammaṇam*): just this is the end of *dukkha*.

This clearly sees 'that sphere', *nibbāna*, as 'that' which is unsupported and objectless, as Paras.8 and 9 above show 'stopped' discernment to be. Even the reference to 'non-functioning' falls exactly into line with this reading: Miln.325–26 (Para.11.21) sees non-functioning as relating to the suspension of the constructing activities, and S.III.54–5 says that this occurs when discernment is unsupported.

(12.12) What of the other aspects of Ud.80? The absence of the four physical elements and of the four formless spheres can be seen as a way of referring to the stopping of *nāma-rūpa*, the sentient body and external 'meaningful forms'. In the formless realms, when these are actual rebirths rather than meditational attainments, only mental phenomena exist. That is, there is no *rūpa*, form, in them, but only *nāma*, intentional mental states. *Nibbāna* as beyond the formless spheres is thus beyond *nāma*. The components of this stop in *nibbāna* as they all depend on stimulation, which in turn depends on a non-stopped form of discernment arising in one of the sense-channels (Paras.8.18–19). The four physical elements, on the other hand, are the primary constituents of *rūpa*. While Ud.80 says that these are absent in *nibbāna*, D.I.223 says, more specifically, that they 'have no footing' in this. This seems to relate to the situation of the stopping of the six sense-spheres, described at S.IV.98: here the six sense-organs stop and cognition of the sense-objects, such as visual form (*rūpa*), 'fade' (Para.11.12). In this situation, '*nāma-rūpa*' in the sense of 'meaningful forms' (see Para.8.11) are not taken as objects by discernment: they mean nothing to the person, so that discernment is not 'supported' by them. *Rūpa*, though, is also the sentient form of the person themselves, which is capable of being affected by cold and heat, hunger and thirst etc. (Para.8.16). Such a form is more than the mere collection of the four physical elements (solidity etc.). It must be enlivened and sensitized by the presence of 'vitality', 'heat' and discernment, and also be aided by the mental states comprising *nāma*. If discernment and *nāma* are 'stopped', so will *rūpa* be: it will not act as a body normally does, for the sense-organs will not be sensitive to objects, but be 'stopped'. With discernment stopped, moreover, there will be no 'birth' of a 'share of discernment' containing all the personality-factors, including *rūpa* (Paras.8.23–6). Thus, in the state of *nibbāna*, the physical elements of a person's body may remain, but they do not constitute a sentient organism, and, to such a person, physical (and mental) sense-objects 'fade' into insignificance and 'have no footing' in the objectless discernment.

(12.13) Continuing the analysis of Ud.80, *nibbāna* is beyond any 'world', for it is where the world stops 'in this fathom-long carcase' (S.I.62, Para.5.6). That is, all 'worlds' as moulded by conceit-laden conception, and the interpretations of cognition are transcended.[5] 'Sun-and-moon' are transcended by nibbānic discernment as this is much brighter: it is 'shining in every respect', and is beyond the knowledge of Brahmā, who only holds sway 'as far as sun and moon revolve in their course' (Para.12.4). *Nibbāna* is beyond 'coming', 'going', 'falling away' and 'arising' as these are 'becoming': phases of discernment which only occur when discernment is not stopped (Para.8.8). Such 'becoming' normally occurs between lives (Paras.6.15, 24–8) and between perceptual cycles (Paras.8.8–9). Ud.80 thus says that *nibbāna* is not only beyond any world of rebirth or normal experience, but is also beyond those phases of discernment which lead up to them. *Nibbāna* is also said to be without any 'maintenance', for S.II.66 shows that, without an object, discernment has neither 'maintenance' nor 'support' (Paras.12.8).[6]

(12.14) At this point, discussion of nibbānic discernment might progress in a number of different directions. It is intended, though, to deal with these in the following order. Firstly, further investigation of the nature of nibbānic discernment will be made. Secondly, it will be shown that nibbānic discernment was seen, in the 'early Suttas', to transcend the death of the Arahat. Thirdly, the relationship between nibbānic discernment and the Arahat's normal consciousness will be examined. Finally, Theravāda and Mahāyāna perspectives on the material of this chapter will be discussed.

THE NATURE OF NIBBĀNIC DISCERNMENT

(12.15) Among the epithets of this at D.I.223 and M.I.329–30 are that it is '*anidassanaṃ*', '*anantaṃ*' and '*sabbato pahaṃ/sabbato-pabhaṃ*'. It is 'infinite (*anantaṃ*)' for, like a sunbeam that does not settle anywhere (Para.12.8), it continues infinitely. It is, of course, different from the formless sphere of 'infinite discernment', for this has an object (Dhs.1417): the discernment which itself had 'infinite space' as object in the prior formless state (Vism.331). Nibbānic discernment is 'infinite', on the other hand, because it has *no* object. It is also 'shining in every respect (*sabbatopabhaṃ*)' because it must have the brilliance of wisdom (*paññā*), which is said to have the supreme 'shine' (*pabhā*) or 'radiance' (*ābha*) (A.II.139, S.I.6). If D.I.223's reading 'sabbato *pahaṃ*' is taken – even though D.A.II.393 gives '*pabhaṃ*' as an alternative here – then it literally means 'a ghat all round',[7] i.e. 'accessible from all round'. That is, though beyond time and space, it is, so to speak, always 'there' to be realized, being attainable by a variety of meditational routes, or even from deep insight arising from a sermon. Alternatively, '*pahaṃ*' may be seen as a contracted form of '*pajahan*', such that '*sabbato pahaṃ*' would mean 'drawing back from everything'. This would be appropriate as nibbānic discernment can be seen as 'drawing back' from all objects, such that the four elements and various worldly contrasts 'have no footing' in it.

(12.16) This is also close to the meaning of 'non-manifestive (*a-nidassanaṃ*)'. '*Nidassana*' is used variously to mean 'visible',[8] 'appearance/manifestation' (A.IV.305) and 'example', i.e. 'that which shows' (Sn.137). At M.I.127–28, it is said that one cannot, by using paint, make visible forms appear (*-pātubhāvaṃ*) in space (*ākāsa*) because space is '*anidassana*'. This suggests that this term refers to that which is invisible itself, and also incapable of having anything else made to appear on or in it. The translation 'non-manifestive' thus seems accurate. This is appropriate as an epithet for nibbānic discernment as this is 'where' *nāma-rūpa* stops and the four elements 'have no footing'. It is such that these have nowhere to 'place' themselves with respect to it, so as to 'appear' or 'be manifest'. Indeed, nibbānic discernment is 'not reached by the solidness of solidity . . . by the allness of the all' (Para.12.4). When it is taken as an object of attention, in the signless state, it is known when 'in solidity, he is not cognizant of solidity', and when the cognition of solidity etc. is 'made clear/destroyed' (Paras.11.27–8). It is also that which is experienced when the constructing activities do not construct each personality-factor into the state of itself (Para.11.20).[9] This all suggests that nibbānic discernment is a state beyond all limiting particulars: a state in which there are no constructing activities to direct discernment onto any item such as 'solidity' or even 'everything'. All such are seen as wholly impermanent/ephemeral, *dukkha*/ worthless, not-Self/insubstantial: not worth latching onto as a supporting focus or 'sign'. All are supposed 'supports' which produce limitation and do not actually help a person 'swim' across the flood of *dukkha* (Para.12.10). As seen in Para.2.10, the personality-factors are, respectively, like a lump of foam, a bubble, a mirage, a hollow plantain tree, and a conjurer's illusion. Even to take the 'signless', *nibbāna*, as itself an object of attention is to hold back from fully experiencing it. The signless state which has *nibbāna* as object is still a constructed state: it holds up *nibbāna* as the supreme state to-be-attained. Yet it does not quite reach the *total* letting-go, even of *nibbāna*, which allows *nibbāna*, objectless discernment, to be wholly realized. *Nibbāna*, like all else, is empty of 'Self', and must be positively recognized as such. When it is so recognized, any subtle clinging to it ends, and it is then fully realized.

(12.17) Such *nibbāna*, of course, is also seen as a form of 'discernment' (*viññāṇa*). As it has no *ārammaṇa* or object,[10] it does not have anything, as such, to discern. And yet it is still seen as a type of *viññāṇa*, perhaps here as knowledge (*-ñāṇa*) which is apart (*vi-*) from all else. While such a form of discernment is very hard to conceive of (Foreman, 1990), this is no reason for it not being *nibbāna*, for *nibbāna* is very hard to conceive of! The peculiar nature of nibbānic discernment means, in fact, that it cannot be seen as part of the discernment personality-factor (or causal-link). This is because this factor/link is defined as the six discernment-collections (Para.9.4), which all occur in perceptual processes and thus have objects.[11] They are, moreover, part of the 'all' (Para.12.5), while nibbānic discernment is 'not reached by the allness of the all'. That nibbānic discernment stands apart from the discernment which is a personality-factor, is also indicated by S.III.54–5 (Para.8.8). Here, discernment is not mentioned among the personality-factors which discernment takes as supporting objects, but then it *is* mentioned among the factors for which unsupported discernment has no attachment. This suggests that the 'supported' discernment is itself the normal personality-factor, while 'unsupported' discernment, in abandoning all such supports, also transcends supported-discernment, i.e. the discernment personality-factor. Similarly, at S.III.9–10 (Para.7.18), the personality-factors other than discernment are the 'home' for a 'home-haunting' discernment which has attachment for them, but an enlightened person is a 'home-abandoner' without attachment for these or even (normal) discernment. That the discernment personality-factor does not encompass *all* forms of discernment is also indicated by S.III.87 (Para.8.4), which says that while the constructing activities construct each of the first four personality-factors into the '*state of* (*-ttāya*)' itself, it only constructs discernment into '*what is meant by* (*-tthāya*)' discernment.[12] Thus when the constructing activities stop, the first four personality-factors are *absent*, but discernment only stops being what is normally meant by 'discernment', the personality-factor of that name. Clearly, though, ordinary discernment has the *potential* for transcending into the nibbānic state. Such a potential is best seen as embodied in the 'brightly shining *citta*' discussed in chapter 10.

(12.18) It has been seen at Para.7.15 how the complexities of the conditioned personality-factors are generated from the interaction of the six 'elements' (*dhātus*): discernment, space (*ākāsa*) and the four basic physical elements (solidity, cohesion, heat and motion). In *nibbāna*, this interplay is stopped. Nevertheless, *nibbāna* – objectless, unsupported discernment – is likened to space in various ways. Para.12.16 shows that space is also 'non-manifestive', and it is also capable of being 'infinite', as in the formless 'sphere of infinite space'. What is more, M.I.424 actually says that it is 'not supported (*patiṭṭhito*) anywhere' (cf. Miln.388). The Sarvāstivādin school went so far as to see space as unconstructed, like *nibbāna*, though the Theravādins insisted that *nibbāna* was the sole unconstructed state.[13] The similarity between the two states seems to be that just as space is a physical void, but not nothing (it is a basic element), so *nibbāna* is a mental void (*suññatā*; Paras.11.28–9), but not nothing: it is infinite discernment, with no object to limit it.

(12.19) Nibbānic discernment is where the vortical interplay of (conditioned) discernment and *nāma-rūpa* no longer spins out the conditioned realm of *dukkha* (Paras.7.17–20). While a monk 'abandons home for homelessness', nibbānic discernment is 'homeless' in a more radical sense, and truly 'dwells alone', being 'seclusion (*viveko*)' (Paras.3.9–10; 7.18). Of course, such 'aloneness' cannot be seen as the state of a 'lone individual'; for there is nothing in *nibbāna* that would allow individuation. There is nothing in 'one person's' *nibbāna* to separate it from that of another 'person'. As it is beyond time and spatial location, there can only be one *nibbāna*, however or whenever, or by whoever it comes to be experienced.

UNSUPPORTED DISCERNMENT AND *NIBBĀNA* BEYOND DEATH

(12.20) The above discussion of *nibbāna* has focussed on it as a transcendent state experienced during life, but it can be seen to apply equally to *anupādisesa nibbāna*, that which lies beyond the death of the Arahat (not 'after' it, for that implies *nibbāna* exists in time). A passage at Ud.9, on a recently dead Arahat, echoes a number of the passages discussed so far:

> Where cohesion, solidity, heat and motion have no footing (*na gādhati*),

There stars do not shine, the sun is not made manifest (*na ppakāsati*),
There the moon appears not, no darkness is there found,
So when the sage, the brahmin, by wisdom knows by himself,
Then he is freed from form and the formless, from pleasure and pain.

Here is a state where the physical elements 'have no footing' (D.I.223; Para.12.3), and there is an intrinsic radiance (M.I.329–30; Para.12.4) outshining sun and moon (Ud.80; Para.12.11), beyond the elements of form and the formless (Ud.80). As the cited passages have been shown to concern *nibbāna* as 'stopped', 'unsupported' discernment, then Ud.9 implies that this exists beyond the death of the Arahat.

(12.21) A passage at S.I.121–22 (cf.S.III.124) also shows this. It describes how Godhika comes to kill himself after persistently struggling, but failing, to attain *nibbāna*. The Buddha, immediately knowing of his suicide, nevertheless says that he had 'attained *nibbāna* (*parinibbuto*)'. That is, Godhika had attained this at the moment of his death, a type of such attainment referred to at Para.6.22. The Buddha then goes with some monks to where Godhika's body is and where a smokiness is seen going in every direction. The Buddha explains:

> This, monks, is Māra the evil one, who is seeking for the discernment of the clansman Godhika: 'where is the discernment of the clansman Godhika supported (*patiṭṭhitan*)?'. But, monks, with an unsupported discernment (*appatiṭṭhitena . . . viññāṇena*), the clansman Godhika has attained *nibbāna*.

This clearly seems to refer to unsupported discernment as existing beyond the death of an Arahat, with such a form of discernment being tantamount to attaining *nibbāna*. An alternative interpretation would be to see the unsupported discernment as existing before or at the moment of death.[14] However, as it has been independently shown that unsupported discernment is *nibbāna*, it would not be destroyed by death even if it had existed before it. In any case, the context clearly shows that Māra is looking for where Godhika's discernment is 'supported' *after death*. It is thus appropriate that the reference to his discernment being unsupported should also be to a state beyond death. Māra expects Godhika to be 'supported' in some form of rebirth, as he has elsewhere found dead people to be (M.I.327). The Buddha points out, though, that through attaining *nibbāna*, Godhika was beyond all such supports, in an 'unsupported' state beyond Māra's reach. In an abstract philosophical sense, the conditioned factors of his personality were an 'all' which were equivalent to 'Māra' (S.IV.38–9). On attaining *nibbāna*, however, Godhika's unsupported discernment was 'beyond the allness of the all'.

THE RELATION OF NIBBĀNIC DISCERNMENT TO THE ARAHAT'S NORMAL STATE

(12.22) Given the radical, transcendent nature of nibbānic discernment – in life and beyond death –, how is it related to an Arahat's normal state, which, as seen in chapter 11, is still affected by certain types of *dukkha*? An aspect of this is the question of how the nibbānic state is entered and left. S.II.66, at Paras.8.5 and 12.8, shows that discernment only has an object and support because the constructing activities of willing, planning and having a latent tendency direct it to one. Para.8.12–13 also shows that the arising of discernment at the start of a perceptual cycle is dependent on attention. It is thus appropriate to say that, when a person's awareness of all available objects as being impermanent, *dukkha* and not-Self becomes very strong, such objects will be turned away from as unworthy of continued attention. For one who is not yet an Arahat, or the Arahat simply 'reviewing' *nibbāna*, this will mean discernment takes *nibbāna* as object. But when constructing activities do not direct discernment onto even such a lofty, but not-Self, object, then nibbānic stopping ensues. For one who is already an Arahat, this stopping will be relatively easy, for an Arahat has destroyed all latent tendencies, or deeply ingrained dispositional errors. All he or she needs to do to enter stopping is to methodically attend to phenomena as not-Self etc. (Para.11.15), and thus stop willing and planning. To emerge from the nibbānic state, on the other hand, all that seems necessary is to will/plan once more. S.II.66 in fact says that discernment has an object if a person; a) wills, plans and has a latent tendency; or b) plans and has a latent tendency; or c) just has a latent tendency. Discernment is objectless when all three are absent. While the text does not specifically say so, it would seem that, in the case of the Arahat, willing (*cetanā*) (or planning) alone would be sufficient to re-activate the normal flow of conditioned processes in a person.

(12.23) For this to be the case, the Arahat must, of course, have *cetanā*. A potential problem, here, is that an Arahat does not generate any new karmic results, and *cetanā* is given as the definition of karma (A.III.415). According to the Abhidhamma, an Arahat's discernment is never karmically active, but is either in the form of results of past karma, or of neutral 'functional' states. It seems appropriate to say, however, that *cetanā* is karma only when it is still accompanied by latent tendencies. Certainly a living Arahat still has some constructing activities – of which *cetanā* is typical (S.III.60) –, for S.III.112 refers to these as among the *dukkha* processes that end at his death. Besides willing, desire (*chanda*) is also normally present in the Arahat, for at S.V.12–13 the Buddha says that he enters a state in which desire is quieted, implying that it was still there to quiet. It is, then, through the absence or presence of willing that the nibbānic state is entered and left by the Arahat.[15] His being able to enter nibbānic stopping 'at will' could be seen as an aspect of his freedom.

(12.24) Once discernment is no longer stopped, it can take a variety of objects as support, whether a sense object or one experienced in *jhāna* or the formless attainments. In the stopping of cognition and feeling, however, there would seem to be no object *or* discernment (Paras.10.15–19). As this is a situation very akin to nibbānic stopping, it is no wonder that undergoing it often leads directly on to becoming an Arahat (Paras.11.13–14). In the signless state, on the other hand, discernment has the subtlest of objects as support, *nibbāna* itself (Paras.11.25–6). Other wholesome 'supports' include the four 'foundations of mindfulness' (D.III.101). Again, it is said that a certain Arahat on his alms-round was 'supported in the essence (*sāre patiṭṭhitaṃ*)' (Ud.4), with 'virtue, meditation, wisdom and freedom', being described as four 'essences' (*sāras*) (A.II.141). Such references, demonstrate that 'unsupported' (*appatiṭṭhita*) discernment is not the same as an Arahat's normal non-clinging, non-fixated state of mind; for they show that even an Arahat has a 'supported' mind in normal consciousness. Admittedly, the 'early Suttas' do contain one reference to a *citta* which is '*apatiṭṭhita*' while in normal consciousness, but here it relates to the practice of 'guarding the sense doors', which is part of the path – being an aid to virtuous conduct – not its goal (S.V.74). The passage refers to a person's *citta* as inwardly 'well composed/settled' (*susaṇṭhita*) in the face of sense objects, so that pleasant ones do not give rise to attachment, and in response to unpleasant ones, he is 'not discontented, his *citta* is not *patiṭṭhita* (*apatiṭṭhita-citto*), his mind is not undone (*ādīna-mānaso*), his heart has no ill-will (*avyāpanna-cetaso*)'. Here, the commentary explains '*apatiṭṭhita-citto*', 'a *citta* not hard/rough (*atiṭṭha-*) because of defilements' (S.A.III.145–46). That is, in *this* context, a *citta* which is '*patiṭṭhita*' is one which responds in a sharp way, overly focussed on an object of dislike. Of course, one can be without such reaction-against-the-unpleasant without thereby having a mind which is totally 'unsupported'. So this is not a case of a person's discernment being fully 'unsupported' in normal consciousness.

(12.25) An alternative perspective on some of the above is offered by Rune Johansson, who gives what could be called a 'layer' model of the enlightened mind. He holds that if the 'discernment, non-manifestive, infinite . . .' passage describes *nibbāna*, it must describe an ever-present 'layer' of the Arahat's *citta* which is different from the 'surface layer which consists of everyday processes, perceptions and reflections' (1969: 77). He also sees such passages as describing 'a deeper and more permanent level of consciousness, which can be characterised as a background of understanding, calm confidence and freedom from desire' (p.53–4). He uses such a model to account for the fact that, as well as 'stopped' discernment, an Arahat has 'conscious processes as long as he lives' (p.77). The model is inappropriate, however, for it has been shown that the Arahat's ordinary discernment is the very process which is stopped, along with all other mental content, in nibbānic stopping. Discernment, then, cannot be simultaneously stopped and unstopped. Only the timeless realm of *nibbāna*, as 'seen', for example by the Stream-enterer (Para.11.24), exists 'all the time', but then this is 'there' even for ordinary people, who lack any knowledge of it. For an Arahat to 'participate' in this, however, his normal consciousness must be transcended.

(12.26) What might be called a 'pseudo-layer' model is for the mind to rapidly alternate between an objectless and with-object state. This is unlikely, though, as entry to the objectless state requires specific attention to phenomena as not-Self etc. Nevertheless, an Arahat who preserved strong insight could possibly have perceptual cycles which alternated between ones having objects (worldly or even *nibbāna*) and those without. Having said this, it seems that even the Buddha needed to withdraw from normal activities for a period in order to re-enter *nibbāna* (Para.11.10). To walk down the road with the mind hopping in and out of a stopped, objectless state, might possibly be a risky, or at least very slow, process! Perhaps in a meditative sitting, such alternation would be possible.

(12.27) What, though, of the relationship between nibbānic discernment and the *bhavaṅga* discernment/brightly shining *citta* investigated in chapter 10? Neither of these is the same as the normal six kinds of discernment arising in the processing of physical or mental objects. Nibbānic discernment is 'shining in every respect', while *bhavaṅga* is 'brightly shining'. Moreover, S.III.54–5 (Para 8.8), has been cited in the proof of both a *bhavaṅga*-like 'root' discernment (Paras.10.6–7) and of the unsupported nibbānic discernment (Para.12.9). How, then, are the two related? Could they be:

i) the same, in all people, with only the Arahat coming to know such a *nibbāna*-within?
ii) the same, in the case of the Arahat only? so that between each perceptual cycle, the Arahat's mind always enters an objectless state, while at certain times *all* object-directed processes are suspended?

The first of these possibilities is ruled out, however, by the view that *bhavaṅga* has an object, as asserted both in developed Theravāda theory (Vism.458) and S.III.54–5, which implies that even *bhavaṅga*-like 'root' discernment is 'planted' in *nāma-rūpa*, taking it as object. Moreover, Paras.10.31–3 make clear that, even when the brightly shining *citta* (*bhavaṅga*) is uncovered by defilements, when the mind is poised for the higher knowledges, it still has to go *on* to attain *nibbāna*. So such a radiant *citta* cannot be an 'underlying' *nibbāna* present in all. As regards the second possibility, this is ruled out by the Theravādin Abhidhamma; for *Paṭṭhāna* I.411 (CR.461) says that *bhavaṅga* is 'grasped at (*upādiṇṇa*-)', giving no indication that this is not a universal statement applying even in the case of the Arahat. As Dhs.1211–12 sees what is 'grasped at' as the fruition of karma, it must be a product of constructing activities. Therefore whatever is 'grasped at' is constructed, and cannot be the same as the unconstructed discernment which is *nibbāna*. A second argument, here, is that there is 'coming and going' of discernment – i.e. becoming (Para.12.13) – only when discernment has an object (S.III.54–5). As *nibbāna* is objectless and without 'coming and going' (Ud.80), there can be no 'becoming' there. As such 'becoming', in Sutta language, is what is later referred to as *bhavaṅga* (Para.10.8), it is highly improbable that *bhavaṅga* could exist in, or be *nibbāna*.

(12.28) *Bhavaṅga*/brightly shining *citta* cannot be seen as *nibbāna*, then. It is, nevertheless, the 'natural' state of mind which, when uncovered by defilements, is the ideal springboard for the attaining of *nibbāna* (Para.10.32). As seen at Paras. 10.33–6, it thus became part of the basis for Mahāyāna ideas on the Buddha-nature. In the 'early Suttas', it is a radiant level of mind which, when uncovered, is that from which the non-manifestive, nibbānic discernment, 'shining in every respect', can flash forth, destroying the possibility of any more defilements arising. For the Arahat in normal consciousness, the shining *citta* is thus ever free of defilements, but in nibbānic stopping, even this conditioned state of discernment is transcended.[16] *Nibbāna* is like a fire that has gone out (Para.11.5) – with more fuel (the personality-factors) left to burn, in the case of *nibbāna* in life, but with none in the case of *nibbāna* beyond death. *Bhavaṅga*, on the other hand, is like the root of a burning fire or, in dreamless sleep, fire latent in fuel (Paras.10.24).

THERAVĀDIN PERSPECTIVES

(12.29) The classical Theravādin view, as expressed from the time of early interpretative texts – the Canonical Abhidhamma, the *Paṭisambhidāmagga* and the *Niddesa* – is other than that developed in this and the last chapter. The only kind of realization of *nibbāna* that these texts envisage is the knowledge of it *as an object*. It is seen as known in this way by the four 'Paths' (*magga*s) and the four 'Fruits' (*phala*s). These technical Abhidhamma terms relate to the four grades of sainthood: Stream-enterer, Once-returner, Non-returner and Arahat. In the case of each of these, a momentary Path-*citta* is said to arise, with *nibbāna* as object, and then a few moments of Fruit-*citta* follow, which also take *nibbāna* as object. The basis of this developed view can be seen in the statements that all the Paths and Fruits have an object (*ārammaāṇa*) (Dhs.1408) and that *nibbāna* – as 'dispassion' (*virāga*) or 'freedom' (*vimutti*) – is this object, with the Paths and Fruits being 'supported (*patiṭṭhito*)' in it (Ps.II.140ff.). Not only this, but the Theravādin view sees discernment as 'stopped' at the time of *all* the Paths and Fruits. This is seen from Nd.II.245, in its comment on Sn.1037, 'Where sentiency and body (*nāmañ ca rūpañ ca*) are stopped without remainder, by the stopping of discernment, here, this is stopped' (cf. D.I.223). The full comment is:

> By the stopping of discernment (which comes) from constructing activities (*abhisaṅkhārā viññāṇassa*) by the knowledge of the Path of Stream-entry, sentiency and body which

would arise in the round of rebirth of inconceivable beginning, setting aside seven becomings [ie. lives], here these stop. . . . By the stopping of discernment (which comes) from constructing activities by the knowledge of the Path of Arahatness, sentiency and body which would arise (after death), here these stop. By the stopping of the last discernment of the Arahat attaining *nibbāna* in the element of *nibbāna* without-remainder-of-the-grasped-at, wisdom, mindfulness, sentiency and body, here these stop.

The aspect of this which sees 'stopping' as only a partial affair has already been criticised at Para.11.8. A further criticism is that *nibbāna* during life is clearly seen as unconstructed (*asaṅkhata*) (Para.11.17), and D.III.275 sees 'constructed' and 'arisen from conditions (*paṭicca-samuppannaṃ*)' as synonyms (Para.11.18). *Nibbāna* during life, as unconstructed, is therefore 'where' *all* aspects of the conditioned links of Conditioned Arising (*paṭicca-samuppāda*) stop: not where some stop and some remain as before.

(12.30) In the Abhidhamma, it is said that Conditioned Arising still operates at the time of the Paths and Fruits, with discernment being in the form of conceptional-discernment[17] As seen above, the type of discernment the Theravāda *does* see as stopping at the time of the Paths and Fruits is that which comes from the constructing activities. Steven Collins discusses this commentarial idea of '*abhisaṅkhāra-viññāṇa*' in some detail (1982: 205–08). He cites the commentary (Sn.A.505–06) on 'stopping of discernment' at Sn.734 (Para.11.11) as saying that this is the stopping of 'construction-consciousness born together with karma'. He goes on to argue that '*abhisaṅkhāra-viññāṇa*' can refer to both construct*ive* and construct*ed* discernment. He then says that when *nibbāna* during life is attained, 'then *constructive*-consciousness is completely destroyed and no further life will be constructed', but that '*constructed*-consciousness' continues, as a result of past karma, until the death of the Arahat (p.207). The trouble with this Therāvada interpretation is that i) it ignores the fact that Sutta passages on the 'stopping' of the discernment link (Paras.12.8–9) give not the slightest hint that they are talking about anything other than the 'stopping' of *all* forms of discernment. If discernment is not wholly stopped, and if it still has an object and support, then the normal flow of conditioned processes will continue, and *nibbāna* will not be fully realized. Moreover, it has already been argued (Para.12.23) that an Arahat in normal consciousness must have some types of constructing activities (in order to perform any actions). So his discernment is *not* only in the form of the results of past constructing activities. As for the view that the Paths and Fruits of the non-Arahat (and even the Path of the Arahat) have *nibbāna* as object, this is unobjectionable as far as the view of the 'early Suttas' goes. Such knowledge of *nibbāna* is in the signless state, however, and so is 'constructed' (Para.11.25). The Arahat's full participation in *nibbāna*, however, goes beyond all such constructed states, and is also 'where' all constructing activities have temporarily ceased. The Theravādin understanding of the 'stopping' of discernment, and the Arahat's experience of *nibbāna*, is thus out of tune with the perspective found in the 'early Suttas'.

(12.31) The Theravādin Abhidhamma does, though, contain a passage that implies that discernment, were it to be genuinely objectless, would be *nibbāna*. The same passage which says that the Paths and Fruits have an object (Dhs.1408) also lists only two states which have no object: material form (*rūpa*) and *nibbāna*. As discernment is clearly not the same as material form, then it must, if it were to become objectless, be *nibbāna*. Dhs.1309 also includes *nibbāna* (as the 'unconstructed') among those states which are included in '*nāma*': 'sentiency' or, literally, 'name'. As this term, in the Abhidhamma, is normally used to cover any mental state (including discernment, unlike in Sutta usage), this clearly regards *nibbāna* as in some sense a mental state. Nevertheless, Dhs.1511 says that *nibbāna* is 'not *citta*'. While *citta* is normally synonymous with discernment, this statement need not, on its own, rule out that the nibbānic discernment of the 'early Suttas' is *nibbāna*. This is for three reasons. Firstly, because nibbānic discernment is not what is normally 'meant by' discernment (Para.12.17). Secondly, because the Abhidhamma sees *citta* as a term covering only the six forms of sense-discernment and the mind-organ (*mano*) (Dhs.1510): none of which is nibbānic discernment. Thirdly, because, as such discernment is unconstructed, it can hardly be said to be a '*citta*' or 'mind-*set*': a discernment 'set up' by the constructing activities such as *cetanā* (willing), and with such states accompanying it (Paras.7.2, 9–11).

(12.32) Some twentieth century Theravādin writers express a view not unlike the one developed in this chapter. In 'A Dialogue on *Nibbāna*', the Burmese layman S.Z.Aung portrays a hypothetical debate on *nibbāna*. Here, one monk-debater expresses the view that 'a nibbānic being consists of the fruitional consciousness of highest Ariyanship solely occupied with its own tranquillity as object' (p.253). This says that *nibbāna* is a form of consciousness/discernment, though one with an object, yet the monk also says 'The subject and object are merged in one reality, *nibbāna*' (p.251). Similar ideas are also present in the Thai meditation tradition. Speaking of the 'unshakeable state of meditation' of the reputed Arahat Acharn Mun, Acharn Mahā Boowa states:

> Within such a lofty condition, mind rests with dharma and dharma with mind; mind is dharma and dharma is mind. . . This condition is the entire extinction of the mundane world (1976: 140).[18]

As A.III.35 explains the Dhamma/Dharma refuge as *nibbāna*, this seems to say that, in a certain state, an Arahat's mind is the same as *nibbāna*, and the conditioned world is ended. Mahā Boowa also states that 'the *Citta* by itself has no *Dukkha*' (1980: 13), that the pure *citta* of the Arahat is 'permanent' (p.30), but 'the permanence (unchangingness) of the pure *Citta* is not what the world understands "permanence" to mean' (p.37), and that the pure *citta* is different from the brightly shining *citta* (p.35). There is thus clearly a strand of Theravādin thought which is open to the type of interpretation developed in this chapter. The fact that early Theravādin exegetical texts do not support this interpretation need not be taken as a fatal objection to it. As has been seen in chapter 6, such texts are also out of tune with the 'early Suttas' on the subject of an 'intermediary existence' between lives. Because a Sutta is among those collected by the Theravādins does not mean that they must therefore have the best interpretation of it!

MAYĀYĀNA PERSPECTIVES

(12.33) Aspects of Mahāyāna thought, in fact, are akin to the interpretation developed in this chapter. In the Yogācāra school, the aim is to overcome the delusive splitting of experience into the duality of a 'grasper' and the 'graspable': i.e. an inner 'subject' and outer 'objects'. This is because it teaches that all that is known is is *citta-mātra*, or 'mind-only'. All that is ever actually experienced is an unbifurcated flow of *citta*s and accompanying mental qualities. The subject-object split is a misinterpretation of this: both a Self-subject and 'outer' objects are projections for which there is no good evidence. When this is fully realized, a state beyond the error of dualism is reached. As Sthiramati's commentary on Vasubandhu's *Triṃśatikā* v.28 puts it:

> It is thus that there arises the knowledge (*jñānam*) which is homogenous, without object (*-anālambya-*), free from discrimination (*nirvikalpam*) and supramundane. The tendencies to treat the object and subject as distinct and real entities are forsaken, and thought (*cittam*) is established in the true nature of one's own thought (*sva-citta-dharmatāyām*).[19]

The following verse of the *Triṃśatikā* itself says:

> That indeed is the supramundane knowledge
> When one has no mind (*acitto*) that knows ,
> And no object for its support (*'nupalambho*);
> It follows the revulsion of basis . . .
>
> (Kochumuttom, 1982: 160).

As such an enlightened *citta* ('thought'/'mind') is contentless, it is hardly what is normally meant by '*citta*'. In this, it is like the stopped discernment of the 'early Suttas', which is not what is normally meant by 'discernment' (Para.12.17). The Yogācāra perspective also sees *nirvāṇa* as an object-transcending state of discernment. As stated by the *Laṅkāvatāra Sūtra* (p.62), 'Nirvāṇa is the Ālayavijnāna where revulsion takes place by self-realization', such that 'the getting rid of discriminating (*vikalpasya*) conceptional discernment – this is said to be Nirvāṇa . . . when conceptional discernment is got rid of, the seven discernments are also got rid of' (p.126–27). Here, the *ālaya-vijñāna* is the underlying 'home-' or 'store-discernment' which projects out of itself the other forms of discernment (*vijñāna*s) which appear to be aware of objects. When this situation is experientially understood, there is a 'revulsion' or turning about, in the store-discernment, and the whole system collapses. It is then known that 'The triple world is no other than discrimination, there are no external objects (*bāhyamarthaṃ*)' (p.186). The *Vimalakīrti-Nirdeśa Sūtra* likewise says, on the non-dual enlightened state, 'That which arises from an object (*ālambanaprabhāvita*) is duality. The absence of an object (*nirālambana*) is non-duality' (Lamotte, 1976: 200).

(12.34) Such passages are clearly supportive of the idea of *nibbāna* as an objectless mental state, as argued in this chapter. The Yogācāra idea of the world of 'objects' as a mere projection, though, does not find support in the 'early Suttas', which merely say that sense-input comes to be distorted by the interpreting mind (Paras.5.5–11), with 'supporting' objects being unreliable (Para.12.10). Mahāyāna texts also talk of *nirvāṇa* in terms of a *citta* which is 'unsupported': '*apratiṣṭhita*', the Sanskrit equivalent of Pāli '*appatiṭṭhita*'. The *Vajracchedikā Prajñā-paramitā Sūtra* clearly sees Buddhahood, the genuine *nirvāṇa* in the Mahāyāna, as such an unsupported *citta*:

> Therefore then, Subhuti, the Bodhi-being, the great being, after he has got rid of all perceptions (*-saṃjñā-*), should raise his thought (*cittam*) to the utmost, right and perfect enlightenment (*samyaksambodhau*). He should produce a thought which is unsupported by forms (*na rūpa-pratiṣṭhitam*), sounds, smells, tastes, touchables or mind-objects, unsupported by dharma, unsupported by no-dharma, unsupported by anything. And why? All supports have actually no support (*yat pratiṣṭhitam tad eva-apratiṣṭhitam*). It is for this reason that the Tathagata teaches: By an unsupported Bodhisattva should a gift be given, not by one supported by forms, sounds, smells, tastes, touchables or mind-objects (Conze, 1958: 54, with 1957: 41–2).

This passage partly refers back to an earlier passage where is is said that the Bodhisattva should 'not be supported anywhere' when he gives a gift, i.e. he 'should give gifts in such a way that he is not supported by the notion (*-samjñāyām*) of a sign (*nimitta-*)' (p.26). The production of an 'unsupported thought' is also referred to in section 10.c of the text, with Conze seeing this as 'final Nirvana', the 'last stage a Bodhisattva can reach' (p.47). Such passages clearly see *nirvāṇa* as a state where a person has no cognition/perception/notion (Sanskrit *samjñā*, Pāli *saññā*), particularly none focussed on a perceptual 'sign', and yet has an operative *citta*: one which is not 'supported' on anything. As it is not 'supported' on Dharma, it must, surely, not even be supported on signless *nirvāṇa*, but simply be this. Nevertheless, the Sutra sees this as possible at the time of (or immediately after?) action in the world, e.g. giving a gift. This is because everything is seen as 'empty' of inherent existence or essence. One with true wisdom sees that there is no substantial thing there to act as a genuine 'support' of the mind: 'all supports have actually no support'. His giving is a spontaneous action performed in a space where all supposedly 'solid' 'things' and 'people' are seen as empty essence-less fluxes, which present nothing for the mind to cling to or fixate on.

(12.35) In his Rome edition of the Sanskrit text (p.95–6), Conze offers a long list of 'other possible translations' for the term *apratiṣṭhita*:

> **I.** Derived from relations between bodies: 1. not rely on anything; 2. unsupported by anything, or unsupported anywhere; 3. not dependent on anything, or nothing to be depended upon; 4. not stand about anywhere; 5. not be established anywhere; 6. not carried by anything; 7. not fixed on anything; 8. not rest on anything; 9. not lean on anything; 10. not hold onto anything; 11. not abide in anything, or, not intent on anything abiding anywhere; 12. not attached to anything; 13. not cling to anything.
>
> **II.** Derived from emotional experiences: 14. not settling down anywhere; 15. make yourself nowhere at home; 16. not seek a secure basis anywhere; 17. seek no refuge, or security, anywhere; 18. not rejoice in anything.
>
> **III.** Derived from social relationships: 19. expect no help from anything; 20. trusting in nothing (except perfect wisdom); 21. without believing in anything.

Such an explanation could be seen as describing a state where the mind is both totally self-reliant and fluidly moving through the world without 'sticking' to any particular item, a state of total 'letting go' and non-clinging. It is notable, though, that none of this implies that the 'unsupported' *citta* literally has no object, only that it does not construe its 'objects' in such a way as to cling to them. As argued at Para.12.24, though, the 'early Suttas' see the 'unsupported' discernment as not identical with the normal non-clinging state of the Arahat, for this is one which is still 'supported'.

12.36 The *Aṣṭasāhasrikā Prajñā-pāramitā Sūtra*, one of the earliest Mahāyāna texts, also refers to an 'unsupported' state:

> Nowhere did the Tathagata take his stand, because his mind sought no support. He stood neither in what is conditioned, nor in what is unconditioned, nor did he emerge from them (Conze, 1973: 98).

The text recommends that the Bodhisattva should train himself in this way, 'As the Tathagata is stationed, so will I stand, well placed because without a place to stand on' (p.98). This is the state of 'standing in emptiness', where a person 'does not take his stand on' any of a long list of items, including the factors of the path, Arahatship and Buddhahood (p.97).

(12.37) The notion of 'standing' neither in the conditioned world nor in the unconditioned, *nirvāṇa*, is taken up in the Yogācāra term for the type of *nirvāṇa* favoured by the Mahāyāna: *apratiṣṭhita-nirvāṇa*, 'non-abiding *nirvāṇa*', which is seen as different from the two 'elements' of *nirvāṇa* discussed in the Pāli texts (see Para.11.2). In his detailed discussion of *apratiṣṭhita-nirvāṇa*, Gadjin Nagao (1981) sees it as the only *nirvāṇa* attained by Bodhisattvas or *tathāgata*s (p.62). The basic idea is that it is a state where a Bodhisattva attains *nirvāṇa* (in life), due to his wisdom, but through his compassion, he has no intention of passing away into *nirvāṇa* beyond death. This would be to abandon beings in *saṃsāra* (the round of rebirths). At death, he thus remains in *saṃsāra*, though is undefiled by it, so as to continue helping others. This applies to a Bodhisattva from stage eight of the ten-stage Bodhisattva-path, when the Bodhisattva is irreversibly destined for Buddhahood (p.66). Nagao sees such a *nirvāṇa* as one which is not 'dwelt in' or 'clung to' (p.64). The advanced Bodhisattva dwells in/clings to neither *nirvāṇa* nor *saṃsāra*, for he has attained the non-dual 'equality wisdom' that knows that they are not really different (p.67). Nagao goes on to discuss the way in which this non-abandoning of *saṃsāra* is done. This is to be reborn 'willingly, volitionally' (*saṃcintya-*) in a way which is not driven by karma or defilements, as it is for all other types of being (p.68–71). Though he knows *saṃsāra* is not ultimately real, the Bodhisattva manifests himself 'in' 'it' to help the 'beings' there. The *Laṅkāvatāra Sūtra* (p.118–19) describes how the advanced Bodhisattva, having attained 'revulsion of the basis', i.e. *nirvāṇa,* enters a meditative concentration in which he attains two forms of *manomaya-kāya*, or mind-made body. With the first of these, he can travel at will to 'Buddha-lands' throughout the universe, and with the second, he can take on the form of a variety of class of beings, in the round of rebirths, to help others towards liberation. Such a mind-made body is not a substantial entity, for nothing is this, but is like a conjurer's magical illusion, 'The personality which a Bodhisattva assumes is not real, and yet it is perceived when he works for the benefit of beings'.[20]

(12.38) The above ideas are clearly not identical with those of the 'early Suttas', but contain interesting echoes of them. It has been argued, above, that the state of nibbānic stopping is entered by the suspension of willing, and left by the resumption of willing. This accords with the idea of the advanced Bodhisattva manifesting himself in *saṃsāra* 'at will'. However, whereas the 'early Suttas' see the full realization of *nibbāna* as an 'unsupported', objectless state of discernment, where other mental factors are absent and activity in the world does not seem possible, the Mahāyāna sees 'non-abiding' *nirvāṇa* as compatible with action in the world. Only if the Arahat rapidly alternated between objectless, nibbānic discernment and object-directed states of discernment (cf. Para.12.26) could these two perspectives be brought together. To do this, of course, could be seen as a case of being 'unsupported' in either *nibbāna* or *saṃsāra*. However, it has been argued that, even in the nibbānic state itself, the Arahat is 'unsupported', i.e. he does not take even *nibbāna* as an object of his discernment, but *is nibbāna*. Only when the mind takes *nibbāna* as an object is it 'supported' in it, according to the 'early Sutta' perspective. As the Mahāyāna sees the Arahats as inferior to the Bodhisattvas, the former were seen as attaining an inferior '*nirvāṇa*'. The Mahāyāna view, here, could be taken to mean that the Arahat is 'supported' in *nirvāṇa*, i.e. merely takes it as the object of his knowledge, and is attached to it as something that he will only fully enter at death. A being who had already entered it during life, however, by attaining an 'unsupported' discernment/*citta*, would know that this state could be fully entered at any time, without immediately bringing rebirth to an end. In that case, further rebirths – taken purely out of a motive of compassion – would be no impediment to continuing to fully experience *nirvāṇa*. The 'early Suttas', though, contain no hint of an enlightened person choosing to remain in *saṃsāra* after death. From the perspective of the 'early Suttas', the unsupported nibbānic state would be either dwelt in for specific, limited periods, or perhaps a state which rapidly alternated with normal consciousness. In the Mahāyāna perspective, though, *saṃsāra* and *nirvāṇa* are not ultimately different, so it makes sense to say that the Bodhisattva can be 'in' *nirvāṇa* and *saṃsāra* literally simultaneously.

(12.39) This chapter has shown that, in the perspective of the 'early Suttas', *nibbāna* is a radically transformed state of discernment. By contemplation of *all* worldly phenomena, however subtle, as ephemeral, unsatisfactory and insubstantial (impermanent, *dukkha* and not-Self), and thus as unworthy of attention, discernment first comes to have world-transcending *nibbāna* as a supporting object. When there is letting go even of this, the mind stops all willing, and discernment is not directed by constructing activities onto *any* objects. Being thus unconstructed, it *is nibbāna*. In this state it is 'stopped', not being what is normally meant by 'discernment' (*viññāṇa*), and not the same as the normal discernment personality-factor. It is discernment from which all limiting objects have dropped away, so that it is infinite, limitless. Like space, on which nothing can be drawn, it is 'non-manifestive': objects 'gain no footing' in it. Normally meaningful forms have no way of placing themselves in respect of it so as to be apprehended, for they have faded into insignificance. No worldly quality, be it the 'solidness of solidity' or the 'allness of the all' can touch it, for it is 'not reached by' any of them. When itself apprehended as an object, this is done in a 'signless' state where even in such phenomena as solidity, no 'solidity' is recognized: such perceptual 'signs' are transcended as 'supports' which are in fact unreliable. They do not genuinely help a person 'swim' across the current of *dukkha* to the 'other shore', the unconstructed *nibbāna*. Nibbānic discernment is a state of blissful 'seclusion' from all worldly phenomena, but it is not something 'alone' in a world of 'others'. *Nibbāna* is beyond the possibility of number and counting: the same unique *nibbāna* is realized by all Arahats.

(12.40) Such nibbānic discernment exists whenever the Arahat fully experiences *nibbāna* during life, and also exists when the *dukkha* personality-factors finally drop away at the Arahat's death. In either case, nibbānic discernment is without *nāma-rūpa*, the sentient body, for even in life the stopping of discernment totally suspends the operation of body-sentience, feeling, cognition and the constructing activities. In the infinite emptiness which is nibbānic discernment, these simply cannot arise. The Arahat, though, can re-activate them by leaving the nibbānic state, through the arising of willing. He or she can also re-enter this state by ceasing to will or plan. While it is possible that an Arahat might rapidly alternate between the nibbānic and non-nibbānic state, there do not seem to be any positive indications of such an alternation in the 'early Suttas'. These suggest that time had to be set aside for re-entering the nibbānic state. While the first experience of the nibbānic state might only have lasted a few seconds, this would have come after a period of meditation or listening to a sermon, in which a certain type of attention was developed.

(12.41) In the saṃsāric state, the normal flow of conditioned, *dukkha* phenomena is spun out by the vortical interplay of discernment and *nāma-rūpa*, both internal (the sentient body) and external (meaningful forms). Within this vortex, the brightly shining *citta* continues as a pure basis which, when uncovered by defilements, presents an ideal opportunity for nibbānic discernment to flash out of it, overcoming the gravity-pull of *nāma-rūpa*, and transcend all constructedness. Here, the vortex of *dukkha* ceases. As is said at S.I.15:

> Where solidity, cohesion, heat and motion find no footing,
> Hence ebb the flooding tides
> Here the round does not turn
> Here *nāma* and *rūpa* are stopped without remainder.

Here discernment is no longer trapped in the saṃsāric vortex by dependence on *nāma-rūpa*, but is liberated. Just as a huge amount of energy is released when an atomic nucleus is split, so the transcending of *saṃsāra* releases a potential pent-up within it. The radiant, infinite, unconstructed Dhamma, nibbānic discernment, is released once the dance of constructed discernment and *nāma-rūpa* cease to generate the realm of the born, dying and constructed.

(12.42) Prior to the attainment of the unconstructed state, a person does not have nibbānic discernment already within him or her; only the conditioned form of discernment is found in him then. Yet nibbānic discernment always exists, in a timeless sense, as the unconstructed Dhamma, ever open to being realized. When a person comes to finally do this, in the Arahat's first full experience of *nibbāna*, or later repetitions of this, the timeless realm is 'participated' in: a timeless, unconstructed space takes over in the place 'where' the 'person' was. In this, that which had been the constructed personality-factor known as discernment comes to transcendentally 'stop', and in doing so is identical with the timeless, unique, unconstructed Dhamma.

(12.43) The textual Theravāda tradition has, however, been reluctant to see *nibbāna* as a type of *citta*/discernment, although it has acknowledged that it is a mental state (*nāma*). The reluctance may well be due to wanting to avoid the danger of misinterpretation: taking such a *citta*/discernment as a metaphysical Self, so as to be a focus of clinging and empty speculation. As seen at Para.2.16, though, the Theravāda sees *nibbāna* as sharing many of the qualities of a

Self, as it is said to be permanent, happy, undisintegrating, not hollow, an essence, and not dependent on another. In the 'early Suttas' nibbānic discernment is in *some* ways like the Upaniṣadic Self (*Ātman*), which is said to be a form of *vijñāna* experienced when *nāma-rūpa* fall away (PU.6.5, MU.3.2.7–8). Yet *nibbāna* is not seen as the creator which has the factors of the world and personality 'supported (*pratiṣṭhitaḥ*)' in it, as is the Self (PU.6.4 and 6). Again, nibbānic discernment partially resembles the absolute of Hindu Advaita Vedānta philosophy, this being a Self which is *Sat-cit-ānanda*: Being-consciousness-bliss. Yet while *nibbāna* is a form of blissful consciousness, it is not a '*citta*' in the sense of a conditioned 'mind-set'. It is the 'real (*santaṃ*)' (e.g. M.I.436), though is not seen as Being, the essence of existence. In particular, it does not reside in people, even Arahats, as an unchanging Self-essence. Indeed, it is only attained by a person when *everything*, even *nibbāna* itself, is known as being empty of any supposed Self or essential 'I'. It is beyond all I-ness, empty even of the possibility of the thought 'I am' arising in it. This can *only* arise with respect to the conditioned personality-factors, and even here, it is a delusion (Para.1.31).

(12.44) Strands of the Theravāda practice tradition, though, continue to be willing to see *nibbāna* as a state of *citta*/discernment, and the Mahāyāna tradition has emphasized that the enlightened mind is without any supports to latch onto, and even one without any objects. In the Mahāyāna, though, apparent 'objects' are no real objects separate from a subject. Or they are seen as empty, essence-less 'supports' which are no real supports: they are just the unconstructed seen by the distortions of the ignorant, constructing mind. From this perspective, true letting go, *nirvāṇa*, lies in continuing in the flow of apparently constructed phenomena, so as to help the beings who do not yet have the option of transcending it. Such an possibility is not discussed in the 'early Suttas', but the idea of re-activating a conditioned personality even after the death of an Arahat is not totally ruled out.

(12.45) The 'early Suttas' have only a limited amount to say on *nibbāna*, for their main concern is the practical one of how to attain it: through cultivating moral virtue, developing the powers of a calm and concentrated mind, and attaining insight into the nature of the world. Nevertheless, if what is said on *nibbāna* is analysed and inter-related into a coherent pattern, the perspective developed in this and the previous chapter emerges. To do this properly, passages have to be carefully interpreted in the light of other related ones. Doing this shows that what is said on *nibbāna* is not such as to make it wholly enigmatic and incomprehensible. If it was, it would probably never have *been* said, for the Buddha affirmed that he only taught what was both true and spiritually useful (Para.I.17).

13

SEEKING THE *TATHĀGATA*

A tathāgata is deep, immeasurable, hard to fathom as is the great ocean . . . (M.I.486–87).

(13.1) In chapter 1 of this work, it was shown that the 'early Suttas' did not accept a real, permanent Self, but saw everything, including *nibbāna*, as not-Self. In chapter 12, it was also shown that the 'early Suttas' saw *nibbāna*, during life and beyond death, as objectless, unconstructed discernment. These two perspectives will now be drawn on in analysing a number of passages which affirm that, during life, the *tathāgata*, or enlightened person, is 'immeasurable', 'inscrutable', 'hard to fathom', and 'not being apprehended'. The implications of the Buddha's refusal to specify a *tathāgata*'s state after death will then be explored, rounding off the earlier discussion of the 'undetermined questions' in chapters 5 and 6.

(13.2) Before focussing on key passages on the *tathāgata*, it is first necessary to clarify which persons the word refers to. The Buddha often used it when talking of himself as an enlightened being, rather than as the individual Gotama (ch.1, note 5). In general '*tathāgata*' is used specifically of the Buddha, the one who discovers and proclaims the path to *nibbāna* (A.II.8–9, S.III.65–6), with the '*tathāgata*, Arahat, perfectly and completely enlightened one' being contrasted with a 'disciple of the *tathāgata*' (D.II.142). Nevertheless, '*tathāgata*' *is* sometimes used of any Arahat.[1] S.V.327, for example, discusses the 'dwelling of a learner' and that of a *tathāgata*, and explains the second by describing the qualities of an Arahat. At M.I.139–40 and 486–87, moreover, there is a switching between talk of a '*tathāgata*' and of 'a monk whose mind is freed thus', as if they were simple equivalents. '*Tathāgata*' literally means 'thus-gone' or 'thus-come', probably meaning one who is 'attained-to-truth' or 'whose-nature-is-from-truth'. In the Suttas, the word was used by both Buddhists and non-Buddhists as a term for someone who had attained the highest goal of the religious life: 'a *tathāgata*, a superman (*uttama-puriso*), (one of) the best of men, attainer of the highest attainment' (S.III.116).

THE 'UNTRACEABILITY' OF THE *TATHĀGATA*

(13.3) A key passage on the mysterious nature of a *tathāgata* is at M.I.486–87. Here, Vacchagotta tries to get the Buddha to answer the 'undetermined questions' on the state of a *tathāgata* after death: on whether he then 'is', 'is not', 'both is and is not', or 'neither is nor is not' (see Paras.I.8 & 5.12). The Buddha explains that these are 'undetermined' by him and that a *tathāgata* is without the latent tendency to conceit (*mānanusaya*). Vacchagotta persists in his questioning, though, changing the wording to ask 'where does a monk whose mind is freed thus arise (*upapajjati*)?'. The Buddha handles these questions in the same way as the original questions on a *tathāgata* after death: 'arise', 'does not arise', 'both' or 'neither' simply 'do not apply'. He then explains that 'This Dhamma is deep (*gambhīro*), difficult to see, difficult to understand . . .' and then likens the asking of such questions to asking which direction an extinguished fire had gone in: east, west, north or south. As such questions are inappropriate – for an extinct fire goes in no direction but to a state beyond designation (Para.10.3–4) –, so are those on the death of an enlightened monk. The Buddha then says:

> Even so, Vaccha, that material form by which one defining a *tathāgata* might define him, that material form for a *tathāgata* is abandoned (*pahīnam*), cut off at the root, made like a palm tree stump that can come to no further existence and is no more liable to rise again in the future. Freed from reckoning by material form (*rūpa-saṃkhā-vimutto*) is a *tathāgata*, he is deep, immeasurable, hard to fathom (*gambhīro appameyyo dupariyogāho*) as is the great ocean.[2]

The passage then repeats that 'arise' etc. do not apply, and then reformulates the above with each of the remaining personality-factors in place of 'material form'.

(13.4) This passage is indeed a very rich one. While given in the context of questions on the state of a *tathāgata* beyond death, it is clearly also making important statements about a *tathāgata* during life. The status of a *tathāgata* beyond death will be discussed below.

The present discussion will focus on the *tathāgata* during life, analysing several of the things said above. The meaning of a *tathāgata* as 'freed from being reckoned by' any of the personality-factors, even in life, is made clear by S.III.35. This explains that 'That for which a monk has a latent tendency, by that is he reckoned (*yaṃ . . . anuseti tena sankhaṃ gacchati*), what he does not have a latent tendency for, by that is he not reckoned'. This is explained in respect of 'having a latent tendency for' any of the personality-factors. What might this mean? The 'latent tendencies' (*anusaya*s) are such things as the 'I am' conceit, referred to above, and attachment, irritation and spiritual ignorance (M.III.285). These are all deeply ingrained ways in which the mind clings to and becomes involved in conditioned phenomena. An enlightened person, however, being without such tendencies, gives no clue as to what he is about. He cannot be 'reckoned' or 'named', through assessing his favourite personality-factor, as, say: 'a very physical person', 'a man of feeling', 'an intellectual', 'a schemer, a planner' or 'a discerning person, a connoisseur'. This situation is because, even in life, a *tathāgata* has 'abandoned' the personality-factors. This is explained to mean that he has no 'desire and attachment' (*chanda-rāga*) for them (S.III.27), with such 'abandoning' leading to much future happiness (M.I.140). The personality-factors are simply a 'burden' (S.III.25–6), and the enlightened person is one with 'burden dropped' (M.I.139). He or she does not hang on to the personality-factors as if they had permanence, satisfactoriness or Self in them. He does not identify with them as if they were a true Self or I, but sees them as merely conditioned phenomena. He is thus a 'man of nothing', not clinging to anything, whether internal to 'his' personality-factors or external to them (Para.3.14).

(13.5) The meaning of the *tathāgata*'s being 'immeasurable' is illustrated by A.I.266. Here, one is 'easily measured (*suppameyyo*)' if one is 'frivolous, empty-headed, a busy-body of harsh speech, loose in talk, lacking concentration, of flighty mind, with senses uncontrolled'; one is 'hard to measure' if one lacks these characteristics, but is 'immeasurable (*appameyyo*)' if one is an Arahat. Such a person clearly gives nothing away as to what he is about. He or she has destroyed attachment, hatred and delusion, which are each 'productive of the measurable (*pamāṇa-karano*)' (M.I.298). Having 'abandoned' the personality-factors, he is thus 'escaped from, unfettered by, released from' them and 'dwells with a mind (*ceto*) made to be without boundaries' (A.V.152). For a *tathāgata*, attachment etc. no longer limit the range and scope of his mind, so as to make it a bounded, measurable quantity (see Paras.3.13–16). Going beyond the range of other beings, he thus cannot be found by them:

> He has abandoned reckoning and did not attain to measuring,
> He has cut off craving, here, for the sentient body . . .
> Gods and humans do not succeed when searching (for him)
> Here or beyond, in heavens or in any dwelling (S.I.12).

This is because, as explained in the verses leading up to this, he is beyond all forms of 'conceit', or limiting I-centred thought. As he does not identify with any limited set of phenomena, his mind cannot be pinned down within the ambit of any such limitation. As expressed in Para.3.14, 'When a person lets go of everything, such that "his" identity shrinks to zero, then *citta* expands to infinity'.

(13.6) What might be called the 'untraceability' of the *tathāgata* is referred to in several other passages. For example, at M.I.139–40 it is said that several powerful gods:

> do not succeed in their search (to find): 'Dependent on this (*idaṃ nissitaṃ*) is the discernment of a *tathāgata*'.[3] What is the reason for this? In this visible world, monks, I say of a *tathāgata* that he is 'inscrutable (*ananuvejjo*)'.

Elsewhere, one of these gods, Inda, is told that to have discernment 'dependent' on something is to grasp at it, while to have discernment which is not 'dependent' is to attain *nibbāna* (S.IV.102). M.I.138, just prior to the above passage, refers to being 'dependent' on views, and Sn.849 links 'dependence' to having preferences. A *tathāgata*, though, does not grasp at anything, whether by views, preferences or in any other way. He is thus beyond the ken of the unenlightened, particularly Māra: 'For whatever they grasp at in the world, by just that Māra follows a man' (Sn.1103). Māra cannot 'see' a person who regards the world as 'empty' of Self (Sn.1119) or who knows that the body is ephemeral, like froth or a mirage (Dhp.46), and his 'army' cannot 'succeed in their search' for one who recognizes the personality-factors as not 'I' or 'mine' (S.I.112). Such a person cannot be 'found' even when in normal consciousness, for they do not invest an 'identity' anywhere. When they take *nibbāna* as the object of their mind, 'dependent' on it in what must be a non-grasping way (S.IV.367), they are even harder to trace. When nibbānic stopping is itself entered, discernment is not 'dependent' in any sense and the 'inscrutability' of a *tathāgata* is even deeper.

THE 'HARD TO FATHOM' *TATHĀGATA* AND DHAMMA

(13.7) The M.I.486–87 passage cited above refers to both the *tathāgata* and Dhamma as 'deep' (*gambhīra*). An investigation of the link between these two helps show that the 'immeasurable' *tathāgata* is 'hard to fathom', but not totally '*un*fathomable', as '*duppariyogāho*' is usually translated (e.g. MLS.II.66). While ordinary gods and humans cannot search out a *tathāgata*, as they are looking in the wrong way, a Stream-enterer can. A Stream-enterer is one such as Upāli, for whom:

> the dustless, stainless Dhamma-eye arose to him that: whatever is of the nature to arise (*samudaya-dhammaṃ*), all that is of the nature to stop (*nirodha-dhamman-*). Then the householder Upāli, as one for who Dhamma is seen, attained, known and fathomed (*pariyogāḷha-*) . . . (M.I.380).

A passage at S.III.120 shows that to 'see' Dhamma is in fact to 'see' the nature of the *tathāgata*:

> Enough, Vakkali! What is there for you in this vile visible body? Who, Vakkali, sees Dhamma, he sees me; who sees me sees Dhamma.

As, when talking of himself as an enlightened being, the Buddha generally referred to 'the *tathāgata*', rather than 'me', the 'me' of this can be read as 'the *tathāgata*'. That is, Stream-entry is an experience in which the 'deep' *tathāgata* is seen by seeing the 'deep' Dhamma. Dhamma is '*difficult* to see' (M.I.487), but *is* 'seen' and 'fathomed' at Stream-entry. From this, it is clear that it is also an experience in which the '*hard* to fathom (*dup-pariyogāho*)' *tathāgata* is 'fathomed' (*pariyogāḷha-*). The *tathāgata*'s nature is only 'unfathomable' to one who lacks the Dhamma-vision of a Stream-enterer.

(13.8) What, though, is the Dhamma which is seen at Stream-entry? Para.11.24 makes clear that it is Conditioned Arising and *nibbāna*. How can the *tathāgata*'s nature be seen here? It is not likely to be seen in seeing Conditioned Arising, for this is the very process by which *dukkha* arises. It makes more sense to say that seeing Dhamma's aspect as *nibbāna* means that a *tathāgata*'s nature is seen. For while a *tathāgata understands* Conditioned Arising, it is through the experience of *nibbāna* that attachment etc. are destroyed and he *is* a *tathāgata*/Arahat. That is, *nibbāna* is the nature of the *tathāgata*; it is 'Arahatness', that which is the defining characteristic of an Arahat (Para.11.6). Now as 'seeing' Conditioned Arising alone is enough to 'see' Dhamma (Para.8.25), so it also makes sense to say that simply 'seeing' *nibbāna* is to 'see' Dhamma. Thus Stream-entry is where there is 'seeing' Dhamma as both the Conditioned Arising of *dukkha*, and as *nibbāna*, the *dukkha*-cessation which is the nature of the *tathāgata*. Stream-enterers and members of the Sangha-refuge are all 'plunging into the deathless (*amataṃ vigayha*)' (Sn.228), i.e. *nibbāna*. They 'plunge into (*vi-gāhati*)' *nibbāna* and thus 'fathom (*pari-o-gāhati*)' the *tathāgata*'s nature.

(13.9) This indicates a very close affinity or identity between *nibbāna* and the *tathāgata*. Of course, the terms do not denote precisely the same, for '*tathāgata*' is used as a term for a type of person, whereas '*nibbāna*' is not. Nevertheless it is through having fully experienced *nibbāna*, and being able to repeat this, that a person is a *tathāgata*. It is the mysterious objectless discernment that is his nature. Karel Werner (1988: 91–3), has commented on such an interpretation as developed by myself in an earlier version of this chapter (1983). While accepting that *nibbāna*/Dhamma can be seen as the 'true nature' of every *tathāgata*, he holds that this cannot mean that a *tathāgata* attains identity with this by 'merging with or becoming it', such that there is 'the complete non-existence of himself as a particular *Tathāgata*'. He goes on to say that 'we have to accept a plurality of *tathāgata*s whose status and inner nature is the same whether they are "alive" or not'. I would differ with him on this. While *tathāgata*s in normal consciousness are clearly different people with different characters, when they experience *nibbāna* – in life or beyond death – there can be no way in which there can be any differentiation between 'different' *tathāgata*s. Such differentiation can only pertain to the conditioned world of space and time, not to the realm of the unique unconstructed element, *nibbāna*. The only way a *tathāgata* can remain different from 'other' *tathāgata*s and *nibbāna*, is by keeping his constructed personality-factors going. This is confirmed by material discussed by John S. Strong regarding unorthodox beliefs on Arahats in parts of Burma and Thailand (1992: 12–14 & 236–52). One text, the *Lokapaññatti*, dating from the eleventh or twelfth century, says that the Arahat Upagutta, who lived at the time of emperor Asoka, still lives on, dwelling at the bottom of an ocean, as a protector that can be called on by devotees. He is seen as still existing as an individual, but this is precisely because he is said *not* have attained *parinibbāna*, i.e. he has never entered *nibbāna* beyond death.

(13.10) Werner goes on to postulate a 'personality structure' which can be 'filled with empirical contents in saṃsāric conditions, while in the state of enlightenment its "filling" is nibbānic', such a 'structure' being the '*purisa*' or 'person'. I find no evidence for such a concept in the 'early Suttas'. The concept is more or less the same as the 'person' (*puggala*) of the Personalists (Puggala-vādins), whose ideas have been shown to be misinterpretations (Paras.1.36–42). Werner holds that the main Buddhist objection to such a theory was that it was not helpful in the task of spiritual development. This is not the case: Paras.1.36–7 show that it was objected to because it was a clear misunderstanding of the Buddha's teachings.

(13.11) The *tathāgata*'s relationship with Dhamma is clearly that of having 'become Dhamma', as can be seen in what follows. Thag.491 affirms:

> The seven Buddhas are rid of craving, without grasping, merging into destruction (*khay-ogadhā*), by whom, having become Dhamma (*dhamma-bhūtehi*), venerable, this Dhamma was taught.

That is, all Buddhas (Gotama and those of past ages) have merged into and become the unconstructed Dhamma, that which destroys craving and makes them enlightened beings. Thus D.III.84 says that 'these are designations of the *tathāgata*, "one having Dhamma as body (*dhamma-kāyo*)", "one having the supreme as body (*brahma-kāyo*)", "Dhamma-become (*dhamma-bhūto*)", "become the supreme (*brahma-bhūto*)" . . .'. This, of course, not only applies to a Buddha, but also to any Arahat, for S.III.83 says that Arahats are 'become the supreme', a synonym of Dhamma-become in this passage.[4] Both the Buddha and Arahats have 'become' *nibbāna* in their experience of it, and also embody Dhamma, in the sense of the Holy Eightfold Path, the 'Dhamma-vehicle' or 'supreme-vehicle' (Para.3.3).

(13.12) This interpretation fits the context at D.III.84, for the Buddha says, just prior to the quoted passage, that one whose faith in the *tathāgata* is 'settled, root-born, established, firm' is one who is 'a genuine son of the Lord, born from his mouth, born of Dhamma, created by Dhamma, heir of Dhamma'. A person of such firm faith is clearly at least a Stream-enterer, one who has entered the 'stream' of the Holy Eightfold Path (S.V.347) and is endowed with 'unwavering confidence' in the three refuges: the Buddha, Dhamma and the Holy Sangha of Stream-enterers and other saints (S.II.68). In having confidence in the Dhamma, they have confidence in the Holy Eightfold Path and *nibbāna* (A.II.34–5). *These*, then, are most likely to be the Dhamma which D.III.84 sees the Buddha as having as 'body', or as having 'become'. It is notable that A.II.34–5 also says that the Holy Eightfold Path is the 'best' (*agga*) of all constructed states and that *nibbāna* is the best of *all* states, whether constructed or unconstructed. This accords with D.III.84 implying that the Dhamma is the 'supreme' (*brahma-*). It may well be that D.III.84 is saying that the Buddha has the supreme constructed state, the Path, as his 'body',[5] and has 'become' the supreme of all states, *nibbāna*. That is, the Buddha has two sides to him (as do Arahats). His nature is *nibbāna*, which is itself without any 'body', for it is the stopping of all constructed states. But when the Buddha is in a non-nibbānic state, he manifests his nature by a 'body', or personality, which is redolent with factors of the Path. Like all Arahats, he is endowed with (A.V.16), and is awakened to (D.III.279) the 'five Dhamma-groups (*dhamma-kkhandhā*)': those of virtue, meditation, wisdom, liberation, and knowledge-and-vision of liberation. Stream-enterers and other members of the Holy Sangha are still working to complete such an uplifting set of Dhamma-qualities (It.106–08). Nevertheless, they have been taught Dhamma-as-Path by the Buddha, and actually 'seen' his Dhamma-nature. They are thus 'born' from the Buddha's mouth as Stream-enterers etc. and are 'created' by the Dhamma that they have heard and 'seen'. The Dhamma which the Buddha and Arahats have 'become' is the unconstructed, *nibbāna*, and their 'body' is the Holy Eightfold Path which leads to the full experience of this. *Nibbāna* is their nature, and they continue to live and act from the Path-Dhamma that is the way to this.

THE *TATHĀGATA* AS 'NOT BEING APPREHENDED'

(13.13) At S.IV.380–84, S.III.116–19 and S.III.109–12 are three parallel passages which deal in considerable detail with the *tathāgata* and his relationship with the personality-factors, this being in the context of the questions on his state after death. The first passage occurs after a Sutta parallelling M.I.486–87, on the *tathāgata* as 'deep, immeasurable, hard to fathom'; the second and third occur immediately prior to the Sutta on 'he who sees Dhamma sees me'. These passages are thus a good test of the interpretation developed so far, and in turn allow this to be deepened. At S.IV.380–84 and S.III.116–19, the Buddha chides Anurādha for holding that a *tathāgata*'s state after death can be declared in some other way apart from the four standard, and unacceptable, views: 'is', 'is not', 'both', or 'neither'. At S.III.109–12, Sāriputta chides Yamaka for holding that an Arahat 'is cut off and perishes when his body breaks up, after death he is not'. In both cases, the chiding begins in the same way. Firstly, it is said that one should see the personality-factors as being impermanent, *dukkha* and not-Self,[6] so that one can then go on to become an Arahat, i.e. a *tathāgata*. Then Anurādha and Yamaka are led to admit that they do *not* regard a *tathāgata* in any of the following ways:

i) as the same as any of the personality-factors
ii) as 'in' any of them
iii) as 'apart from (*aññatra*)' any of them
iv) as all of them listed together[7]
v) as 'this one who is formless, feelingless, non-cognitive, without constructing activities or discernment (*arūpī avedano asaññī asaṅkhāro aviññāṇo*)'.

The Buddha and Sāriputta then continue:

> Anurādha/Yamaka, as here in this visible world, truly, reliably, a *tathāgata* is not being apprehended by you (*te . . . saccato thetato tathāgato anupalabbhiyamāno*), is it proper for you [to explain in the way you are being chided for?].[8]

The passages then end in the following ways. In one, the Buddha tells Anurādha that he declares only *dukkha* and the cessation of *dukkha*: i.e. only *dukkha* ends at the death of an Arahat. In the other, Yamaka says that now 'Dhamma is understood' and that, if asked on the state of a *tathāgata* after death, he would simply say that the impermanent, *dukkha* personality-factors have ceased, and not that an Arahat was destroyed at death.

(13.14) These passages seem particularly insistent that only *dukkha* ends at the death of a *tathāgata*. This accords with an insistence, at M.I.140 (Para.1.22), that no 'real being (*santo satto*)' – i.e. no substantial Self-entity – ends then: for no such entity can be found to exist. On the other hand, the passages suggest that the '*tathāgata*' is not apprehendable in regard to the (*dukkha*) personality-factors. That is, while they end at a *tathāgata*'s death, they are the *only* things which end then: not the *tathāgata*'s mysterious nature. This latter point is supported by Yamaka's saying, at the end of the discourse, that it was now the case that 'Dhamma is understood (*abhisameto*)'. This wording indicates that he had now become a Stream-enterer [9]: at S.III.135, a monk wanting to 'see' Dhamma – i.e. attain Stream-entry – is given a teaching (on Conditioned Arising and its stopping) such that Dhamma was likewise 'understood' by him.[10] That is, as a result of the teaching he had been given, Yamaka now *saw* Dhamma, and thus saw the nibbānic nature of a *tathāgata*. Up until this realisation, it was still the case that the *tathāgata* was 'not being apprehended by' him, but he now saw the true *tathāgata* in seeing Dhamma/*nibbāna*.

(13.15) It is by Stream-entry, then, that the true nature of the *tathāgata* is apprehended and the four misconceived views on the *tathāgata* after death are abandoned. As S.IV.390 says, one who 'sees' the 'stopping of becoming' – i.e. *nibbāna* (A.V.9) – does not hold any of these views. This is because a Stream-enterer a) sees the nature of a *tathāgata* in seeing *nibbāna*, and b) has insight into Conditioned Arising, seeing the world as a stream of Self-less conditioned phenomena. This insight means that a Stream-entry destroys (D.II.252) the 'views on the existing group' (*sakkāya-diṭṭhi*), i.e. views which relate a Self to the personality-factors in some way (Para.I.8). Such views are the very thing which are said to lead people into asking the four 'undetermined' questions on the *tathāgata*'s destiny (Para.5.12). To hold such views means that, not only is a Self seen as somehow residing in one's own personality-factors, but a *tathāgata* is taken as a such a substantial, permanent Self. To ask what happens to a *tathāgata*-Self after death, however, is to ask a question to which all the apparently possible answers 'do not apply', for such a thing cannot be found to exist during life. The question is misconstrued, like 'have you stopped beating your wife?' addressed to an innocent man.

(13.16) In order, then, to help Anurādha and Yamaka towards Stream-entry and abandonment of the views on a *tathāgata*' destiny, they are led to reflect that: i) the personality-factors are not-Self and, ii) the *tathāgata* is not a 'Self' related to the personality-factors as in the various 'views on the existing group'. That is, the *hard*-to-apprehend *tathāgata* is *not* a 'Self', which is *totally* 'inapprehensible', as it is a baseless, self-contradictory concept (Paras.1.17–34). At this stage, Anurādha and Yamaka have put down the deluded views characteristic of the 'ordinary person' (*puthujjana*), but have not yet destroyed them. It seems that they are at the level of the eighth holy person: one practising for the realization of the fruit which is Stream-entry (A.IV.372; cf. Para.11.7). Once Stream-entry is attained, though, Self-views are completely destroyed, and *nibbāna*, the *tathāgata*'s nature, is seen/apprehended/fathomed. As unconstructed, this lies beyond the constructed phenomena that were the breeding-ground for the Self-delusion, a delusion which is a key factor in the very process of the construction of limited, *dukkha* processes.

(13.17) If a *tathāgata*'s nature is *nibbāna*, though, and this is objectless discernment, is this not to take the '*tathāgata*' in one of the five ways rejected at Para.13.13? A careful examination of these shows that this is not so. View i) is to regard the *tathāgata* as one of the personality-factors, just as the first type of existing-group-view takes a Self to be one of these. The real nature of a *tathāgata*, though, is objectless discernment, which is neither a Self nor is it identical even with the discernment personality-factor (Para.12.17). View ii), taking a *tathāgata* as 'in' any of the personality-factors, parallels the fourth type of existing-group-view: taking a Self as 'in' one of the factors. But objectless discernment is both Self-less and does not lie 'in' any of the factors. View iii), on a *tathāgata* as 'apart from' each factor, is a little harder to interpret. Nevertheless, S.III.130 (Para.1.32) sees saying 'I am' any of the factors, or 'I am apart from' any of them, as equivalent to having existing-group-view. That is, holding that a *tathāgata*/Self is 'apart from' each personality-factor is a way of covering any remaining types of existing-group-views which have not already been specifically spelled out. Thus view iii) of Para.13.13 means that a *tathāgata* or Self is 'endowed with' some factor or contains it.[11] Objectless discernment, though, is both Selfless and is where all the conditioned personality-factors cease, so that it cannot be said to 'contain' them or be 'endowed with' them. View iv), taking a *tathāgata* as all the personality-factors together, is like having the attitude 'I am' with respect to all the factors, which S.III.130 cites as a delusion which goes further than that of the existing-group-views.[12] Again, objectless discernment is no Self or 'I' and is not equivalent to the totality of the personality-factors.

(13.18) What, though, of view v) at Para.13.13? This takes a *tathāgata* as lacking the qualities of all the personality-factors: could not this be said of objectless discernment? If so, the rejection of such a view is surely a rejection of such discernment being the 'nature' of a *tathāgata*. But what does view v) actually *mean*? One could see view iv) – the *tathāgata* is all the factors – as a generalisation of view i) – he is one or other of the factors. Similarly, one can see view v) as a generalisation of view iii) and perhaps ii): a *tathāgata* is 'apart from' all of the factors, as he contains them all, is endowed with them all, or perhaps is in them all – but is not, himself identical with any of them. This interpretation seems to be confirmed by a passage at Miln.26, concerning the non-findability of 'Nāgasena' taken as a real Self or true 'Person'. Nāgasena says that 'he' is not a) any of the personality-factors, b) the totality of the factors (i.e. view iv. on a *tathāgata* does not apply to him) or c) 'apart from' all the factors. Here, taking the Nāgasena-Self as 'apart from' all the factors seems to be like taking the *tathāgata*-Self as in view v). So, what does this show? That the rejected view v) is one that takes a *tathāgata* as 'apart from' all the personality-factors: not the *same* as any of them but yet containing or being endowed with them all. To 'contain' or be 'endowed with' a personality-factor does *not* amount to *being* it, as is made clear by Ps.I.144–45. It is like a flower having a scent or a tree having a shadow: the flower is not the scent and the tree is not the shadow. Thus something which is supposed to stand beyond all the personality-factors but 'has' them can still be said, itself, to lack the qualities of them. But it is not correct to say that objectless discernment is like this. It is beyond all the personality-factors, yes, but it does not have them as its properties nor does it contain them. When discernment is objectless for a person, the personality-factors do not exist, and when they exist, discernment is not objectless.[13]

(13.19) The discussion of the last two paragraphs thus shows that, not only is the *tathāgata*'s nature not any kind of Self, however subtle, but that the non-acceptance of views i)–v) at Para.13.13 does not rule out taking the *tathāgata*'s nature as objectless discernment.

Indeed it is just this which is left when all other ways of trying to apprehend the true *tathāgata* are stripped away. It is Stream-entry which is the break-through which destroys Self-views, the basis of these misconceptions, and simultaneously allows the apprehension of what a *tathāgata* really is: objectless, unsupported, unconstructed, deathless, nibbānic discernment.

NIBBĀNIC DISCERNMENT AND THE VIEWS ON A *TATHĀGATA* AFTER DEATH

(13.20) What, then, of the Buddha's non-acceptance of the four views on the state of a *tathāgata* after death:

i) 'after death, the *tathāgata* is (*hoti tathāgato param maraṇā ti*)'
ii) 'after death, the *tathāgata* is not (*na hoti* . . .)'
iii) 'after death, the *tathāgata* both is and is not (*hoti ca na hoti* . . .)'
iv) 'after death, the *tathāgata* neither is nor is not (*neva hoti na na hoti* . . .)'.

Clearly, such views were unacceptable primarily because they were held by those who took the *tathāgata* as a Self,[14] as well as due to the fact that asking which of them was correct was a timewasting side-track from spiritual development (M.I.426–31). Apart from these considerations, though, does the Buddha's response to these views rule out any type of concept of a *tathāgata* beyond death, whether positive or negative? In particular, does it rule out taking a *tathāgata* beyond death as objectless, unsupported discernment? For Paras.12.20–21 have argued that this still exists beyond the death of an Arahat, according to the 'early Suttas'. To investigate this issue, it is necessary to assess carefully the meaning and implications of the above four views. Only then can it be seen what the non-acceptance of the views amounts to.

(13.21) The easiest to asses is view ii). Para.13.13 shows this to mean that an Arahat 'is cut off and perishes when his body breaks up, after death he is not'. This is clearly the view of the 'Annihilationist', who holds that both 'fools and the wise' are totally destroyed at death (D.I.55), due to the non-existence of rebirth for any being. Such an Annihilationist view is one which posits some kind of Self (D.I.34) or substantial 'real being' (M.I.140) which is then 'cut off' at death. As a view about what happens to a self-contradictory

'Self'-entity, view ii) is meaningless. As a denial of the general fact of rebirth, though, it can be seen as false. Moreover, as Sāriputta so strongly insists on the inappropriateness of this view (Para.13.13), and it is emphasized that *only dukkha* ends at the death of an Arahat, the total non-existence of a *tathāgata* beyond death seems to be ruled out.

(13.22) What, then of view i)? As view ii) is its opposite, it is likely that view i) is a form of 'Eternalism', the opposite of Annihilationism. That is, view i) takes the *tathāgata* as some kind of Self which survives death and continues eternally. That this is so is indicated by S.III.215–20, which says that the four views on the *tathāgata* after death arise from clinging to the personality-factors, and that this also leads to views on the precise qualities – regarding form, formlessness, suffering and happiness – of the 'unimpaired' Self after death. Sn.1075 in fact asks, if one 'gone to the goal' 'does not exist (*natthi*)' or is 'eternally unimpaired'. That is, is a *tathāgata* after death annihilated, or does he continue as an eternal Self? Sn.1076 replies that neither of these – clearly equivalent to views ii) and i) – pertain, for 'there is no measuring one who has gone to the goal'. View i) not only holds that a *tathāgata* is an eternal Self, but also implies that its eternal existence is in some form of rebirth. This is shown from M.I.486 (Para.13.3), where the question-form of the view is replaced by 'where does a monk arise (*upapajjati*) whose mind is freed thus?'. As (non-enlightened) beings are said to 'arise' in a rebirth, this shows that, in the context of the questions and views on a *tathāgata* after death, '*hoti*', or 'is', is equivalent to 'is reborn'. Indeed, at Ps.I.154, '*hoti*' in this context is synonymous with 'persists (*tiṭṭhati*)', 'arises (*uppajjati*)' (a term replaceable by '*upapajjati*'), and 'is produced (*nibbattati*)'. The last of these terms is close to '*abhinibbatti*', which is used in the definition of 'birth', i.e. the start of a rebirth, at S.II.3.

(13.23) It is notable that Ps.I.154 does not list '*atthi*' or 'exists' among the synonyms of '*hoti*' in the context of questions on the *tathāgata* after death. All the synonyms are ones which suggest continuation in a world of change. i.e. in the conditioned world. '*Hoti*' is in fact a contracted form of '*bhavati*', meaning both 'is' and 'becomes', again suggesting a context of change. '*Hoti*' is the word used to say that one thing or person 'is' something or other, e.g. 'the brahmin is a minister' or 'the Self, unimpaired after death, is formless' (S.III.219). In sum, it is a word used of something continuing in a world of change, having a particular worldly identity. To say that a *tathāgata* beyond death '*hoti*' is to imply that he is a permanent Self which continues eternally in time, within the cycle of rebirths, and 'is' one or other conditioned phenomenon. This is inapplicable to a *tathāgata* whose nature is *nibbāna*. *Nibbāna* is said to 'exist (*atthi*)' (Ud.80), but '*hoti*' is never applied to it. '*Atthi*', then, can be applied to that which 'exists' in a timeless sense, just as objectless discernment does. Miln.73, in fact, is quite happy to say that, even after his death, the 'Lord' 'exists (*atthi*)', being like a fire that had gone out and has gone beyond designation (Para.10.4). So while '*hoti*' is inapplicable to a *tathāgata* beyond death, there seems to be no reason why '*atthi*' should not be applied to him.

(13.24) All of this implies that it is perfectly acceptable to see the *tathāgata* as existing beyond death in the form of Selfless, unsupported, objectless discernment, which has transcended all rebirths and the conditioned world of time. Of course, view i) on a *tathāgata* after death is still unacceptable. If it takes a *tathāgata* as a Self, the view is absurd, for it then concerns what happens after death to a totally inapprehensible, self-contradictory supposed entity ('Self'). If, apart from this, it takes a *tathāgata* as reborn, it is simply false.

(13.25) An examination of the remaining two views accords with this analysis. View iii), 'both is and is not', is simply the view that part of the *tathāgata* continues after death in a rebirth. At M.II.233, there is a view that the Self is both eternal and non-eternal, while D.I.21 gives an example of such a view: the physical senses are a non-eternal Self, which is destroyed at death, but discernment or *citta* is an eternal Self, which is not so destroyed. Thus view iii) is one which takes a *tathāgata* as two Selves: material form and mind, with only the mental Self surviving death – in what would be a 'formless' rebirth. Belief in more than one 'Self' (centres of identity?) was also held by some Annihilationists (Para.1.10), but they held that they were *all* destroyed at death.

(13.26) What, then, of view iv): 'neither is nor is not'? Such 'neither . . . nor' expressions in the Pāli Suttas are used to refer to any state where something hovers between presence and complete absence, just as we might say of a balding man that he is 'neither bald nor not-bald'. Such usage can be clearly seen in the case of the 'sphere of neither-cognition-nor-non-cognition'. This meditational state, and parallel rebirth, is just beyond the 'sphere of nothingness', which is the 'extreme point of cognition' (D.I.84), but is yet different from the 'cessation of cognition and feeling' and the realm of 'non-cognizant beings' (D.II.69). That is, it is a meditational experience, or a rebirth, in which there is neither an active state of cognition, nor a complete lack of it. In it, cognition exists in only an attenuated form. How, then, does this shed light on why someone should hold the view 'after death, a *tathāgata* neither is nor is not'? If they took a *tathāgata* as a Self which was, in life, cognition, but after death was 'neither with nor without cognition' (M.II.231), being reborn in the realm of neither-cognition-nor-non-cognition, then this view on a *tathāgata* would seem appropriate to them. Alternatively, if they saw him as a Self which was, in life, the 'material form' (*rūpa*) personality-factor, but held that the *tathāgata*-Self 'neither has form nor is formless' after death (S.III.219), then this view would again seem appropriate. That is, if a) person takes a *tathāgata* as a particular personality-factor, seen as a Self, and b) such a factor-Self is seen to exist only in an attenuated state after death, due to the type of rebirth attained, then, c) that person would naturally hold that a *tathāgata* 'neither is nor is not' after death. However, a *tathāgata*'s nibbānic nature is neither a Self nor any personality-factor, and he can be related to no kind of rebirth after death. Indeed, all four views on the state of a *tathāgata* after death are set aside because:

> as to the reason, the ground for declaring him 'with form', or 'without form', as 'with cognition' or 'without cognition', or 'neither with nor without cognition' – if such reasons, such grounds, should cease in every way, entirely, wholly and utterly without remainder, declaring him by what would you declare him as 'with form' or . . . ? (S.IV.402. cf. Sn.1076).

That is, for a *tathāgata* after death, there is absolutely no basis for applying to him the categories of the personality-factors, or of the types of rebirths where particular factors are present or absent.

(13.27) Taking a *tathāgata* as a Self means that the four questions on his state after death become meaningless: questions about what *actually* happens to a mythical entity after 'it' dies. If this inbuilt misapprehension is put to one side, however, the views that the questions propose can all be seen to be *false*. This is because they hold, respectively, that after death a *tathāgata* is:

i) reborn in his entirety
ii) annihilated in his entirety
iii) partly reborn and partly annihilated,
iv) reborn in his entirety, but in a very attenuated form, e.g. in the

realm of neither-cognition-nor-non-cognition, the subtlest of rebirths.

As seen at Para.13.13, Anurādha is criticized for trying to 'declare' a *tathāgata* after death in some *other* way than 'is', 'is not' 'both' or 'neither'. This is because these views exhaust all the logical possibilities of what happens to a *tathāgata* after death: *if* he is taken as a Self which is reborn or annihilated. There *is* no 'other way', if one is working from these presuppositions: the *tathāgata*-Self must be either reborn, annihilated, both, or neither. If these presuppositions are jettisoned, though, as they are at Stream-entry, all four views are seen as inapplicable. The *tathāgata*'s not-Self nibbānic nature is seen, so that it is understood that he is neither reborn in any way, however subtle, nor annihilated. Yet, beyond rebirths, a *tathāgata* can be said to exist. This is not 'after' death, for that implies existence in time, subject to conditions, but 'beyond' it, beyond all time and change. Beyond death, a *tathāgata* exists in the form of nibbānic discernment: objectless, unsupported, non-manifestive, stopped, unborn, deathless, infinite, radiant, and blissful.

(13.28) In sum, the different elements of this chapter come together as follows. One who is not yet a Stream-enterer, an 'ordinary person' (*puthujjana*), is a person with some variety of existing-group-view. That is, he or she explicitly or implicitly identifies some aspect of the personality-factors as a permanent, substantial Self. Such a Self or 'real being' is seen as either destroyed at death or as continuing in some form. Such views inevitably affect a person's understanding of an enlightened person. He or she is taken to have an enlightened Self which is either destroyed at death or continues eternally in time. Such misconception leads to holding one or other of the four views on the *tathāgata* after death, or to persistently wondering *which* of these is true. The 'ordinary person' is unable to fathom or apprehend what a *tathāgata* is, for a *tathāgata* grasps at nothing as 'Self' or 'I', and has let go of all the personality-factors, i.e. of everything which is normally taken as 'Self' or 'I'. He is thus beyond measure or reckoning: he does not betray himself as this or that kind of person by identifying with any limited group of phenomena. Thus neither major gods nor Māra can search him out or pin him down. This is especially so when his active contemplation of *everything* as not-Self leads to 'his' discernment being objectless.

(13.29) At Stream-entry, a person destroys Self-views by insight into the conditioned arising of all personality-factors. He or she also 'sees', fathoms and plunges into *nibbāna*, the unconditioned Dhamma which is the *tathāgata*'s nature. Due to insight into conditionality, the four views on the *tathāgata* after death are completely abandoned. Due to seeing *nibbāna*, the *tathāgata* is directly known. On becoming an Arahat, a person is himself a *tathāgata*. He does not just 'see' Dhamma, but *becomes* it. In his full experience of *nibbāna*, 'he' *is* Dhamma/*nibbāna*, in the form of objectless discernment. The first full experience of this destroys all lingering vestiges of the 'I am' attitude and other latent tendencies, so that the Arahat is 'deep, immeasurable, hard to fathom as is the great ocean'. Without latent tendencies, he is beyond reckoning and immeasurable, even in normal consciousness, when he has Dhamma, in the sense of the Path, as his 'body'. At death, the conditioned personality-factors, which are all *dukkha*, simply fall away, but no 'real being', no Self is destroyed: for there never was one to be destroyed. Free of all causes of rebirth, a *tathāgata* is beyond all conditioned states, even those of the Path, but he is not destroyed. That which first made him enlightened – objectless, unsupported discernment – is a timeless reality which is in no way affected by the death of 'his' personality-factors. Beyond time, beyond the bodily remains of a *tathāgata*, it exists as the unique unborn, deathless element: radiant, infinite, blissful, objectless discernment. That is, it is the reality first glimpsed at Stream-entry and then fully participated in by the Arahat whenever his personality-factors are stopped in nibbānic realization.

(13.30) The above is the perspective which emerges when the jigsaw of scattered passages on the *tathāgata* and *nibbāna* are pieced together. I hope I have shown that all the pieces fit properly, and that there are no pieces left over. Standing back, one can then see the whole picture. Of course, gaining an intellectual view of this picture is different from experiencing the reality that it depicts! That requires another kind of approach, which comes from steadily treading the path of virtue, meditative calm, and insight. Nevertheless, an intellectual map of the goal will hopefully be both interesting in itself and of no hindrance to those treading the path. This will be the case, though, only if what has been said here, based on the teachings ascribed to the Buddha, does not become the basis for misconceptions. In my reading of the Buddha's formal 'silence' on the *tathāgata*'s destiny, I have therefore sought to guard against any such Self-related misconceptions, by emphasizing that the relevant texts see 'Self' as a wholly baseless concept. As the Buddha held that he taught only what is true and spiritually useful (M.I.395), I hope that my reading of the teachings ascribed to him are useful in both a spiritual and scholarly sense. Every silence in the midst of discourse has a particular meaning, and I hope to have shown what the Buddha's silence meant. In this, I go further than Collins (1982: 135–36), who holds that this is beyond the remit of the scholar. From my reading of the texts, it *is* possible for the methods of scholarship to deduce this meaning.

(13.31) The Theravāda tradition's exegetical texts have certainly kept closer to the Buddha's formal silence than I have done. The Mahāyāna, on the other hand, has referred to the Buddha as still existing after death as a heavenly-type being, in the form of a *Sambhoga-kāya* or 'Enjoyment body'. As such, he is seen as responding to prayer and devotion in various ways. This puts more into the silence than the Sutta-based interpretation of this chapter would warrant. As regards the Theravada tradition, devotion to the Buddha is seen as beneficial, but not because he actually responds to it: it is beneficial in itself (Miln.95–101). Nevertheless, the Theravāda certainly holds that something of the Buddha's power remains in the world after his death. Such power is associated with *paritta*s and the Buddha's bodily relics. *Paritta*s are protective chants – mostly certain short sermons of the Buddha – which are seen to contain a beneficent truth-power: power which is activated when a *paritta* is devoutly chanted or listened to (Harvey, 1990: 180–82 & 1993b). They can be seen to represent the power of the the Buddha's 'Dhamma-body', the Holy Eightfold Path. At a physical level, something of the Buddha's purity and power is seen to have been absorbed by his relics (Harvey 1990b). Their power, though, will eventually wear out. The Theravāda holds that 5000 years after the death of the Buddha, when knowledge and practice of Dhamma has faded away in human society, Gotama Buddha's influence on earth will have ended. Then all his scattered relics will converge, by their own power, at the foot of the tree under which he attained enlightenment. Forming the image of a Buddha, they will then disappear in a flash of light (Vibh.A.433). This is known as the *parinibbāna*, or passing into *nibbāna*, of the relics!

14

CONCLUSION

(14.1) What, then, has this exploration of the thought-world of the 'early Suttas', and related later Buddhist texts, shown us? Part I investigated how the 'early Suttas' both did and did not accepted 'self' (*attā*), depending on the sense given to this word. It is clearly held that, within what might be called the 'empirical self', i.e. the five personality-factors, no permanent, substantial, autonomous, metaphysical Self can be found. Such a Self is not explicitly denied, however, for a key aspect of the process of spiritual development is to carefully examine everything that is taken as 'Self' or 'I', and then 'let go' of it when it is clearly recognised to be not-Self. A bald denial of Self would short-circuit this very practical and self-transforming exploration. The 'early Suttas' in a sense actually *use* the deep-seated illusion of Self (this being an example of 'skilful means'). Its ideal of perfection is used as a criterion against which all else can be measured. In this way, non-attachment to everything can be fostered by the recognition that this . . . this . . . this . . . *everything* is not-Self. In the total letting-go that this leads to, *nibbāna* is realized. While this is still not-Self, it is like a Self in many respects – permanent, blissful, not dependent on anything – though lacking the crucial aspect of I-ness. The attitude 'I am' can only arise with respect to the personality-factors and is a *mistake* even here. So *nibbāna* is the Self-like goal which is attained when attachment to all not-Self phenomena ceases, and the full-blown Self-ideal has been abandoned as a deep-rooted but ultimately baseless human aspiration. This aspiration is to find that which is an inviolable true identity, a permanent, blissful state of total autonomy, where 'I' rests content in itself. The irony is that seeking such a state breeds suffering, for it tries to combine the uncombinable: I-centred-ness and genuine, secure happiness. To attain the second, which is *nibbāna*, the first must be abandoned. When this is done, though, the empirical personality comes to be very strong: a 'developed self'. An Arahat is a 'big person' precisely because the limiting I-delusion has been jettisoned. This leaves space for the unhindered working of the many Dhamma-qualities whose development culminated in the Arahat's state.

(14.2) Chapter 4 shows that seeing a person as a Self-less set of processes does not undermine questions of moral responsibility or continuity of character. In spite of the changes taking place in a person, some character-patterns are repeated, even over many lives, before they are worn out or replaced by others. The process-view of a person, then, does not see personality as a chaotic flux, but as a law-governed moving pattern which only changes in so far as supporting conditions change. The complex of conditions arises out of an interaction of those internal to a person's own stream of psycho-physical processes and those from the external world. Some of the 'external' conditions, though, will be influenced or generated by internal processes, present or past (karma). The person-process is not an isolated self in an alien world, but one which is changed by, and changes, its environment.

(14.3) As seen in chapter 5, the empirical self not only objectively affects its surrounding external world, but also generates (consciously and unconsciously) its own subjective image of this world, which it then lives in as 'reality'. It lives in a world of its own making by a) tuning into a particular level of consciousness (by meditation or the rebirth it attains through its karma) which has a particular range of objects – a world – available to it, b) selective noticing from among such objects, and c) then processing what has been sensed to form a distorted interpretative model of reality: a model in which the 'I am' conceit is a crucial reference point. When *nibbāna* is experienced, though, all such models are transcended: the world stops 'in this fathom-long carcase'.

(14.4) As seen in chapter 6, a real and sustaining feature of the empirical self is the 'life-principle', whose crucial component is the personality-factor known as discernment (*viññāṇa*). This is particularly prone to being taken as a permanent Self, a metaphysical Life Principle, but is, in fact, a changing and conditioned state. It is not destroyed by death, though, but flows on, accompanied by other factors, as the key feature of the subtle spirit (*gandhabba*) which exists in the intermediary period between rebirths. This intermediary existence is shown to be an idea supported by the 'early Suttas' though not by the Theravādin transmitters of these texts. The 'early

Suttas' see it as a craving-driven period of 'coming and going', wandering in search of a new rebirth for the 'I am' delusion to feed on. It is a period, though, in which the most quick-witted type of Non-returner can destroy this delusion, and attain *nibbāna*, before another rebirth ensues.

(14.5) Part II presents what might be seen as a largely psychological analysis of reality: both of the conditioned state of personality, which generates suffering, and the nibbānic state which transcends this. Chapter 7 shows that the 'early Suttas' saw a person as a cluster of mental and physical processes centred on discernment, also seen as a succession of mind-sets (*citta*s). *Citta* is in some sense the functioning centre of the empirical self, but it is not a unitary self consistently working to a stable goal. While steering the general flow of the person-process, is not actually in charge of itself. It is like the captain of a vessel who can never quite make up his mind where he wants to go, or a succession of captains (some of which keep returning) that each think that they have always been at the helm. *Citta*, then, represents a number of competing, but related, mind-sets. Spiritual development helps make them more consistent and integrated. In more analytical terms, a person is seen as a combination of discernment and the sentient body (*nāma-rūpa*), which latter comprises all the personality-factors other than discernment. These interact in such a way that discernment is influenced, maintained and buffeted by the sentient body it engenders, enlivens and directs. The constant interplay of these two generates a vortex of changing states which spins out *saṃsāra*: the conditioned realm of moment-to-moment, day-to-day and life-to-life existence. Chapter 8 analyses the details of this interplay, with the constructing activities, such as will, moulding a person and directing discernment onto a variety of objects from within the accompanying sentient body and external meaningful forms (both '*nāma-rūpa*'). In this, attention acts to select the objects to which prior activities have given the mind an inclination. Once discernment finds a particular object, it conditions the sentient body to continue in a way which is focussed on that, whether this be from moment to moment in the process of perceiving the world, or from life to life.

(14.6) Chapters 9 and 10 examine the nature and activity of discernment/*citta* according to the 'early Suttas' and developed Theravādin theory. Chapter 9 shows that discernment works hand-in-hand with cognition (*saññā*) in the perceptual process, each making its own contribution to the complete perception. Discernment contributes the basic awareness of the presence of an object, and the separation of this into its parts. Cognition contributes the classification and labelling of these as a perceptual interpretation or misinterpretation. Even in the 'early Suttas', the perceptual process was envisaged as a series of states which included different kinds of discernment, a model which is merely refined, but not invented, in the Canonical and later Abhidhamma. Another such 'Abhidhamma' concept is that of *bhavaṅga*, the latent resting state of the mind. Such an idea also has roots in the 'early Suttas', but is, of course, not the same as the idea of a hidden 'Self'. A stratum of 'early Sutta' texts also deals with the 'brightly shining' *citta*, which represents the mind's potential for spiritual development. The perspective of these texts is that, however unstable and variable the *citta* is, however much it is defiled and flows on from rebirth to rebirth (be they good or bad), it has a natural radiance and purity which is only ever obscured, never destroyed. The process of spiritual development is one of weakening these obscuring defilements, by morality and meditative calming, and finally destroying them, by an insight which sees all that they latch on to as impermanent, *dukkha* and not-Self. The final destruction comes with the experience of *nibbāna*, the subject of chapters 11 and 12.

(14.7) Chapter 11 argues that *nibbāna* during life is a timeless experience in which all the personality-factors 'stop'. This is a state where the constant arising (birth) and passing away (death) of the personality-factor processes is transcended. Here, the stopping of the constructing activities means that there is simply the 'unconstructed'. In this state, *dukkha* in *all* senses is transcended. There is not only no physical or mental pain, and no changing states, but there is no *dukkha* in the sense of imperfect, constructed phenomena. This state is not experienced by the Arahat all the time, but he or she can re-enter it during life, and can also be aware of it without entering it. Chapter 12 argues that discernment, the heart of the normal personality-process, is also, when radically transformed, that which is *nibbāna*. When insight into phenomena as impermanent, *dukkha* and not-Self reaches the highest level, the vortical interplay of discernment and *nāma-rūpa* stops, *nāma-rūpa* drops away, and discernment stands without any object, having let go of all of them. Discernment is thus unsupported, unconstructed, infinite and radiant, beyond any worldly phenomenon. This timeless reality can be 'participated in' by the Arahat on occasions when his or her liberated personality is not needed to act in some way within the conditioned world. At death, the conditioned personality-factors fall away, but objectless discernment, *nibbāna*, still timelessly exists.

(14.8) Chapter 13 focusses on the state of the enlightened person before and beyond death. Such a person, having let go of all the personality-factors, is 'deep, immeasurable, hard to fathom as is the great ocean'. He cannot be pinned down in any way, as he has no focusses of attachment or I-identity. He or she cannot be angered, for example, for nothing is 'owned' and so there is no need for an angry 'defence' of 'I-me-mine'. There is no 'I' there to feel threatened by anything. Such a person cannot be fathomed by those who can only think of a person as centred on some I-identity. Those who destroy views on Self/I know the nature of an enlightened person, though; for at Stream-entry they see and fathom the timeless Dhamma, *nibbāna*, which is his nature. The hard-to-fathom enlightened one has become this Dhamma and thus destroyed all limiting defilements. In normal consciousness, his brightly shining *citta* is ever-radiant, and the qualities of the Holy Eightfold Path provide him with a Dhamma 'body' that is a source of teaching and strength for others. When an enlightened person, Buddha or Arahat, dies, all conditioned features of him finally pass away, but his unconditioned nature, nibbānic discernment, timelessly exists. Being beyond the conditioned, this does not lead on to any further rebirth, as normal discernment does. But nor is it destroyed. It exists as timeless *nibbāna*: blissful, *dukkha*-less, unborn, deathless, and unconstructed. It must be seen as beyond anything which could individualise it, for there cannot be more than one timeless, unconstructed state. It is discernment which has transcended its normal limited state by abandoning all objects, even *nibbāna* itself, so as not to be dependent on anything at all. Abandoning all that is constructed, it leaves behind all *dukkha*. It is a discernment which is emptiness: it is totally empty of all 'I-ness', of all defilements, of all impermanent, *dukkha*, constructed states, of all that is normally meant by 'discernment'. And yet the 'early Suttas' still refer to it as a kind of discernment.

(14.9) This interpretation clearly has something in common with the Yogācārin emphasis on discernment (*vijñāna*) as central to both the unenlightened and enlightened state. In contrast to the other main Mahāyāna school, the Mādhyamikas, the Yogācārins were unwilling to see the enlightened state as one of total 'emptiness'. They were also close to the strand of Mahāyāna thought concerning the *tathāgata-garbha*, later known as the 'Buddha-nature'. As seen in chapter 10, the beginnings of such an idea are also found in the 'early

Suttas'. A key Mādhyamika criticism of the Yogacara is that they wrongly privileged discernment as the one thing which stands out 'in' emptiness, as not empty of itself: as if it had an inherent, non-dependent Self-nature. Nevertheless, the 'early Suttas' do contain a clear strand of thought which is willing to see *nibbāna* as a form of discernment. Such an unconditioned discernment, though, is seen as attained by recognising *everything* as empty of Self, and is itself empty of what is normally meant by the conditioned, dependent factor known as 'discernment'.

(14.10) Such different view-points are all, of course, seeking to give the best articulation of the 'middle way' advocated by the Buddha. Conditioned Arising provides a middle way analysis which shows that a person, after death, is neither annihilated nor continues as an eternal Self. This is because the Suttas see a person as reborn by the continuation of a conditioned, changing process. The analysis developed in Part I show that the Suttas chart a middle way not only between full Annihilationism and full Eternalism, but also between partial versions of these. Partial Annihilationism is to say that, though rebirth normally follows death, there are no relatively stable character-patterns passed on from life to life. Chapter 4 shows that such a view is at odds with that of the 'early Suttas'. Partial Eternalism is the view of the Personalists, who posited a subtle 'person' which was neither eternal nor non-eternal, but was the carrier of personal continuity from life to life. Paras.1.36–42 show this to be a misinterpretation of the Suttas. As to what lies beyond the death of an enlightened person, similar extremes are avoided in the 'early Suttas': Annihilation, or the Eternal existence, of a liberated 'Self'. Partial Annihilationism and Eternalism are also possibilities here. The first is to make *nibbāna* so transcendent, and unrelated to the personality-factors of the enlightened person, that *nibbāna* beyond death has no apparent connection to that person. Classical Theravāda seems close to such a view. Partial Eternalism seems to be advocated by the Mahāyāna view of the Buddha as continuing to exist at a heavenly level, albeit with insight into emptiness etc. In this work, I have tried to show that the 'early Suttas', through both hints and explicit passages, see *nibbāna*, in life or beyond death, as unsupported, object-less discernment, thus avoiding both these partial extremes. As advocated at M.I.260, however, one should not cling to any view, however 'purified' or 'cleansed' it is: how much more so to one that may fall short in these regards! All views are not-Self.

APPENDIX

The Theory of the Process of *Citta*s

(A.1) This appendix will show how the theory of the 'process (*vīthi*) of *citta* s' (Vism.22), normally associated with the commentarial writings of Buddhaghosa, was already implicit within the Canonical Abhidhamma of the Theravāda. As seen in ch.9, the early beginnings of such a theory were already present in the 'early Suttas'. The appendix will also give an outline of the fully developed theory, also known as the 'continuity (*-santānaṃ*)' of *citta*s.

(A.2) The earliest Theravādin Abhidhamma text was probably the *Dhammasaṅgaṇi*. As can be seen from Para.7.11, this envisages a series of *citta* s consisting of one of visual-, aural-, nasal-, gustatory-, tactile-, or conceptional-discernment, or the conception-element (*mano-dhātu*), followed by another of these, etc.. The *Vibhaṅga* and *Paṭṭhāna* then outlined the specific sequences in which these *citta* s occurred. At the end of the period of the canonical Abhidhamma, the *Kathāvatthu* explicitly refers to *citta* s as lasting only a moment each, and talks of the 'continuity (*-santati*)' of *citta*s (Kvu.458). The *Milindapañha* also refers to a 'continuity of processes (*dhamma-santati*)', apparently consisting primarily of forms of discernment (Miln.40).

(A.3) The *Vibhaṅga* is the first text to put the *citta*s enumerated in the *Dhammasaṅgaṇi* in some sort of sequence. Dhs.1418 says that there are just three conception-elements, these beings described at Dhs.455, 562 and 566 as the 'fruitions (*vipākā*)' of wholesome or unwholesome karma or as 'functional' (*kiriyā*, i.e. a spontaneous occurrence which is neither karmically active nor the fruition of karma). Vibh.88–9 explains them thus:

> Therein, what is conception-element? Immediately after the cessation of the visual-discernment-element that has arisen,

> there arises a *citta* . . . as appropriate conception-element . . . Or else it is the first act-of-attention (*samannāhāro*) to any process (*sabbe-dhammesu*).

This says that one conception-element succeeds visual-discernment (or any of the other four discernments related to physical sense-organs) and that another is the first act of attention to an object in *any* of the six sense-channels. As, from the *Dhammasaṅgaṇi*, a conception-element cannot be simultaneous with another *citta*, this latter conception-element must *precede* any of the five sense-discernments or conceptional-discernment. As M.I.190 says (Para.8.13), an 'act-of-attention' is needed for a 'share of discernment' to occur in relation to an object. Vibh.89–90 then adds that, after visual-discernment and the following conception-element, there arises 'an appropriate conceptional-discernment-element'. Vibh.320–21 shows that the latter is associated with the generation of karma. This is because it says the five (sense) discernments neither arise consecutively nor simultaneously, nor do they perform wholesome or unwholesome states. As, from the *Dhammasaṅgaṇi*, conception-element is either a fruition or is functional, then only the following conceptional-discernment-element can be what performs wholesome or unwholesome states, i.e. karmas, which generate later fruitions. Given that the five sense-discernments are only fruitions (Dhs.431, 443, 556), the following *citta*-sequence thus emerges in the *Vibhaṅga*:

i) conception-element, as the first act-of-attention to an object → a sense-discernment-element, which is a fruition, → conception-element → conceptional-discernment-element, as that which performs karma.
ii) conception-element, as the first act-of-attention to a mental object → conceptional-discernment-element.

(A.4) The *Paṭṭhāna* considerably extends these *citta*-sequences. As argued by Lance S. Cousins, 'almost all the stages of the consciousness process are precisely specified in the *Paṭṭhāna*' (1981: 41). It introduces the term '*bhavaṅga*' as an apparently already familiar term, and sees it as a fruitional state (Pt.I.368; CR.406–07) which is 'grasped at' (*upādiṇṇa*) and 'favourable to grasping' (*upādāniya*) (Pt.I.411; CR.461). It can be immediately followed by another *bhavaṅga* (Pt. I.313; CR.339), or by 'advertence' (*āvajjana*)

(Pt.I.312–13; CR.338–39). This 'advertence' is said to be a functional state (Pt.I.368; CR.406–07) and to be followed by five-fold-discernment (Pt.I.369; CR.407). 'Advertence' can thus be identified with the conception-element which is the first act-of-attention in the *Vibhaṅga*, and is shown to be the functional, rather than fruitional conception-element referred to in the *Dhammasaṅgaṇi*. The *Paṭṭhāna* also shows that, following after one of the five-fold-discernments, in succession, come fruitional conception-element, fruitional conceptional-discernment-element (Pt.I.411–12; CR.461), and then a functional conceptional-discernment-element (Pt.I.368; CR.407, and Pt.I.312; CR.339). It is also to be noted, here, that Dhs.431–97, in dealing with the fruitions of wholesome states, deals with them in the order visual- . . . tactile-discernment, conception-element, conceptional-discernment-element, conceptional-discernment-element. This suggests that the order was, even in the *Dhammasaṅgaṇi*, taken as partly indicating a set temporal sequence. In the case of the 'conception-door', or mental sense-channel, the *Paṭṭhāna* gives a different sequence from that for the other 'sense-doors': 'advertence', then 'personality-factors producing fruitions' (Pt.I.369; CR.407). The name for the latter, from Ps.II.72 and 73, can be seen to be *javana*, 'impulsion', as these passages refer to 'wholesome karma in the moment of *javana*'. *Javana* is thus clearly what produces fruitions, and is thus the karmically active state. Such states 'producing fruitions' are seen to succeed each other, an unspecified number of times, before being followed by 'emergence', a fruitional state (Pt.I.368 and 369; CR.407). Summarising the above details, along with those previously tabulated, the following *citta*-sequences emerge:

i) *Bhavaṅga* → *bhavaṅga* (etc.) → a functional *citta* accomplishing 'advertence', i.e. conception-element as the first act-of-attention to an object → a fruitional sense-discernment-element → fruitional conception-element → fruitional conceptional-discernment-element → functional conceptional-discernment-element → a sequence of conceptional-discernment-elements as what perform karma, i.e. *javana* → emergence, a fruitional state.
ii) *Bhavaṅga* → *bhavaṅga* (etc.) → a functional *citta* accomplishing 'advertence', i.e. conception-element as the first act-of-attention to a mental object → a sequence of personality-factors producing fruitions, i.e. a series of conceptional-discernment-elements (with any accompanying factors), called *javana* → emergence, a fruitional state.

(A.5) In the *Vimuttimagga* (Ehara et al, 1977: 256), now found only in Chinese, and in the later *Visuddhimagga*, which was partly based on it, the various *citta*s are given names and explanations are added. The sequence, as outlined at Vism.21 and 458–60, is as follows:

a) the continuity (*santāna*) of *bhavaṅga citta*s;
b) a visible form as object (*ārammaṇa*) comes into the eye's range such that there is 'impinging on the eye-sensitivity' and *bhavaṅga* arises and ceases twice, this being the 'disturbance' of *bhavaṅga*;
c) functional conception-element with the function of adverting (*āvajjana*) to the visible form, 'as it were, cutting off *bhavaṅga*';
d) visual-discernment with the function of 'seeing' (*dassana*), with eye-sensitivity as its 'physical basis', which discernment is a fruition.
e) fruitional conception-element with the function of 'receiving' (*sampaṭicchana*) the object;
f) fruitional 'root-causeless' (*ahetuka*) conceptional-discernment-element, with the function of 'investigating' (*santīraṇa*) the object;
g) functional root-causeless conceptional-discernment-element, accompanied by indifference (*upekkhā*), with the function of 'determining' (*votthapana*) what the object is;
h) six or seven 'impulsions impel (*javanāni javanti*)', if the object is vivid. *Javana*s are always carried out by forms of conceptional-discernment-element, be these normal karmically active wholesome or unwholesome *citta*s, Path or Fruit *citta*s, which have *nibbāna* as object, or the 'functional' *citta* specific to an Arahat, who generates no karmic fruits.
i) if the object is very vivid, there is then an occurrence, twice or once, of 'registration' (*tadārammaṇa*), also called 'aftermath *bhavaṅga*', which is fruitional;
a) *bhavaṅga* then resumes its occurrence and continues until interrupted again.

In this sequence, c)–i) all have the same object and comprise the 'process (*vīthi-*) of *citta*s' (Vism.22) or the 'continuity (*-santānaṃ*)' of *citta*s, occurring according to the 'law of *citta*' (Vism.460). All items, a)–i), are also said to be 'modes (*ākārā*)' in which *citta*s 'function (*pavattanti*)' (Vism.457). It is pointed out at Asl.269 that when the mind responds to a weak object, only stage b) or g) may be reached before the mind lapses back into *bhavaṅga*. In the case of the mental sense-channel, the process of *citta*s is curtailed (Vism.458–60):

a) the continuity of *bhavaṅga*;
b) an object of any of the six kinds comes into the range of the conception-door and there is 'disturbance' of *bhavaṅga*;
c) the functional conceptional-discernment-element without root-cause arises, accompanied by indifference, as it were cutting off *bhavaṅga* and accomplishing the function of 'advertence'.

The sequence then jumps to h), i) and a), above. These two sequences simply put names to the *citta*s in the *Paṭṭhāna*, add a few details to them, add 'disturbance' of *bhavaṅga* at the beginning of each, and says that conceptional-discernment-element, rather than conception-element, adverts in the case of the mental sense-channel.

(A.6) In fact, Vibh.88–9 (Para.A.3) does not explicitly say that conception-element adverts in the mental sense-channel, and the *Paṭṭhāna* does not specify whether it is conception-element or conceptional-discernment-element. The functional conceptional-discernment-element which Buddhaghosa uses to perform this function is a *citta* already referred to, at Dhs.574, being also used for 'determining' in the other five sense-channels. In both cases, it is the *citta* which immediately precedes *javana*. This seems appropriate as, in the mental sense-channel, an object will be immediately perceived and 'determined' even at advertence: it does not need to be interpreted but arises as already having a determined meaning. As regards the conception-element of the Suttas, though, the above shows that Buddhaghosa makes this equivalent to various forms of conceptional-discernment-element in the Abhidhamma sense: for *bhavaṅga* and advertence in the mental sense-channel are all carried out by this type of *citta*. Thus at M.A.I.77, on M.I.112, he explains that 'conception' in 'conceptional-discernment arises conditioned by conception and mental objects' is just *bhavaṅga-citta* (with conceptional-discernment as advertence) or '*bhavaṅga*-conception with advertence' (with conceptional-discernment as *javana*). Similarly, at Vism.489, he says, 'conceptional-discernment arises conditioned by *bhavaṅga*-conception, a mental object and attention'.

(A.7) Buddhaghosa's *Visuddhimagga* scheme also mentions two modes of *citta* besides *bhavaṅga* and those arising in the sense-channels, as above.

i) 'falling away' (*cuti*), the last *citta* of a life, and
ii) 'relinking' (*paṭisandhi*), the *citta* occurring at the moment of conception in the womb.

These are referred to at Pt.I.312–13 (CR.338–39) as '*cuti-citta*' and 'rebirth-(*uppatti*)-*citta*', with the latter immediately following the former. Vism.457 explains that the relinking *citta* has the same object as the mind had 'at the time of death', which may be a particular karma done by the person, a symbol of this, or an indication of his next rebirth. Vism.549–50 makes clear that, at the time of death, there is a sequence, in the mental sense-channel, of: disturbance of *bhavaṅga*, advertence to such an object, *javana*s and registration. Alternatively, a fuller process may occur in one of the other sense-channels, with an item associated with unwholesome or wholesome thoughts as object. Next, 'one falling away *citta* arises making *bhavaṅga*'s objective field (*-visayaṃ*) its object (*ārammaṇaṃ*)'. The immediately following relinking discernment(s) (there may be between one and five) take the same object as advertence to registration, not the object taken by the 'falling away' *citta*. The object of this – and of the (past) *bhavaṅga* – is not specified. Nevertheless, after relinking discernment, *bhavaṅga*-discernment takes over, and has the same object as relinking discernment (Vism.458). This implies that the object of *bhavaṅga*-discernment changes from life to life, and is an item associated with the time of death in the previous life:

i) immediately prior to the end of one life, the mind focusses on an object associated with the next rebirth, or good or bad karma already done, or something associated with such actions;
ii) after 'registering' this object, one moment of 'falling away' *citta* follows, with the same object as the *bhavaṅga* of the ending life;
iii) immediately after this, one to five moments of 'relinking' *citta* arise at the very start of the next rebirth, with the same object as in i).
iv) the *bhavaṅga*, or resting-state, *citta* of that life then takes over, with, again, the same object.

It is clear from this that *bhavaṅga is* seen to have an object. Indeed, Asl.278 says that a *citta* may arise without adverting, but not without an object (*ārammaṇa*). *Bhavaṅga* is also said to be of the same *type* as the relinking *citta* at the start of the present life, which varies according to the type of rebirth and past karma (Vism.458; Gethin,

1994). Relinking, *bhavaṅga* and falling away *citta*s are all forms of conceptional-discernment and are karmic fruitions, which may include meditative states (the *jhāna*s or the formless attainments) arising due to past attainment of them. The latter would relate to the *bhavaṅga*s of beings in the heavens of (pure) form and formlessness.

NOTES

INTRODUCTION

1. The present work is based on the author's doctoral thesis, 'The Concept of the Person In Pāli Buddhist Literature', submitted to Lancaster University in 1981. Chapter 3 has previously appeared, in slightly altered wording, as 'Developing a self without boundaries' in BSR., 1 (2), 1983–84, 115–26. An earlier version of ch.13 was published as Harvey 1983. Some material from ch.6 has appeared in Harvey 1986b, and some from chs. 10 and 12 has appeared in Harvey 1989.

CHAPTER 1

1. See also Horner and Coomaraswamy, 1948. Mrs. C.A.F.Rhys Davids also had similar ideas, as e.g. at Kindred Sayings Vol.II p.x and Vol.III pp.ixx.
2. For other examples, see Dhp.103; ; Sn.585, 782, 888; M.I.276, 288; A.II.179, A.III.125 (cf. Dhp.66); S.I.162, 238; D.III.93; Nd.II.79
3. The commentary (M.A.I.38) says that '*nibbāna*' here means 'enjoyment of the five kinds of sensory pleasures', which spiritually immature people take as *nibbāna* (quoting D.I.36 in support). Likewise, the Theravādin Abhidhamma interprets this passage in the same way (Kvu.401). I disagree. At M.I.4, '*nibbāna*' comes at the end of a long list of items (pp.3–4), all of which are subjected to the process of 'conceiving'. The list starts with the four material elements, continues with a number of gods and heavens at an ever higher level of existence, then finishes with, 'the seen . . . the heard . . . the sensed . . . the discerned . . . unity . . . diversity . . . all (*sabbam*) . . . *nibbāna*'. If '*nibbāna*' simply meant enjoyment of sense-pleasures, it would be a rather paltry item with which to round off such an all-encompassing list. Indeed, at A.V.318–19 there is a similar list, culminating with *nibbāna* in a genuine sense. The fact that '*nibbāna*' comes after 'all' at M.I.4 indicates that genuine *nibbāna* is meant there. This is because, at S.IV.27, 'all', meaning all components of a person, is said to be 'subject to death'. As *nibbāna* is the 'deathless', it is the clear contrast to this, and would appropriately come after its contrasting pair in the same way that 'diversity' follows 'unity'.

Though a spiritually immature person has not experienced *nibbāna*, he can still have ideas about it, just as he can have ideas about a refined heavenly sphere, which he probably has not experienced either.

4. both the spellings *anupalabbyamane* (S.IV.384) and *anupalabbiyamāno* (S.III.118) are used.
5. As can be seen e.g. from two parallel passages at S.III.140 and A.II.38–9. One talks of 'the *tathāgata*' and the other of 'I. . .'.
6. Note that Venkataramanan, in his SNS. translation, generally uses the word 'self' rather than 'person'. A non-Chinese reader can only assume that this is his translation of the (or a) Chinese translation of the Sanskrit '*pudgala*', or 'person'. I thus treat his 'self' as equivalent to 'person'.

CHAPTER 2

1. A.A.III.22, cf. S.I.88 and its commentary, S.A.I.271
2. As at Sn.68 and 219. This reading is found in both the Pāli Text Society and Pāli Publication Board editions.
3. C. in Para.2.6 sees 'essence' as 'empty, as not-Self'. It also, though, sees it 'as devoid, as hollow', which Ps.II.238–41 says *nibbāna* is not. This must be because Ps. and Nd. are using either 'essence' or 'devoid, hollow' in different senses.

CHAPTER 3

1. 'Dhamma' must here be used in the sense of 'teaching' (and its practice), as at A.I.218, where a layman praises Ānanda's modesty in teaching by saying, 'here there is no trumpeting his own Dhamma, no depreciating another's Dhamma, but just teaching Dhamma in its proper sphere'.
2. *puñña*, usually translated, somewhat lamely, as 'merit'.
3. *Kāya*, or 'body' may refer to the 'mental-body' (*nāma-kāya*), i.e. the mental components of a person other than *citta*, or to everything in a person other than *citta*, 'mind-and-body' (*nāma-rūpa*) as a whole (see below, chapter 7. A 'developed *kāya*' would then be a person's 'body' of mental states, or their 'sentient body' when developed by spiritual practice. At M.I.239, having a 'developed *kāya*' means that when a pleasurable feeling arises, it does not persists in taking hold of *citta*, through attachment; while having a 'developed *citta*' means that when an *un*pleasant feeling arises, it does not persist in taking hold of *citta*, through grieving. M.A.II.285 sees the first state as developed by Insight (*vipassanā*) meditation, and the second by Calm (*samatha*) meditation.
4. As quoted and translated by Har Dayal (1932: 15–16). On the meditative 'higher knowledges' (*abhiññā*s) as overcoming various barriers, see Para.10.31.
5. And not because he is unaware of objects (at least in normal consciousness: see ch.12).
6. These two aspects might be seen to correspond to the emphases which Mahāyāna Buddhism assigns to 'Hīnayāna' Buddhism and itself, respectively non-attachment and compassionate concern for others.

CHAPTER 4

1. S.III.114–15 uses '*upādiṇṇa*' in a different sense to that at M.I.185: all five personality-factors are seen as '*upādiṇṇa*' when someone has views on them as related to a Self in some way.
2. It is not the case that *everything* is seen as influenced by karma. At S.IV.230–31 (cf. A.II.88, A.V.110 and Miln.134–38), the Buddha denies that all feeling is 'due to what was done earlier', explaining that feelings (by which he evidently means those arising through the body) can arise due to a number of biological or environmental causes, *or* 'born of the fruition of karma'. There are thus many non-karmic causal chains, and only *some* things are directly caused by karma.

CHAPTER 5

1. In some of the '(pure) form' heavenly worlds, specific senses are said to be missing (Vibh.418), while the 'formless' worlds are purely mental, with nothing in them related to the five physical sense-objects.
2. E.g. in the *Avyākata-saṃyutta*, S.IV.374–403.
3. Cf. S.IV.394. See also S.Collins, *Selfless Persons*, pp. 132–33.
4. This is only one of a number of possible routes to the attainment of *nibbāna*.

CHAPTER 6

1. '*Sarīra*' is best translated as 'mortal body' as, unlike other words denoting the body, it is often used of dead bodies (A.III.57 and 323; D.II.141), or even of bones left over after a cremation (D.II.64), i.e. 'relics'. When used of a living body, *sarīra* is that which wears out with old age (Dhp.151), or which becomes lean and pale through grief (Sn.584).
2. Cf. similar language on 'Self' at Para.1.17 and 'being' at Para.1.22.
3. See Jacobi 1973, II: 340: his translation, except for the replacement of 'soul' by 'life-principle'.
4. Even some Annihilationists believed in a 'mind-made' Self. In this, they could be seen as accepting a life-principle which was not the same as the physical body, but which was so strongly dependent on it that it was destroyed at its death. On the general 'mind-body' relationship in the Pāli Canon and later Theravāda texts, see Harvey, 1993.
5. This does not make it like the 'person' of the Personalists, which they saw as related to the personality-factors as fire is to fuel (SNS.182, L'AK.V.234). They saw it as not the same as the personality-factors (Kvu.11–13 and 20), while the life-principle being discussed here is primarily discernment: one of these factors.
6. Note that the Abhidhamma solution to the life-principle/mortal-body problem is to say that the life-principle is, essentially, the 'life-faculty' (*jīvit-indriya*), which comprises *both* a physical and a non-physical 'life-faculty'. Cf. Paras.4.16 and 6.3.
7. There seems to be a particular link between the discernment-nutriment

and the 'doctrine of Self' (*atta-vāda*). The four nutriments are said to depend on craving (M.I.261), which puts them in the same place as 'grasping' (*upādāna*) in the Conditioned Arising sequence. As pointed out by S.Collins (1982: 296), *āhāra* ('nutriment') and *upādāna* are in fact both from verbal roots meaning to 'take up' (*up-ā-dā*, *ā-hṛ*) S.II.3 defines the 'grasping' causal-link as grasping at: sense-desire, views, virtue-and-vows, and Self-doctrine. The first three of these are associated with the first three nutriments: i) 'food-nutriment' is linked to attachment to sense-pleasures (S.II.99), ii) views depend on 'stimulation' (D.I.41–2), the second nutriment, and iii) grasping at virtue-and-vows is obviously associated with attachment to certain forms of mental volition. This leaves 'grasping at Self-doctrine' to correspond to discernment-nutriment.

8. Cf.SNS.187–88, which shows that the Sammitīyas saw the transfer from the personality-factors of one life to those of the intermediary existence as instantaneous, with no gap or overlap.
9. Cf. Para 6.11, on discernment as like air or the wind/breath. It is also seen as a fuelling 'nutriment' for rebirth (Para.6.13).
10. This says, implausibly, 'just in the moment of falling away (*cuti*) he is not arisen (*anuppanno*), from the non-arisen state of relinking-*citta* [i.e. discernment at the time of conception]'.
11. SNS.201 and Kvu.366, with Kvu.A.106.
12. Kvu.366, with Kvu.A.106.
13. This passage is also referred to, in its Sanskrit form, by Vasubandhu (L'AK.II.38–9), though he does not analyse it in any detail.
14. An actual example of an *antarā-parinibbāyī* Non-returner is probably referred to at S.IV.59–60. The attempted Theravādin explanation of A.II.134 is: '"of a kind to take up arising", by which he takes up arising immediately. "Of a kind to take up becoming", the condition for the taking up of arising-becoming' (A.A.III.130). This seems to mean that those with the first fetters are reborn immediately, while those with the second simply have conditions in them for rebirth. This implies that all Non-returners except the highest kind will die as soon as they become Non-returners!
15. For the Sarvāstivādins, there are four kinds of 'becoming': intermediary-becoming; arising-becoming (becoming at the moment of conception); prior-time-becoming (becoming during life, prior to death); and death-becoming (becoming at the moment of death) (L'AK.II.45 and 117. cf. 36).
16. Indeed the Sammitīyas saw the between-lives state as a time for re-adjustment before a new mode of self-expression (SNS.202).
17. At L'AK.II.122, '*saṃbhavaiṣin*' (Sanskrit) is one of the five names for the intermediary existence, along with '*manomaya*', '*gandharva*' and '*(abhi)nirvrtti*'.
18. See SNS.201 and L'AK.II.37 and 122.
19. Wijesekera, 1945, traces the Vedic ancestry of these and many other aspects of the *gandhabba* described in the Pāli texts.
20. Also found at M.II.156–57. Cf. Jat.V.330 and Miln.127 and 129. 'Descent into the womb' could be an alternative rendering of '*gabbhass-*

āvakkanti', but M.A.II.310 quotes M.III.122 in support of '*gabbha*' meaning the being in the womb, the embryo. Also, when D.II.62–3 talks of discernment descending into the womb, the word for 'womb' is '*kucchi*', this being in the accusative, not dative, as '*gabbhassa*' would have be for it to mean 'into the womb'. Note that a passage at A.I.176 sees 'descent of the embryo' as conditioning mind-and-body in the same way that discernment does at D.II.62–3 and elsewhere. An interesting passage at D.I.229 also sees the 'embryo' as being 'ripened' in a previous life.

21. L'AK.II.47 says that the intermediary beings of the sense-desire world eat 'food-nutriment' of a non-gross kind: odour.
22. Cf. Kvu.A.106–07. D.I.195 describes two kinds of bodies which 'have form (*rūpī*)', one of which is mind-made and the other of which is 'gross', comprised of the four great physical elements, and feeding on 'food-nutriment'. If the *gandhabba* had a mind-made body and yet fed on '*subtle*' food-nutriment, so as not to have a 'gross' body, it would be an intermediary between a 'mind-made' and 'gross' body.
23. 1970: 85 & 249–53. For a modern account of 'memories' which purport to concern the experience of a person between lives, see Story 1975: 191–99.

CHAPTER 7

1. *Citta* can also be synonymous with *mano*, the 'mind-organ', e.g. at S.I.53, A.III.336, Sn.161, D.III.103–04, and S.II.94.
2. 1975: 507, note 35 '. . . perception and formations' is his translation of *saññā* and *saṅkhārā*, here translated as 'cognition' and 'the constructing activities'.
3. S.III.80 seems to equate 'the discernment-endowed body' and 'all external *nimitta*s (sensory indications)' with the five personality-factors *wherever* they occur, internal to a particular person or external to him.
4. The Abhidhamma, though, sees it as partly dependent on some aspect of material form. The *Paṭṭhāna* refers to 'the material form supported by which mind-organ-element and mind-organ-discernment-element occur' (I. p.5; CR.I.6). See Harvey, 1993.
5. It might be said that, as *nāma-rūpa* and the six sense-spheres are separate items in the standard Conditioned Arising sequence, then *nāma-rūpa* cannot be the same as the *kāya*, as this is said to include the six sense-bases (Para.7.12). However, many passages on Conditioned Arising (e.g. D.II.62) omit any reference to the sense-spheres, going direct from *nāma-rūpa* to stimulation. The sense-spheres must thus be optionally includable in one or other of these. As they are the sense-organs (S.II.3), five of which are physical, the sense-spheres cannot be included in stimulation (*phassa*), as this is not included in *rūpa* (material form; S.II.3–4). They must thus be included within *nāma-rūpa* in passages where *nāma-rūpa* is said to directly condition stimulation. *Nāma-rūpa* can thus be the same as the *kāya*, with the sense-organs as like the 'gates' of the 'town' of *kāya*/*nāma-rūpa*: in one sense part of it, in another sense different from and dependent on it.

6. In the term '*sakkāya*', 'existing group' or 'own group', '*kāya*' refers to all five personality-factors (M.I.299), thus including discernment. This is another sense of the term, but it does at least show its flexibility: it is not limited in its use to the physical body devoid of mental components.
7. A.K.Warder's rendering, 1970: 108. So far, the more conventional rendering 'mind-and-body' has been used. The suggestion, in the last Para., that the term may sometimes mean 'meaningful forms', will be further discussed at Paras.8.11 and 21.
8. Vism.558, on the *nāma-rūpa* link, agrees, though Vism.438 uses *nāma-rūpa* in a wider sense, to cover all five personality-factors.
9. Cf. the 'discernment-endowed body' of Para.7.13. The passage is also reminiscent of the statement that the world and its origin lie within 'this fathom-long carcase which is cognitive and endowed with conception' (Para. 5.6).

CHAPTER 8

1. See Para.7.5. This parallel suggests that *cetanā* is the principal state whose association with discernment deploys the latter to form an arrangement, a 'mind-set', which is *citta*.
2. That '*ārammaṇas*' here means the 'object' of discernment, as in the Abhidhamma (e.g. Dhs.1) can be shown as follows. A.IV.146–47, having referred to the six sense-organs, six sense-objects (visible forms etc.) and the six forms of discernment (visual discernment etc.), gives, in one manuscript, a summarising verse: 'With respect to the six doors and *ārammaṇa*s, here, and to the discernments. . .'. That is, '*ārammaṇa*' is used as the term for an object that discernment becomes aware of through one of the six sense-'doors'. Again, at A.IV.385, it is said that 'purposeful thoughts (*saṅkappa-vitakkā*)' have *nāma-rūpa* as *ārammaṇ a*. *Nāma-rūpa* must surely be the 'object' of such thoughts. Lastly, at A.III.312, it is said of one who recollects the various good qualities of the Buddha, 'having made this (thought) an *ārammaṇa* . . .': that is, such a thought has been the 'object' of his discernment.
3. '*Patiṭṭhita*' can also mean 'settled' or 'standing', in certain contexts.
4. E.g. at S.II.268, M.III.94–5 and S.IV.147–48.
5. Note that discernment is not dependent on stimulation in the perceptual process (as one might expect), but vice versa, as S.II.73 (last Para.) shows. Stimulation is the meeting of *three* phenomena, not of *two* so as to spark off the production of a third.
6. Cf. D.III.104: 'as a consequence of right *manasikāra*, he touches (*phasati*) a (meditative state of) mental-concentration of such a form . . .'. Here '*phasati*' is the verbal equivalent of '*phassa*', 'stimulation', and the passage indicates that 'attention' leads on to 'stimulation'. Vism.463 says of stimulation:

   > its proximate cause is an objective field (-*visaya*-) that has come into range, because it arises immediately through the appropriate act of attention (*tajjā-samannāhārena*) and a sense-faculty when the objective field is present.

7. In the Abhidhamma, the term is a clear synonym of *manasikāra* (Vibh.321), and in the Suttas, the verbal forms of the two words are used as equivalents (M.I.445). The word itself is derived from '*saṃ*' + '*anu*' + '*āhāra*', and literally means 'thoroughly (*saṃ*) bringing on (*āhāra*) along to (*anu*)'. At MLS.I.236, I.B.Horner renders *samannāhāra* by 'impact'. Apart from not fitting the derivation as well as 'act of attention', this is inappropriate to the context. Though an object may be within the range of the eye but not actually be focussed on so as to produce an 'impact', there is no similar situation with hearing. If a sound is audible it is *heard, unless* one's *attention* is not directed at it. As all the senses are treated in a parallel manner, '*samannāhāra*' must mean something like an 'act of attention' not only in the case of hearing, but in the other five cases too. This translation is that used by P.De Silva, 1973: 12.
8. Seeing the constant arising of discernment and feeling as a kind of recurrent 'birth' is in line with the view of the Burmese teacher Ledi Sayadaw (1914: 158–59):

> The genesis of consciousness belongs to the category birth, which is one ultimate phenomenon, as do all facts of inception, production, origination, propagation, or continual serial genesis. Analogous are mental decay and death, belonging respectively to the categories of the ultimate phenomenon of decay and that of death (p.158–9).

CHAPTER 9

1. And cf. S.II.151, D.II.58–9, D.III.289, A.IV.146–67.
2. An alternative meaning of the six 'discernment-collections' *might* be *all* occurrences of visual-discernment etc. that ever arise in a person. If that were the case, though, then there seems to be no reason why e.g. grasping (*upādāna*), as a causal link, should not be explained in terms of the four 'collections' of graspings of the same type (i.e. all examples of sensual grasping etc.). In fact, '*kāya*' is only used in the explanation of the discernment, stimulation, feeling and craving links (S.II.2–4), and the feeling, cognition, volition and discernment personality-factors (S.III.59–61). In each case, six *kāya*s are listed: the relevant process occurring in each of the six sense-channels. The 'collections' referred to, then, are particularly allied to the six sense-channels, and must refer to the various feelings etc. that can arise in particular sense-channels while processing and responding to a particular object.
3. The number of *bhavaṅga citta*s between each perceptual cycle is not specified in the Abhidhamma or Buddhaghosa's works, but it would make sense to say that it varies in inverse proportion to a person's degree of alertness or wakefulness. The more alert, the quicker he or she adverts to a new object.
4. Elsewhere, Buddhaghosa explains that 'registration' is like 'some water that follows a little after a boat going upstream' (Vism.460), thus showing that, though the mind would normally return to its *bhavaṅga*

state after *javana*, if the object is vivid or very clear, it remains on the same object for a short while to 'register' it.

5. 1976: 331. The OED. gives, on 'Consciousness': '5. The totality of impressions, thoughts and feelings which make up a person's conscious being'.
6. The OED. gives, on 'Consciousness': '3. The state or fact of being mentally conscious or aware *of* anything. 4. Philos. The state or faculty of being conscious, as a condition and concomitant of all thought, feeling and volition'.
7. The concise OED., on 'discern', gives: 'perceive clearly with mind or senses . . .'
8. Dhs.431, 443, 556, Vism.91, 71, 488. This could not be fully investigated in chs.5 or 8 as the differentiation of the functions of discernment in the perceptual process had not then been outlined.
9. I am grateful to Lance S. Cousins, of the University of Manchester (now retired), for suggesting this solution to the problem.
10. A possible problem, here, is that in the process of *citta*s, the conception-element which precedes a sense-discernment, accomplishing the function of 'advertence', i.e. attention, is a *functional* (*kiriya*), not a karmically resultant (*vipāka*) *citta* (see Para.A.5). Nevertheless, attention/advertence may be instrumental in the arising of a karmic result without itself being a karmic result. '*Vipāka*' literally means 'fruition', and so cannot refer to the process instrumental in the arising of an actual 'fruition', just as the 'fruition' of an apple tree is not the blossom, but only the apple. Indeed, not everything arising due to karma is described as a *vipāka*: Dhs.1211 does not use '*vipāka*' for physical states (*rūpa*s) arising 'from karma having been wrought', and Kvu.351–52 has the Theravādin reserving '*vipāka*' as a description applicable only to (some) non-physical states.
11. As seen at Para.9.4, only indifferent feeling arise at the time of seeing, hearing, tasting or smelling: in the case of these senses, pleasant or unpleasant feelings arise as part of the mental reaction to such sense-objects. Such a reaction may include both feelings which immediately and automatically arise, and feelings as part of an active response to an object. Only those which automatically arise can be seen as due to past karma. Such karmically-resultant feelings will be those that arise at the time of the two karmically-resultant conception and conceptional-discernment immediately following e.g. a visual-discernment (Para.9.13). Feelings as part of an active response occur at the time of *javana* discernments.
 Past karma, then, determines what sort of visual objects are noticed, and the feeling-charge that these immediately invoke in the mind. Lance S. Cousins, citing Vism.456, says that the neutral feeling accompanying sense-discernments resulting from wholesome and unwholesome karma are, respectively, 'subtle and will shade towards pleasant feeling', and 'inferior and will shade towards unpleasant feeling' ('The *Paṭṭhāna* and the Development of the Theravādin Abhidhamma', p.31).
12. One cannot use this as a way of making b) plausible, as this would mean that sense-discernments were karmic results principally for this reason. If this were so, the only way that karma would *actively* determine a person's experience would be by determining their rebirth. This would

make the operation of karma a rather crude affair and does not account for the different ways in which different people experience the 'same' situation. This surely is due to karma, in Buddhist terms, as it can be seen as due to dispositions set up by previous actions.

CHAPTER 10

1. See Para.9.12, Appendix and Collins, 1982: 238–47.
2. Buddhism would not, of course, accept fire as an 'indestructible element' but would see it as an element in flux; this would certainly be the Abhidhamma perspective. Nevertheless, some instance of the element would always be present in a material object, so this makes little difference to the general idea of fire.
3. Bareau also reports that the Sautrāntikas accepted subtle (*sūksma*) conceptional-discernment as the root of the five personality-factors (p.156). Kvu.A.122 also indicates that the Andhakas accepted a *bhavaṅga*-discernment.
4. As suggested by C.A.F. Rhys Davids in an editorial note to B.C. Law's *The Debates Commentary*, p.239.
5. As regards the translation of '*aṅga*' as 'characteristic factor' rather than simply 'factor', this can be defended on the grounds that this is the most likely translation, here, of those listed at PED. p.6. As Vibh.145 explains, 'becoming' consists of the four mental personality-factors, so the *Paṭṭhāna* references -simply to '*bhavaṅga*- must be seen as picking out the most prominent factor of becoming, with no qualification seen to be needed. Lance S. Cousins (1981: 24–5) points out that '*bhavaṅga*' is also used as a term for any of the twelve causal links at *Netti-pakaraṇa* p.29, and says that this is the original meaning of the term, from which its usage 'to designate or qualify a particular type of consciousness' derives. His argument, here, is that the discernment causal link is often used to refer to discernment at the moment of conception, which in later theory is very close to *bhavaṅga* in nature. Yet this is not a strong argument, as the discernment causal link is defined as the six discernment-collections. It thus includes visual-discernment-collection etc., which are clearly *not* '*bhavaṅga*' in the Abhidhamma sense.
6. As reported by Nyanatiloka, 1972: 32–3.
7. As translated from the Chinese by Ehara et al., 1977: 256.
8. Note that Lance S. Cousins (1981: 28) suggests, on *bhavaṅga*, that 'We may interpret its continuance throughout life as the natural mode to which the mind continually reverts as indicating its role of "carrying" the essential features of the individual those tendencies which remain apparently unchanged in a particular individual throughout a given life'. See Gethin, 1994 for a development of this idea.
9. 1955: 151, 159, 164, 172 and 240.
10. For a more detailed analysis of this, see Harvey, 1993. Note that S.Collins, says that, for the Theravāda, in cessation 'personal identity is carried by the body, and not by the identity of a continuing level of mind or consciousness' (1982: 257), for 'it is the material life-faculty [*jīvitindriya*] that continues to exist in cessation' (p.230.).

11. A preliminary investigation of the 'brightly shining mind' can be found in Harvey, 1989. References to it by contemporary Theravāda meditation teachers include: Ajahn Chah (1980: 1), and Acharn That Desaraṅsī (1986: 47–8).
12. Cf.D.I.84 and M.I.279–80, where the same simile is used to illustrate the situation of destroying the 'cankers', from the fourth *jhāna*.
13. This *could* also mean 'light to turn' (i.e. turn to the various tasks such as those of the higher knowledges: see below), though its occurrence at A.A.III.317 (Para.10.14) shows it to mean 'quick to change'. A.A.I.59 explains the phrase thus; 'arising quickly (*lahuṃ*), ceasing quickly'.
14. The meaning of '*āgantuka*' is shown by S.IV.219, at which a 'guest-house (*āgantukāgāram*)' where people of various classes come (*āgantvā*) and take up residence is used as a simile for the situation of 'in this body, diverse feelings arise'.
15. The four 'cankers' (*āsava*s) are those of sense-desire, (attachment to) becoming, views, and spiritual ignorance.
16. Note that A.A.I.57 comments 'overgrown with the five hindrances' on the 'turbid' state of *citta* referred to at A.I.8–10, and that A.III.236 compares a *citta* free of vacillation, the fifth hindrance, to a pot of water which is neither muddy nor in a dark place but 'clear, purified, unturbid' and in the light.
17. The six 'higher knowledges' are: exercise of psychic powers (such as walking on water), hearing sounds (human or divine) at a great distance, reading other people's minds, memory of past lives, seeing how others are reborn according to their karma, and knowledge of destruction of the cankers, Arahatship (cf.Para.10.31). The last three of these are the same as the 'threefold knowledge' said to have been attained by the Buddha on the night of his enlightenment.
18. While the first simile suggests that the radiance of *bhavaṅga* comes from the mortal body (*sarīra*), the second avoids this implication.
19. It has been seen at Para.9.19 that 'advertence' or 'attention' in any of the physical sense-channels is generally influenced by past karma. This does not mean, however, that a person has no control over his attention, as that in the conceptional sense-channel is not so influenced.
20. P.222. These three *Laṅkāvatāra* passages are also referred to by W.Rahula, 1978: 98.
21. This can perhaps be related to the idea that *bhavaṅga* is comprised of various *citta*s of the sense-desire, (pure) form or formless worlds (Para.10.9). A form world god, for example, will have a form-world *bhavaṅga*, which might be seen as less amenable to being defiled than is a sense-desire-world *bhavaṅga*.

CHAPTER 11

1. E.g. in the '*Nirvāṇa*' article, by T.P.Kasulis, in Eliade, 1987: 448–49.
2. '*-saṅkhayā-*' *could* mean 'from the destruction', but as, above, the first *nibbāna*-element is *itself* seen to be a 'destruction' (*-kkhayo*), I take '*-saṅkhayā-*' as in apposition to the feminine '*dhātu*', and not as ablative.

3. Cf. D.III.255 which, for '*arahattāya paṭipanno*' has variant readings '*arahatta-phala-sacchikiriyāya*' and '*arahatta-sacchikiriyāya paṭipanno*'.
4. The text on p.61 gives '*nibbidā*' and '*nirodhā*' (twice), though p. p.59 gives '*nibbidāya*' and '*nirodhāya*', with '*nibbidā*' and '*nirodhā*' as variant readings.
5. E.g. M.I.341, A.V.410, Thag.132, It.49, S.III.26, Sn.707.
6. This is when the mind takes *nibbāna* as its object (Vism.700) and 'reviews' it (Khp.A.152). As argued above, the early texts do not seem to support making a distinction between *nibbāna* during life and Arahatness-fruit.
7. M.I.208–09 lists, as 'pleasant dwellings', the four *jhāna*s, the four formless states and then, as the most excellent, the destruction of the cankers in or just after the cessation of cognition and feeling. This does not imply that cessation-attainment is here seen as the highest 'pleasant dwelling' or 'dwelling in bliss'. Only the state where the cankers get destroyed is this. In this passage, though, the reference to the *jhāna*s and then formless states sets up a natural progression leading up to cessation-attainment. Canker-destruction is thus naturally referred to in this context, though cessation-attainment is not the only route to this.
8. This shows that D.J.Kalupahana is wrong when he says that *nibbāna* is, in the Suttas, "*paṭiccasamuppanna* ('causally conditioned')", i.e. not beyond the process of Conditioned Arising (1975: 140).
9. From Sn.732, at Para.11.11, it is clear that the 'tranquillizing/calming of *saṅkhāra*s', in the context of *nibbāna*, relates primarily to the '*saṅkhāra*s' in the sense of 'constructing activities', rather than as 'constructed states'.
10. Or 'what is meant by it', in the case of discernment.
11. A.III.443, on the contemplation of 'all *saṅkhāra*s' as impermanent and *dukkha*, but of 'all *dhamma*s' as not-Self, shows this. '*Saṅkhāra*' is here clearly meant in the sense of a constructed state. The passage says that an advantage of perceiving *dukkha* in all such states is that 'in all *saṅkhāra*s, the perception of *nibbāna* will be present to one as a slayer with drawn sword'. That is, one will see that *nibbāna*, the stopping of all that is *dukkha*, is the destruction of all constructed phenomena.
12. A.A.V.2, on a parallel passage at A.V.7–8.

CHAPTER 12

1. By K.N.Upadhyaya (1971: 352–56), N.Dutt (1971: 283–88 and 1978: 189–91), and Bhikkhu Ñāṇananda (1971: 57–68). A brief account of the present author's views on *nibbāna* and discernment is given as part of Harvey, 1989.
2. Note that the change from '*nirujjhati*' to '*uparujjhati*' cannot be of any real significance as these are synonymous. This can be shown from It.105–06, which makes '*nirodha* of *dukkha*', in prose, equivalent to where *dukkha* '*uparujjhati*' in verse. The two words also occur in prose and verse respectively at D.I.223. The two words also mean the same at Nd.II.159.

3. The PTS. edition of the text, from its lack of an intervening end-quote '*ti*', implies that this speech still comes from Baka. It comes more logically, though, from the Buddha, as the commentary, M.A.II.413 takes it to do. The parallel passage at D.I.223 reinforces this reading, of course.
4. One should not be misled, here, by the instrumental case of '*nirodhena*' into thinking that the stopping of discernment *leads* to *nibbāna*, the destruction of craving, but is different from it. At M.I.53, the stopping of discernment, as of all the other causal links, is that to which the Holy Eightfold Path goes, i.e. *nibbāna*. That is, the stopping of discernment, which also involves the stopping of all the other links, is not part of the path, but its *goal*.
5. The reference to a 'world beyond', of course, does not imply that Ud.80 describes a state not experienced by the Arahat while alive. This can be seen from A.V.320, which refers to a person who is said, in a certain meditation, to be 'in a world beyond, not cognitive of a world beyond'. That is, one can be aware of a 'world beyond', and also transcend it, while alive in this world
6. The reference, at S.III.54–5 (Para.8.8) to 'unsupported' discernment as being 'steadfast (*ṭhitaṃ*)' does not contradict the S.II.66 description of it as without 'maintenance (*ṭhitim*)' (Para.12.8), for S.III.54–5 clearly suggests that such discernment does not 'persist (*tiṭṭhati*)', i.e. it is without a 'maintenance'.
7. A 'ghat' is a flight of steps leading down to a river, where people have easy access to the river.
8. E.g. D.III.217, with Vibh.64, 70f..
9. Except in the case of discernment: see next Para.
10. See ch.8, note 2 for evidence that '*ārammaṇa*' refers to an object of the six senses.
11. Cf. Vibh.428 says that the discernment personality-factor has an object.
12. The PTS. edition records no variant readings on these.
13. Cf.L'AK.II.139, note 1, which quotes a Sanskrit *Sūtra* that refers to space as '*apratiṣṭhitam anālambanam*'. Miln.268 seems influenced by the Sarvāstivādin view in saying that space and *nibbāna* are 'born neither of karma, nor of a cause, nor of physical change'.
14. The context rules out the complication that Godhika might have attained *nibbāna* between lives (see Paras.6.21–5).
15. One is reminded of the idea of Dōgen (1200–1253), founder of Sōtō Zen in Japan, that in meditation, one should sit in a 'purposeless way' (so as to manifest one's intrinsic 'Buddha-nature').
16. Note that *bhavaṅga*/brightly shining *citta*, which occurs unmixed in dreamless sleep, could be seen to correspond to the 'third' state of consciousness referred to in the *Upaniṣads*: dreamless sleep. Nibbānic discernment, on the other hand, might be seen as like the 'fourth (*turiya*)' state, which *Māṇḍūkya Upaniṣad* 7 describes as the 'tranquillisation of elaboration (*prapañcopaśamam*)', for S.IV.370 sees the 'unelaborated (*nippapañcam*)' as synonymous with *nibbāna* during life.
17. Vibh.172–73 and 179, with Dhs.277ff. and 505ff. Bhikkhu Bodhi (1976) argues that, in the Theravādin Abhidhamma, at the time of the Paths and Fruits, there are the 'bare aggregates', i.e. the personality-factors in

the form of the *khandhas* but not the *upādāna-kkhandhas* (lit. 'groups-of-grasping'). That is, when the Paths or Fruits are experienced, the personality-factors (the *khandhas*) exist in a form in which they cannot become the object of anyone's grasping, whether the experiencer's or that of other beings. As the first sermon of the Buddha sums up *dukkha* by saying, 'in brief, the five *upādāna-kkhandhas* are *dukkha*' (Vin.I.10), Bhikkhu Bodhi argues that dukkha must be absent at the time of the Paths and Fruits, as the *upādāna-kkhandhas* are absent then. However, the momentary processes existing at that time are still conditioned, changing ones and 'whatever is impermanent is *dukkha*' (S.II.53). The Paths and Fruits must, thus, still be *dukkha*, both because they consist of impermanent states and, from Para.11.8, because they are conditioned.

18. My thanks to Lance S. Cousins for pointing out this passage to me.
19. Translated by Conze et al (1954: 210). Sanskrit interpolated from Kochumuttom (1982: 160). Paul Griffiths (1990: 87) claims that Asaṅga's *Mahāyāna-sūtrālaṃkāra* sees 'unconstructed awareness' (*nirvikalpa jñāna*) as having an *ālambana*, or object. This object is specified as the "indescribability of things" (*dharmanirabhilāpyatā*), identical with "Thusness of absence of self" (*nairātmyatathatā*; cf. Ps.II.105 at Para.11.30). The content of such an awareness is said to be absence of *nimittas* (p.88), i.e. absence of perceptual 'signs'. Such awareness is also identical with "mirror-like awareness" (*ādarsajñāna*), in which there is no distinction between 'apprehension, and that which is to be apprehended' (p.89). This state, though, is arrived at at the 'path of vision' (*darśanamārga*), equivalent to Stream-entry, which this chapter still accepts as a state having an object.
20. *Mahāyāna-saṃgraha* ii, 27, as translated by Conze et al (1954: 216). For further information on *apratiṣṭhita-nirvāṇa*, see: Lamotte, 1976: 44–5, 229–36, with p.45 note 8 citing various textual references); Lamotte also cites sources in 1939, Vol.II, p.47*–48*, with his translation referring to the concept on pp.259–60; Conze, 1962: 236–37.

CHAPTER 13

1. The PTS. *Pāli Tipiṭakaṃ Concordance*, in fact, gives ': epithet of an Arahant' at the entry on '*tathāgata*'.
2. Cf. a parallel passage at S.IV.376, where it is prefaced by saying that no accountant or 'reckoner (*saṅkhāyako*)' could calculate the volume of water in the ocean, as it is 'deep, immeasurable, hard to fathom'.
3. I.B.Horner, at MLS.I.179, translates: 'This is the discriminative consciousness attached to a Tathāgata'. This is based on the reading '*nissataṃ*' rather than '*nissitaṃ*'. This reading, however, is not found in either the PTS edition of the text or the commentary.
4. As to what '*brahma-*' means here, it can be seen that D.A.III.865 is right to say 'Dhamma is called "*brahmā*" in the sense of the best (*seṭṭha-*)'. At S.V.4–6, people seeing a fine chariot say 'Aha, that is the *brahmā* of chariots (*brahmaṃ . . . yānaṃ*)! That is, the *brahmā* of chariots for beauty'. This shows that, in the Buddha's day, '*brahmā*' had become a general term

of praise, meaning 'best', 'splendid', or 'supreme'. That it is used as a synonym for Dhamma at D.III.84 is appropriate as, just prior to the quoted passage, this refers to Dhamma as the 'best (*seṭṭho*)'. The use of the term *brahmā* is particularly appropriate in the context, as the Buddha is talking to a Brahmin, who had previously said that only Brahmins were genuinely 'born of Brahmā (*brahma-jā*)' (p.81), i.e. born of the god *Brahmā*, the supreme reality according to them.

5. A similar interpretation of the Buddha and Arahats having 'Dhamma as body' is given by the commentary on S.III.120, S.A.II.314, on 'who sees Dhamma sees me'. This explains that 'The nine-fold supramundane (*lokuttara-*) Dhamma, indeed, is the body of the *tathāgata*'. This nine-fold Dhamma is explained, at Ud.A.311, Asl.350 and Thag.A.II.205 as the four Paths, the four Fruits and *nibbāna*. This implies that the state of being fully 'Dhamma-bodied' is attained in stages, as the Paths and Fruits are gradually attained. It also, though, includes *nibbāna* in the Buddha's 'Dhamma-body', whereas my interpretation sees 'Dhamma-become' as a unique reference to this. This has the advantage of seeing 'one with Dhamma as body' and 'Dhamma-become' as not merely synonyms, but as alluding to two aspects of the Buddha. That 'Dhamma-become' relates to *nibbāna* is indicated by the Thag.491 verse, on Buddhas as 'merging into destruction . . . become Dhamma', for *nibbāna* is 'destruction' (of attachment etc.) (Para.11.2).
6. At S.III.120, this is what the Buddha says Vakkali should do, presumably so as to 'see' Dhamma and so 'see' the *tathāgata*. S.III.168 sees 'methodical attention' to the personality-factors as impermanent, *dukkha* and not-Self as the way to become a Stream-enterer.
7. This possibility is omitted at S.III.118.
8. This is also quoted at Para.1.20. On the translation of '*saccato thetato*', see Para.1.18.
9. Dhamma being 'understood' by Yamaka at S.III.112 certainly cannot mean that he becomes an Arahat, for he only does this at the end of the Sutta (p.115).
10. The commentary on this phrase, at S.III.106, sees it as referring to Stream-entry (S.A.II.308).
11. But not, here, that a *tathāgata* or Self is 'in' a personality-factor, as this possibility has already been covered.
12. A Stream-enterer still has the attitude 'I am' with respect to his own personality-factors but one must assume that he does not project this attitude into his understanding of others, or he would not be able to go beyond view iv) on a *tathāgata*.
13. An alternative reading of view v) might be to take it as akin to a view at D.I.32. This postulates a Self which, after death, is both without cognition (*asaññī*, implying a lack of all four mental personality-factors) and without form (*arūpī*). That is, it postulates a Self which is reborn in a kind of quality-less state. View v) would then take a *tathāgata*, in life, as some quality-less Self-essence. The nearest thing, in Buddhist cosmology, to such a quality-less rebirth is that of the non-cognizant (*asañña-*) beings, who lack all four mental personality-factors but do have a subtle kind of form (Vibh.419). But objectless discernment

is no kind of Self-essence, and goes to no kind of rebirth. As it is a form of discernment, albeit of a radically non-normal kind, it is not completely 'without discernment', either.

14. Para.13.15. See also Collins, 1982: 131–37.

ABBREVIATIONS

All references to Pāli texts are to the volume and page number of the PTS. editions, except where otherwise stated (the PTS. retains nearly all these texts and their translations in print). Where A. appears after a text, it refers to its commentary, e.g. S.A. is the commentary to the *Saṃyutta Nikāya*, also known as *Sāratthappakāsinī*. Information on Pāli texts and translations can be found in P. Harvey, *An Introduction to Buddhism*, pp.xiv–xix and 322–23.

A.	*Aṅguttara Nikāya*
Asl.	*Atthasālinī* (commentary on Dhs.)
BPS.	Buddhist Publication Society
BQ.	*Buddhist Quarterly*
BSR.	*Buddhist Studies Review*
BU.	*Bṛhadāraṇyaka Upaniṣad*
CU.	*Chāndogya Upaniṣad*
CR.	*Conditional Relations*, i.e. Nārada's Pt. translation.
D.	*Dīgha Nikāya*
Dhp.	*Dhammapada* (reference is to verse numbers)
Dhs.	*Dhammasaṅgaṇi* (reference is to the section number)
EFEO.	*École Francais d'Extrême-Orient*
It.	*Itivuttaka*
J.	*Jātaka*
JS.	*Jātaka Stories*, i.e. Cowell *et al.*'s J. translation
JIABS.	*Journal of the International Association of Buddhist Studies*
JPTS.	*Journal of the Pāli Text Society*
JRAS.	*Journal of the Royal Asiatic Society*
Khp.	*Khuddakapāṭha*
KU.	*Kaṭha Upaniṣad*
Kvu.	*Kathāvatthu*
L'AK.	*L'Abhidharmakosa de Vasubandhu*, La Vallée Poussin's translation of the Abhidharmakośa
M.	*Majjhima Nikāya*
MAn.IV.	*Minor Anthologies IV*, i.e. Horner and Gehman's *Vimānavatthu* and *Petavatthu* translations.
Miln.	*Milindapañha*
MLS.	*Middle Length Sayings*, I.B.Horner's translation of M.

MoB.	Motilal Banarsidass
MU.	*Muṇḍaka Upaniṣad*
Nd.I.	*Mahāniddesa*
Nd.II.	*Cullaniddesa*
Netti.	*Nettipakaraṇa*
OED.	*Oxford English Dictionary*
Para.	Paragraph number in this book
PBR.	*Pāli Buddhist Review*
PED.	*Pāli-English Dictionary,* Rhys Davids and Stede
PEW.	*Philosophy East and West*
PP.	Path of Purification, i.e. Nanamoli's translation of Vism.
PPB.	Pāli Publication Board
PU.	*Praśna Upaniṣad*
Ps.	*Paṭisambhidāmagga*
Pt.	*Paṭṭhāna* (PPB edition, reference is to marginal pagination)
PTS.	Pāli Text Society
Pug.	*Puggalapaññatti*
Pv.	*Petavatthu*
S.	*Saṃyutta Nikāya*
Skt.	Sanskrit
Sn.	*Sutta-Nipāta*
SNS.	*Sāmmītīyanikāya Śāstra*: translation of this text by K.Venkataramanan
Thag.	*Theragāthā* (reference is to verse number)
Thig.	*Therīgāthā* (reference is to verse number)
UCR.	*University of Ceylon Review*
Ud.	*Udāna*
Vibh.	*Vibhaṅga*
Vin.	*Vinaya*
Vism.	*Visuddhimagga*
Vv.	*Vimānavatthu*

BIBLIOGRAPHY

Ācariya Mahā Boowa (1980) *The Dhamma Teachings of Ācariya Mahā Boowa in London*, translated by Bhikkhu Paññāvaddho from the Thai, 'for free distribution', no publisher.

Acharn Mahā Boowa Nyanasampanno (1976) *The Ven. Phra Acharn Mun Bhuridatta Thera, Meditation Master*, 'for free distribution', Wat Pa Barn Tard, Thailand.

Acharn That Desaraṅsi (1986) *Only the World Ends*, 'for free distribution', Wat Hin Mark Peng, Sri Chiangmai, Nongkhai, Thailand.

Ajahn Chah (1980) *A Taste of Freedom – Selected Dhamma Talks*, 'for free distribution', Wat Pah Nanachat, Ampher Warin, Ubon Rajathani, Thailand, The Sangha.

Aung, S.Z. (1918) 'A Dialogue on Nibbāna', *Journal of the Burmese Research Society*, Vol.VIII, part III, 233–53.

Aung, S.Z, and Rhys Davids, C.A.F. (1910) *Compendium of Philosophy*, (transl. of *Abhidhammattha-saṅgaha*) London, PTS..

Bareau, A. (1955) *Les Sectes Bouddhiques du Petit Véhicule*, Paris, EFEO..

Bhattacharya, K.(1973) *L'Ātman-Brahman dans le Bouddhisme Ancien*, Paris, EFEO..

Bhikkhu Bodhi (1976) 'Aggregates and Clinging Aggregates', PBR., 1 (1): 91–102.

—— (1978) 'The Meaning of the Word "Tathāgata"', PBR., 3 (2): 65–83.

Collins, S.(1982) *Selfless Persons – Imagery and Thought in Theravāda Buddhism*, Cambridge University Press.

—— (1990) 'On the Very Idea of the Pali Canon', JPTS., XV: 89–126.

Conze, E. (1951) *Buddhism – Its Essence and Development*, Oxford, Cassirer (2nd paperback edition: 1974).

—— (1957) *Vajracchedikā Prajñāpāramitā*, text, Serie Orientale Roma, Rome, Istituto Italiano per il Medio ed Estremo Oriente.

—— (1958) *Buddhist Wisdom Books*, (transl. of *Vajracchedikā* and *Hṛdaya* Perfection of Wisdom *Sūtras*), London, George Allen and Unwin.

—— (1962) *Buddhist Thought in India*, London, George Allen and Unwin.

—— (1967) *Thirty Years of Buddhist Studies*, Oxford, Cassirer.

—— (1973) *The Perfection of Wisdom in Eight Thousand Lines and its Verse Summary*, (transl. of *Aṣṭasāhasrikā Prajñāpāramitā Sūtra*) Bolinas, Four Seasons Foundation.

—— (1975) *Further Buddhist Studies*, Oxford, Cassirer.

Conze, E. et al (1954) *Buddhist Texts Through the Ages*, New York and Evanston, Harper & Row.

Cousins, L.S. (1973) 'Buddhist *Jhāna*: its Nature and Attainment According to the Pāli Sources', *Religion*, 3 (Autumn): 115–31.

—— (1981) 'The *Paṭṭhāna* and the Development of the Theravādin Abhidhamma', JPTS, IX, ed. K.Norman.

Dayal, H. (1932) *The Bodhisattva Doctrine in Buddhist Sanskrit Literature*, London, Kegan Paul (reprinted by MoB, 1975)

De Silva, P. (1973) *Buddhist and Freudian Psychology*, Colombo, Lake House Investments Ltd..

Dutt, N. (1971) *Early Monastic Buddhism*, 2nd. edn., Calcutta, Mukhopadhyaya (1st edn. 1960).

—— (1978) *Mahāyāna Buddhism*, Delhi, MoB..

Ehara N.R.M., Soma Thera and Kheminda Thera (1977) *The Path of Freedom – Vimuttimagga of the Arahant Upatissa*, translated from Chinese, Kandy, BPS..

Eliade, M., ed. (1987) *The Encyclopaedia of Religion*, New York, Macmillan, and London, Collier Macmillan.

Freemantle, F., and Chōgyam Trungpa (1978) *The Tibetan Book of the Dead – The Great Liberation Through Hearing in the Bardo*, Boulder, Colo., Shambhala.

Forman, R.K.C., ed. (1990) *The Problem of Pure Consciousness Mysticism and Philosophy*, Oxford University Press.

Gethin, R. (1994) '*Bhavaṅga* and the Rebirth According to the Abhidhamma', in *The Buddist Forum, Vol. III, 1991–93*, eds. T.Skorupski and U.Pagel, London, School of Oriental and African Studies: 11–35.

Griffiths, P.J. (1987) *On Being Mindless – Buddhist Meditation and the Mind-body Problem*, La Salle, Ill., Open Court.

—— 'Pure Consciousness and Indian Buddhism', pp.71–97 in Forman, R.K.C.,

Grimm, G. (1958) *The Doctrine of the Buddha*, 2nd. edn., translated by Bhikkhu Silacara, Berlin, Akademie Verlag (German original: 1915).

Harvey, P. (1983) 'The Nature of the Tathāgata', in *Buddhist Studies, Ancient and Modern*, ed. P.Denwood and A.Piatigorsky, London, Curzon, and Totowa, NJ., Barnes and Noble: 35–52.

—— (1986) 'Signless Meditations in Pāli Buddhism', JIABS., 9 (1): 25–52.

—— (1986b) 'The Between-lives State in the Pāli Suttas', in *Perspectives on Indian Religion Papers in Honour of Karel Werner*, (Bibliotheca Indo-Buddhica No.30), ed. P.Connolly, Delhi, Sri Satguru Publications: 175–89.

—— (1987) 'The Buddhist Perspective on Respect for Persons', BSR., 4, (1): 31–46.

—— (1989) 'Consciousness Mysticism in the Discourses of the Buddha', in *The Yogi and the Mystic Studies in Indian and Comparative Mysticism*, ed. K.Werner, London, Curzon, and Riverdale, The Riverdale Company: 82–102.

—— (1990) *An Introduction to Buddhism – Teachings, History and Practices*, Cambridge University Press.

—— (1990b) 'Venerated Objects and Symbols of Early Buddhism', in *Symbols in Art and Religion – The Indian and Comparative Perspectives*, ed. K.Werner, London, Curzon, and Riverdale, The Riverdale Company: 68–102.
—— (1993) 'The Mind-body Relationship in Pāli Buddhism – a Philosophical Investigation', *Asian Philosophy*, 3 (1): 29–41.
—— (1993b) 'The Dynamics of Paritta Chanting in Southern Buddhism', in *Love Divine- Studies in Bhakti and Devotional Mysticism*, ed. K.Werner, London, Curzon, and Riverdale, The Riverdale Company: 53–84.
Holmes, K.H. and K. (1985) *The Changeless Continuity*, 2nd.edn. (transl. of the *Ratnagotra-vibhāga Śāstra*), Eskdalemuir, Scotland, Karma Drubgyud Darjay Ling.
Horner, I.B. (1936) *Early Buddhist Theory of Man Perfected– A Study of the Arahan*, London, Williams and Norgate.
—— (1971) 'Attā and Anattā', *Studies in Comparative Religion*, 7 (1): 31–3, also in *Middle Way*, 45 (2), 1970, 66–9.
—— (1977) 'Theravāda Buddhism', in *The Concise Encyclopaedia of Living Faiths*, ed. R.C.Zaehner, London, Hutchinson.
Horner, I.B. and Coomaraswamy, A.K. (1948) *The Living Thoughts of Gotama Buddha*, London, Cassell.
Jacobi, H. (1973 reprint) *Jaina Sūtras*, Part I and II, Sacred Books of the East Vols. XXII and XLV., Delhi, MoB..
Jayatilleke, K.N. (1949 & 1950) 'Some Problems of Translation and Interpretation I and II', UCR., 7: 208–24 and 8: 45–55.
—— (1963) *Early Buddhist Theory of Knowledge*, London, George Allen and Unwin.
—— (1974) 'The Logic of the Four Alternatives', PEW., XVII: 69–83.
—— (1975) *The Message of the Buddha*, ed. N.Smart, London, George Allen and Unwin.
Johansson, R.E.A. (1965) '*Citta, Mano* and *Viññāṇa* – a Psychosemantic Investigation', UCR., 23: 165–215.
—— (1969) *The Psychology of Nirvana*, London, George Allen and Unwin.
—— (1979) *The Dynamic Psychology of Early Buddhism*, London, Curzon.
Jones, J.G.(1979) *Tales and Teachings of the Buddha– the Jātaka Stories in Relation to the Pāli Canon*, London, George Allen and Unwin.
Kalupahana, D.J. (1975) *Causality – the Central Philosophy of Buddhism*, Honolulu, University Press of Hawaii.
Karunadasa, Y. (1967) *The Buddhist Analysis of Matter*, Colombo, Department of Cultural Affairs.
King, W. (1964) *In the Hope of Nibbāna– an Essay on Theravāda Buddhist Ethics*, La Salle, Ill., Open Court.
Kochumuttom, T.A. (1982) *A Buddhist Doctrine of Experience– a New Translation and Interpretation of the Works of Vasubandhu the Yogācārin*, Delhi, MoB..
La Vallée Poussin, L. de (1971) *L'Abhidharmakośa de Vasubandhu* (6 vols), Bruxelles, Institut Belge des Hautes Etudies Chinoises.
Lamotte, E. (1939) *La Somme du Grande Véhicule d'Asaṅga* (*Mahāyānasaṃgraha*), Vol.II, Louvain, Bureaux du MusÇon.

—— (1976) *The Teachings of Vimalakīrti*, (Lamotte's 1962 French translation of the *Vimalakīrti-nirdeśa*, rendered into English by S.Boin), London, PTS..

Ledi Saydaw (1914) 'Some Points on Buddhist Doctrine', JPTS.: 115–69.

Masefield, P. (1979) 'The *Nibbāna-Parinibbāna* Controversy', *Religion*, 9 (Autumn): 215–30.

Nagao, G.M. (1981) 'The Bodhisattva Returns to This World', in *The Bodhisattva Doctrine in Buddhism*, ed. L.S.Kawamura, Waterloo, Canada, Wilfred Laurier University Press: 61–79.

Ñāṅamoli Bhikkhu (1975) *The Path of Purification*, (Vism. transl.), Kandy, BPS, and (2 vols.) Berkeley, Calif., Shambhala, 1976.

Ñāṇananda (1971) *Concept and Reality in Early Buddhist Thought*, Kandy, BPS..

Nārada, U. (1969) *Conditional Relations*, (transl. of Pt.) London, PTS..

Nyanaponika (1969) *The Heart of Buddhist Meditation*, London, Rider.

Nyanatiloka (1972) *Buddhist Dictionary– Manual of Terms and Doctrines*, 3rd. edn., Colombo, Frewin.

Paul, D.M. (1980) *The Buddhist Feminine Ideal– Queen Śrīmālā and the Tathāgata-garbha*, Missoula, Montana, Scholar's Press.

Pérez-Remón, J. (1980) *Self and Non-Self in Early Buddhism*, The Hague, Mouton.

Pieris, A. (1979) 'The Notions of *Citta*, *Attā* and *Attabhāva* in Pāli Exegetical Writings', PBR., 4 (1-2): 5–15.

Radhakrishnan, S.(1978) *The Principal Upaniṣads*, (texts and translations), London, George Allen and Unwin.

Rahula, W.(1978) *Zen and the Taming of the Bull*, London, Gordon Frazer.

Reat, N.R. (1987) 'Some Fundamental Concepts of Buddhist Psychology', *Religion*, 17 (Jan.): 15–28.

Rhys Davids, T.W. and C.A.F.(1910) *Dialogues of the Buddha*, Vol.II, (transl. of D.II) London, PTS. (in 5th. edn by 1971).

Robinson, R.H. (1970) *The Buddhist Religion*, Belmont, Calif., Dickenson, 1st edn.

Saddhatissa, H. (1970) *Buddhist Ethics*, London, George Allen and Unwin.

Sarathchandra, E.R. (1958) *Buddhist Psychology of Perception*, Colombo, Ceylon University Press.

Schrader, F.O. (1904-05) 'On the Problem of *Nirvāṅa*', JPTS.: 157–70.

Spiro, M. (1970) *Buddhism and Society– a Great Tradition and its Burmese Vicissitudes*, New York, Harper and Row, and London, Allen and Unwin, 1971.

Stcherbatsky, T. (1919) 'The Soul Theory of the Buddhists' (translation of the *Abhidharmakośa*'s refutation of the views of the Personalists), *Bulletin de l'Académie des Sciences de Russie*, 13 (12–18): 823–54 and 937–58.

Story, F. (1975) *Rebirth as Doctrine and Experience*, Kandy, BPS..

Strong, J.S. (1992) *The Legend and Cult of Upagupta– Sanskrit Buddhism in North India and Southeast Asia*, Princeton and Oxford, Princeton University Press.

Suzuki, D.T. (1932) *The Lankavatara Sutra* (translation), London, Routledge and Kegan Paul.

Upadhyaya, K.N. (1971) *Early Buddhism and the Bhagavadgītā*, Delhi, MoB..

Vaidya, P.L. (1960) *Aṣṭasāhasrikā Prajñā-pāramitā Sūtraṃ*, text, Dharbhanga, Mithila Institute.

—— (1963) *Laṅkavatāra Sūtraṃ*, text, Darbhanga, Mithila Institute.

Venkataramanan, K. (1953) '*Sāmmītīyanikāya Śāstra*', translation from Chinese, with an introduction, *Visva-Bharati Annals* (of Visva-Bharati University, Bihar, India), 5: 154–243.

Warder, A.K.(1970) *Indian Buddhism*, Delhi, MoB..

Wayman, A. (1974) 'The Intermediate-State Dispute in Buddhism', in *Buddhist Studies in Honour of I.B.Horner*, ed. L.Cousins et al, Dardrecht, Holland, D.Reidel Publishing Co..

—— (1976) 'Regarding the Translation of the Buddhist Terms *Saññā/Saṃjñā, Viññāṇa/Vijñāna*', in *Malalasekera Commemoration Volume*, ed. C.O.H. de Wijesekera, Colombo, Malalasekera Commemmoration Volume Editorial Committee.

Werner, K. (1988) 'Indian Concepts of Human Personality in Relation to the Doctrine of the Soul', JRAS., no.1: 73–97.

Wijesekera, O.H. de A. (1945) 'Vedic Gandharva and Pāli Gandhabba', UCR., III (1): 73–107.

Williams,P. (1989) *Mahāyāna Buddhism – The Doctrinal Foundations*, London and New York, Routledge.

INDEX AND GLOSSARY

Reference to 'early Sutta' texts, being numerous, are only listed when a particular Sutta, *Nikāya* or section of a *Nikāya* has been mentioned by name in this work.

References are to paragraph numbers and note numbers, e.g. 10.7, 8, 11.1, 6n.2 = chapter 10 paragraphs 7 and 8, chapter 11 paragraph 1, chapter 6 note 2.

I. = Introduction, A. = Appendix.
Ab. = a Canonical Theravādin Abhidhamma text
My. = a Mahāyāna school or text
Sy. = a Śrāvakayāna (non-Mahāyāna) school of Buddhism
Any text without an explanation following it is part of the Theravādin Sutta collection.

Abhidhamma, Theravādin (and see, *Dhammasaṅgaṇi*, *Kathavatthu*, *Paṭṭhāna*, *Puggalapaññatti* and *Vibhaṅga*), I.13–15, 2.9, 4.2, 12, 16, 5.8, 11, 6.18, 20, 22, 7.10–11, 14, 16, 8.3, 9.2, 4, 12–14, 15–17, 19–20, 21, 10.9, 29, 12.23, 27, 29, 30, 31, 14.6, Appendix, 1n.3, 7n.4, 8n.2, n.7, 9n.3, 10n.2, 12n.17
Abhidhammattha-Vibhārani (late Theravādin Abhidhamma text), 10.11
Abhidharmakośa (of Vasubandhu, giving Vaibhāṣika Sarvāstivādin view), I.15, 1.37, 38, 41, 42, 4.1, 3, 13, 5.18, 6.31, 32, 33, 34, 6n.5, n.13, n.15, n.17, n.20, 12n.13
Adam and Eve, 1.47
advertence (the mind's first turning towards an object), 9.12, 15, 10.12, 14, 27, 28, A.4, 5, 6, 9n.10, 10n.19
agent of action, 2.9, 4.4
Aggañña-sutta, 4.19, 10.38
air, 6.10–11, 35
Ājīvakas (a fatalist religious movement), I.2, 4.4
Akaniṭṭha heaven (highest of the 'pure abodes', qv.), 6.21, 24
Alagaddūpama-sutta, 1.17–25
ālaya-vijñāna ('home-' or 'store-discernment', a Yogācāra concept), 10.35, 12.33
all (*sabbaṃ*, the entirety of normal, conditioned reality), 5.5, 12.4, 5, 17, 21, 39, 1n.3
alone, dwelling, 3.9, 14, 16, 7.18, 12.19, 39
Anatta-lakkhaṇa-sutta, 2.2, 7, 9
Andhakas (Sy.), 10.n.3
Aṅguttara Nikāya, I.13, 6.38
Annihilationism (denial of any kind

tathāgata beyond death), 11.2, 3–4, 31, 12.5, 20–1, 28, 13.1, 9, 14.10; and *bhavaṅga*, 12.27–8; and cessation-attainment, 11.13–14; and *citta*, 12.2, 25, 31, 32, 33–4; and Dhamma, 11.24, 12.32, 13.8, 12, 29, 14.8; and discernment, ch.12, 13.1, 6, 17, 27, 14.7, 8, 9, 10; in life, 11.5–12, 17–22, 31, 12.5, 9, 22–8; in the Mahāyāna, 12.33–4, 37–8, 44; non-different from *dukkha*?, 11.30, 12.37; as object of insight, 11.24–30, 12.6, 16, 25, 29, 30, 38, 39, 13.6, 8, A.5, 11n.6; as 'permanent', 2.13, 11.22, 14.1; as 'seclusion', 3.10; and Self, 1.2, 3, 5, 15–16, 34, 35, 2.6, 13–17, 3.1, 12.22, 26, 43, 13.1, 14.1; as signless, undirected, emptiness, 11.29–30, 31; and space, 12.18; as 'stopping' (*nirodha*), 8.1, 26, ch.11, 12.1, 3, 5, 7–9, 12, 13, 16, 18, 25, 29, 30, 38, 39, 40, 41, 13.15, 14.7, 11n.11; and the *tathāgata*, 13.8–9, 14–17, 29; beyond time and space, 12.15, 19, 20, 25, 42, 13.9, 23, 29, 14.7, 8; as unitary/unique, 11.20, 31, 12.42, 13.9, 14.8; and world, 5.11, 14–15, 18–20

Niddesa, I.14, 2.7–12, 3.6, 10, 11.8, 12.29, 1n.2, 12n.2

Non-returner (type of saint), I.4, 6.21–25, 11.6, 14, 24, 12.29, 14.4, 6n.14

nothing, man of, 3.14, 16, 13.4

nothingness, sphere of (a formless realm), 13.26

not-Self (*anatta*/*anātman*; and see marks), I.7–11, chs.1–2, 3.15, 4.3, 12, 21, 22, 5.11, 6.1, 11, 12, 15, 37–8, 7.19, 11.15, 28, 12.16, 22, 39, 13.1, 4, 6, 13, 15, 16, 17, 24, 28, 14.1, 6, 7, 9, 10, 2n.2, 11n.11, 12n.19, 13n.6

nutriments, 1.42, 6.13, 34, 8.8, 10.6, 6n.7

object (*ārammaṇa*; and see subject and object), 7.5, 8.5, A.5, 8n.2; and attention, 8.1213, 19, 8n.7; *bhavaṅga* has one, 10.12, 12.27; at death, A.7; and feeling, 9.4, 9n.11; in formless states, 12.15, 24; merged with subject in *nibbāna*?, 12.32; *nibbāna* as an, 11.24–30, 12.6, 16, 22, 25, 29, 30, 38, 39, 13.6, 8, A.5, 11n.6; *nibbāna* has none (and see objectless), 12.17; 'seeing through' of, 11.27–8; as 'split up' by discernment, 9.17; as a 'support' for discernment, 6.15, 7.19, 8.5, 8–9, 11, 12, 12.22, 24, 35, 39, 14.5; as tuned into, 5.11, 20; unconstructed awareness has one, 12n.19; in Yogācāra thought, 12.33, 44

objectless state, 12.8, 9, 10, 11, 12, 13, 15, 16, 17, 26–7, 31, 33, 39, 13.1, 17–19, 20, 24, 27, 28, 29, 14.7, 10

Once-returner (type of saint), I.4, 11.6, 12.29

ordinary person (*puthujjana*; one lacking in spiritual insight), I.8, 13.16, 28

ownerless, 2.7, 4.17, 6.4, 7.4, 14.8

pain, 9.4, 11.9, 14.7

Pāli Canon, I.12, 13,

parinibbāna (passing into *nibbāna*, especially at death), 11.8, 13.9

paritta chants, 13.31

Path, Holy Eightfold, I.5, 3.3–4, 16, 5.18, 11.10, 16, 13.2, 12n.4; as *Dhamma*, 13.11, 12, 29, 14.8

Paths, the four, 9.10, 12.29, 30, A.5, 12n.17, 13n.11

Paṭisambhidāmagga, I.14, 2.8, 10, 13–15, 2.13–15, 8.2, 11.19, 28, 30, 12.10, 29, 13.18, 23

Paṭṭhāna (Ab.), 6.18, 9.12, 19, 10.11, 28, 12.27, A.2, 4, 5, 6, 7n.4, 10n.5

perception (*saññā*; and see cognition), 9.5

seclusion, 3.10, 12.19, 39
Self (*atta/ātman*) (and see not-Self), I.2, 7–11, ch.1, 6.8–9, 38, 10.10, 35, 11.25, 29, 12.42, 13.1, 4, 6, 15–30, 14.1, 6, 8, 10, 4n.1, 6n.2, n.4, n.7, 13n.11, n.13; criteria of, 2.6–12; and discernment, 1.3, 6.8, 13, 29, 14.4, 6n.7; Higher or Great, 1.2, 1.5, 1.13; idea of, 2.3; as inapprehensible, 1.3, 17–25, 13.16, 24; and life-principle, I.2, 6.2, 3, 12, 14.4; Lower, 1.2, 1.5, 17; and world, 5.2–3, 12, 16, 19, 20
self, empirical, 1.1, 6–14, 28, 34, 50, ch.3, 4.1, 2, 7.1, 7, 14.1, 3, 4, 5; as developed, 3.6–7, 16, 14.1; as great, 3.4, 16, 4.21; and world, 5.5–7
self-contained, 3. 8–10, 14
self-control, 3.2, 3, 7, 15
sense-channels (visual etc.), 9.2, 4, 10.2, 7, 14, 12.12, A.4, 6, 7, 9n.2, 10n.19
sense-desire (*kāma*), realm of, I.3, 3.11, 6.16, 24, 10.9, 6n.21, 10n.21
sense-spheres (*āyatana*s; the six senses), I.6, 6.20, 7.13, 15, 8.22, 10.6, 7n.5; stopping of, 11.12, 12.8, 12
senses; and cessation-attainment, 10.16; as deceptive, 5.9; as 'gates' of the body, 5.11, 20; and (pure) form realm, 5n.1; as 'Self', 5.3
senses and objects; and the Arahat, 3.9, 13, 15, 11.2; stopping of, 11.12; and cognition and discernment, 9.17; as conditioning discernment, 6.13, 7.18, 20, 8.12, 14, 19, 21, 9.2, 4, 10.2, 40, A.3, 12n.11; and *nibbāna*, 11.26, 12.12; and stimulation, 8.12, 19, 21, 9.3, 11.2; and world, 5.6–7
sensual pleasure, five strands of (*kāma-guṇa*s), 3.2, 5.6, 7, 15, 1n.3, 6n.7
sentiency (*nāma*), 7.14, 16, 8.12, 18–19, 21, 12.12, 31, 43, 3n.3
sentient body (*nāma-rūpa*, and see mind-and-body), I.6, 7.13–14, 8.11, 12, 13.5, 7n.5, n.9, 8n.2; and *citta*, 1.9, 7.8–9; and discernment, 6.9, 14, 31, 7.6, 13–20, 8.1, 5, 8, 9, 11, 15–21, 22, 24, 26, 12.19, 41, 14.5, 7, 6n.20; stopping of, 11.8, 12. 3, 7, 8, 12, 16, 29, 40, 41, 14.7
signless (*animitta*) state, 11.16, 25–30, 31, 12.16, 24, 30, 34, 39
signs (sensory indications), 11.25, 27, 28–9, 12.16, 34, 39, 12n.19
similes: atom-splitting, 12.41; blind men and elephant, 9.7; border town, 6.27, 7.12, 7n.5; captain(s) of ship, 14.5; carpenter, 9.7; chariot, 1.22, 38; children and coins, 9.10, 13, 16; conch, 6.10; diamond-like mind, 3.8, 16; engine, 8.19; fire, 1.37, 4.3, 5, 6.19, 23, 28, 10.25, 10, 38, 12.28, 13.3, 6n.5, 10n.2; fire-drill, 6.10; flood-crossing, 12.10, 16, 39, 41; flower and scent, 1.32, 13.18; fruit of a tree, 9n.10; gold, 10.23–4, 35; guest house, 10n.14; home, 7.18–19, 8.26, 10.12, 17, 12.17, 19; iron ball, 6.10; iron bit, 6.23; lamp, extinction of, 11.5; lotus, 3.8, 16; mirror, 10.26, 12n.19; monkey, 10.14; ocean, 1.49, 3.6, 13.3, 29, 13n.2; rocket, 2.4; reed and sheath, 6.5–6; root, 10.6–7, 10, 12.27; salt in water, 3.4; seed and fruit, 4.2, 3, 5, 6, 5.17, 6.16, 28, 31, 8.8, 10.6; soup and its ingredients, 7.16; spider, 10.12; sun, 10. 26, 12.11, 13, 20; sunbeam, 12.8, 15; turtle, blind, 4.10
skilful (*kusala*), see wholesome
skilful means, 2.3, 14.1
sleep, 6.29–30, 10.9, 10, 13–14,